D1447130

The Kremlin's Nuclear Sword

THE RISE AND FALL OF RUSSIA'S
STRATEGIC NUCLEAR FORCES, 1945–2000

STEVEN J. ZALOGA

SMITHSONIAN BOOKS
WASHINGTON, DC

In memory of two friends who provoked my interest in Soviet military technology, Janusz Magnuski and Jim Loop.

This book may be purchased for educational, business, or sales promotional use. For information, please write: Special Markets Department, Smithsonian Books, P.O. Box 37012, MRC 513, Washington, DC 20013.

Copy editor: Tom Ireland
Production editor: Robert A. Poarch
Designer: Janice Wheeler

Library of Congress Cataloging-in-Publication Data
Zaloga, Steve
    The Kremlin's nuclear sword : the rise and fall of Russia's strategic nuclear forces, 1945–2000 / Steven J. Zaloga.
        p.   cm.
    Includes bibliographical references and index.
    ISBN 978-1-58834-007-4 (cloth) ISBN 978-1-58834-484-7 (paperback)
    1. Strategic forces—Soviet Union. 2. Strategic forces—Russia (Federation). 3. Soviet Union. Raketnye voæska strategicheskogo naznacheniëì—History. 4. Russia (Federation). Raketnye voæska strategicheskogo naznacheniëì. I. Title.
UA776.R3 Z35 2002
355.02′17′094709045—dc21   2001049092

British Library Cataloguing-in-Publication Data is available

Manufactured in the United States of America
19 18 17 16 15 14   5 4 3 2

Contents

SMITHSONIAN HISTORY OF AVIATION AND SPACEFLIGHT SERIES

Dominick A. Pisano and Allan A. Needell, Series Editors

Since the Wright brothers' first flight, air and space technologies have been central in creating the modern world. Aviation and spaceflight have transformed our lives — our conceptions of time and distance, our daily routines, and the conduct of exploration, business, and war. The Smithsonian History of Aviation and Spaceflight Series publishes substantive works that further our understanding of these transformations in their social, cultural, political, and military contexts.

Preface

The terrible heart of the Cold War was the nuclear arms race. Until recently, its history has been told from only a single perspective, that of the United States. The Soviet side of the story has long been an enigma, and Western accounts have been based on the tiniest fragments of information, strung together with a great deal of speculation and conjecture. This situation has dramatically changed since the collapse of the Soviet Union in 1991.

This book deals with the development of the Soviet Union and Russia's strategic nuclear forces. The primary focus is on the offensive forces, though some coverage of strategic defensive forces is of course necessary. The intercontinental ballistic missile force is at the center of this study, since it was by far the most important element of the Soviet Union's forces.

On reading an early draft of this study, a friend of mine jokingly referred to it as "a billion dollar book": it contains information that U.S. intelligence agencies spent billions of dollars trying to obtain. During the Cold War, no subject was kept a more closely guarded secret than the Soviet Union's strategic nuclear weapons. It went so far that even the names of the missiles, bombs, and submarines were considered a state secret, to say nothing of more important issues such as their technical characteristics and performance. Besides the weapons themselves, their design, the decision-making policy, and plans for their employment were all off-limits except to a very narrow circle of top Soviet officials. Since the end of the Cold War, the secrecy around these issues has lessened considerably, though it most certainly has not disappeared.

English-language accounts of Soviet nuclear forces have traditionally focused on two subject areas: arms control and strategic nuclear doctrine. Arms control was the most accessible facet of Soviet nuclear weapons policy since it involved the interaction of American diplomats with their Soviet counterparts. Nuclear doctrine was not as closely guarded as more technical subjects since the Soviet government wished to convey state policy to its rivals.

This book provides an account of Soviet and Russian strategic nuclear forces from a different perspective. Its primary focus is the development of Soviet strategic nuclear weapons technology from the vantage point of the Soviet aerospace industry and the related institutions of the Soviet armed forces. This approach was taken for several reasons. Although the Russian state archives are more open than they were during the Cold War, most state records dealing with this theme are still inaccessible. In contrast, there has been a torrent of new information on this subject from other sources, especially from the Russian aerospace industry and key military institutes.

The second reason for taking this perspective is its novelty and importance. During the Cold War, details on the design bureaus and research institutes were so tightly classified that even the CIA had only the faintest impression of their role in Soviet defense affairs. Due to the lack of information, there was a tendency to portray Soviet defense decision making as an ideal process: the central organs of the Communist Party, state, and military carefully formulated their doctrine, and from this issued requirements to the industry, which faithfully carried out their decrees. As this study suggests, Soviet defense decision making was not so rational, well organized, or centralized. The Soviet military industries played a far more central role in defense decision making than has been previously recognized and was the primary source of technological innovation. A more popular caricature is that the military's insatiable appetite for ever more baroque weapons was at the heart of the Cold War arms race. In fact, the Soviet military was frequently an impediment to technological innovation due to the difficulties of absorbing radically new technology into a force manned by poorly educated conscripts. Finally, details of the weapons program help to illuminate broader issues of state policy and military doctrine. There is considerable debate about Soviet policy and intentions during many critical phases of the Cold War, and the weapons programs are the most tangible manifestation of these policies.

The relaxation of secrecy on these themes has been erratic and unorganized. While the end of the Cold War has certainly diminished security concerns, openness about defense subjects has never been a Russian trait. To put this in some perspective, data on Soviet weapons production in World War II was not declassified until the mid-1990s. Soviet General Staff studies of many World War II battles are still classified. No Soviet war plans are available except for some examples from the 1930s. Even in the past few years, the state police have warned Russian authors against writing about many Cold War weapons programs, even about weapons that are obsolete and have been retired.

The release of information about the Cold War weapons programs has come not so much from Russian historians as from the weapons designers and their institutions. There have been two principal reasons for this. To begin with, the engineers and staff of these institutions are extremely proud of their accomplishments during the Cold War, and resentful of their anonymity. The designers of relatively simple weapons, such as the rifle designer Mikhail Kalashnikov of AK-47 fame, have been heralded as Russian national heroes, while engineers of far more sophisticated and important weapon systems have had their accomplishments cloaked in secrecy for decades. This rationale alone could not overcome the tendency of the Russian state police to censor anything dealing with nuclear weapons. However, by the mid-1990s, a more practical reason had emerged. The Russian defense industries were in catastrophic decline. Orders from the Russian government for new weapons had evaporated due to the collapse of the economy and the state budget. One of the few bright spots was the Russian space industry, since the U.S. government was pouring in funding for Russian participation in the International Space Station. To American firms, the organization of the Russian aerospace industry was a complete mystery. Gradually, the Russian design bureaus and aerospace plants began to release publications detailing their past accomplishments and current capabilities in hopes of participating in these international ventures. Since the space industry and the missile industry are one and same, this shed considerable light on the history of the Cold War arms race. Some key industry leaders have published their memoirs, and many design bureaus have released accounts of their past accomplishments.

A similar process took place in the Russian armed forces. There was considerable pride on the part of commanders and military leaders about their accomplishments in the Cold War, which had previously been hidden from public view. This encouraged the armed forces to push back the boundaries imposed by state censors. The 300th anniversary of the founding of the Russian fleet in 1996 provided a rationale for a flood of publications on the history of the Soviet fleet and the Soviet ship-building industry. Similarly, the fortieth anniversary of the founding of the Strategic Missile Force in 1999 was occasion for a surge of publications about its history. The appearance of these other sources has made it possible for Russian scholars to examine this sensitive subject.

Over the past decade, I have been able to talk to hundreds of Russian and Ukrainian engineers involved in the Cold War programs. While wary of discussing technical issues, they were extremely helpful in explaining the process and motivation of many weapons programs.

This is one of the first books in English to refer to Soviet nuclear weapons by their Russian names, not by their more familiar U.S. or NATO intelligence designations. So the Soviet ICBM known in the West as the SS-11 is referred to in this book by its Russian designation, UR-100. Initially, this will be jarring to readers unfamiliar with the Soviet designations, but it is a necessary and timely change in dealing with Cold War history. As the Russian archives gradually become more open, historians will have to become familiar with the Russian terms for their weapons. For example, some recent accounts of the Cuban Missile Crisis, based on newly released archival documents, have been confusing due to lack of familiarity with Russian military terminology. Recent Russian books on this subject have also shifted to the use of these formerly secret Russian designations. Appendix 3 lists the various designations applied to these weapons in hopes of making this process less troublesome. The names of the various design bureaus have been simplified somewhat in this account to avoid confusing readers. Soviet design bureaus had multiple classified and unclassified names, which frequently changed through time. Indeed, the recent history of one rocket engine design bureau was preceded by an entire page listing the many names under which the bureau had been known over the past half century! So, where possible, this account uses the name of the founding general designer of the bureau for the organization, a practice that the Russians themselves follow.

I am indebted to many friends and colleagues for their assistance on this project over the past decade. Special thanks go to David Markov and Andrew Hull of the Strategy, Forces, and Resources Division of the Institute for Defense Analyses for their support and encouragement over the years. David Isby and Joseph Durant have been instrumental in keeping me abreast of the latest revelations from the Russian defense press. Norman Friedman has provided a great deal of practical advice on the technical issues examined in this book. Charles Vick of the Federation of American Scientists has provided generous support from his own considerable knowledge of the Soviet space program. Joshua Handler of Princeton's Center for Energy and Environmental Studies has been most helpful in sharing material from his own extensive research in Russia. Asif Siddiqi, Dwayne Day, Piotr Butowski, David Woods, and Barney Dombrowski have all provided helpful comments and material. And William Burr and Jeffrey Richelson of the National Security Archives at George Washington University have been most helpful in sharing the results of their own extensive research into Cold War history.

1.   Revolution in Military Affairs
1946–1953

In May 1945 the Red Army was at the pinnacle of its power, standing victorious in the smoldering ruins of Berlin. After four years of savage warfare with Germany, it had vanquished the strongest European continental power. The Red Army was the largest in the world, with over 430 rifle divisions, 20 cavalry divisions, and 32 tank and mechanized corps.[1] It was armed with 89,600 field guns, 27,300 armored vehicles, and 115,600 combat aircraft.[2] The communist dream of spreading the world revolution was now a tangible possibility. But Soviet power would advance on the inexorable power of the Red Army, not on the intellectual fantasies of the Marxist dialectic. Then in August 1945, "Plump came the atomic bomb. The balance which now seemed set and steady was rudely shaken. Russia was balked by the West when everything seemed to be within her grasp. The three hundred divisions (of the Red Army) were shorn of much their value."[3]

There was a palpable change of mood in Moscow. The U.S. ambassador cabled Washington: "Suddenly, the atomic bomb appeared and [the Soviets] recognized that it was an offset to the power of the Red Army. This must have revived their old feeling of insecurity." A correspondent stationed in Moscow in 1945 recalled that news of the Hiroshima bomb "had an acutely depressing effect on everybody. . . . Some Russian pessimists dismally remarked that Russia's desperately hard-won victory over Germany was now as good as wasted."[4] An official in the bomb program later recalled, "Stalin was really enraged, [it was] the first time during the war that he lost control of himself. . . . He perceived the collapse of his dream of expansion of socialist revolution throughout all Europe, the dream that had seemed so real after the capitulation of Germany and that was invalidated by the "carelessness" of our atomic scientists."[5] Joseph Stalin ordered Soviet scientists to accelerate their own bomb program; no resources would be denied. The machine age of warfare had given way to the nuclear age.

The late Stalin years saw the Soviet Union evolve from a regional power to a global superpower. The triumph of the Red Army in 1945 helped erase the memory of a century of humiliating Russian defeats. From the Crimean War of 1854, Russia had been beaten even by its smaller neighbors in the 1904–5 Russo-Japanese War, World War I, and the 1920 Russo-Polish War. It was by no means certain that the Soviet Union would emerge from World War II in any position to challenge the United States. The human and material cost of the war had been staggering, with over twenty-five million dead and the towns and cities of the western Soviet Union burned-out ruins. The Soviet Union was the only major victor to emerge from the war with a major loss in its productive capacity, with nearly a quarter of its prewar assets destroyed.[6] Stalin's ambitions remained unabated, and the wartime alliance between the Soviet Union, the United States, and Great Britain quickly degenerated into the Cold War.[7]

By 1945 new military technologies had dramatically altered the face of battle. In the space of a century, there was a fundamental change in the power of weapons. The muzzle-loaded cannon, capable of firing a small, high-explosive shell a few hundred yards, was the most potent weapon of the nineteenth century. By 1900 the effective range of all weapons was still no greater than the range of human eyesight. The First World War saw the beginning of change. Innovations in communications, improvements in gun technology, and new tactics permitted cannon to engage targets beyond human eyesight to ranges of over ten miles. The airplane and zeppelin, while still primitive tools of war in 1918, were harbingers of long-range warfare. By the end of the Second World War, the revolution was reaching its climax. A strategic bomber was capable of delivering an atomic bomb several thousand miles. The battlefield was no longer a muddy line of trenches a few miles deep, but encompassed the entire globe. This represented a fundamental revolution in military affairs. To challenge the United States, the Soviet Union needed to embrace the revolution. This was a formidable task, because the Soviet Union was not in the forefront of military technology at the end of World War II and particularly weak in the areas most crucial to the new way of war.

The Soviet and American responses to the nuclear revolution were quite different, shaped by contrasting military cultures. The Soviet Union was a traditional continental power, that is, its army was the paramount element of its armed forces. In this respect, it was similar to other continental powers like Nazi Germany. Its air force was subordinated to the needs of the army, and its navy was weaker still. The United States was a maritime power in the tradition of Britain, and the war had seen air power added as a crucial element in American military doctrine.

Great navies traditionally have had a global outlook, and this tradition was absorbed by the U.S. Air Force as well. As a result, the institutional culture of the U.S. armed forces was already aligned to the notion of long-range power projection. In contrast, the Red Army lacked such traditions, and it had to be initiated from the top.

In the Shadow of War

The Red Army emerged from World War II as the savior of the Russian people from German annihilation. The great victory was one of the few indisputable successes of Soviet Russia and became a sacred memory for the postwar generation. The victory validated Stalin's hypermilitarization of the economy, and no Soviet leaders questioned the need to maintain strong armed forces.[8] Yet in spite of its enormous power, the Red Army of 1945 was in many ways archaic, depending more on size and brute force than on tactical or technical prowess. Some tactical innovations such as deep operations by tank and mechanized formations had been accepted with enthusiasm and employed with considerable skill. But the great victory helped hide the fact that modernization of the Red Army during the war was spotty. The Soviet Air Force was unable to dominate the tactical battlefield in a manner comparable to the Anglo-American forces and lacked the capability to conduct long-range bombing campaigns against the German heartland. The advent of the atomic bomb accentuated these weaknesses.

Stalin's public pronouncements in the 1940s suggested a willful refusal to embrace the nuclear revolution. Soviet military doctrine remained centered on the "permanent operating conditions," an unimaginative and traditional policy that emphasized the stability of the rear, troop morale, and the quantity and quality of divisions and weapons.[9] Yet Stalin's public utterances about military policy also contained a strong element of deception. Stalin publicly discounted the value of atomic weapons in war to undermine American efforts to use their nuclear monopoly to intimidate the Soviet Union. From his spies, Stalin knew that the U.S. atomic arsenal was small.[10] As long as atomic bombs were scarce, warfare in the early years of the nuclear age did not appear to be substantially different from warfare in the concluding years of the machine age.

Contrary to public pronouncements, Stalin clearly understood the value of atomic weapons and had authorized an expensive crash program at the end of World War II. During a conference on the bomb program late in 1946, Stalin gave a more candid appreciation of the bomb's merit: "Atomic bombs were the cheapest means of war."[11] The atomic bomb was only one element of the crash program. It was of little value if it could not be delivered against its intended targets, so means of delivering the bomb were also given high priority. Stalin's military plans also focused on the need to defend the Soviet Union from the threat posed by the new generation of strategic weapons and the long-range bomber, whether armed with conventional or atomic bombs. So air defense was also assigned a high priority in the late 1940s. The Soviet program to develop strategic offensive weapons took considerable time to emerge, while strategic defensive weapons—interceptor aircraft, air defense radar, antiaircraft guns—were nearer to realization. As a result, they took up a larger share of Soviet defense procurement through the Stalin years. Starting in August 1945, Stalin created three special organizations to manage the development of these new strategic weapons: Special Committee No. 1 under Lavrenty Beria for the development of nuclear weapons, Special Committee No. 2 under Georgy Malenkov for the development of missiles, and Special Committee No. 3 under Maksim Saburov for strategic air defense.[12]

A major impediment to the development of a new generation of Soviet strategic nuclear weapons was the backwardness of Soviet defense industries. The Soviet Union had managed to win its war against Nazi Germany in large measure due to the strengths of its industries, which had outproduced its opponents in tanks, fighter aircraft, guns, and ammunition. The wartime emphasis had been on quantity over quality. A limited number of conventional weapons were given priority, while expensive and unproven new technologies were treated as unaffordable luxuries. As a result, in 1945 the Soviet Union was behind countries such as the United States and Britain in defense technology. Soviet radar technology was poor and for nearly a decade depended on lend-lease British and American designs.[13] As a result, the Soviet Union had virtually no experience in the conduct of electronic warfare. In aviation technology, the Soviet Union was one of the few major powers not to field a jet fighter by the end of the war, and its early postwar jet fighters depended on derivatives of captured German engines or imported British designs. Soviet aviation technology had been forced to rely on plywood for much of its airframe construction and was behind in the application of aluminum and light alloys in airframe construction. Aircraft power-plant design had stagnated, particularly in the area of high-horsepower engines and turbochargers, which were essential in heavy-bomber design. Soviet histories have promulgated the myth that the Katyusha multiple-rocket launchers formed the technological basis for postwar Soviet missile development.[14] However, the Katyushas were a technological dead end, because their primitive solid-fuel propellant was too heavy and inefficient to power modern guided missiles.

Two other factors presented major hurdles to the development of new strategic weapons. The enormous human and material losses suffered by the Soviet Union during the war years required it to reconstruct its major cities and industries in the vital western regions. This was not a burden shared by the United States, which had escaped the war unscathed by war on its own soil. Given the choice between civilian reconstruction or the new weapon programs, Stalin gave the military programs priority. The two largest civil engineering programs in the late Stalin years were the construction of the nuclear reactor facilities near Chelyabinsk and Krasnoyarsk.

Soviet industry had been built up around its military plants in the 1930s, and its civilian industries were weak and backward. The new arms race depended upon a steady flow of technological innovation in a broad range of areas, including composites and alloys, chemicals, and electronics. These innovations often appeared first in the American civilian economy, which proved a rich resource for the defense industries. This was seldom the case in the Soviet Union, and the lack of a vigorous civilian high-tech sector acted as a constant drag on the Soviet defense industries.

Building the Bomb

Although Soviet scientists were aware of the possibilities of the military use of nuclear energy since the late 1930s, research on nuclear weapons prior to World War II was on a very small scale and without strong government support.[15] Some senior scientists regarded it as "breaking away from practical work" for the defense industries, and it was viewed in some quarters as "false science."[16] As the war drew nearer, and the threat of German development of a nuclear weapon was suspected, attitudes began to change. A central coordinating committee called the Uranium Commission was formed in June 1940 but was viewed as too small by the younger generation of scientists. Cowed by Stalin's purges, the senior physicists were unwilling to press for too expensive a program. The head of the prestigious Leningrad Physics-Technology Institute, Abram Ioffe, concluded that "if mastery of missile technology is a matter for the next fifty years, then the employment of nuclear energy is a matter of the next century."[17] In any event, the outbreak of the war in June 1941 put a complete end to the nuclear program, because the main labs in Leningrad were soon surrounded and the staff diverted to more pressing needs.

The new catalyst for the program came from the extensive Soviet espionage network. On 4 November 1941, Lavrenty Beria, the head of the Soviet NKVD secret police, received a coded telegram from the London embassy indicating that theoretical work on a uranium bomb was being undertaken in England.[18] Stalin remained skeptical of this information, but Beria continued to collect reports until a more convincing case could be made. The material was corroborated by the rival GRU military intelligence service, which received information from the German émigré scientist Klaus Fuchs, who was working on the British bomb program.[19] In

May 1942 Beria went to Stalin with the new espionage evidence, and after a meeting with senior Soviet scientists, Stalin ordered the start of a Soviet atomic bomb program.

The Soviet bomb program was headed by a young physicist, Igor Kurchatov.[20] With a budget of only R 20 million, the Soviet program was a very small program compared to the Anglo-American, German, and Japanese efforts.[21] The center of the uranium bomb research was a new organization in Moscow, code-named Laboratory No. 2 of the USSR Academy of Sciences. At the end of 1943, there were only about fifty people on the staff, and only twenty scientists. Even as late as the summer of 1945, the bomb program had little priority, little funding, and little equipment.[22] A program to begin the mining and processing of uranium ore did not start until November 1942 and had little initial success. While uranium deposits were discovered in remote regions of the Soviet Union, resources were too scarce during the war to engage in a significant mining operation. The Soviet government approached the United States to obtain enough uranium oxide ore to construct an atomic reactor similar in size to the first American one in Chicago. Realizing the intentions of the purchase, the Americans stalled, consenting in 1944 to the shipment of only a thousand pounds of uranium salts and two pounds of low-grade uranium metal in an attempt to "smoke out" the scope of the Soviet program. In spite of the paltry resources, the Soviet program made some significant progress if for no other reason than the steady stream of espionage material. By 1945 the Soviet spy nets had placed several agents in the U.S. Manhattan project at Los Alamos and scattered in the other sites in the United States, Canada, and Europe.[23] Kurchatov later stated that the work of the espionage agencies accounted for half the success of the Soviet atomic bomb program.[24]

By 1945 the success of the espionage ring had allowed Beria to usurp administrative control over the program. The growing power of his police empire provided much of the human and material resources needed to accelerate the program. As the end of the war freed up resources, the NKVD expedited uranium mining operations in Central Asia in the Fergana Valley using labor camp prisoners. A "special regime camp" was set up on the outskirts of Chelyabinsk in the Ural Mountains to begin work on a secret factory for uranium processing. This began a pattern of the use of GULAG labor in the early Soviet bomb program.

The Bomb Program Accelerates

Prior to 1945 Stalin had a very limited appreciation of the revolutionary nature of the atomic bomb. He began to pay more attention in 1945 as evidence mounted that the Anglo-American Manhattan program was on the brink of success. At the 24 July 1945 Potsdam Conference, the new American president, Harry Truman, cryptically informed Stalin that the United States had a "new weapon of unusual destructive force." Stalin said that he was "glad to hear it" and hoped that it would be put "to good use against the Japanese." Truman and Churchill were left with the impression that Stalin did not comprehend the new weapon's significance. This was not the case, and at an August 1945 meeting with Kurchatov and other senior officials, he pleaded, "Comrades—a single demand of you. Get us atomic weapons in the shortest time possible. As you know, Hiroshima has shaken the whole world. The balance has been broken. Build the bomb—it will remove the great danger from us!"[25] In late August 1945, a new organization to manage the bomb program was formed entirely separate from the rest of the defense industry, called the First Chief Directorate of the USSR Council of People's Commissars (PGU pri SNK).[26]

The design of the bomb itself was immeasurably helped by the espionage material, which provided details on the basic configurations developed by the United States. Although bomb design presented the most obvious challenge, the task of mining and processing uranium to fuel the bomb was the most complicated and expensive element of the effort. The mining and chemical processing operations alone would cost billions of rubles and require the labor of tens of thousands of workers.[27] Stalin gave Beria two years to carry out the program, with a test explosion set for 1948.

Occupied Germany contained a wealth of resources useful for the Soviet atomic bomb program, including scientists, laboratory equipment, and uranium deposits. The Germans had not been very successful in bomb design but had made key breakthroughs in uranium processing technologies.[28] The Germans had begun tapping uranium deposits in central Europe, such as in Czechoslovakia, providing an early source for uranium ores. By the end of 1945, Soviet scientists had collected a hundred tons of uranium oxide, the first substantial amount of uranium acquired by the Soviet atomic project.[29] Several German physicists would play a vital role in the design of uranium separation technology.[30] Two German labs were organized in the Soviet Union as part of the NKVD network of "special camps": Object A at Sinop, near the city of Sukhumi on the Black Sea, and Object G near Agudzeri.[31] A Russian scientist involved in the bomb program later concluded that German aid in the form of the captured scientists, uranium, and laboratory equipment accelerated the Soviet bomb program by as much as five years.[32] Without the German aid, and without the data obtained from the United States through espionage, the bomb program probably would have taken the ten years estimated by U.S. intelligence instead of the four years it actually took. The effort to recruit members of the Japanese atomic bomb program at the Konan development center in Manchuria were less successful, though Japanese mines in North Korea later proved a fruitful source of fissionable material.[33]

With a wealth of detail on the Anglo-American bomb effort, Kurchatov expanded the Soviet investigation beyond the original gun configuration, like the Hiroshima bomb, to include the plutonium-implosion configuration, like the Nagasaki bomb. The potential use of plutonium for the bomb was the most important lesson of Beria's intelligence efforts, because it would be easier to extract than U-235. This espionage discovery enabled the Soviet Union to explode a bomb at least two years sooner than if they had continued to pursue their own gun-configuration bomb fueled with uranium. Plutonium could be produced within the reactor that Kurchatov was building in Laboratory No. 2 in Moscow. The process of chemically separating the plutonium from the reactor output was less of a technological hurdle than the complex uranium isotope separation techniques being developed by the captive German scientists. Kurchatov had a broad appreciation of the relative costs of the different approaches from intelligence material and published reports on the American effort.[34] The CIA concluded in 1956 that "if outside information [from espionage] had not been made available, the Soviets simply could not have had the time to do the required basic research in reactor and weapons design and produce a weapon in the period it was accomplished."[35] Espionage saved the Soviets considerable time in basic research by removing the need to explore expensive and unproductive blind alleys that had already been explored and rejected by the Americans, and to concentrate their efforts into the most productive avenues of development using proven technologies. On the other hand, the espionage material would have been of little value except in the hands of a group of skilled physicists and engineers prepared to exploit it.

In 1946, the main hurdle facing the Soviet atomic bomb program was the lack of sufficient uranium ore. The uranium problem was so severe that some American military leaders, including the head of the Manhattan Project, Maj. Gen. Leslie Groves, believed that it would take the Soviets twenty years to build their first bomb. Erroneous wartime assessments had concluded that the combined Soviet and Czech deposits would total only about 5 percent of the world's uranium supply. U.S. teams operating in Germany in 1945 had managed to scour up much of the German uranium, and to further stymie the Soviet effort, an Anglo-American effort was undertaken to buy up the world's uranium stocks and preempt Soviet purchases.[36] The U.S. assessments were mistaken, since they did not appreciate the full scope of uranium deposits in central Europe, and they were unaware of the large uranium deposits in the Soviet Union. By 1950 about 100,000 miners and other workers had become involved in uranium mining in the USSR, nearly all from the GULAG forced labor camps. Occupied Germany proved to be the most productive source of uranium, about 45 percent of Soviet production, according to later CIA estimates. European sources accounted for over three-quarters of the uranium extracted by the Soviet program through 1950 (table 1.1).

Table 1.1

Soviet Uranium Extraction, 1946–50 (tons)[37]

	1946	1947	1948	1949	1950	Total
Soviet ore supply	37	1,430	2,540	3,970	5,500	13,477
European ore supply	0	340	1,140	1,870	3,220	6,570
Total ore supply	37	1,770	3,680	5,840	8,720	20,047
Soviet uranium extracted	50	129	182	278	417	1,056
European uranium extracted	60	210	452	989	1,640	3,351
Total uranium extracted	110	339	634	1,267	2,057	4,407

As supplies of uranium were mined and processed, they were shipped to Kurchatov's lab in Moscow. The first refined uranium became available in January 1946, intended for the creation of a nuclear reactor.[38] The construction of the F-1 reactor was an enormously expensive undertaking, costing about $120 million, or about half the Soviet nuclear weapons budget in 1947, according to CIA estimates. The reactor design was based on the American Hanford test reactor because it was suitable for plutonium production, while the first American reactor, the Fermi pile in Chicago, was not. The first controlled nuclear chain reaction in the USSR took place on 25 December 1946. The successful completion of the reactor represented the first of three key hurdles the Soviet bomb program had to accomplish. The next two stages of the program were already under way: the production of sufficient fissile material to fuel the first bomb, and the design of the bomb itself.

Plutonium production for the first Soviet atomic bomb was undertaken at Combine No. 817 in Kyshtym, code-named Chelyabinsk-40. A related plant for chemically separating the plutonium was code-named Chelyabinsk-65.[39] Part of the Chelyabinsk-65 plant was constructed under one of the neighboring lakes, with massive concrete reinforcement to harden it against an American air attack. The first production reactor took eighteen months to assemble and finally became operational on 10 June 1948.[40] An accident in June 1948 shut it down for over a month. Due to the high priority afforded the program, the repairs were undertaken without proper radiation protection for the workers, leading to extensive radiation poisoning. More than two thousand workers were diagnosed with radiation sickness in the first few years of operation due to the lack of suitable protection. The complete lack of environmental safeguards led to contamination of the nearby river system, and about 124,000 people in the neighboring region were affected by radiation sickness by 1952. While environmental safeguards would later improve, the atomic program would leave Russia with a legacy of radioactive despoilation of vast regions of the Urals. The first batch of plutonium for the bomb program was delivered in February 1949, but it took several more months to machine the actual warhead core.

By 1949 construction had begun on two additional reactors at Chelyabinsk-40, bringing the total to three in 1952. A second major facility for the manufacture of fissionable materials, Combine No. 815 (Krasnoyarsk-26), was built near the small Siberian village of Zheleznogorsk beginning on 26 February 1950.[41] Its plutonium-production reactors were placed in deep underground bunkers. It was one of the largest Soviet construction projects to date, involving the work of over 100,000 soldiers and 65,000 GULAG workers.[42] Plutonium production began in 1958, several years later than at Kyshtym.

A special design bureau was formed to develop the bomb on 8 April 1946 and code-named KB-11 (Design Bureau-11).[43] It was located at the new Arzamas-16 facility at the old Sarov monastery, near the industrial city of Gorky. The team was headed by Yuly B. Khariton, who led Soviet bomb design through most of the following four decades.[44] An outline of the bomb design was submitted on 25 July 1946.[45] At least two bomb designs were approved, a direct copy of the American Fat Man plutonium bomb designated as RDS-1, or Izdeliye 501 (Item 501), and an original Soviet design designated RDS-2, or Izdeliye 601. Stalin insisted that the proven American design receive priority with a test scheduled for 1 January 1948, to be followed by a test of the Soviet design on 1 June 1948. Continued delays in processing the ore delayed the test program by more than a year. A site in the Kazakhstan deserts to test the new bomb, code-named Semipalatinsk-21, was chosen in 1948.[46] The first bomb was tested from a 50 m (160 ft) high steel tower. The first test of the RDS-1 bomb, code-named Pervaya Molniya (First Lightning), was conducted on 29 August 1949 and had a yield of about twenty-two kilotons.[47]

The detonation of the first Soviet atomic bomb was not publicly announced, and the United States learned of it from atmospheric sampling. U.S. intelligence agencies had not been expecting the first detonation for several more years. There was a tangible impact on both U.S. and Soviet foreign policy. Possession of the bomb gave Stalin more confidence in dealing with the United States. Recent accounts of the origins of the Korean War suggest that Stalin was willing to support the North Korean invasion of South Korea in June 1950 in part due to the belief that possession of an atomic bomb by the Soviet Union would deter the United States from making any response.

On 3 March 1949 Stalin authorized the funding for the first twenty atomic bombs, to be produced at the Avangard plant in Saransk in 1949–50 at a rate of ten annually.[48] Two or three more test bombs were constructed, and a verification test of one of these bombs was conducted in 1950. It failed.[49] After changes to the design, the first three modified RDS-1 (Item 501M) bombs were completed in December 1951 at the KB-11 lab. These first bombs were never actually deployed with air force units but were kept disassembled in special warehouses. Due to lingering problems, only five series-production bombs were completed.[50] The KB-11 design bureau also developed their RDS-2 design, an original Soviet plutonium implosion design. It was tested at Semipalatinsk on 24 September 1951 under the code name Second Lightning, exploding with a yield of thirty-eight kilotons. Stalin did not publicly announce the detonation of the bomb, though the United States soon learned on the basis of trace elements detected in the atmosphere.

The Uranium Problem

Although the first plutonium bombs had proven successful, the potential yield of such devices was less than that possible with a bomb fueled by uranium or a composite uranium-plutonium core. Uranium separation had been given lower priority in the rush to build the first bomb, and additional resources were shifted to this effort in 1950, after the demonstration of the first successful plutonium fission bombs.

As in the American case, the 1948 decision to proceed with a uranium gaseous-diffusion separation plant took place before the actual technology had been perfected.[51] Development of the technology was undertaken by a number of design bureaus in Leningrad.[52] The Combine No. 813 (Sverdlovsk-45) facility was constructed in the village of Rusnoi, northwest of Sverdlovsk. Serious problems delayed uranium production until the beginning of 1951.[53] The difficulties plaguing the Sverdlovsk-45 project forced the development of alternative methods, especially electromagnetic separation. By the time that the electromagnetic separation facility was ready in 1952, the problems with the gaseous-diffusion plant had been overcome. The potential use of centrifuges was also examined but not seriously pursued. As a result, gaseous diffusion became the Soviet Union's primary uranium-extraction technology in spite of its energy inefficiencies. Due to the enormous cost of creating the Soviet uranium and plutonium processing industry, the atomic bomb program was one of the most expensive military programs of the Stalin years. The funding for the program was so secret that it has not been possible for Russian scholars to precisely determine the amount. The best estimate is that it cost about R 64.8 billion in 1951–55, or about 10 percent of the defense budget.[54]

With uranium becoming available, Khariton's KB-11 design bureau began to develop the RDS-3 composite-core bomb. This used a mixed core, with about 7 kg (15.4 lb) of uranium and 3.5 kg (7.7 lb) of plutonium. Such a bomb design offered the possibility of a higher yield than any of the all-plutonium bombs tested up to that stage.[55] The RDS-3, the first Soviet atomic bomb dropped from an aircraft, was delivered by a Tupolev Tu-4 bomber over Semipalatinsk on 18 October 1951. Its yield was double that of the first Soviet A-bomb, at about forty-two kilotons.[56] A total of three production RDS-3 bombs were completed by March 1952. An improved version with neutron injection, called the RDS-3I, was tested on 23 October 1954 and produced a yield of sixty-two kilotons. The serial production of the RDS-3 began alongside the RDS-1 at the Avangard plant in 1953 at an initial rate of twenty per year.[57] To manage the new bomb-manufacturing plants, in 1955 the nuclear industry created the Main Directorate for the Manufacture of Special Ammunition, better known as the 6th GU-MSM. In spite of this vast effort, the Soviet Union had less than a dozen bombs in stock at the time of Stalin's death in 1953.

Building a Strategic Offensive Force

At the end of the Second World War, the heavy bomber was the only means to deliver nuclear weapons. The Soviet Union was far behind the United States and Britain in 1945 and had to create such a force from scratch. The Soviet Air Force had developed a sizable heavy-bomber force in the 1930s based around the Tupolev TB-3 bomber.[58] But the air force did not sustain sufficient interest in long-range strategic bombing. The bomber designers were imprisoned during the Great Purge, and strategic bombing fell from Stalin's favor. At the outset of the war in 1941, there were only four heavy-bomber regiments, and their poor technical state and the obsolescence of their aircraft rendered them largely ineffective.[59]

For all intents and purposes, the Soviet Air Force lacked a strategic-bomber force during the war. Only a single type of heavy bomber, the Petlyakov Pe-8, was produced during the war, and only ninety-three were completed.[60] At no point during the war did Soviet heavy-bomber strength exceed thirty heavy bombers, at a time when the Royal Air Force (RAF) and the United States Army Air Forces (USAAF) were conducting one thousand plane raids on Germany.[61] During World War II, the Long-Range Aviation branch of the Soviet Air Force was mainly assigned to the tactical bombing role, supporting army operations. Unlike Britain's RAF or America's USAAF, the Soviet Air Force did not have a practical doctrine for the strategic bombing of enemy industrial targets. The Soviet Air Force did launch a number of propaganda raids on Berlin and other central European cities during the war, but they were very small in scale and little more than a nuisance.[62]

The problems confronting the Soviet strategic-bomber force were both doctrinal and technological. Stalin had shown an aversion to strategic bombing, and resources were concentrated on tactical aviation instead. The main technological problem was the lack of powerful, fuel-efficient engines. This was also the bane of the German strategic-bomber program, and a difficulty that would continue to plague Soviet strategic-bomber development for the next two decades. Stalin made several requests to the United States for delivery of strategic bombers as part of the lend-lease program, but these were turned down.[63] At the end of the war, the Soviet Long-Range Aviation Force was still nothing more than a tactical air force, unable to carry out deep bombing operations, and equipped mostly with short-range bombers.[64] It was reorganized in 1946 in anticipation of becoming a true strategic-bomber force.[65]

On 7 September 1943 Andrei N. Tupolev's OKB-156 design bureau was authorized to start work on a new strategic bomber called Aircraft 64 with an effective range of 6,000 km (3,700 mi) while carrying an eight-ton bomb load. The requirement was based on Soviet intelligence information on the American B-29 bomber. While Tupolev's design studies were being undertaken, three intact B-29s landed in the Soviet Union after being damaged during raids on Japan.[66] The United States requested their return, but the requests were ignored. The three aircraft were flown to test facilities in central Russia in late 1944 for trials. During the spring of 1945, Stalin decided that it would be more prudent to copy the American design than to develop Aircraft 64, and on 6 June 1945 Tupolev was ordered to start the process. Delays in the program and lingering efforts on the canceled Aircraft 64 by Tupolev's design staff were among the ostensible reasons for the purge of aviation minister A. I. Shakurin and the head of the Long-Range Aviation Force, Gen. A. A. Novikov, in 1946.[67] The high priority afforded the bomber program was closely tied to the initiation of the Soviet atomic bomb program. As a result, supervision was turned over to the head of the secret police chief, Lavrenty Beria, who also headed the atomic bomb program.

By Soviet standards, the bomber program was a massive effort. A total of sixty-four design bureaus and research institutes, as well as nine hundred factories, were eventually involved in the development and production effort. Many compromises had to be made, since the American aircraft was manufactured to English measurement, not metric measurement.

The first test flight occurred near the Kazan production plant in May 1947, and by the summer of 1947, ten aircraft had been delivered to the main air force test center at Zhukovsky, outside Moscow. When accepted for service use, the B-29 copy was designated as the Tupolev Tu-4. The first three of the new Tu-4 bombers took part in the annual Soviet Aviation Day air show over Tushino air base on 3 August 1947. The display confused Western intelligence agencies, which were unsure whether the aircraft were simply the three missing B-29s. U.S. Air Force leaders initially dismissed reports that the Russians had managed to copy the B-29

The first nuclear delivery system for Soviet atomic bombs was the Tupolev Tu-4 heavy bomber. It was nearly identical to the American Boeing B-29 Superfortress. This example is preserved at the Russian Air Force museum at Monino.

as preposterous; the magnitude of such an effort was deemed to be outside the capability of Soviet industry. But the presence of a fourth transport aircraft, the Tu-70, based on the B-29 design, suggested that production had begun.

The first twenty Tu-4 bombers were completed by the end of 1947, and testing concluded in the summer of 1948.[68] Production was extended to two more plants.[69] The first Tu-4 strategic-bomber regiments entered service in 1949. The Tu-4 bombers were plagued with problems, not altogether surprising in view of its revolutionary technologies. The difficulties with the Tu-4 manufacturing program underscored a significant difference between the Soviet and American defense effort. While the U.S. designers could often turn to the robust civil economy for advanced materials, tools, and subcomponents, the Soviet designers were usually forced to develop everything themselves, down to the raw materials. This was a hindrance to the Soviet designers and a curse to the Soviet citizen, since technologies developed inside the defense industry did not necessarily leak back out into the impoverished civil economy. The problem of copying a foreign design was that by the time it entered service, it was already obsolete. By 1952 the U.S. Air Force had fielded the B-47 jet bomber, which had the range and payload of the

Tu-4 but much superior performance. Furthermore, the Strategic Air Command was already fielding the B-36 bomber, the first truly intercontinental bomber, which could reach targets in the Soviet Union from the United States.

Until the advent of first Soviet atomic bombs in 1949, the Tu-4 was armed with conventional high-explosive bombs. Some Tu-4's were modified for atomic weapons delivery under the designation Tu-4A (A = *atomny*). The modifications included insulation and heat control of the bomb bay, as well as a weapons arming and control system. A total of 1,000 Tu-4 bombers were ordered, but only 847 were completed by the time production ended in 1952. The premature end of Tu-4 production was due to the lessons of the Korean air war in 1950–53. In 1950 the Soviet Union began committing several of its MiG-15 jet fighter regiments to combat over Korea.[70] Large-scale battles with B-29 formations took place in April and May 1951. Later in the year, the threat posed by the MiG-15 proved so great that B-29s were withdrawn from daylight bombing missions and restricted to nighttime attacks.[71] The American bombers did not manage to shoot down a single Soviet jet fighter over Korea, a failure that had obvious implications for any intended missions by Soviet bombers against the American air defense network.[72] The lessons of the Korean air war created a nagging doubt in the mind of Soviet defense planners about the survivability of bomber aircraft in modern battlefield conditions.

By 1953 the Soviet Long-Range Aviation Force had deployed three air armies and one independent bomber corps equipped with the Tu-4.[73] When initially deployed in the late 1940s without atomic bombs, the Tu-4 bomber force was capable of little more than harassment attacks against the United States.[74] As nuclear weapons became more widely available in the mid-1950s, the Tu-4 began to be recognized by United States defense officials as a more serious threat, though one with distinct limitations.

The performance of the Tu-4 was markedly poorer than that of the B-29, on which it was based. The Tu-4 was heavier than the B-29 due to problems in the copying process. In addition, it was based on early versions of the B-29 that did not have the performance of later versions, including the greater fuel capacity. Finally, Soviet air operations were hampered by the use of low-octane fuel, even though the B-29 engines were optimized for the use of high-octane fuel. Under normal operating conditions, the Tu-4 could reach targets only 1,525 km (945 mi) away from its base on a round-trip flight.[75] The optimal location for bomber attacks on the United States would have been the upper Chukotsky Peninsula, in the northern Pacific area, such as the airbase at Anadyr, the closest point from the USSR to the U.S.A. From Anadyr, a Tu-4 could reach central Alaska and portions of northwestern Canada, but not even as far as northern Washington state. The alternative was a one-way mission. A Tu-4 taking off from Anadyr on a one-way mission could attack targets in the northwestern United States. The northeastern United States could not be reached on one-way flights, even those launched from bases in the northernmost portions of the European USSR, such as the Kola Peninsula. One-way missions were conceivable, and the U.S. Air Force planned one-way missions against the USSR for its B-47 medium bombers during these years.

Another alternative was aerial refueling. The combat radius of a Tu-4 refueled in midair would be extended to a maximum of 4,000 km (2,500 mi), enabling it to reach targets on a one-way mission through much of the western and northern United States. The first efforts to develop aerial refueling capability began in 1948, and the first test took place on 16 June 1949.[76] Following extensive trials and several different versions of the system, only three Tu-4 bombers were converted to the tanker role, starting in 1952, because the system was far from ideal.[77] So there were never enough of these tankers to stage anything more than a token raid on the United States.

The almost complete lack of atomic bombs until 1954 forced the Soviet Air Force to consider the possibility of having to use conventional bombs in strategic air strikes. To enhance their effectiveness, guided bombs were developed to arm the Tu-4 starting in 1950.[78] These programs were headed by Aleksandr D. Nadiradze, who would later lead the Soviet Union's solid-fuel ballistic-missile program. Flight tests of the Kondor guided bomb began in September 1954 from Tu-4 bombers. By the time that the Kondor became available, nuclear bombs had become more plentiful, so the guided-bomb effort slipped into limbo.

Early Nuclear War Plans

Once the Soviet nuclear industry was on the verge of manufacturing atomic bombs in quantity in 1953, Stalin began the first steps to prepare the armed forces for employing them against the United States in the event of a war.[79] The initial schemes were unrealistic to the point of being ludicrous. In the summer of 1952, air force marshal P. F. Zhigarev was ordered by Stalin to begin preparations for the formation of a hundred bomber divisions that could be forward deployed on the Arctic ice beyond the North Pole to strike at targets in the United States.[80] Because there were only a dozen Tu-4 heavy-bomber divisions, Stalin insisted that they be formed with other bombers, such as the new Tu-16 and IL-28 jet bombers.

The Soviet Navy became involved in the scheme with some equally preposterous proposals. In the late 1940s navy officers came up with the idea of seizing forward American air bases in remote locations such as Alaska or Greenland rather than creating air bases on the inhospitable Arctic ice packs. The air bases would be captured by a submarine task force, and then the Tu-4 bombers would be flown to use the bases as forward-staging areas for attacks on the continental

United States.[81] In 1948 the Soviet Navy authorized the development of the Project 621 amphibious assault submarine.[82] The submarine contained enough equipment and men to fight a small battle, including 10 tanks, 16 trucks, 14 artillery pieces, and 745 naval infantry, all of which could be landed using bow ramps. The submarine even contained three Lavochkin La-11 fighter aircraft that could be launched by catapult from the deck to provide air cover. Senior navy officials were skeptical about the practicality of the design, and it was canceled before construction began. The project was revived in 1952 due to Stalin's interest in possible air operations against the United States. The new Project 626 submarine was smaller, with a more realistic cargo capacity. It included a telescoping tower in the sail, which could punch through Arctic ice and was wide enough to permit troops to climb from inside the submerged submarine up to the surface. The whole idea of operating from Arctic bases was preposterous due to the difficulty of transporting supplies and equipment, and the scheme was abandoned following Stalin's death in 1953.

Stalin's interest in intercontinental power projection did force the Soviet Air Force in 1952 to begin training for transpolar operations against the United States from three bases in the Arctic in 1952: Dickson Island in the Kara Sea, Mys Shmidta on the Chukchi Sea, and Providenia on the Chukotsky Peninsula.[83] Weather conditions were too severe to permit year-round basing, and rail lines to support the base with fuel and equipment were nonexistent. As a result, Soviet strategic bombers were not permanently stationed in the Arctic. In 1953 specially modified Tu-4 bombers began to conduct reconnaissance flights over the polar region to gain experience in transpolar flights and secure additional navigational data.[84] A series of 1957 flights by special reconnaissance TU-4R versions included missions toward Spitzbergen in Greenland, over Franz Josef Island, and toward the northern Canadian coast.[85]

Aside from its range limitations, the viability of a Tu-4 attack against the continental United States was further undermined by the rapid growth of U.S. strategic defenses. While U.S. air defenses in 1949 were not particularly impressive, the alarm caused by the first appearance of the Tu-4 bomber led to a crash program to improve continental air defense. These defenses posed a serious threat to the Tu-4 even if a few bombers could reach the United States. The technical solution to the air defense problem was the use of stand-off missiles launched from the bomber instead of free-fall bombs. Such missiles could be released from distances beyond the effective range of American air defense missiles or guns. Work on a bomber-launched missile for the Tu-4 began in the late 1940s. The first to be tested were improved copies of the German V-1 Buzz Bomb. These were developed by Vladimir Chelomey's OKB-51 design bureau in Tushino and were called the 10Kh and 14Kh. Chelomey's buzz bombs were not particularly successful, but the designer would emerge a decade later during the Khrushchev years as one of the major ballistic-missile and space-system designers.

Early Strategic Defenses

In the late 1940s and early 1950s, the Soviet Union embarked on one of the most sophisticated and expensive weapons development programs of the early Cold War years, larger even than its nuclear weapons program.[86] Faced by the threat of U.S. and British strategic-bomber forces, Stalin ordered the creation of an interlocking system of strategic air defenses. During the Stalin years, far more funding was directed to strategic air defenses than to the offensive bomber program— about 15 percent of the annual military expenditures, compared to 6 percent for the bomber effort and 10 percent for the atomic bomb program.[87] In August 1950 Stalin ordered the formation of the Third Main Directorate of the Council of Ministers, to speed up work on strategic defense.[88] This system required the creation of a nationwide network of radar stations to detect incoming aircraft, and a command-and-control network to collate the data from these stations and pass it on to other elements of the system to intercept the enemy bombers. Soviet radar production more than quadrupled between 1950 and 1955, and funding increased more than tenfold.[89] The three primary combat elements of the defense system were new radar-directed antiaircraft guns, surface-to-air missiles, and jet fighter aircraft.

This high-tech solution was forced on the Soviet Union by studying the wartime German experiences in repelling Anglo-American strategic-bomber attacks with conventional artillery and fighter aircraft, which largely failed. Although the levels of attrition of the bombers was sometimes quite high, such air defenses could not prevent the vast majority of bombers from reaching the target area. This was bad enough when bombers were armed with conventional high-explosive bombs, but even less adequate when confronting bombers carrying atomic weapons.

The Soviet Air Force quickly appreciated that existing Soviet piston-engine fighters would have little hope against contemporary American bombers such as the B-29, and so attention turned to a new generation of jet fighters. After a number of false starts, in 1949 the Soviet Union began a massive manufacturing program for its new Mikoyan MiG-15 fighter, based on copies of an imported British jet engine. A total of 13,056 were manufactured, making it one of the most widely manufactured combat aircraft of the postwar years.[90] This aircraft was soon put to the test in the skies over Korea, and by the spring of 1951, its successes against American B-29 bombers convinced many in the Soviet Air Force that the days of manned bombers were over.

In spite of the successes of the MiG-15, it was still only a clear-weather, daylight fighter. For poor weather and at night, other methods were still necessary until all-weather interceptors became available, late in the 1950s. As a short-term solution, the army began a program to field radar-directed antiaircraft guns in 1948.[91] German antiaircraft guns had not proven particularly effective in 1944–45, but it was presumed that the use of radar direction and the new radar proximity fuze would considerably enhance their effectiveness. The proximity fuze was another acquisition from the espionage program against the United States in World War II, and most of the early Soviet air defense radars were copies or derivatives of wartime American and British designs.[92]

A U.S. Army study in 1958 concluded that Moscow had the densest antiaircraft-gun defenses of any location, heavier even than the densest concentrations in Germany in 1945. Soviet efforts to expand the antiaircraft belts around major cities continued well into the 1950s. Five antiaircraft divisions were added in 1951 to cover the frontiers with NATO, followed by another four divisions in 1953 to expand coverage of Leningrad and the industrial regions of the Donbass and Urals. Indeed, U.S. intelligence estimated that the antiaircraft-gun effort alone cost about R 150 billion in 1946–61, about five times the cost of the intercontinental bomber program.[93] Continued reliance on this obsolete and largely ineffective technology was testament to the power of institutional inertia in the Soviet armed forces. It should be pointed out that the Soviet Army did not disband its last horse cavalry divisions until the Khrushchev reforms of 1957.

In the long term, more hope was placed on surface-to-air missiles, and Soviet engineers began by studying German designs in late 1945 and 1946.[94] In 1948 Stalin ordered the initiation of a program to use advanced technology to defend Moscow against bomber attack.[95] After failed attempts to copy German missile designs, an entirely new system called the Berkut was started in 1950.[96] The Berkut strategic air defense system was intended to defend Moscow against an attack by one thousand bombers.[97] This requirement was based, no doubt, on the scale of raids launched by Britain and the United States against key German cities in 1943–45. The requirement reveals Stalin's lack of sophistication in military technology. With the advent of the atomic bomb, massed raids were a thing of the past, since a small number of nuclear-armed bombers could accomplish the same task.

The S-25 Berkut system was declared operational in August 1957. In spite of its shortcomings, the development and construction of the S-25 system was a remarkable accomplishment in view of the relative lack of sophistication of Soviet military electronics at the end of World War II. Nikita Khrushchev nicknamed the Berkut the Moskovsky Chastokol (Moscow Palisades), unknowingly pinpointing

During the early 1950s the Soviet Union spent as much on strategic-defense programs as on offensive forces. The single most expensive element of this program was the S-25 Berkut air defense missile network ringing Moscow, called SA-1 Guild by NATO. This missile and radar antenna from the system are preserved at the museum at Khodynka Field in Moscow.

its central problem. The system layout was ill-conceived, being spaced equally around the periphery of Moscow. This meant that at the most likely points of bomber attack, the north and west, the thin layer of defenses could be overwhelmed during an attack, or the defenses breached by preliminary attacks prior to the main bomber waves. The system could only engage subsonic targets, even though supersonic bombers were beginning to appear on the scene by the time of its deployment. Finally, in the mid-1950s, both the United States and Soviet Union were developing stand-off missiles such as the American AGM-28A Hound Dog. These posed a threat, since they were much smaller radar targets than a bomber and enabled the bomber to fire the missile from outside the lethal envelope of the Berkut. These shortcomings, as well as its high cost, led to rejection of the idea of extending the system to Leningrad in the late 1950s. The S-25 network remained in service for another two decades, though its effectiveness was always suspect. It was gradually replaced by more modern missiles.

The Strategic Balance in 1953

At the time of Stalin's death in 1953, the Soviet Union had managed to create the core of a strategic intercontinental nuclear force. Its most substantial accomplishment was the creation of its nuclear weapons industry, an enormously expensive enterprise in terms of money and human lives. The product of the new nuclear industry did not immediately transform the Soviet Union into a superpower like the United States. Few bombs were manufactured before 1954, and the Soviet Union's ability to deliver these weapons was too circumscribed by the limitations of its weapons technology, particularly in the area of heavy bombers. The backwardness of the Soviet aviation industry did not permit the development of intercontinental capability in the Stalin years, though the Tu-4 bomber program served as a seed for future programs. The next step in the race to superpower status would be the Soviet attempt to develop means for intercontinental nuclear weapons delivery. The Soviet Union's least impressive accomplishment in the Stalin years was its strategic defense program, which was horribly expensive, technically unsound, and bound for premature obsolescence.

The shortcomings of the Soviet strategic nuclear forces were so severe that it is doubtful that Stalin ever seriously considered their employment in a strike against the United States. Stalin was deterred from doing so by the far larger and more robust U.S. strategic forces, notably the U.S. Air Force's Strategic Air Command (SAC). In 1953, SAC had 185 B-36 bombers, able to hit targets nearly anywhere in the Soviet Union from bases in the United States.[98] In addition, SAC had 575 medium bombers, such as the B-47, that could reach the USSR from bases in Europe and the Pacific. At a time when the Soviet Union possessed less than a dozen bombs, the U.S. nuclear arsenal, with its 1,350 nuclear bombs, could have conducted a retaliatory strike on the USSR of unimaginable horror.[99]

2.   Bomber vs. Missile

1953–1959

Following the death of Stalin in 1953, a power struggle took place in the Kremlin, and Nikita Khrushchev eventually emerged as the new Soviet leader. The strategic programs started under Stalin did not immediately attract Khrushchev's attention because of his focus on the consolidation of his power and the lack of any immediate controversies over the course that the strategic-weapons programs would take. To an important extent, this was a period when technology was the primary driver in strategic-force decisions, since technological limitations largely dictated the shape and capabilities of the forces. It is sometimes called the "era of the chief designers," because it was a time when weapons engineers like Sergei Korolyov, Tupolev, and others played the predominant role in shaping the Soviet strategic forces. As in the United States, many different technological approaches were examined to determine which were viable and which were not, including strategic bombers, cruise missiles, ballistic missiles, and submarine-launched missiles.

The post-Stalin years saw the Soviet Union begin a sustained effort to reach superpower status. Its nuclear industry was on the verge of producing weapons in significant quantity. Soviet bomb designers kept pace with their American rivals in the next stage of the arms race, the development of thermonuclear fusion weapons. Intercontinental bombers finally entered Soviet service, but an unexpected rival to the bomber appeared in the form of missiles. The history of the strategic missile undermines the stereotype that Soviet weapons programs were tightly managed by the military and party leadership. Ballistic-missile development was pushed forward by the enthusiasm of the engineers and the budding aerospace industry and won only the most grudging support of the military. In the end, it was the launch of the first earth satellite, the Sputnik, that finally convinced Khrushchev that future Soviet military power would be based on the nuclear missile. This culminated in the formation of a new combat arm, the Strategic Missile Force (RVSN), in December 1959.

The Second Bomber Generation

In the spring of 1951, Stalin canceled further work on piston-engine bombers in favor of jet bombers, based on the experiences of the Korean air war. On 28 February 1951 the head of the Soviet Air Force, Gen. Pavel F. Zhigarev, had reported to Stalin that the air war over Korea had shown that propeller-driven bombers like the American B-29 and its Soviet copy, the Tu-4, were defenseless against the new jet fighters.[1] At the time, the Tupolev design bureau was working on its Tu-85 propeller-driven bomber, which had range sufficient to reach most industrial cities in the northern United States, and with refueling to reach virtually all of the United States. But there was some doubt that it could survive in the face of improving American air defense. Stalin was undoubtedly aware through intelligence sources of the U.S. Air Force's program to develop its first intercontinental jet bomber, the Boeing B-52 Stratofortress. Tupolev had a meeting with Stalin on this issue, but Tupolev insisted that Soviet jet technology was insufficiently mature to mass-produce jet engines efficient enough to power an intercontinental bomber. Tupolev was heavily involved in developing a new medium-range jet bomber, the Tu-16, which gave him considerable insight into the problems of designing bombers with intercontinental range. Stalin was infuriated that Soviet engineering could not keep pace with American technology. In March 1951 he ordered that a new design bureau be organized, headed by Vladimir Myasishchev, to design the first Soviet intercontinental jet bomber.[2] Ultimately, Tupolev was proved correct. Tupolev's turboprop propulsion scheme was a more practical alternative for intercontinental range given the limitations of Soviet jet engine technology in the early 1950s. Although Stalin was aggravated by Tupolev's stubbornness, he had enough respect for his skills that he permitted development of both Tupolev's turboprop Tu-95 and Myasishchev's jet-powered 2M to proceed. The requirement called for the delivery of a five-ton nuclear fission bomb and an unrefueled bomber range of 16,000 km (10,000 mi). Neither of these bombers was ready prior to Stalin's death in 1953.

Stalin gave Myasishchev two years to get his bomber design into the air and, to speed things up, gave him carte blanche to recruit promising young engineers from the Moscow aviation academies and design bureaus. Myasishchev had been an active designer for nearly a decade, but his previous design bureau had been closed in the postwar consolidation. None of his designs had ever been accepted for series production. He developed a reputation for conceiving imaginative and futuristic designs, but designs that could not be manufactured using existing Soviet technology. Myasishchev too often made rosy assessments of forthcoming propulsion technology and based his aircraft around new power plants that were not yet proven. His lack of realism proved to be a fatal flaw in many of his designs, as would prove to be the case again with the new strategic jet bomber. His new bureau, designated OKB-23, was set up adjacent to State Aviation Plant No. 23 in Fili, on the outskirts of Moscow. This was a clear indication of the priority afforded the program. Fili was one of the premier Soviet aviation factories, dating back to the 1920s, and one of three plants in the Soviet Union with experience in large-aircraft construction. The other two plants, in Kazan and Kuibyshev, were already committed to Tupolev bombers.

The first Myasishchev 2M bomber prototype was completed in January 1953. As Tupolev had predicted, the aircraft's range was barely half the requirement, only 9,000 km (5,500 mi). Such a range made it incapable of flying a two-way mission to the United States unless it was refueled, and the design did not incorporate aerial refueling equipment. When Khrushchev visited the plant to inspect the new bomber, he was shown a chart of the 2M's proposed flight profile against U.S. targets. The final stage of the flight took the bomber over Mexico, where the crew was expected to bail out, on the assumption that Mexico would be neutral. Khrushchev rebuked Myasishchev for such a preposterous scheme and instructed him to rectify the plane's problems. In spite of its inadequacies, the 2M was placed into production at the Fili aircraft plant in 1954 on a small scale under the military designation of M-4. It is better known in the West as the Bison A.

The prototype M-4 flew over Red Square during the 1954 May Day parade, giving the U.S. Air Force a good scare. On 13 July 1955 Western military attachés in Moscow were invited to the annual air show at the Tushino airbase. A wave of ten M-4 bombers passed overhead, followed later by two more waves of nine aircraft each. This suggested that the Soviets had almost thirty bombers already in service and it had reached quantity production. As some of the more skeptical Western attachés suspected at the time, it had all been a ruse. In fact, only ten aircraft had been ready for the air show, and they had been flown around in circles to create the illusion of greater numbers. Thirty-one M-4 bombers were completed at the Fili plant between January 1955 and June 1956, not including the first two prototypes. They were handmade in small production batches, and like many advanced designs of the period, they had a troubled service history. There were nine major accidents in 1955–58, finally leading the air force to withdraw the aircraft from service for a time. In the early 1960s the surviving twenty-five bombers were converted into aerial tankers to support other strategic-bomber units.

Stalin insisted that the Tu-4 be replaced by a jet bomber, even though Tupolev told him it was technologically impossible. The rival Myasishchev design bureau developed the 2M Bison bomber, which, as Tupolev had predicted, had inadequate range to reach the United States. (Courtesy Aviadata)

A major redesign program followed in 1956, called the 3M and M-6, substituting improved engines to extend its range to 12,000 km (7,500 mi). Called the Bison-B by NATO, the 3M was also the first variant of the Myasishchev bomber designed for aerial refueling. With aerial refueling, its range could be extended to 15,000 km (9,300 mi) to meet the air force requirement.[3] In spite of the range improvement, the 3M suffered from serious shortcomings in engine durability. The engines required depot overhaul every 100 flight hours or less, and this drastically diminished the operational value of the 3M. An expensive series of rebuilding efforts conducted through the late 1950s were only partially successful in redeeming the design. The 3M showed a more sophisticated approach to tactical problems, being the first version of the Bison to be fitted with an electronic warfare system to challenge U.S. air defenses.[4] Curiously enough, it was also the first Soviet aircraft with "stealth" features, using a special radar-absorbent paint derived from wartime German technology, coating its wing leading edges and other surfaces. Through 1960, 116 Bison bombers of all models were manufactured. There were never more than 60 Bison bombers in service with the Long-Range Aviation Force due to accidents and the conversion of many of the troublesome early M-4 aircraft into tankers.[5] In 1962, at peak strength, there were 57 3M bombers and 25 M-4 tankers in line regiments. The fate of the Myasishchev bomber was sealed due to its indifferent performance, reliability problems, and cost.[6]

The Tu-95 Bear Strategic Bomber

The first genuinely successful Soviet bomber with intercontinental range was the Tupolev Tu-95, better known by its NATO code name, Bear. The design of this aircraft can be traced back to preliminary design studies started in the summer of 1948 to explore the flight characteristics of a heavy strategic bomber with a swept-wing design.[7] The final pair of designs envisioned four jet engines or four turboprops. The version with four turboprops offered an intercontinental range of 13,000 km (8,000 mi), while its jet analog offered a range of only 10,000 km (6,200 mi), below the threshold necessary to reach targets in the depths of the United States. Tupolev was given the green light for his proposed turboprop strategic bomber on 11 July 1951, and it was on the basis of the initial work that he rebuffed Stalin's demand for a jet bomber.

The most important new element of the Tu-95 design was a new type of power plant, the turboprop engine, which used a jet engine to power the propellers. In the United States, Boeing had considered a similar turboprop configuration when designing its new B-52 strategic bomber, but had rejected it.[8] The first Tu-95/1 prototype was completed in September 1952 with less powerful engines than in-

Tupolev argued for a more conservative approach for the first intercontinental bomber, using turboprop propulsion instead of jet propulsion. The resulting Tu-95A Bear bomber proved to be a more robust and dependable aircraft than its rivals, and the later Tu-95MS version is still in service. This is a preserved example at the Monino museum.

tended, since new technology proved to be troublesome.[9] The first flight was conducted on 11 November 1952, and the prototype was lost due to an engine fire in late 1953. The definitive Tu-95/2 had its first flight on 16 February 1955.

The successful flight trials of the original Tu-95, combined with the delays and poor performance of the rival Myasishchev bomber, led to the government's decision in January 1955 to put the Tu-95 into series production. Production was undertaken at the Kuibyshev plant, and the first two production Tu-95's came off the assembly lines in October 1955. Thirty-one Tu-95 series-production bombers were built through 1957, called Bear-A by NATO. Due to engine and propeller problems, production shifted to the use of the more refined NK-12M engine, resulting in the Tu-95M. These went into production in 1957, and nineteen were completed when production ended in 1958. Some consideration was given to the development of an improved version of the Tu-95, called the Tu-96, which could cruise at a higher altitude, 17,000 m (56,000 ft), to evade U.S. jet interceptors. However, by the time that the prototype flew in January 1956, it was obvious that such altitudes offered no protection against air defense missiles, and the project was dropped.[10] The most adventurous propulsion option for the Tu-95 was an experimental nuclear power plant version begun in December 1955 under the code name Samolyot 119 Lastochka (Swallow), which would have given the bomber virtually unlimited range.[11] The design never proved practical due to the radiation hazards posed to the crew, and it was abandoned after a nonflying test bed was built.

The Tu-95 first became operational with heavy-bomber regiments in late 1955, replacing older Tu-4 bombers. It was not officially accepted for service until August 1957 due to lingering teething problems. The new aircraft were assigned to the 106th Heavy-Bomber Aviation Division at Uzin. A second division was added in 1957 as the first was completing its equipment phase (table 2.1).

The Soviet Air Force was not entirely happy with the Tu-95M when first in service, due mainly to the overstressed engines, low engine durability, and problems with the sophisticated contra-rotating propellers. There were a string of modification efforts through the early 1960s. The lack of experience of the Soviet Air Force in conducting operations over the Arctic soon became clear. When deployed to Arctic forward-staging bases during the biannual exercises, the Tu-95s proved to be a major maintenance burden for these minimally equipped bases. One of the biggest headaches was the aircraft oil system, which would freeze up in the intense winter conditions. This required the aircraft to be hooked up to engine-oil preheaters while on the ground. Few of these forward bases had such extensive ground handling equipment, and the alternative was to start and run the engines every few hours to heat up the oil. However, due to the low life expectancy of the early engines, this was less than an ideal solution. Eventually, improvements in oil chemistry solved the problem.

Table 2.1

Intercontinental Bomber Order-of-Battle, 1960

Division	Base	Aircraft Type
22nd Heavy-Bomber Aviation Division	Engels, Russia	
101st Guards Heavy-Bomber Aviation Regiment	Engels	M-4, 3M
203rd Guards Heavy-Bomber Aviation Regiment	Engels	M-4, 3M
79th Heavy-Bomber Aviation Division	Semipalatinsk, Kazakhstan	
1223rd Heavy-Bomber Aviation Regiment	Semipalatinsk	Tu-95M
1226th Heavy-Bomber Aviation Regiment	Semipalatinsk	Tu-95M
106th Heavy-Bomber Aviation Division	Uzin, Ukraine	
409th Heavy-Bomber Aviation Regiment	Uzin	Tu-95M
1006th Heavy-Bomber Aviation Regiment	Uzin	Tu-95M
182nd Guards Heavy-Bomber Regiment	Mozdok	Tu-95M

The early bombers were not particularly user-friendly and reflected the Soviet Air Force's lack of experience in conducting long-range strategic bombing missions. The cabins of the aircraft were painted black, and the pilots sarcastically referred to themselves as "tank officers" due to the dank and dingy interior. The seats were ill-suited to long-duration flights and there was neither a toilet nor a galley in the aircraft. Nevertheless, the crews had generally good morale, because the strategic-bomber divisions were considered a vital element of the air force and were assigned more experienced crews than average. Due to their importance, the bomber regiments were given considerable flight time, often two ten-hour night missions a week, and up to 1,200 flight hours annually.[12] Training flights included frequent missions into the Arctic to practice transpolar strikes against the United States. The Soviet Air Force did not fly its missions with armed nuclear weapons, as did the U.S. Strategic Air Command. Usually, a squadron of each regiment was kept on alert duty, called "sitting on the hole" by the crews, because the bombers were deployed unarmed on a specially prepared section of the runway with servicing trenches under the aircraft. On orders to prepare to attack, the bombs had to be transferred from special bunkers on the base and loaded into the aircraft from the servicing trench below the bomb bay, a process that could take two hours.[13] This elaborate procedure was followed because the early bomb storage facilities were controlled by special KGB custody units until 1959, when new army custody units were given control. The bomber regiments were first armed with the RDS-4 Tatyana, a fission bomb with a yield of forty-two kilotons. There were plans to replace this with the 400-kiloton RDS-6S thermonuclear bomb, but the design proved flawed. This was followed by the RDS-37, a 2.9-megaton thermonuclear bomb, which became the main weapon through most of the late 1950s and 1960s. This was excessive for some missions, so the less powerful RP-30 and RP-32 200-kiloton bombs were ready for some missions. On being armed, the bombers were deployed to forward-staging bases such as Anadyr, on the Chukotsky Peninsula opposite Alaska.

In spite of their technical problems, the Tu-95 and 3M bombers finally gave the Soviet Union its first real intercontinental capability. This capability was limited both by the small size of the force compared to its American rival and the inexperience of the Soviet Air Force in training, deploying, and operating a force of this type. The Soviet Air Force did not regularly keep any of its aircraft on airborne alert, as did the U.S. Strategic Air Command, in part due to lingering durability problems with the engines and the difficulties of operating from the remote Arctic bases, and in part due to concerns over control of the weapons.

The presumption that strategic bombers would form the vanguard of the new strategic forces began to be challenged in the mid-1950s, about the time of Khrushchev's consolidation of power. Early Soviet nuclear weapons doctrine was preoccupied with asserting negative control over the weapons, that is, in being certain that they would not be used without Kremlin approval. The sociopathic violence of the Stalin years had left deep scars on the Soviet populace, and many officers had personal or family exposure to the purges and political repression. This led to the creation of a system supervised by the KGB to ensure that a disgruntled officer could not commandeer an aircraft and weapon and use it against targets in Russia itself. There was significant concern in the Kremlin over command and control of the bomber force and its nuclear weapons, both in peacetime, due to accidents, and in wartime, due to the difficulties of communicating with the force.

The United States benefited from its naval tradition and its global alliance network. Radio relay stations were accessible to the U.S. military through much of the northern hemisphere, which made communication with forward-deployed bombers possible. But in the Soviet case, once the bombers left Soviet air space, they were quickly beyond effective radio communication. Finally, the initial displays of the Myasishchev and Tupolev bombers in Moscow air exhibitions had provoked the United States into an expensive but highly potent modernization of its strategic air defenses.

By the late 1950s Soviet bombers would face not only supersonic fighters, but also a new generation of air-to-air missiles. Even the early American missiles, like the Falcon, could hit the bombers from ranges outside the defensive armament of the Tu-95 Bear bomber. The Genie missile was on the verge of deployment, and its nuclear warhead was so powerful that the missile was not even guided: a near miss was more than sufficient. Equally important, the U.S. Army had begun fielding surface-launched missiles to act as a final layer of defense for any bombers surviving the onslaught of the fighters. These missiles, the Nike-Ajax and Nike-Hercules, could strike the bomber from dozens of miles away from the intended target. The possibility that the Soviets might launch a surprise attack with their bomber force prompted the United States to erect an elaborate network of radars, interceptors, and missiles to protect American cities and bases from bomber attack. The North American Air Defense Command erected the DEW (Distant Early Warning) line across Canada and the United States.

The Kremlin was well aware of these programs, and they had a similarly lavish program of their own. Soviet assessments of their own strategic air defense network presumed a very high rate of success against existing bombers and cruise missiles.[14] By the late 1950s, there was a growing conviction that the defensive missiles of both sides would seriously undermine the viability of strategic bombers.

The most significant challenge to the bomber came in the form of the intercontinental ballistic missile (ICBM). In the early 1950s, missiles were not a serious challenge to bombers since they did not have enough range. Furthermore, the early atomic bombs were so large that an intercontinental missile seemed decades in the future. The most important breakthrough came in nuclear warhead design. The advent of small thermonuclear weapons weighing under five tons completely changed the prospects for the ICBM. Besides solving the weight problem, the thermonuclear weapons also solved the accuracy problem. Early missiles were lucky to impact within ten miles of their target. But the new thermonuclear fusion bombs offered a hundredfold increase in power, from the forty-kiloton yield of typical fission bombs of the early 1950s to the five-megaton thermonuclear fusion weapons at the end of the decade.

Initial Thermonuclear Bomb Designs

Early ideas about fusion bombs in the Soviet Union came from espionage and internal Soviet studies, and the espionage materials dominated early work.[15] The early American H-bomb concepts had substantial flaws, which were not resolved in the United States until the early 1950s, and so the spy material may have served to confuse, rather than assist, the Soviet effort. Nevertheless, it made it clear that the United States was working on this concept, and Soviet designers had to presume that the United States would eventually succeed. The initial work on the Soviet thermonuclear fusion bomb began in 1947–48. The decision to proceed with a major thermonuclear bomb program took place after Stalin and Beria reviewed espionage material from Klaus Fuchs on 13 March 1948, indicating that the United States was proceeding with a fusion bomb. In June 1948 a special research group at the Physics Institute of the Academy of Science (FIAN), headed by Igor Tamm, was formed to undertake the research.

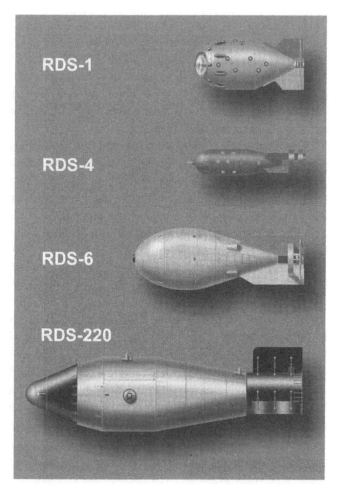

Soviet atomic bombs, 1949–59.

The designers of early thermonuclear bombs envisioned using an atomic bomb as a trigger to provide the needed heat and compression to initiate the thermonuclear reaction of a layer of liquid deuterium between the fissile material and the surrounding chemical high explosive. The Tamm group realized that a lack of sufficient heat and compression of the deuterium would result in an insignificant fusion of the deuterium fuel. Andrei Sakharov's study group at FIAN in 1948 came up with a second concept in August–September 1948. Adding a shell of natural, unenriched uranium around the deuterium would increase the deuterium concentration at the uranium-deuterium boundary and the overall yield of the device, because the natural uranium would capture neutrons and itself fission as part of the thermonuclear reaction. This idea of a layered fission-fusion-fission bomb led Sakharov to call it the *sloika,* or layer cake. It was also known as the RDS-6S, or Second Idea Bomb. Studies of light hydrogen isotopes led to the decision to use lithium deuteride as the fusion fuel in the early designs.[16]

The RDS-6 Second Idea bomb was not a fully evolved thermonuclear bomb in the contemporary sense, but an intermediate step between pure fission bombs and the thermonuclear "supers." The energy of the fission explosion created momentary fusion of part of the lithium deuteride fuel, thus "boosting" the explosion's power by about 20 percent. The U.S. program examined a similar concept in its "Item" detonation on 21 May 1951.

The Soviet thermonuclear development efforts followed a different course than in the United States due to a three-year lag in making the key breakthrough of radiation compression, which led to the supers.[17] Instead of proceeding with a single-stage fusion bomb, the United States decided to skip ahead to a two-stage fusion bomb using radiation compression that would deliver higher yields in the megaton range. In the interim, an advanced, 500-kiloton, high-yield fission bomb was developed as a stopgap.[18] In the Soviet case, the analog RDS-7 advanced fission bomb was not further developed, and instead, the single-stage, 400-kiloton RDS-6S, the Layer Cake, proceeded as the main effort.

In the United States, Stanislaw Ulam and Edward Teller's discovery of radiation compression took place in January 1951, while in the Soviet Union, the analog Sakharov Third Idea radiation compression theory was not developed until March–April 1954. Engineering development of the RDS-6 was approved by a Council of Ministers decree on 26 February 1950, an action triggered in part by the decision on 31 January 1950 by President Harry Truman to authorize the American superbomb. Although planned for testing in 1952, detonation of the first boosted bomb was delayed a year. The prototype RDS-6S Layer Cake design was detonated on 12 August 1953, producing a yield of 400 kilotons, about ten times more powerful than any previous Soviet test.

There was considerable confusion in the United States about exactly what sort of bomb the Soviet had managed to detonate, a boosted bomb, or a true super. The United States detonated its first super using radiation compression on 1 November 1952, code-named Mike. It had a yield of 10.4 megatons, about twenty times greater than the RDS-6S detonated in 1953. However, the Mike device was a so-called wet design using deuterium sustained in a liquid state by an enormous refrigeration system. The Mike design was much too large to convert into a practical weapon. The final stage in the American program was a so-called dry design, using lithium deuteride as the fusion fuel, but a radically different approach in bomb design. Some American analysts mistakenly concluded from the airborne debris that the Soviets had skipped the first stages and were already testing a device of the final stage, a true dry super. However, the intelligence community soon realized that the fourth Soviet test was an equivalent of the aborted 1946 Teller Alarm Clock idea, not a fully evolved thermonuclear super.[19]

Following the development of the RDS-6S design, Sakharov proposed an upgraded version called RDS-6SD. Some of the concepts behind this effort proved faulty, and the design was neither built nor tested. Along with the RDS-6S Layer Cake design, the Soviet team had been working on the RDS-6T Truba (Tube) concept, a Soviet analog of Edward Teller's "classical super," which they had learned about from espionage. This proved to be a dead end.

In March and April 1954, Sakharov began work on what he dubbed the Third Idea, a two-stage thermonuclear bomb, analogous to the American dry super. The Third Idea used the radiation wave of a fission bomb, not simply heat and compression, to ignite the fusion reaction, and paralleled the discovery made by Ulam and Teller. Unlike the RDS-6S boosted bomb, which placed the fusion fuel inside the primary A-bomb trigger, the thermonuclear super placed the fusion fuel in a secondary structure a small distance from the A-bomb trigger, where it was compressed and ignited by the A-bomb's x-ray radiation. The KB-11 Scientific-Technical Council approved plans to proceed with the design on 24 December 1954. Technical specifications for the new bomb were completed on 3 February 1955, and it was designated the RDS-37.

There was some controversy over funding further research on the RDS-37 due to the amount of computational effort and experimentation that would be required, as well as the diversion of talent away from weaponizing the earlier RDS-6S bomb design. While the KB-11 design bureau was mesmerized by the revolutionary design, the head of the Ministry of Medium Machine Building, Vyacheslav Malyshev, was primarily interested in immediate manufacture of the RDS-27, a 250-kiloton-yield version of the RDS-6S "classical" first-generation thermonuclear bomb, which was intended for use on the new R-7 ICBM. Kurchatov was severely reprimanded for his lack of control over Khariton and the unauthorized RDS-37 program at KB-11.

The Kremlin was so unhappy with the whole superbomb affair that an effort began to set up a competitor to Khariton's unruly KB-11. Ostensibly, the second nuclear weapons design bureau would generate new ideas and accelerate thermonuclear weapons research. Malyshev disagreed, arguing that it would simply dissipate limited talent and resources. One of the unspoken objectives of the effort was to reduce the influence of Jewish scientists. The leadership of KB-11—Khariton, Yakov B. Zeldovich, and others—were Jewish. Even after Stalin's death, there was a general trend toward reducing the numbers of Jews in critical defense industry leadership posts. The new design bureau was authorized on 31 July 1954. In February 1955, during another round of Kremlin infighting, Malyshev was removed as head of the Ministry of Medium Machine Building, ostensibly due to his failure to establish the second nuclear weapons design bureau. In fact, his removal resulted from the downfall of his chief supporter in the Kremlin, Georgy Malenkov. The new design bureau, designated NII-1011, was established at the closed facility of Chelyabinsk-70.[20] The original bomb design center, KB-11, was soon dubbed Israel, and the new NII-1011 design bureau Egypt—a taste of the "anti-Zionist" campaign under way in the Kremlin in 1956.

The RDS-27 boosted bomb was successfully tested from a bomber on 6 November 1955 at Semipalatinsk. This was followed on 22 November 1955 by a test of the RDS-37 superbomb. The device exploded with a yield of 1.6 megatons, almost a hundred times greater than the first Soviet atomic bomb six years before. The United States had exploded a comparable dry super a year earlier. But the gap between the United States and the Soviet Union was closing. More to the point, with a weapon of this magnitude, the race was over. Thermonuclear bombs would be perfected: made lighter, more reliable, and more compact. But the Soviet Union now had a weapon that could destroy any target in the United States.[21]

Early Missile Development

Although bombers were viewed as the most likely delivery system for nuclear weapons until the mid-1950s, they were not the only contender. The second alternative was the missile. The German use of missiles in the concluding year of World War II was a clear harbinger of the future. However, early missiles suffered from an even more severe range problem than did the bombers. The German V-1 cruise missile and V-2 ballistic missile had a range of only a few hundred miles and were beyond the manufacturing capabilities of Soviet industry until the late 1940s. Stalin had originally pinned his hope on one of the fantastic German wonder-weapons, the Sanger "interpodal" bomber. This manned, rocket-propelled cruise missile was designed to fly to the edge of space and skip along the outer atmosphere before reentering the atmosphere to drop its payload a continent away. The concept was derided as fantasy by Soviet engineers, and Stalin had forgotten it by the end of the 1940s.

In 1945 the nascent Soviet missile industry began to study German wartime missile technology. The German V-1 cruise missile was copied by the later Chelomey 10Kh series of cruise missiles. They were not built in any significant number due to political infighting.[22] German ballistic-missile technology would prove more fruitful.

In May 1946 Stalin formed Special Committee No. 2 to oversee the development of new strategic offensive weapons while Special Committee No. 1 worked
on the design of the first Soviet nuclear weapons.[23] It consolidated a number of
missile-design groups that had been formed toward the end of World War II, including the Raketa group. In March 1946 the Supreme Soviet approved a new
five-year plan, which contained an ambitious missile program to complement
the atomic bomb effort. The program envisioned reestablishing German V-2 missile production in the Soviet Union as the first stage of a program to develop a
long-range missile capability.

The cream of the engineers connected with rocket and missile research were
organized into a new group to scoop up German wartime missile technology. The
first members of the team arrived in Berlin in August 1945. The Soviets established the Institut Rabe as the German wing of the program in occupied Germany.[24] It included the main V-2 production facility at Nordhausen, as well as
several subsidiary factories and development agencies. The main aim of the Soviet program was to reestablish V-2 production at Nordhausen as a first step toward creating V-2 missile production inside the Soviet Union at a later date. The
German operation assembled thirty V-2 missiles by September 1946, which it
shipped to the new State Central Launch Site No. 4 (GTsP-4) at Kapustin Yar, east
of Stalingrad. The Soviet Army formed its first ballistic-missile brigade in July
1946. The Soviet troops learned the operation of V-2 missiles from German veterans. This brigade was mainly intended to serve as a teaching establishment to
form further missile units once quantity production began in the Soviet Union.

Missile research in the Soviet Union was concentrated at NII-88 (Scientific Research Institute-88) in Kaliningrad in the Moscow suburbs. This old artillery plant
was under the administrative control of the Soviet Army's highly respected artillery research arm, the GAU (Main Artillery Directorate). In August 1946 Sergei
Korolyov was appointed chief designer of Special Design Bureau-1 (OKB-1) at
NII-88 and assigned to lead the first serious attempt to modernize the German
A-4, a project called K-1.[25] This small organization would prove to be the seed for
the Soviet missile and space program.

Korolyov had been active in prewar rocket research but was junior enough to
have survived Stalin's purge of the rocket engineers in 1937–38. He was sent to
the Kolyma GULAG camp but saved when the police decided to form special
prison design bureaus. He worked with Tupolev's aircraft design bureau through
the war years before being set free in 1945 and given the rank of colonel. Korolyov would go on to be the single most important engineer in the Soviet missile
program in the 1950s, heading the work on nearly all the major programs, including the rocket that launched the Sputnik satellite and the first manned spacecraft.

Other design bureaus were established at the same time to develop related missile technology. Among the most important was the OKB-456 rocket engine bureau in the Moscow suburb of Khimki, headed by Korolyov's former prison bureau chief, Valentin Glushko.

With the task of preparing experimental V-2 missiles in Germany largely complete, in October 1946 the Soviet government forcibly transferred the German missile engineers to a special research facility at Gorodomlya Island near Moscow. They were kept isolated from the Soviet engineers, although Korolyov and other senior engineers frequently consulted with them on many issues. The German engineers captured by the Red Army did not have the stature of the Wernher von Braun team in the United States, and the Soviet engineers were adamant in their refusal to allow the Germans to play a significant role in actual missile design. Nevertheless, their experience was useful, and they were not allowed to return to East Germany until the mid-1950s.

Korolyov was called to the Kremlin for a personal meeting with Stalin on 14 April 1947. Stalin authorized the production of V-2 missiles, called R-1, in the Soviet Union using Soviet components once tests of V-2 missiles assembled from German components were completed. The first missile was ready on 18 October 1947 and was launched successfully at Kapustin Yar. Some twenty R-1's were test fired between the end of October and the beginning of December 1947. Following the tests, Korolyov's team was mainly involved in establishing the indigenous Soviet production lines for the V-2, involving some thirty-five research institutes and eighteen factories, mainly in the Moscow area.

Korolyov's success in this effort was in no small measure due to an astute recognition that a missile program would require the cooperative efforts of a number of design bureaus and was too big a project to be handled by a single bureau. This was not the traditional approach in Soviet aviation engineering, where the aircraft design bureau dominated the process. Korolyov's OKB-1 was one of the few Soviet missile-design bureaus to succeed in translating German technology into Soviet weaponry. Most of the other bureaus followed the traditional practices, which proved ineffective. At the heart of Korolyov's management approach was his informal Council of Chief Designers, consisting of the Big Six of Soviet rocketry: Korolyov, of OKB-1 (missile design); Valentin Glushko, of the OKB-456 in Khimki (rocket engine design); Vladimir Barmin, of NII-3 at the Kompressor Plant in Moscow (ground support and launching equipment); Viktor Kuznetsov, at NII-944 (gyroscopes); Nikolai Pilyugin, at NII-885 (inertial guidance); and Mikhail Ryazansky, at NII-885 (radio-command guidance). The Chief's Council, as it was also known, would play a central role in Soviet missile and space development over the next two decades. In parallel to the industry's NII-88, the army's missile research institute—the NII-4 in Bolshevo—concentrated on the tactical requirements for future missiles, as well as developing methods for the army's testing, training, and deployment of the new ballistic-missile weapons.[26]

Small-scale production of the R-1 ballistic missile began in 1948. On 17 September 1948 the first test launch of a Soviet-manufactured R-1 failed, and the first successful test followed on 10 October 1948. Testing continued through 1950, and the R-1 missile system was accepted for use by the Soviet Army on 28 November 1950. Production of the R-1 missile was far from assured. The influential head of the GAU (Main Artillery Directorate), Marshal Nikolai Yakovlev, was firmly opposed to series production and deployment. Yakovlev felt that the new ballistic missiles were inordinately expensive, too cumbersome to use, and not militarily effective. This view was shared by many of the more conservative senior leaders of the artillery branch. One general remarked that if his troops were given as much alcohol as was used to fuel a single R-1 missile, they could capture any town! In spite of their lack of enthusiasm, Stalin and senior leadership of the armed forces pressed ahead with the missile program, recognizing it was only a first step in a more ambitious scheme to field long-range missile weapons. Yakovlev was overruled, and in December 1951 he was arrested on other matters.[27] His view was shared by the U.S. Army, which also tested German V-2's. The U.S. Army was more successful in blocking V-2 production in the United States and insisted on waiting until missile technology was sufficiently mature to field a less cumbersome weapon.

The handmade R-1 test missiles were not suitable for service use, so on 1 June 1951 the defense ministry approved plans to open a new missile facility on the grounds of the Dnepropetrovsk Automobile Factory (DAZ) No. 586.[28] The Dnepropetrovsk plant would eventually become the Soviet Union's largest ICBM plant.

Production of the R-1 was quickly followed by production of an evolutionary improvement, the R-2, which had more range. The most significant technical change of the R-2 was the partial substitution of a monocoque fuselage, in which the fuselage skin itself was used for fuel storage, rather than a separate internal fuel tank. This saved considerable weight. The weight of the R-2 increased only 50 percent, but the range doubled, to 600 km (370 mi). The most significant tactical change was the substitution of a separable warhead, which cured the tendency of the R-1 to disintegrate on reentry into the atmosphere. The first test flight of an R-2 took place at Kapustin Yar in September 1949. Testing continued through the summer of 1951, and the missile was accepted for service on 27 November 1951. The first series-production missile was completed in June 1953, and the R-2 began entering the new missile brigades shortly afterwards (table 2.2).

Table 2.2

R-1 and R-2 Missile Production[29]

1951	1952	1953	1954	1955	Total
76	237	544	308	380	1,545

The successful completion of the R-2 missile marked the end of the apprenticeship stage for Korolyov's team. It was the last Soviet missile where the basic design was German or based primarily on German innovations. Future designs, though certainly influenced by German technology, would take on an increasingly Soviet flavor. The completion of the R-2 also marked a watershed in the applications of missiles for the Soviet Army. Both the R-1 and R-2 were improved V-2's, with similar operational qualities. The next generation of missiles would be more carefully tailored to the operational requirements of the Soviet Army. It would also be the first generation to carry nuclear weapons.

Early Missile Deployment

Prototypes of the R-1 missiles became available in the fall of 1950, permitting the formation of the first regular Soviet missile unit at Kapustin Yar under the cover name of the 23rd Special-Purpose Engineer Brigade (OSNAZ) of the Supreme High Command Reserve (RVGK). Through March 1953 six special-purpose brigades were formed. The R-1 and R-2 brigades were based around two launch battalions, each with a single launcher.[30] Only twenty-four R-1/R-2 launchers were deployed with active Soviet Army missile brigades, a very small force. Even after the conclusion of the test program, the missile brigades had an active program of test launches for training purposes. Through January 1956 there had been sixty-two launches of the R-1 and forty-one launches of the R-2 (table 2.3).

The early R-1 and R-2 missiles were armed only with high-explosive warheads. They were not initially armed with nuclear warheads for a variety of reasons, including low reliability, the heaviness of early Soviet nuclear devices, and the relatively small number of warheads available until series production of the RDS-3 began in 1954. As a result missile advocates expressed some interest in alternative types of warheads with improved combat effectiveness. The idea arose to use warheads armed with nuclear reactor waste. Such a warhead could contaminate larger areas than would be damaged by conventional high-explosive warheads, and abundant supplies of nuclear waste products were available from the new Soviet nuclear processing facilities.

Table 2.3

Ballistic Missile Units of the Supreme High Command Reserve (RVGK), 1951–54

Initial Formation	1954 Deployment	Post-1954 Designation
22nd OSNAZ Brigade RVGK	Medved, Leningrad Military District	72nd Engineer Brigade RVGK
23rd OSNAZ Brigade RVGK	Kamyshin	73rd Engineer Brigade RVGK
–	Belokorovich, Carpathian Military District	77th Engineer Brigade RVGK
–	Belokorovich, Carpathian Military District	80th Engineer Brigade RVGK
54th OSNAZ Brigade RVGK	Kapustin Yar	85th Engineer Brigade RVGK
56th OSNAZ Brigade RVGK	Kiev Military District	90th Engineer Brigade RVGK

In the early 1950s, two warheads filled with "military radioactive agents" were tested.[31] The Geran (Geranium) warhead was filled with radioactive liquid, and at a preselected altitude, the warhead would burst open and the liquid spray out as radioactive rain. The Generator warhead used a large number of small containers that would smash on impact with the earth, much like a submunition warhead. In 1953 two R-2 missiles were launched with the Geran and Generator warheads. The test launches of both missiles were a success, and trials lasted from 1953 to 1956.[32] However, the available records provide little to determine whether the Geran and Generator were deployed. Following the start of series production of nuclear warheads at the Avangard plant in 1954, a nuclear fission warhead was developed for the R-2. Test flights of an R-2 missile with a suitably lengthened nose section were conducted in November 1955, and the warhead was accepted for service in 1956. The availability of a nuclear fission warhead for the R-2 may account for the disappearance of radioactive waste warheads.

The First Nuclear Missile

By 1950 Soviet missile advocates had become determined to field a weapon with a significantly greater range than the existing R-1 and R-2, capable of striking targets in Europe, and one reliable enough to be armed with a nuclear warhead. This system, designated the R-5, was also developed by the Korolyov design bureau at NII-88. The R-5 missile was another step forward in the basic V-2 evolution. It weighed only about a third more than the R-2 but had double the effective range.

This was accomplished by the use of a more efficient engine. The design effort proceeded very quickly, because Korolyov favored proven technologies due to the marginal reliability of missiles at this time. The first test flight of the prototype R-5 missile took place on 2 April 1954. The conventionally armed version of the R-5 was not accepted for service in significant numbers. It was soon followed by the R-5M version, which introduced redundant flight-control features to ensure high reliability when carrying a nuclear warhead. Trial production of test R-5M missiles began at the new Southern Machine Building Plant (Yuzhmash) at Dnepropetrovsk in the winter of 1954–55, where the earlier R-1 and R-2 missiles had been manufactured. Tests of unarmed R-5M missiles began at Kapustin Yar on 20–21 January 1955. Twenty-eight test launches were conducted through February 1956, with only one pad explosion in the series. The state commission accepted the R-5M missile on 11 January 1955, paving the way to the first test of a Soviet missile armed with a nuclear warhead. A first test of a missile armed with a live nuclear warhead was conducted at Kapustin Yar on 20 February 1955. The test was only a partial success, because the temperature control of the warhead compartment did not work properly, and the fission warhead did not detonate at full yield. However, the missile itself was proven, and it was accepted for service in the Soviet Army on 21 June 1956.

The R-5 was first deployed on a temporary basis with existing RVGK brigades in 1956, and the nuclear-armed R-5M was first deployed in 1957.[33] In 1955 the Politburo authorized the first forward deployment of a nuclear-armed missile system beyond Soviet soil in Germany, which would allow the missiles to strike targets deep in Europe. This could not be accomplished immediately due to delays in the R-5 program and the need to adequately train the new missile troops. The first forward deployment of a nuclear-armed Soviet missile brigade did not take place until early 1959. The 72nd Engineer Brigade was surreptitiously deployed near the East German city of Furstenberg on a mission of "special state importance."[34] There was evidently some concern about deploying nuclear weapons so close to NATO, and the brigade was pulled back in August 1959 to Gvardeisk, in former East Prussia on the Baltic coast. Another R-5M brigade became operational at Simferopol on 10 May 1959. At peak strength, four regiments were armed with the R-5M, each with a nominal strength of twelve missile launchers.[35] The RVSN began reequipping these units in 1966 with improved missiles, and the R-5M was retired in 1967.

The successful development of the R-5M also had important repercussions in the missile industry. Korolyov was allowed to split away from NII-88, and his OKB-1 became an independent design bureau. In the hierarchy of the Soviet defense industry, institutes like NII-88 were generally smaller than design bureaus and oriented toward basic research and advanced development of new technologies, but not the design of actual weapons. Engineering and manufacturing development were the responsibility of the design bureaus, like Korolyov's new OKB-1. Unlike the American aerospace industry, where engineering and manufacturing development were part of a larger corporation which also undertook series production, in the Soviet Union, the two functions were separate. Korolyov's bureau had a small plant attached to it to construct the first few test samples of missiles, but once production was authorized by the government, series manufacturing was conducted at a separate plant. This difference would have important consequences in the course of Soviet missile development.

Intercontinental Capability: Cruise or Ballistic Missiles?

The R-5M gave the Soviet Union the capability to strike targets with nuclear warheads to a distance of 1,200 km (750 mi). While this was a major leap forward compared to the relatively primitive R-1 and R-2, it did not provide an adequate capability to cover U.S. bomber bases in the United Kingdom, Japan, or the Pacific. A research program had been under way since 1947 on a missile called the R-3, with a range of 3,000 km (1,900 mi). However, this design study never progressed to engineering development. In 1950 the Council of Chief Designers conducted a study program entitled "Experimental Development Perspectives of Various Types of Long-Range Missile of 5,000–10,000 km Range and 1–10 Ton Warheads" to examine far more sophisticated alternatives.

The design studies convinced Korolyov that single-stage missiles such as the R-3 and R-5 did not have sufficient potential for truly long-range missiles. Since the late 1940s, Glushko's engine design bureau had been working on a 100-ton-thrust engine, which was powerful enough for a long-range single-stage missile. But the program was not successful. Soviet metal technology of the time was not advanced enough to build large-volume combustion chambers able to withstand the heat, shock, and vibration of such a large-thrust engine. Two-stage configurations were also considered, but Soviet and German designers favored the use of so-called packet designs, with strap-on boosters around a central core, partly because of their conviction that powerful single engines could not be designed for the foreseeable future, and also concern over the reliability of igniting second-stage engines in the vacuum of space or the upper atmosphere. An underlying but largely unspoken aspect of this study program was the desire by Korolyov and several other prominent missile engineers to develop a missile large enough to support space exploration missions, even though they had been unable to win sanction for such missions from the government.[36]

In December 1951 and January 1952, a series of meetings were held in Moscow to discuss the status of current ballistic-missile studies. The studies concluded that a 200-ton missile using a central core and four strap-on boosters could deliver a three-ton payload within an intercontinental range of 8,500 km (5,300 mi). However, the missile would not be very accurate, and the nuclear warheads of the time were not powerful enough to make up for the shortcomings in accuracy.

Intelligence about American ballistic-missile programs further affected the debate. The U.S. Air Force was not pursuing intercontinental ballistic missiles with the single-minded purpose of the Soviets, convinced that manned bombers were the only reliable delivery system for thermonuclear bombs. But a missile program was under way in the United States—the XSM-64 Navaho intercontinental cruise missile. Navaho used a ballistic rocket to boost a supersonic cruise missile high into the atmosphere. The idea of using an atmospheric cruise missile was attractive for one principal reason. If an air-breathing ramjet were used to power it, it would not have to carry its own oxidizer, thereby lowering the weight of the missile by more than half.[37] By lowering the weight of the missile, a smaller rocket engine could be used in the first stage. In the case of the Navaho, the rocket engine had a thrust of twenty-five tons—well within both American and Soviet rocket engine technology of the time.

The Korolyov bureau had already looked at a similar design as a fallback in case their own ballistic-missile designs continued to be stymied. The Korolyov proposal differed from the American Navaho in configuration, but the basic concept was the same.[38] Initial work began on this missile in 1952, but in April 1953 the project was taken out of Korolyov's hands so that his design bureau could concentrate on ballistic missiles. Two aviation bureaus were given the assignment to develop the intercontinental cruise missile: those headed by Myasishchev and Lavochkin.

The development of the Myasishchev Buran and Lavochkin Burya cruise missiles completely changed the complexion of the Soviet strategic-missile program. Korolyov now realized that he was in a race, not only with the Americans, but with other Soviet designers as well. He had already been leaning toward abandoning the R-3 in favor of a true intercontinental ballistic missile, one with a range capable of reaching the United States. The initiation of the competitive cruise-missile program in April 1953 forced his decision.

In February 1953 Korolyov had been authorized to begin drawing up a proposal for a 170-ton missile capable of reaching 8,000 km (5,000 mi). In the spring of 1953 he unveiled his R-6 intercontinental ballistic-missile design, which consisted of a central core missile with four R-5 missiles strapped to the sides to provide additional thrust. Korolyov won approval to proceed with study of this missile in May 1953. In October 1953, following the detonation of the first Soviet thermonuclear bomb, a meeting of senior officials was convened to examine the progress of the nuclear-missile program and the implications of the recent bomb

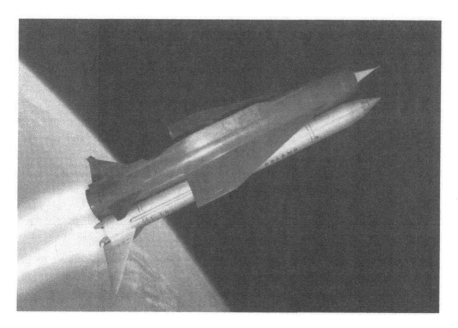

Intercontinental cruise missiles were a potential rival of ballistic missiles but never entered service. This illustration shows the Lavochkin La-350 Burya. The rocket boosters propelled the cruise missile during the initial leg of the flight, after which they separated. On reentering the atmosphere, the cruise missile was powered by a ramjet. This missile reached the test-flight phase, but it had already been overtaken by ballistic missiles.

test. The new fusion bomb partly solved the accuracy problem due to its sheer destructive power, and the nuclear scientists were certain that they could trim the weight and size of the devices to fit into future missile designs.

Malyshev, the head of the nuclear program, was skeptical of Korolyov's R-6 proposal, since to date they had only managed to fire missiles to ranges of about 500 km (310 mi) with 35-ton-thrust engines. The proposed new 8,000 km–range missiles with 250-ton-thrust rocket engines seemed overly ambitious. Malyshev was deeply suspicious of Korolyov's motives in suggesting the new missile and accused him of attempting to develop a space booster disguised as a military missile. Furthermore, Malyshev was convinced that by the time the R-6 was ready, a thermonuclear weapon would be available for deployment with considerably greater power than existing fission weapons. Korolyov was instructed to reconfigure the design so that instead of delivering a one-ton fission warhead 8,000 km, the missile could deliver a five-ton thermonuclear warhead to the same range.[39]

Ustinov, responsible for the missile program, supported the Korolyov ICBM proposal on the condition that the tests on the nuclear-armed R-5M be concluded successfully. The revised missile configuration was dubbed the R-7, and unofficial approval came later in 1953.[40] By February 1954 the overall configuration of the R-7 missile had been completed to the satisfaction of the chief designers. The successful test launch of the first R-5M missile in April 1954 paved the way for formal approval of the R-7 program, and on 20 May 1954 it was officially sanctioned.

The authorization decree from the Council of Ministers was the most important single event in the political decision-making process for new weapon systems. Due to the nature of the centrally planned economy, it was vital to incorporate future manufacturing plans into future economic plans at the earliest possible date. Besides authorizing the design of the new weapon, these decrees also initiated the first plans for manufacturing the weapons. As weapon systems became more complex, early involvement by the industrial ministries was essential. Unlike traditional weapons, which were manufactured by the plants of a single industry, the new missiles required a broad range of technologies that crossed ministerial boundaries and took years of preparation.

As an offshoot of the studies of ICBM designs, several of the chief designers were urging that more serious attention be paid to other forms of missile propulsion and fuels. Efforts were already under way on liquid-fuel rocket engines using storable, hypergolic fuels with nitric acid as the oxidant instead of the cryogenic fuel combination that had been used to date, consisting of kerosene and supercold liquid oxygen.[41] The advantage of hypergolic fuels was that the propellants could be stored at normal temperatures, meaning that the missile could be left in a fueled state for days at a time. In contrast, cryogenically fueled missiles were awkward to use on the battlefield, since under normal temperatures, the liquid oxygen began to boil off, requiring complicated systems to vent and then replace it.

Korolyov was unenthusiastic about the hypergolic fuels for a variety of reasons. To begin with, the fuels were less energetic than the liquid-oxygen/kerosene engines. The specific impulse of existing hypergolic engines was on the order of 215 seconds, while the cryogenic engines were significantly better, at about 250 seconds.[42] At a time when Soviet engine designers were trying to squeeze as much thrust as possible from their engines, this was a significant concern if longer ranges were needed. In addition, Korolyov was not happy about the use of oxidizers such as nitric acid, which he dubbed "the devil's venom," since it was extremely toxic and attacked metallic and synthetic materials in the engine and storage tank. The threat of inadvertent leaks and resulting fires was a risk he did not want to take, compared to the manageable consequences of liquid-oxygen leaks. Korolyov's adamant refusal to seriously study hypergolic-fueled rocket engines for ICBMs led to acrimonious debates with the military and other designers. It would eventually lead to the so-called civil war of the chief designers in the late 1950s.

Minister of Armaments Dmitry Ustinov was placed in an awkward position. He appreciated Korolyov's brilliant leadership of the missile program, but he was also under pressure from Malyshev, other designers, and the military to tailor the missiles to their needs as well. As a compromise, in June 1954 Ustinov supported a move to open a second ballistic-missile design bureau. Mikhail Yangel, the head of NII-88 and one of the supporters of storable fuel, was delegated to head the new SKB-586 at the Dnepropetrovsk missile plant.[43] Yangel's new assignment was intended to invigorate a 2,000 km (1,200 mi) intermediate-range missile called the R-12, which had begun at NII-88 in 1950, and in so doing, to direct more attention to alternate forms of propulsion. This was part of a broader effort by the Khrushchev administration called "doubling."[44] The aim was to ensure that there were at least two design bureaus in every major category of weapons. This introduced a measure of competition between the bureaus and prevented the type of confrontation that Stalin had with Tupolev in 1952 over the intercontinental jet bomber. In Khrushchev's mind, it was another tool to ensure the primacy of the Communist Party over the unruly technocrats in the defense industry.

The design of Korolyov's R-7 was surprisingly rapid, taking only about three years. Glushko's OKB-456 in Khimki had already been studying a pair of single-chamber engines for a packet design like the R-7, even though early firing tests in 1952 were a failure. A less challenging configuration was selected, using several smaller combustion chambers clustered together, fed from a common turbopump. Guidance and trajectory planning also presented a significant technological challenge. Never before had a missile been fired such enormous distances. An inertial guidance system of the type used by the V-2 was suitable for flights of a few hundred miles. But its inherent inaccuracies, acceptable at short ranges, would lead to gross inaccuracies at the ranges contemplated for the R-7. Even if it was armed with a powerful thermonuclear weapon, it would still have to land within a few miles of the target. Under the new scheme, the missile would be controlled by the inertial platform during the initial launch phase. As the missile began its ascent, it would be tracked by radar, and the radio correction system would send midcourse updates to the flight-control system twenty to thirty seconds before the central engine core shutdown to insert the missile into its final ballistic trajectory. The system was designed to achieve an accuracy of 5 km (3 mi), well within the lethal blast diameter of a thermonuclear bomb.[45]

For the new missile program, the Soviet government decided to erect a new and more elaborate test center for the intercontinental missiles than the existing site at Kapustin Yar. The site finally selected was near the Tyuratam railroad station in the Kazakhstan desert. It was isolated enough to discourage spying, and sparsely populated. In later years, when the Soviet Union publicly announced the site of origin of the first space flights, it was called Baikonur, even though the town of Baikonur is 400 km (250 mi) from the missile launchpads. The misnaming of the site was typical of Soviet security precautions of the time. Baikonur/Tyuratam would be the center of the Soviet missile and space program until the collapse of the Soviet Union.

Prior to the R-7, Soviet ballistic missiles had employed wheeled trailers and simple launch deflector pads like that used with the German V-2. These were clearly inadequate for so large a missile as the R-7. In 1955 the Barmin design bureau was assigned the task of developing the new launch site at Tyuratam, including the enormous launch complex itself, as well as related support facilities such as the assembly and preparation hangers.[46] This program led to the legendary Tyulpan (Tulip) launch structure so characteristic of Soviet launch sites even today. At the base of the Tyulpan was an enormous concrete foundation and exhaust trough, nicknamed the Stadium. This deep chasm vented the hot exhaust gas from the rocket engines away from the launch pad. The excavation of the Stadium required the removal of over a million cubic meters of earth. As was the case with American ICBM programs of the period, the support and launch facilities were far more costly to field than the missiles themselves, on the order of ten to one. This would eventually prove to be the undoing of the program.

While the Tyuratam site was under construction, initial tests of missile components began in 1955. Korolyov's design style was typical of Soviet aircraft designers of the 1940s, placing more emphasis on equipment tests than on paper analysis. Following static tests of the engine, in January 1956 a mock-up of the missile minus the strap-on boosters was static fired in August 1956, and a complete engine packet in the winter of 1956–57. In December 1956 the first prototype R-7 missile was delivered to the Tyuratam test range. On 15 May 1957 the first R-7 finally lifted off the pad. At T+98 seconds, with all of its five engine clusters firing, the missile exploded over the test range.[47] Further failed launches followed on 9 June and 12 June 1957. Finally, in the early morning hours of 21 August 1957, an R-7 lifted off and successfully continued toward the Pacific Ocean. All systems worked properly, and the world's first flight of an intercontinental ballistic missile was successfully completed. The R-7's dummy warhead disintegrated before impacting in the Pacific Ocean some 6,400 km (4,000 mi) downrange. This was not a surprise, because Korolyov's team had not yet completed design of the reentry vehicle. The Soviet government publicly announced they possessed an ICBM on 27 August 1957, not mentioning, of course, the warhead failure. The announcement had little impact in the United States, being widely regarded as propagandistic bombast.

It would take another two years before the first R-7 missile was deployed in service. After its amazing launches in 1957, the R-7 missile program degenerated into a morass of technical problems, cost overruns, and schedule slips. The problems with the missile itself were compounded by its complicated basing. Korolyov and his team successfully overcame the problem with the reentry vehicle

Photographic reconnaissance played a critical role in the Cold War. This image, taken from a U-2, shows the Tyulpan launch pad of the first Soviet ICBM, the R-7A, at the Tyuratam proving ground. The enormous chasm behind the launch pad, which funneled the hot exhaust gas away, was dubbed the Stadium by its designers. (Courtesy Central Intelligence Agency)

on the test flight of 29 March 1958. Although the reentry vehicle survived for the first time, its accuracy was atrocious, about 50 km (30 mi) from the target. In March 1959 a final series of military R-7 acceptance trials were conducted from the Baikonur proving ground, trying out new warhead configurations to ensure a more acceptable accuracy. One of the more alarming accidents took place during a full-range test on 30 May 1959, when the command to shut off the engines failed, and the missile flew some 2,000 km (1,200 mi) beyond the impact zone near Kamchatka, almost landing on U.S. soil in the Aleutian islands off Alaska. For the next few months, R-7's were launched at a rate of one a week. The R-7 was officially accepted for service by a government resolution on 20 January 1960.

In the meantime, work was under way on the secret launch sites for the missile. Due to the range limits of the original version of the R-7, the bases had to be situated in northern Russia to minimize the distance to targets in the United States. The plan was to deploy twelve launchers at Plesetsk, followed by four similar bases in northern Russia. Plesetsk was in a sparsely populated forest region south of the Arctic port city of Arkhangelsk. Construction work at Plesetsk began on 15 July 1957, even before the first successful flight. Due to its northern location, construction was a nightmare. The winters were long and cold, preventing construction work for nearly half the year. Soil conditions were atrocious. Much of the land was covered with swamps that froze in the winter and thawed in the summer, oozing mud and belching natural gas. To gain firm foundations for the massive missile structures, it was necessary to scrape the soil down to the underlying bedrock. But nature resisted these assaults, flooding the excavated roadways and construction sites with mud during the spring thaws and after heavy rains. To avoid these problems, several of the launcher sites were built on costly man-made extensions on a bluff over the Yemtsa River. The base construction proved far more expensive than anticipated and was far behind schedule.

In a special Kremlin meeting in 1958, a furious Khrushchev threatened to cancel the program due to the delays and the huge cost overruns. Each launch site was projected to cost about a half billion rubles, that is to say, about 5 percent of the annual defense budget.[48] This experience was not unique: the cost of U.S. ICBM launch sites declined sevenfold between the first and second generation.[49] The alternative was to wait until a new missile was ready. Such work was already under way, and it would have sufficient range to be launched from bases in more temperate regions of Russia. Korolyov indicted that improvements to the R-7 would extend its range and allow it to be launched from a site further south.

But Khrushchev was not appeased. As a compromise, he allowed the completion of the first four launch platforms at the R-7 base in Plesetsk, while work on the remaining eight pads at Plesetsk and all of those at the other four locations were canceled.[50] It was a momentous decision, because it would be at least four years before any of the newer missiles would be ready. As a result, there were never any more than six R-7 missile sites on alert, the four at Plesetsk and two of the three test launchers at Baikonur. The first strategic-missile unit became operational at Plesetsk on 9 February 1959, as soon as the first launchpad was completed.[51] On 15 December 1959 the first R-7 was test fired from Plesetsk. The full complement of six launchers was not ready until 1961, almost five years after the first successful test launch. Serial production of the R-7A missile did not begin until 1959, when thirty were ordered, followed by an order for seventy-five more in 1960.[52] The five-year plan envisioned building only 210 R-7A missiles through 1966, some of which were intended as space boosters.

The decision to sharply curtail the first ICBM program was influenced by other factors as well. When the R-7 ICBM program had been initiated in 1954, it was presumed that the R-7 would be launched from secret bases. However, by 1958 the overflights by the CIA's U-2 spy planes had begun to uncover the Soviet missile bases, and the secret base at Plesetsk was likely to be discovered. The enormous and cumbersome R-7 took nearly twenty hours to prepare for launching, and the missile's cryogenic fuel system meant that it could not be left on alert for more than a day.[53] This meant that the Soviet missile force could not be kept on permanent alert status, and could be destroyed on the ground even by subsonic strategic bombers before the missiles could be launched. They were even more vulnerable to a surprise attack by new American ICBMs.

Both Korolyov and Khrushchev were aware that overhead spying would not go away, even though the Soviet PVO-Strany Air Defense Command, responsible for defending national air space, was in the process of fielding the new S-75 antiaircraft missile to deal with the U-2. Korolyov had been authorized on 12 April 1957 to begin developing the Soviet Union's first reconnaissance satellite, and there was little doubt that the Americans were working on a similar system. Inadvertently, the Sputniks had established a critical precedent: space was beyond national borders, permitting unfettered overflight anywhere over the globe.[54] The U-2 overflights were known to Khrushchev and a narrow circle of senior leaders, but the implications of the overflights for the security of the missile bases was not widely appreciated in the design bureaus at the time.

The advent of nuclear-armed intercontinental missiles injected a dangerous degree of instability into superpower relationships. Attacks from the new missile sites were not survivable, and the time available to senior national leadership to make decisions in a crisis was greatly compressed. A land-based ICBM would take less than thirty minutes to travel between the United States and the Soviet Union. In the 1960s the Kremlin had no way to detect the launch of an American ICBM, and the missile might not be detected until a few minutes before its actual arrival, if at all. This was not enough time for Khrushchev to pass instructions to the Soviet force to launch its missiles. Since the Soviet bomber force did not fly regular alert patrols, the bombers could be destroyed on the ground as well. Combined with the restrictive control that the KGB exercised over nuclear warheads, the Soviet strategic nuclear force was extremely vulnerable to a preemptive U.S. strike.

Missile Alternatives

In spite of the problems with the R-7 ICBM, Khrushchev had few other attractive alternatives. The strategic cruise-missile program had been even slower and more troublesome than the ICBM program. Naval ballistic missiles were already starting to enter service, but they had significant shortcomings.

The first successful launch of the R-7 ICBM led Khrushchev to cancel the rival strategic cruise-missile program in November 1957. Myasishchev's RSS-40 Buran missile was canceled outright, because none of the missiles had been completed. The Lavochkin V-350 Burya was allowed to continue to the flight trials stage since several missiles had already been built. The first test flight, on 1 August 1957, was a failure shortly after takeoff. During 1957–60, nineteen launches were conducted, of which fourteen were successful. In March 1960 a test missile reached a range of 6,500 km (4,000 mi) and demonstrated accuracy of within 10 km (6 mi) of the target.[55] The Lavochkin Burya was a significant technological achievement due to its advanced ramjet propulsion, its pioneering technologies in materials that could withstand the heat of high supersonic flight, and its novel astronavigation guidance system. But such cruise missiles offered nothing over ballistic missiles. In particular, they were viewed as far more vulnerable to American air defenses than ballistic missiles due to their slow terminal speeds. One curious detail about the program is that U.S. intelligence appears to have been completely ignorant of the project.

Although the main focus of Soviet strategic-weapons development was strategic bombers and land-based missiles, naval alternatives were also examined. It is generally not realized that the Soviet Navy was the first to test a submarine-launched ballistic missile and the first to deploy ballistic-missile submarines. However, this proved to be only a short-term advantage, because the Soviet Navy selected a primitive design with substantial tactical drawbacks. In contrast, the U.S. Navy refused to be pushed into adapting army missiles to the submarine environment, preferring to develop a missile specifically designed for submarine launch. As a result, when the new Polaris missile system was deployed in the early 1960s, it was a generation ahead of the Soviet Navy's efforts.

The Soviet Navy had begun to study the launch of missiles from submarines in 1949. The P-2 submarine would have been armed with Soviet copies of the Ger-

The early Soviet missile submarines had their launchers in the sail. This is a Project 611AV (Zulu V), which was armed with two R-11FM missiles. The covers of the launcher are barely evident on the top of the sail, above and to the right of the ship number. (Courtesy U.S. Navy)

man V-1 cruise missile and V-2 ballistic missile. The concept never progressed beyond paper studies. In August 1953 the senior navy leadership began discussions about incorporating missile weaponry into future ship and submarine designs. Authorization to begin work on a submarine-launched ballistic missile (SLBM) won Council of Ministers approval on 26 January 1954 under the code name Volna. The missile was entrusted to Sergei Korolyov's OKB-1, while the work on the related submarine was undertaken by Nikolai Isanin's submarine design bureau in Leningrad.

Due to the pervasive sense of urgency, Korolyov decided to begin with an existing missile rather than design a new missile specifically for submarines. The only Soviet missile small enough for submarine launch was the army's R-11, better known as the Scud A. The technological challenge of the submarine missiles was not with the missile itself, but rather with the launcher. Ideally, the missile should be launched from a submerged position, so that the submarine would not be detectable before launch. This posed a substantial challenge, since neither side had any practical experience in the dynamics of a missile being fired underwater. The U.S. Navy decided to conduct studies on this issue before proceeding with the design of a weapon. The Soviet Navy decided that it would prefer to field a missile as soon as possible, even if the launch method was less than ideal. Korolyov's bureau was already burdened with the high-priority ICBM program, which reinforced the tendency toward a conservative approach. The launch method was simple. The missile would be stored in the sail of the submarine, and once the submarine surfaced, the R-11FM missile would be elevated out of its tube to the top of the sail and fired.

The major difficulty of such a launch method was sea motion. The R-11's accuracy was entirely dependent upon the missile being steady and completely vertical at the moment of launch. Should the missile be tilted even a fraction of a degree, it would miss its intended target by miles. The second accuracy problem had to do with the uncertainties of the launch point. Soviet submarines during the 1950s lacked a sophisticated inertial navigation system, and shore-based radio navigation systems could not reach the patrol areas in the Atlantic and Pacific.[56] To overcome these problems, the new missile submarines were fitted with a stabilized launch platform called the Horn and Hoof and an elementary inertial navigation system code-named Saturn. These were not enough, and poor accuracy plagued the design. The land-launched version of the R-11 missile had a circular error probability (CEP) accuracy of 3 km (1.9 mi), meaning that half of all R-11 missiles fired at a given target would strike within a 3 km radius of the target. Due to the motion of the ship and the uncertainties about the launch point, the naval R-11FM had a CEP of 7 km (4.3 mi), more than double that of the land-based version. The R-11FM was originally tested from a modified version of the Project 611 (Zulu) diesel electric submarine. The first launch was conducted on 16 September 1955, and eight more test launches took place later in the year.

The testing was prolonged and troubled. The R-11FM missile was loaded into the submarine with its fuel tanks already filled, including the highly corrosive oxidant. The fuel tanks were specially coated to prevent the oxidant from eating through the metal for at least three months of storage inside the submarine. But the coating often proved inadequate, and the nitric acid ate its way through joints and piping and leaked. The oxidant was not only highly toxic, it also ignited violent fires.

At the completion of the first series of tests, a conference was held by the new head of the Soviet Navy, Adm. Sergei Gorshkov, attended by the representatives of the design bureaus responsible for the Volna project. Admiral Gorshkov remained skeptical of the concept due to safety hazards, poor accuracy, and the difficulty of operating the system. But the program was vigorously supported by the minister of the defense industries, Dmitry Ustinov, who saw it as a pioneering effort to deploy nuclear missiles aboard submarines. In spite of navy objections, Ustinov won Kremlin approval to deploy the missile submarines. Beginning in 1957 seven Project 611 submarines were modified to launch the R-11FM missile. The test program ended in 1958, and the R-11FM missile was accepted for production in February 1959. On 6 October 1959 Nikita Khrushchev witnessed a test launch from a submarine in the Pacific Ocean. During the Khrushchev years, the deployment pattern of Project 611AB typically consisted of four submarines with the Northern Fleet and two with the Pacific Fleet.

The mediocre performance of the naval R-11FM missile prompted the Soviet Navy to study other approaches, especially cruise missiles. This paralleled work by the U.S. Navy, which began developing the Regulus submarine-launched cruise missile in the late 1940s. The Soviet effort was a competitive development program between the Beriev and Chelomey design bureaus. Georgy Beriev's design bureau was best known for its seaplanes but had been pushed into missile design by Khrushchev's growing obsession with missiles. The Chelomey design bureau won with its P-5 Progress (SS-N-3 Shaddock) design. This multirole design was eventually fielded for strategic strike missions and tactical antiship missions. The Soviet Navy also promoted the massive Ilyushin P-20 cruise missile, with a 2,000 km (1,200 mi) range, but it never progressed beyond the drawing board, because a submarine could only carry a single missile.

The problem with both the early SLBMs and the naval cruise missiles was that they were short-ranged. This inevitably meant that they would have to run the gauntlet of NATO antisubmarine-warfare forces to position themselves for strikes against the continental United States. Added to this problem was the short endurance of early Soviet submarines. They seldom stayed at sea more than thirty days, which meant that they could not maintain standing missile patrols. They would have to foray from their ports days before a nuclear strike, conduct their mission, and return. The command-and-control problem of these forces was even more tenuous than for the bomber force. Direct communication with the submarines once they went on patrol was very uncertain, because the existing Soviet naval radio system could not reach deep into the Atlantic. The idea that submarines would be ordered to sea with a mission to carry out nuclear strikes against the United States several days hence, with no assurance that they could be recalled or retargeted, caused the Soviet General Staff severe anxiety. The Kremlin had little faith that this force would play a key role in initial nuclear strikes against the United States. As a result, Soviet missile submarines did not pose a serious challenge to the land-based ballistic-missile force in the late 1950s.

Khrushchev's New Look Defense Policy

The decision to afford priority to land-based missiles over strategic bombers and missile submarines was strongly influenced by a broader pattern of circumstances. The events that followed the first launch of an ICBM in August 1957 highlight the serendipitous nature of the early strategic technology.

Korolyov, as the military had long complained, did in fact have an agenda for space science. In 1956 he convinced the Kremlin to allow him to modify a R-7 missile to launch an artificial earth satellite. Khrushchev would not give his final approval to the diversion of a military missile to space frivolities until after the successful launch of the first ICBM. He rewarded Korolyov with permission to launch the first earth satellite into orbit on 4 October 1957. The launch of the Sputnik had unexpected consequences in shaping the Soviet strategic programs. The worldwide clamor and jubilation over the Sputnik, and the consternation in the United States, profoundly affected Nikita Khrushchev. Many foreign observers saw the Sputnik launch as evidence of Soviet leadership in science and technology, a view that resonated among first-generation Soviet communists. It seemed proof that the Soviet Union was the vanguard of the new century.

The launch of Sputnik created considerable alarm in the United States and Europe, and created the impression that the Soviet Union was in the lead in a new phase of the strategic arms race.[57] Due to Soviet secrecy, little was actually known about the Soviet space program, and the intelligence gap forced Eisenhower to permit further U-2 flights over the Soviet Union in spite of the increasing risk that they would be shot down. The European NATO countries were so concerned about the apparent Soviet lead that at a December 1957 meeting, they encouraged the United States to establish a stockpile of nuclear weapons in Europe and insisted upon the forward basing of U.S. medium-range missiles in Europe as a counterweight to Soviet action.[58] The Eisenhower administration was forced to accelerate the U.S. missile programs, even though Eisenhower himself was skeptical of a Soviet lead in the arms race.[59] The "missile gap" controversy would play a major role in the 1960 presidential election in favor of the more alarmist views of the Democratic candidate, John F. Kennedy. The widespread miscalculation of the pace of the Soviet program, exacerbated by Khrushchev's belligerent rhetoric and Soviet secrecy, was the critical catalyst in accelerating the nuclear arms race in the late 1950s and early 1960s. The Sputnik scare reversed the defense plans of the Eisenhower administration, forcing an increase in defense expenditures instead of the planned contraction.

The strong international reaction to Sputnik sparked Khrushchev's enthusiasm for nuclear-missile weapons at a time when he was wrestling with other defense dilemmas.[60] Khrushchev was predisposed to view missiles as a panacea to defense problems. Early in his administration, he had used the advent of new antiship missiles as a rationale to curb Stalin's expensive naval shipbuilding program. Khrushchev saw no use for a blue-water navy, and antiship missiles offered the perfect excuse. Korolyov's space spectacular reinforced his predisposition. One of Khrushchev's most pressing problems was to lift the dead weight of Stalin's military expansion during the Korean War. Khrushchev had become convinced of the need to cut the fat out of the Soviet defense budget to help stimulate the domestic economy, while at the same time retaining or expanding Soviet military might in the face of American efforts. The Soviet Union was beginning to feel the demographic shadow of the tremendous loss of human life in World War II. Labor resources were shrinking, and the armed forces absorbed an inordinate share of the labor force.

Missiles offered a panacea. Khrushchev began to believe that missiles were a cost-effective alternative to conventional weapons. Antiship missiles were an alternative to the gun-armed cruisers favored by Stalin. Tactical ballistic missiles were an alternative to conventional artillery. Antitank missiles would doom tanks. Surface-to-air missiles would doom strategic bombers, and so on. In many respects, it was a revival of the *jeune école* from earlier in the century, which saw inexpensive torpedo boats and coastal submarines as the replacement for traditional battleship navies. Like the *jeune école,* Khrushchev's missile mania was based on a naive view of the nature of military revolutions. Yet because of the concentration of power in his hands, Khrushchev was able to act.[61] In place of the bloated army, he decided to field nuclear-armed intermediate-range missiles able to hit targets anywhere in Europe. The first major cuts in the personnel strength of the army since Korea were carried out, and the number of army divisions was reduced.[62] In many respects, Khrushchev's policies were an echo of Eisenhower's New Look defense policy.

Due to the growth of the Soviet gross national product, Khrushchev was able to keep defense expenditures close to the levels of the late Stalin years, though they shrank substantially as a fraction of the state budget. From a peak expenditure of R 124.2 billion in 1953, when it constituted 31.2 percent of state expenditures, the defense budget fell to R 96 billion in 1960 and constituted only 11.1 percent of state expenditures.[63]

One of the immediate impacts of Khrushchev's missile mania was the reorientation of the Soviet defense research establishment. Any major weapons design bureau wishing to survive needed to have a missile program; any bureau resisting this effort was threatened with disappearance. After their failure with the strategic cruise-missile program, both the Lavochkin and Myasishchev aircraft bureaus were closed and their personnel shifted to the new missile bureaus. Aircraft bureaus such as those headed by Artyom Mikoyan, Beriev, and Sergei Ilyushin were assigned cruise-missile projects. Tupolev was directed to develop unmanned spy aircraft and cruise missiles. The Vasily Grabin artillery bureau was shut down and merged with Korolyov's OKB-1 to develop solid-fuel ICBMs. Boris Shavyrin's mortar-design bureau was shifted to antitank missiles, as was Aleksandr Nudelman's aircraft-armament design bureau. Lev Lyulev's naval gun design bureau was shifted to naval and air defense missiles. Several tank-design bureaus, although not closed, were tasked with developing missile-armed tanks or tank chassis for tactical ballistic-missile launchers. Much of their skilled engineering personnel was drained to assist on the missile programs. In addition, many new design bureaus sprang up to satisfy Khrushchev's call for revolutionary technological change.

The shift in defense resources was startling. In 1958 missile procurement represented R 460 million, or 6.2 percent of weapons procurement. By 1965 it had increased almost tenfold, to R 4.1 billion, and represented nearly 53 percent of total Soviet weapons procurement.[64] Space expenditures saw similar rates of growth, rising more than tenfold, from R 17.2 million in 1957 to R 179.8 million in 1961.[65]

Who Controls the Strategic Force?

By the end of the 1950s, the future configuration of the Soviet strategic forces was beginning to take shape.[66] This was due in part to technological successes and failures of the development programs over the past decade, but also to strong institutional biases in the Soviet armed forces. The Soviet ballistic-missile force was clearly the front-runner. The R-5 intermediate-range missile and R-7 intercontinental missiles were by no means mature weapon systems, but they held out the hope for a reasonably robust nuclear delivery system that had a high probability of being able to carry out their mission in the face of existing American defenses. In contrast, both the strategic-bomber force and the submarine missile force were plagued by questions about their ability to reliably carry out their mission, their vulnerability to hostile defenses, and the difficulty of integrating them into a secure command-and-control system.

Soviet attitudes toward the three branches was undoubtedly affected by the institutional biases of the various services.[67] The Soviet Army, and the Ground Forces in particular, held a predominant sway within the General Staff.[68] As in other continental armies, the General Staff dominated policy making in the Soviet armed forces. Institutions of the Ground Forces, namely the GAU Main Artillery Directorate, had managed the early strategic-missile programs.[69] After some initial skepticism, parts of the army were becoming comfortable with the missile as a long-range artillery weapon, and the control of the missile force by army officers was no doubt reassuring to the General Staff. In contrast, the General Staff was not enthusiastic about the navy's role in the strategic mission, holding it in contempt for their minimal role in the Great Patriotic War of 1941–45. The Soviet submarine force, the largest in the world at the outbreak of the war in 1941, had been bottled up by the Germans until the Soviet Army drove the Wehrmacht back beyond the Soviet borders in 1944. There was little confidence in army circles that the modern submarine would perform any better when faced by aggressive U.S.

and NATO antisubmarine-warfare forces. Khrushchev disagreed, and supported submarine development in face of army skepticism.

A similar attitude applied toward the Soviet Air Force. The strategic-aviation force had attempted to conduct a limited strategic campaign against Berlin in 1941, but the lack of suitable aircraft and heavy attrition rendered it little more than a token gesture. Although the postwar years had seen the addition of aircraft with true intercontinental capability, there was still considerable doubt about whether these forces could conduct long-range missions against the United States in the face of modern air defenses. The 1951 air campaign in Korea revealed that even the experienced U.S. Strategic Air Command had a hard time when faced with jet interceptors.

Khrushchev did not rule out a role for the Soviet Air Force in the future missile force. In the summer of 1958 he offered the head of the air force, Gen. Konstantin Vershinin, a deal under which the intermediate-range missile force would come under air force control in return for support in drastically cutting back the number of air force squadrons as part of his economy measures.[70] The air force leaders made a counterproposal, suggesting that the air force convert some of its squadrons to carry nuclear-armed cruise missiles, take over some of the ballistic-missile force, and convert some bomber units to ground-launched cruise missiles. The air force threw away its chance. The army adamantly opposed allowing the air force to muscle in on the missile force, and in the end the air force was forced into heavy personnel and unit cuts, and got no share of the new ballistic-missile units. Instead, two of its proudest long-range bomber armies were converted to missile armies, along with six aviation divisions, and they were removed from air force control. The shifting balance between aircraft and missiles in the strategic role was evident from the disposition of nuclear warheads. In 1958 missiles were carrying 54 percent of the nuclear warheads, and aircraft the remainder; a year later, the missile share had already risen to 70 percent.[71]

Following the first successful launch of a R-7 ICBM from the new base at Plesetsk, on 17 December 1959 Khrushchev announced the formation of the RVSN, the Strategic Missile Force.[72] The new force was to take precedence over the army, navy, air force, and air defense force. While this antagonized the victors of Stalingrad, Kursk, and Berlin, no doubt the fact that the troops of the RVSN wore the khaki uniform of the army and that its senior leadership was made up almost entirely of Ground Forces generals lessened the insult.

The Soviet configuration stood in complete contrast to the American experience. The U.S. Army was pushed out of the strategic-forces debate by the end of the 1950s, with the resources going instead to the U.S. Air Force and the U.S. Navy. The strategic mission was a natural match for the existing U.S. Air Force air power doctrine, and the U.S. Navy likewise was imbued with the global power projection role. None of the existing Soviet combat arms was at all comfortable with a global mission, and the prize slipped out of their hands.

In spite of its impressive title, the Strategic Missile Force was in fact a very tiny force. At the end of 1959 only seven missile brigades were on duty, armed with only thirty-six short-range R-5M missiles, and the three partially equipped R-12 regiments. Only two intercontinental R-7 launchpads were operational. A major expansion was planned, based on units that were being disbanded as part of Khrushchev's force cuts. By the end of 1959, twenty-two additional missile brigades were in various stages of formation. These were drawn from the six disbanded air force divisions and eleven disbanded army divisions as well as a hodgepodge of training schools and other units.

The Soviet army was completely unprepared for so massive a venture. The Politburo decided that missiles sites should be no closer than 30 km (19 mi) from any major town or city so that a nuclear attack could not destroy both. As a result, the new missile units were deployed in remote areas, where the officers and men lived in tents. Living conditions were harsh, and the conscript troops were too poorly trained to deal with the sophisticated new weapons and their deadly chemical contents. Changes were needed almost immediately, and the missile units received a larger than normal share of officers to deal with such sophisticated equipment. A crop of young new officers were dragooned into service, fresh out of engineering schools. Several air force and army maintenance schools were closed and their staffs and students used to bolster the technical support elements of the missile force. Readiness in the missile units was low, and accidents were frequent. But the force was beginning to create a core of specialized missile officers who would be better prepared for the next stage of missile expansion.

In spite of the tiny size of the RVSN at the end of 1959, it marked the culmination of the revolution in military affairs begun with the development of the A-bomb in 1945. Khrushchev's decisions in 1958–59 shaped the basic configuration of Soviet strategic nuclear forces for the remainder of the century. U.S. strategic forces are often described as a triad: a stool with three equally important legs. The Soviet forces can be more properly portrayed as a tricycle: a single big wheel, the RVSN Strategic Missile Force, and two smaller wheels, the submarine force and the strategic bombers.

3.   Deploying the First Generation
1960–1965

Nikita Khrushchev's final years in power, from 1960 to October 1964, saw the first successes in deploying a nuclear force with real capability to strike targets in the United States. Khrushchev's ambitions to deploy a viable nuclear deterrent were frustrated by the poor management of Soviet weapons programs and the continuing technological gaps between the U.S. and Soviet aerospace industries. Spurred on by Khrushchev's intemperate "missile rattling" diplomacy and the missile gap controversy of 1960, the U.S. strategic forces began to race ahead. The first generation of Soviet ICBMs, deployed in 1961–64, proved so poorly suited to the rapidly changing strategic environment that the program had to be curtailed. This created a Soviet "missile gap," which was a significant and often overlooked catalyst in the 1962 Cuban Missile Crisis. The humiliating outcome of the Cuban crisis had an important consequence in subsequent Soviet strategic-weapons development by ending the debate about the primacy of strategic nuclear weapons in superpower relations. Even before the Cuban missile crisis, Khrushchev had to accede to the military's demands for a larger and more potent second generation of missiles. Advocates of a minimum deterrence strategic doctrine in both the United States and the Soviet Union lost out to those advocating larger and more powerful missile forces, provoking the massive nuclear arms race of the late 1960s.[1]

Matching Rhetoric with Missiles

Like Eisenhower, Khrushchev became convinced that nuclear war would be a cataclysmic event that had to be prevented at any cost.[2] He believed that the Soviet

Union would need a nuclear arsenal both to deter the United States from attacking the Soviet Union and to balance any U.S. attempts to use its nuclear arsenal as a political tool in the international arena. In the late 1950s Khrushchev viewed a modestly sized force—200 to 300 ICBMs—as an adequate deterrent against the United States.[3] Due to the cost of the associated launch complexes, ICBMs were extremely expensive weapons systems at the time. So in order to achieve economic savings, Khrushchev was forced to believe that a modest ICBM force would be a viable deterrent against the United States.

In spite of all of Khrushchev's rhetoric about the primacy of strategic missiles, the Soviet Union was falling behind in the nuclear arms race. By 1960 the United States had gained a lead over the Soviet Union in strategic nuclear forces, though this was not readily apparent to either Washington or the Kremlin. Neither side had a mature missile force, and the United States' advantage rested in its more mature and extensive strategic-bomber force. Khrushchev had dismissed the Soviet bomber force as obsolete and irrelevant, and delegated it to secondary missions.

As mentioned earlier, the first Soviet ICBM, the R-7A, had proven to be a failure due to the high cost of its basing and its prolonged launch cycle. This led to a severe curtailment of the program in 1958. Preliminary studies of a new generation of strategic weapons had begun even before Khrushchev trimmed back the size of the R-7 deployment. The new Yangel design bureau in Dnepropetrovsk was showing promise with its development of its R-12 (SS-4) intermediate-range ballistic missile. On 17 December 1956 the Council of Ministers authorized Yangel to begin studies of a new ICBM using the storable fuels pioneered with its R-12 design. The aim of the new program was to field a missile that could be ready for launch within thirty minutes of an alert, not the twenty hours of the R-7 missile. At the same time, Korolyov's design bureau was encouraged to examine novel propulsion technologies for intercontinental missiles beyond the R-7. His staff began to design a missile powered by a nuclear engine, called the YaRD, and began to examine solid-fuel missiles.[4] The research program was also broadened to include aviation design bureaus, with efforts by the Beriev, Pavel Sukhoi, and Myasischev bureaus.

The draft design of Yangel's new R-16 ICBM was completed in January 1958. In April 1958 the Council of Chief Designers concluded that several technical developments warranted the acceleration of the new missile programs. In particular, the weight of nuclear warheads had decreased substantially since the requirement documents for the R-7 had been written in 1954.[5] As a result, the designers projected that the new missiles would be only a third the weight of the R-7. This had important consequences in the cost of the system as a whole, since a smaller missile would require less elaborate basing equipment, further driving down costs. After the experience of the R-7A launch complex, reduced basing costs were a major consideration in the design of the next ICBM.

On 28 August 1958 Yangel was authorized to begin engineering development of the R-16 missile. Korolyov continued to argue with senior government leaders that the storable-fuel propulsion system chosen by Yangel was not proven and that the program therefore was a high risk compared to the cryogenic fuels he favored for his missiles. In spite of the failure of the R-7A, Korolyov still held considerable influence with Khrushchev and other senior leaders, and his recommendations could not easily be ignored. He proposed that a cryogenically fueled ICBM could be developed with a short reaction time, no worse than the Yangel R-16, through the use of special high-speed fuel pumps. The Soviet government gave initial approval for Korolyov's parallel R-9 missile project on 13 March 1959.[6]

While both new missiles offered significant advantages over the R-7, their requirements were driven more by the technical considerations of the designers than by the tactical considerations of the missile force. When the requirements were written up in 1957–58, no real institutional authority within the armed forces had the technical expertise to examine future needs for such weapons. The autocratic and paranoid style of Soviet leadership, inherited from the Stalin period, meant that major weapons decisions tended to be kept within a very narrow circle around Khrushchev and his immediate advisers. Khrushchev followed in Stalin's footsteps by taking a direct and personal role in all major weapon decisions, including even tactical weapons such as tanks, but his conception of the future Soviet missile force was rudimentary.

Unlike Eisenhower, Khrushchev made little effort to call in outside experts to review the general direction of Soviet strategic programs, and there is no evidence of a Soviet equivalent of the U.S. Gaither Commission of 1957.[7] As a result, the Korolyov R-9 and Yangel R-16 missiles proved to be technically competent designs when they were fielded in 1962–64, but as a weapon system they would prove to be fatally flawed. The preoccupation of the designers with fielding a system with low basing costs led them to ignore the desirability of silo basing and the survivability that this would afford.

The U.S. attitude was very different. With work on reconnaissance satellites well underway, the Gaither Commission concluded that in the future, all missiles bases would be vulnerable to attack. The only practical way to shield the missile from a nuclear blast was to protect the missile underground in a hardened launcher. As a result, the U.S. Air Force began to deploy their missiles in silos a generation sooner than the Soviets, largely as a result of the Gaither Commission recommendations. The first silo was designed for the Titan I, which was placed on an elevator, lifting it outside the silo for launch. Subsequent experiments concluded that the missile could be safely fired from the silo by venting the hot exhaust gases away from the missile. This mode was used with the new Minuteman I ICBM in 1962 and would become standard with nearly all ICBMs in the following years.

Korolyov's last attempt at liquid-fueled ballistic missiles was the R-9A (SS-8), which was deployed in small numbers in the mid-1960s. It is often confused with the Yangel R-26, which was shown at parades in Moscow but never deployed. This example is displayed in front of the Central Armed Forces Museum in Moscow.

The origins of Soviet missile silos are in dispute. In his memoirs, Khrushchev claimed to have come up with the idea in the summer of 1958, and that Korolyov and Barmin dismissed the plan as unworkable. In September 1958 Khrushchev's son Sergei showed him an illustration of one of the American silos, and this led to another confrontation with the missile engineers, during which they finally agreed to begin a program.[8] This account is not entirely plausible, because Korolyov was already familiar with silo launch from his work on submarine-launched ballistic missiles, and an underground launch configuration was one of the options studied for the R-7 ICBM.[9] What is far more likely is that the designers had not given serious consideration to silos due to a lack of a perceived need and the higher costs that silos entailed compared to simple surface launchers. The upshot of the controversy was that midway in the program, Khrushchev insisted that the missiles under development be deployed in silos. This was not immediately possible, since initial basing designs were already well under way, and considerable testing would be required. As a compromise, Khrushchev accepted that the new ICBMs would first be deployed in vulnerable but relatively inexpensive surface launchers, but that silo basing would follow as soon as practical. This lack of foresight would undermine the credibility of the new ICBM force even before it reached the test phase. The first experiments with silo basing were conducted quickly, and a Yangel R-12 intermediate-range missile was launched from an experimental Mayak silo on 31 August 1959 at Kapustin Yar. However, the first missile silos were not ready for use until 1963.

Neither the Korolyov R-9 nor the Yangel R-16 missiles progressed as quickly as Khrushchev would have liked. Korolyov's design bureau was swamped with work, including the many space programs and the continuing work on the R-7A missile. Likewise, Yangel's bureau was committed to both the R-12 (SS-4) and R-14 (SS-5) intermediate-range missiles. The R-12 proved to be the first Soviet nuclear-armed missile to be deployed in more than token numbers. Testing of the new design concluded in late 1958, and it was accepted for service on 4 March 1959. The first R-12 missile regiments began to be deployed in May 1959. By the summer of 1960, the RVSN had 248 launchers and 31 regiments deployed.

Until 1960 the RVSN missile force was made up of only a handful of units equipped with the obsolete R-1, R-2, and R-5 missiles. The force structure was considerably reinforced when Khrushchev ordered the conversion of two former bomber army headquarters to missile army headquarters, as well as the first three strategic-bomber divisions. The early divisions were oriented primarily against targets in Western Europe, including forward-deployed U.S. bomber bases, British strategic-bomber bases, and other targets. These units were deployed primarily in Belorussia and Ukraine. A single division was deployed in the Far East, which could reach targets in Japan. Due to their limited range, the R-12 missile units

The vulnerability of the U-2 spy plane led to its replacement by the KH-4 Corona satellites in the early 1960s. This photo of the Soviet missile base at Saryuzek was taken by a Corona satellite on 17 September 1971. The base housed a missile brigade equipped with the R-14U silo-based intermediate-range ballistic missile, which first became operational in 1965. (Courtesy National Reconnaissance Office)

contributed little to the strategic balance of forces between the Soviet Union and the United States. They *were* instrumental in training a generation of Soviet missile crews in the day-to-day realities of missile operation. The intermediate-range ballistic missile (IRBM) force was envisioned as a substitute for the Ground Forces in defending the Soviet Union against NATO attack. While it may seem preposterous that the Kremlin had any fears about a NATO attack on the Soviet Union, the war-scarred generation of Soviet leaders could not escape the stranglehold of bloody memories. The IRBM force could not entirely replace the Ground Forces, but it would provide a rationale for trimming back their size to a more economical level (table 3.1).

The Nedelin Disaster

The first head of the RVSN was Marshal Mitrofan Nedelin. He had commanded one of the first R-5 missile brigades and had subsequently headed the GAU Main Artillery Directorate, responsible for the early missiles. Nedelin was favored by Khrushchev due to his enthusiasm for the new missile weapons, an attitude not widely shared among the hidebound tank generals of the Soviet Army. Nedelin had headed the studies in early 1959 that advocated the new missile force, and Khrushchev rewarded him with command of the RVSN in December 1959.

In October 1960 Yangel's new R-16 ICBM was ready to begin tests at the Tyuratam proving ground.[10] Initial attempts to launch the missile on 23 October 1960 failed. Safety procedures indicated that the missile should have its fuel removed before repairs were undertaken. But the toxicity of the nitric acid oxidant made this a time-consuming and dangerous operation. Nedelin authorized the crew to continue to work on the missile, but it would have to be launched within the next day for fear that the oxidizer would begin to eat through seals and piping. In haste to complete repairs on 24 October 1960, safety procedures were ignored, and a large number of senior personnel, including Nedelin and many of Yangel's top aides, remained around the missile. Yangel and one of the range officers walked away for a few moments to smoke behind a bunker, several hundred yards from the missile. Safety checks of the electrical firing circuits were under way, and a flaw in the wiring accidentally triggered the second-stage engine. The exhaust blast from the engine smashed open the fuel tanks below it and detonated the fuel and oxidizer. The fireball incinerated Nedelin and seventy-three other engineers and officers, including Yangel's senior aide and the Soviet Union's top missile guidance designer.[11] It was the largest single missile launch disaster in Soviet history, and the only one involving senior missile designers and army leaders. The accident was hushed up and Nedelin's death attributed to an airplane crash.

Table 3.1

Intermediate-Range Missile Force Organization, 1960

New RVSN Unit	Former Unit	Location	Commander (July 1960)
50th Missile Army	**50th Strategic Air Army**	**Smolensk**	**Gen. Col. F. I. Dobysh**
32nd Kherson Missile Division	12th Engineer Brigade RVGK	Postavy	Gen. Maj. V. F. Frontov
Gomel Guards Missile Division	72nd Engineer Brigade RVGK	Gvardeisk	Gen. Maj. A. I. Kholopov
29th Vitebsk Guards Missile Division	85th Eng Brigade RVGK	Shulyai	Gen. Maj. A. A. Kolesov
Orlovsko-Berlin Guards Missile Division	25th LRA Division	Valga	Gen. Maj. N. K. Spiridenko
43rd Missile Army	**43rd Strategic Air Army**	**Vinnitsa**	**Gen. Col. G. N. Tupikov**
Svriskoi Missile Division	15th Eng Brigade RVGK	Mozyr	Gen. Maj. G. L. Osyukov
Sevastopol Missile Division	22nd Eng Brigade RVGK	Lutsk	Gen. Maj. V. I. Fadeyev
Missile Division	73rd Eng Brigade RVGK	Kolomya	Gen. Maj. I. F. Dibrova
Bryansk-Berlin Missile Division	83rd LRA Division	Pruzhany	Gen. Maj. F. L. Chernyavsky
9th Missile Corps	**Khabarovsk UAP**	**Khabarovsk**	**Gen. Maj. I. T. Shmelyov**
Missile Division	96th LRA Division	Ussuriisk	Gen. Maj. I. F. Presnyakov

Yangel's fortuitous absence from the launch site prevented the total decapitation of one of the two Soviet ICBM design bureaus. In spite of the heavy losses of key engineers, the program was not seriously delayed, since it was already in the test phase. It took about three months to restore the launch site and conduct a state inquiry into the accident. There was a very different atmosphere in the Kremlin since Stalin. Khrushchev was well aware that his own pressure on Nedelin and Yangel to speed up the program had as much to do with the catastrophe as any particular technical problem, and rather than look for scapegoats, the commission quickly isolated the technical problems and took steps to remedy them. There was none of the repression so common in the Stalin period, and the program continued with a high level of urgency.

The first successful launch of the R-16 took place on 2 February 1961. Curiously enough, U.S. intelligence did not detect a successful launch until the second launch, on 2 April 1961.[12] After this second successful test, Yangel offered to put the missile immediately into service using simple launch pads. Such a short test program was unprecedented and gives some idea of the urgency with which the Kremlin viewed the program. The R-16 missile system was accepted for service by government decree on 20 October 1961, but testing continued until February 1962. One expedient unit was put on duty in April at the test site, and four regiments were declared operational on 1 November 1961.

In spite of its considerable advance over the R-7A, the R-16 compared poorly to contemporary U.S. ICBMs such as the new Titan I. The Titan I was designed from the outset for silo basing and entered service about the same time as the R-16 in 1962. The Titan I had an extremely fast readiness rate: it took only about fifteen minutes to launch once it received the command. In contrast, the first R-16 regiments were deployed at soft sites, that is, surface launchers were not shielded from nuclear attack. On normal duty the missiles were stored in hangers near the launch pad, which were protected by earthen berms. On orders from the Kremlin, the missiles were towed out to the launch pad, erected, and fueled. This took one to three hours. Each launch site consisted of two missile hangers and launch pads, since two missiles shared a common fueling system in order to drive down cost. This exacerbated the vulnerability of the sites to attack, since it placed two launchers within the blast radius of a single nuclear weapon. In the event of a crisis, the R-16 missiles could be erected and fueled in advance of a launch order. However, their corrosive nitric acid oxidant limited the amount of time they could be kept in this state to a few days. After this, they would have to have the fuel removed in a laborious and dangerous process, and the missile would be sent back to the factory for rebuilding. Even in an alert posture such as this, the R-16 had a relatively slow reaction time due to the poor durability of its inertial guidance systems. While American systems were kept running continuously while on alert duty, Soviet systems were not durable enough to do so.[13] As a result, a fueled U.S. missile could be ready to fire three to five minutes after receiving the launch instruction, while the Soviet R-16 missiles had to wait up to twenty minutes as the gyros were spun up and the inertial guidance system aligned.

Korolyov's parallel R-9 ICBM program had started after Yangel's R-16 and reached the test phase seven months later. The first flight test of the R-9 from Tyuratam took place on 9 April 1961 and was a complete failure. The first successful launch was conducted on 21 April 1961. Korolyov proposed deploying small numbers of R-9 missiles on simple pad launchers near the existing R-7A launch sites.[14] The idea was to provide a means to rapidly increase the number of available ICBM launchers by taking advantage of the existing infrastructure, since the R-7 and R-9 shared a common fueling system. This did not take place due to lingering test problems. The third test flight failed only three seconds after launch due to an engine failure, and the missile crashed to the pad, severely damaging it. The continuing problem was Glushko's RD-111 engine. Bitter exchanges over

The first-generation Soviet ICBMs, 1957–67

this issue between Glushko and Korolyov led to the estrangement of the two engineers. These incidents helped ignite the "civil war of the chief designers," an escalation of the long-running debate over storable versus cryogenic fuels. Glushko finally refused to work on later Korolyov projects in spite of Khrushchev's personal intervention to calm down relations between the two design bureaus. While it did not have great impact on missile programs, Glushko's refusal to participate in Korolyov's later N-1 superbooster for the moon program was a major factor in the Soviet Union's loss of the moon race with the United States later in the decade.

The R-9 test program continued to be marred by problems, often involving the complicated ground support equipment used to rapidly fuel the missile. This led to many more test launches than with Yangel's R-16. During the two sets of trials, from March 1962 to February 1964, there were thirty-nine launches, of which twenty-six were judged successful.[15] The most serious failure occurred in February 1964, when a fully fueled missile toppled over after launch, blowing up the launch pad. U.S. intelligence took a more jaundiced view of the test program. Of the thirty-two launches in the first two test series that the United States monitored, it concluded that fifteen were marred by accidents or other failures, and only seventeen were successful.[16] The R-9A was finally accepted for service on 21 July 1965, nearly two years after the R-16 and nearly four years behind schedule.

Even before the testing had been completed, it was clear that the R-16 was the more versatile of the two missiles. It used the type of storable fuel sought by the military, and its fuel-handling equipment was considerably less extensive than the complicated high-speed pumps needed for Korolyov's R-9. Although the two missiles cost about the same, the launcher system for the R-9 was about double the cost of the R-16 launcher system.[17] As a result, series production of the R-16 began at the Yuzhmash plant in Dnepropetrovsk and the Polyot plant in Omsk in January 1962. The R-16 was the first Soviet ICBM to be deployed in large numbers. Indeed, Russian historians consider the R-16 and its competitor, the R-9, to be the first generation of Soviet ICBMs.[18] Already in 1961, the two main ICBM plants at Kuibyshev and Dnepropetrovsk were put on an around-the-clock, three-shift work schedule to increase production.[19]

Bigger Bombs

By the end of the 1950s, the Soviet arsenal had a sophisticated range of nuclear warheads. However, many of the devices were large and unwieldy, and the military continued to seek the development of new, lighter types that more efficiently used the expensive and scarce fissile material.

The testing of very large thermonuclear weapons at Semipalatinsk raised disturbing environmental problems due to the proximity of many small towns and villages. As a result, a more remote test site in a less inhabited region of the country was sought. The Arctic island of Novaya Zemlya in the Barents Sea was selected by a decree on 31 July 1954.[20] It was used for high-energy tests (i.e., those of more than a few megatons yield) and a variety of other specialized exercises, including naval underwater nuclear tests. The first test was conducted on Novaya Zemlya on 21 September 1955, a 3.5-kiloton underwater detonation. A series of high-yield aerial tests was conducted in 1957, including a 2.9-megaton blast on 6 October 1957, examining a new thermonuclear warhead for the R-7A ICBM. Testing continued at an accelerated pace in 1958 to complete designs for the warheads of a new generation of ICBMs, including the R-9 and R-16. By the end of the 1950s, the Soviet nuclear weapons industry was an enormous enterprise, with over ten thousand scientists scattered between the ten closed cities of the "nuclear archipelago." The Ministry of Medium Industry, the cover name for the Soviet nuclear industry, continued to grow through the 1960s. Although it included the civilian nuclear power industry, the bulk of its resources were devoted to the nuclear arsenal. Run as a fiefdom by Minister E. P. Slavsky since 1957, its annual budget was exceeded only by those of the Russian and Ukrainian republics.[21]

The accelerated pace of nuclear tests in 1958 was influenced by Khrushchev's decision to declare a unilateral test ban in the autumn of 1958. But relations between the superpowers were still so tense that treaties to limit nuclear arms seemed in the distant future. There was a notable thaw in relations in 1959, raising hopes of a formal agreement on banning atmospheric tests. The collapse of the planned Paris meeting between Eisenhower and Khrushchev following the May 1960 shoot-down of a CIA U-2 spy plane froze relations yet again.

Soviet nuclear testing resumed in January 1961, in part due to pressure from the Soviet military and in part due to the lack of a reciprocal response in the West. There were several firsts in 1961, including the first underground detonation at Semipalatinsk on 11 October 1961 and the first detonation of an antiballistic-missile (ABM) warhead in space on 27 October 1961. The space tests caused some alarm, because they revealed the vulnerability of Soviet missiles to the electromagnetic pulse (EMP) effects from a distant warhead, which could disable the missile electronics or lead to a premature fizzle of the warhead. Of the 112 tests in the 1961–62 series, about half were thermonuclear devices, and the remainder were fission devices. In the early 1960s missile warheads were being developed by two design bureaus: KB-11 and NII-1011.[22] Following the conclusion of the moratorium in 1961, NII-1011 tested nine nuclear weapons in fourteen tests that it had developed during the test moratorium, while KB-11 conducted forty-five tests. Although the two design bureaus had been organized originally for competitive purposes, in fact NII-1011 was heavily dependent on KB-11 for much of its development and acted as a subcontractor for some programs.

One of these was the RDS-220 Superbomb, the most powerful nuclear weapon ever detonated. This 150-megaton device, designed by Andrei Sakharov in 1955–56, was also the largest ever constructed: about 2 m (6.5 ft) in diameter and 8 m (26 ft) long, weighing about twenty-five tons. To permit the bomber to escape the detonation, the bomb had to be dropped using an enormous set of four parachutes, each with a canopy of 400 sq m (4,400 sq ft). Initial tests of the parachute using a simulated twenty-five-ton load were unsuccessful. The nuclear testing moratorium of 1958 provided additional time to improve delivery. On 30 October 1961 a specially modified Tu-95N bomber dropped the experimental RDS-220 thermonuclear bomb over the range at Novaya Zemlya. Due to concerns over its potential effects, the yield of the weapon was dialed down to 50 megatons for the test, which it achieved. There does not appear to have been any serious plan to mass produce this weapon. Its main value for the Kremlin was propaganda, and its main value for the military was to examine the outer limits of feasible yields. The nuclear tests that followed the moratorium examined a number of high-yield weapons, up to twenty-five megatons, which would be used to arm future ICBMs.

Missile Submarines Founder

The Soviet Navy was deploying nuclear missiles at a faster rate than the Strategic Missile Force, but these contributed little to the strategic balance with the United States. The Soviet Navy's ballistic-missile programs were a muddle of confused priorities and poor planning.

Korolyov eased his way out of SLBM design by shifting this work to the associated SKB-385 design bureau, headed by young Viktor Makeyev in Miass.[23] The original submarine-launched missile system, the D-1 with the R-11FM missile, was too primitive to be deployed on regular patrols. The next generation of submarine ballistic missiles was based around the R-13 missile and D-2 complex, which entered development in August 1956. This missile system was a further evolution of the R-11FM, intended mainly to extend its poor range from 150 km (90 mi) to 600 km (370 mi). It was also the first Soviet SLBM deemed reliable enough to be test fired with a nuclear warhead. In spite of these advantages, it was a poorly conceived design, still cursed by Korolyov's reluctance to develop a missile capable of being launched from underwater. Like its predecessor, the R-13 had to be elevated out of the sail of the submarine for launch. Furthermore, the associated submarines carried only three missiles each.

While this effort was taking place, a parallel program called the D-3, with the R-15 missile, was undertaken by Yangel's design bureau. This missile used a somewhat more advanced launch system, permitting the missiles to be fired from within their launch tubes, though not from underwater. However, the design was doomed by the requirement to carry the same enormous 5.5-ton warhead of the R-7 ICBM. The resulting missile and its large and expensive Project 639 submarine were canceled before leaving the drawing board.

The Soviet Navy was so desperate for a nuclear ballistic missile that Makeyev's unimpressive R-13 missile was accepted for service in October 1961. Two submarines were developed to carry it, the conventional Project 629 (Golf) and the Project 658 (Hotel). Twenty-six submarines had been deployed with it by 1963, only eight of the nuclear Project 658 class, due to their high cost.[24] The navy held out great hope for the nuclear Project 658 class, since the nuclear powerplant offered nearly unlimited underwater cruising. This made it far easier to evade NATO

In its haste to develop intercontinental nuclear strike capability, the Soviet Navy rushed a variety of liquid-fuel submarine missiles into service in the early 1960s. The R-13 (SS-N-4), to the left, and the R-21 (SS-N-5) are preserved at the Central Armed Forces Museum in Moscow.

antisubmarine forces and opened up the possibility of conducting a standing missile patrol off American shores. This concept proved unattainable due to the unreliability of the reactor.

Although the D-2 missile system was not officially accepted for service use until the autumn of 1961, the first Project 658 submarine, the K-19, went operational with the Northern Fleet in November 1960. In June 1961, while conducting a patrol in the Norwegian Sea north of Scotland, the K-19 suffered a major reactor failure, which led to the deaths of nine of the crew from radiation poisoning and nearly to the loss of the submarine. The K-19 had to be towed back to Soviet waters and thereafter was known by the grim nickname Hiroshima. The nuclear powerplant on the Project 658 was so troublesome that a rebuild program had to be undertaken in 1965–70, called the Project 658M. The unreliability of the nuclear submarine fleet put an end to attempts to establish a standing missile patrol off the American coast until 1966. As a result, during the early 1960s, the Soviet submarine missile force was primarily assigned to targets in Europe and Japan, and did not contribute to the Soviet-American nuclear balance until late in the decade.[25]

By early 1958 the navy had recognized that the D-3 system and R-15 missile were doomed, and that Makeyev's D-2 system with R-13 was far from ideal. So Yangel's design bureau began work on the new D-4 system, which included the liquid-fuel R-19 missile with a range of 1,000 km (600 mi) for the Project 639 submarine, and the R-20 missile with a range of 600 km (370 mi) for the Project 629 submarine. Both could be launched from underwater. Hardly had the program begun, when in May 1959 Khrushchev ordered Yangel to accelerate work on the R-16 ICBM, and so ordered a halt to work on their submarine missiles.

As a result, all work on the liquid-fuel SLBM effort was shifted to Makeyev's bureau in Miass. Makeyev's redesigned R-21 missile for the D-4 system was ready for testing late in 1962. This was the first Soviet SLBM that could be launched from underwater.[26] The R-21 was intended to rearm both the diesel electric Project 629 (Golf I) and the nuclear-powered Project 658 (Hotel I) submarines, previously fitted with the unsatisfactory R-13 missile. The R-21 was eventually deployed on thirteen conventional Project 629 submarines and seven nuclear Project 658 submarines between 1966 and 1971. With their reactors finally fixed, these were the first Soviet submarines deemed mature enough to conduct missile patrols off the American coast, starting in 1966. These submarines carried only three missiles each, compared to the contemporary U.S. George Washington submarine, which carried sixteen Polaris missiles, and they were inferior in every other respect, including missile accuracy and submarine silencing. It took fully twelve minutes to fire the three missiles, during which time the submarine would be vulnerable to detection and attack.[27]

The travails of the Soviet submarine force were due in no small measure to wretchedly poor planning, the lingering effects of Korolyov's conservatism in missile design, and the inability of the navy to stand up to Khrushchev's pressure to rapidly deploy missile weapons. In contrast, the U.S. Navy refused to be bullied into deploying inadequate liquid-fuel missiles on submarines, waiting until the technology for the compact Polaris missile was ready. As a result, in 1960, the U.S. Navy leapfrogged over the Soviet designs with the George Washington–class submarines, armed with sixteen solid-fuel missiles. It would take the Soviet Union a decade to catch up, after billions of rubles had been squandered on thirty-seven completely inadequate missile submarines.

Disinheriting the Air Force

The Soviet bomber force continued to stagnate, largely due to Khrushchev's conviction that it was obsolete. As a palliative, the air force had begun to work on cruise missiles that could be launched from the bombers. Khrushchev's main complaint was that the bomber could not survive in the face of fighters and anti-aircraft missiles. The cruise missile countered antibomber defenses, since they could be launched from hundreds of miles away, outside the range of ground based missiles.

The first of these, the Mikoyan Kh-20 "Tsar missile" (AS-3 Kangaroo), entered trials in 1957 and entered service in October 1959.[28] It was an enormous missile, based on contemporary MiG-19 jet fighter design. It could be carried only on the Tu-95 Bear bomber, because the Myasishchev 3M did not have enough ground clearance to fit in its bomb bay. As a result, the final production batch of sixty-seven Tu-95 bombers manufactured in 1959–65 were configured as the Tu-95K, capable of carrying a single Kh-20 missile under the fuselage. Myasishchev began development of his own cruise-missile design to arm his bomber, the M-61, but it was not completed before his bureau was closed. The last gasp of the bomber advocates came in the form of yet another overly ambitious Myasishchev project, the cruise-missile-armed M-50 (Bounder) supersonic bomber. The program started in July 1955 with an aim of producing a supersonic bomber with a range of 12,000 km (7,400 mi), or 15,000 km (9,300 mi) with aerial refueling.[29] The M-50 proved to be a complete flop, with a range only half that of the requirement. To save his bureau, Myasishchev began to turn toward missiles. He was no more successful in this endeavor, and his bureau was finally gobbled up by one of the new missile-design bureaus in 1960.

Khrushchev remained unconvinced that the cruise missiles were any more survivable than the bombers themselves. Nevertheless, they gave a patina of modernity to the bomber force. The commander of the Long-Range Aviation Force, Gen.

Myasishchev's final attempt to redeem his design bureau was the M-50 Bounder strategic bomber, which was intended to replace the flawed 3M Bison. Its range was so poor that Khrushchev closed the bureau in 1959 and turned over its facilities to Chelomey's missile bureau. The sole example is preserved at the museum at Monino in the suburbs of Moscow.

Vladimir A. Sudets, managed to avoid the dissolution of the three strategic-bomber divisions by pandering to one of Khrushchev's pet concerns. Khrushchev was long bothered by the U.S. Navy's capability to attack the Soviet Union with its carrier battle groups. Sudets convinced Khrushchev that the strategic bombers would make ideal anticarrier weapons if armed with a new generation of antiship missile. As a result, Khrushchev's cuts did not affect the bomber divisions equipped with Tu-95M and Myasishchev 3M bombers, but their intercontinental strike mission became secondary. By way of comparison, the U.S. Air Force in 1961 had 1,495 bombers that could strike targets in the Soviet Union from bases in Europe and the United States, while the Soviet Union had a force of only a tenth the size.

The 1962 Missile-Gap Crisis

The Soviet Union's intercontinental strike force in 1960–61 remained very small. By the end of 1961, the RVSN had six R-7A and ten R-16 launchers operational, and by the end of 1962 this had risen to only fifty-six. While the Soviet Union was

Table 3.2
United States–Soviet Strategic-Weapons Balance, 1960–64

	1961	1962	1963	1964
United States				
B-52 intercontinental bombers	555	615	630	600
B-47, B-58 medium bombers	940	890	665	560
Bomber subtotal	1,495	1,505	1,295	1,160
Atlas ICBM	28	57	126	113
Titan ICBM	0	21	67	108
Minuteman	0	0	160	600
Polaris SLBM	48	96	144	224
Missile subtotal	76	174	497	1,045
Soviet Union				
Tu-95M bombers	95	104	112	115
3M bombers	79	78	76	74
Bomber subtotal	174	182	188	189
R-7A ICBM	6	6	6	6
R-16 ICBM	10	50	114	172
R-9A ICBM	0	0	2	11
Missile subtotal	16	56	122	189

deploying its first generation of ICBMs, the United States was racing ahead with its own program. In contrast to the failed R-7, its American analog, the Atlas ICBM, was deployed in significant numbers. The final Atlas F squadrons, deployed in 1962 and 1963, were based in hardened silos. These were followed in 1962 by the new liquid-fueled Titan I, also deployed in silos. From the Soviet perspective, the greatest threat came from the new Minuteman missile. The Minuteman was the cutting edge of missile technology. It was a small, inexpensive, solid-fuel missile, ideally suited for silo basing. Its low cost meant that it could be deployed in massive numbers (table 3.2).

By late 1961 Khrushchev's missile rattling had come back to haunt him. Instead of the Soviet Union manufacturing missiles like sausages, it was the United States that was doing so. The only missiles being manufactured in large numbers were the intermediate-range missiles like the R-12, which could only reach targets in Europe. The public disclosures in late 1961 of the American plans to deploy a large force of the new Minuteman missile highlighted the growing gap in intercontinental nuclear power between the two superpowers. Moscow was now beginning to face its own missile gap, and unlike the 1960 U.S. missile gap, this one was real.

The missile gap argument had been a potent political weapon in the 1960 American presidential elections. The U.S. Air Force, projecting a very large Soviet missile force by the mid-1960s, wanted a new force of 2,500 Minuteman ICBMs. The mistaken American views about Soviet missile force intentions was exacerbated by Khrushchev's frequent and intemperate boasts and threats about the power of his growing missile force. It took some time for the American missile gap controversy to evaporate, and in the meantime, the U.S. Congress was insistent on a major missile deployment program. After considerable debate, the U.S. secretary of defense, Robert McNamara, proposed a future U.S. force structure in the autumn of 1961, and it became public by December 1961.[30] McNamara's figure of 900 to 1,000 Minuteman missiles was considered by many to be the minimum force that an irate Congress would accept.[31] More than any other decision, it would establish one of the boundaries of superpower force levels for decades to come. In addition, the U.S. Navy's ballistic-missile force was set at forty-one submarines, each with sixteen Polaris missiles.

Khrushchev's high expectations for the new R-16 missile force were beginning to lose their luster when compared to the American effort. As the new R-16 missiles were being deployed, the RVSN began to take a close look at the tactics of missile warfare and were disheartened by the conclusions. Khrushchev's view on nuclear doctrine were not particularly complicated, and centered on the notion that even a modest force of ICBMs would serve as an adequate deterrent to prevent the United States from initiating a full-scale nuclear attack. By 1961 Khrushchev's original plans for a small force of 200–300 ICBMs had been given up. On 30 May 1961 the Kremlin had approved a decision to organize a further twenty-four RVSN missile divisions, in addition to the ten divisions organized in July 1960. Of these, the first seventeen were armed with the R-12 or R-14 intermediate-range missiles, while the remaining seventeen were intended to be armed with R-16 or R-9 ICBMs.

While Khrushchev's views dominated most state policy, the Soviet military began to examine strategic doctrine in a more systematic way.[32] Unlike the United States, where civilian analysts at institutions such as Rand played an important role in formulating doctrine, Soviet doctrine was the domain of the military. Two institutions predominated in these discussions: the NII-4 MO in Bolshevo, the RVSN's primary think tank; and the Soviet General Staff, which has traditionally been responsible for formulating military doctrine. The Soviet Army's strategic doctrine in the Khrushchev years was heavily influenced by Marshal V. D. Sokolovsky's seminal work, *Voyennaya strategia (Military Strategy)*. Given the significant technological limitations of the time, idealized doctrine presented few real guidelines for the essential tactical decisions of nuclear war fighting such as strike initiation and targeting. Furthermore, Soviet nuclear doctrine was constrained by obvious U.S. superiority in the means to deliver nuclear strikes against the USSR versus the likely Soviet response through most of this period.

An underlying theme in Soviet war planning during the Khrushchev years was the concept of "initial period of war." Although this is an essential element in all strategic thinking, it had particular resonance in Soviet thinking of the Khrushchev years due to the catastrophic lessons of recent Russian wars. Both the 1905 Russo-Japanese War and the 1941 Soviet-German war had begun with a surprise strike by the opposing forces, and there were similar examples for other countries, notably the 1941 Pearl Harbor attack. The devastating consequences of the German assault in 1941 was painfully etched into the minds of all Soviet military leaders of the Khrushchev period. This dark memory had an inestimable effect on nuclear war planning.

Three basic tactics existed for an initial period of strategic nuclear war: preemption, launch-on-warning, and launch-on-attack. Ideally, Soviet war planners desired to have intercontinental missiles able to carry out preemptive counterforce strikes against U.S. strategic forces. Soviet studies of the initial period of war suggested that allowing the enemy to strike first would invite destruction. Although cultural and doctrinal factors led to a preemptive war-fighting preference, this policy was not without its severe shortcomings. To begin with, it ran against Khrushchev's view that the primary intention of the force was deterrence. In any event, Soviet strategic forces in the early 1960s did not have a high probability of eliminating the U.S. nuclear strategic forces without triggering a devastating counterstrike. This was due to the larger size and greater sophistication of U.S. strategic forces; inherent shortcomings in the reliability of Soviet strategic forces, especially the bomber and submarine forces; and intelligence shortcomings regarding targeting, post-strike assessment, and follow-on strikes. During the Khrushchev years, no Soviet nuclear weapon system had counterforce capability. This was not only a matter of accuracy but also of intelligence. Soviet missiles of the early 1960s were not accurate enough to knock out hardened U.S. missile silos. Furthermore, it is open to question whether the Soviet Union had acquired sufficient space reconnaissance capability to carry out such strikes, even if missile accuracy were not a problem.[33] While the Soviet strategic forces may have preferred the preemptive strike tactic, it was inherently untenable.

Recognition of the shortcomings of a preemptive tactic gradually forced the Soviet General Staff to consider other options, especially launch-on-warning.[34] However, the shift toward a launch-on-warning posture required substantial improvements in both missile technology and Soviet command and control. The existing generation of ICBMs took too long to launch even when on alert status. Flight time from the U.S. missile fields to the Soviet fields was twenty-two to thirty minutes, while typical launch preparation time for the R-9 or R-16 was at least thirty minutes. In addition, the lack of adequate early-warning sensors at the time meant that the first warning of the attack at best would take place under ten minutes from impact, and might not actually occur until the detonation of the first wave of U.S. missiles. To achieve the technical means to permit launch-on-warning, missile reaction times had to be substantially shortened, and the technical means of early warning had to be substantially improved. The recent 1961–62 nuclear tests also raised the alarming specter that the United States might initiate an attack with a series of nuclear blasts in the upper atmosphere aimed at disrupting the Soviet command network by electromagnetic pulse. Even with improvements in place, there were no assurances that the missile force could be launched in time to escape a U.S. missile attack. Launch-on-warning was inherently risky.

The final alternative was launch-on-attack. Under this doctrine, the missiles had to be placed in survivable basing so that at least a significant fraction of the force would survive an American preemptive attack. Launch-on-attack held little attraction for Soviet planners in the early 1960s, since U.S. superiority in strategic nuclear weapons might effectively destroy most if not all of the Soviet strategic forces before they could launch a retaliatory blow, due to the poor basing decisions of the 1950s.

As the first generation of missiles was in the process of being deployed in late 1961, the RVSN had already concluded that they were completely inadequate in the face of the accelerated U.S. program and could not carry out any plausible scenario envisioned in war-fighting doctrine. Industrial problems persisted due to the novelty of the technology, and there were serious bottlenecks in the manufacture of critical subcomponents, especially electronics and engines.

The American plans for a large force of Minuteman missiles created a crisis for Khrushchev and the Soviet military leadership. Instead of the small but expensive force of ICBMs that was expected by Khrushchev, the United States was racing ahead to a fundamentally new level of strategic weapons based around large numbers of cheap and survivable missiles. The size of the new force suggested that they would not be aimed solely at major political and urban centers, but that they might be sufficient in number to be used against the weakly defended Soviet ICBM soft launchers, posing a preemptive counterforce threat. This fear was confirmed by a 16 June 1962 speech by Secretary of Defense McNamara, indicating that the new U.S. forces would be primarily aimed at Soviet offensive nuclear forces. The military leadership was becoming alarmed that Khrushchev's minimalist strategic program would leave them vulnerable to U.S. strategic preemptive attack, while at the same time, his cuts of conventional force structure reduced their capabilities in this regard as well. The Soviet strategic situation in 1962 was "little short of desperate."[35]

In response to the crisis, Khrushchev held a special meeting with senior military leaders in February 1962 at the Pitsunda resort south of Gagra on the Black Sea. The new head of the RVSN, Marshal Kirill S. Moskalenko, presented a damning indictment of the R-9 and R-16 programs.[36] The Soviet industry was hard-pressed to deploy only ten to fifteen launchers in 1962 due to bottlenecks in many key industries. The brash new ballistic-missile designer, Vladimir Chelomey, suggested that the current techniques of missile manufacture were obsolete and that industrial production techniques taken from the experience of the aviation industry should be adopted. This only made matters worse, because it pitted the established missile bureaus, which had traditionally been managed by Ustinov's defense industry ministry, against Chelomey and the aviation ministry.[37] The technical shortcomings of the first generation of missiles ruled out the possibility of simply extending or accelerating their production run to make up the difference between the original small ICBM force and a force adequate to respond to the new U.S. force. Instead, the military began to advocate that the first-generation ICBMs be halted once a modest force was deployed, and the resources directed instead toward a more survivable second generation of ICBMs. Khrushchev was not pleased by the confrontation at Gagra, and in April sacked the RVSN commander, replacing him with Gen. Sergei Biryuzov.

As a result of the confrontation between Khrushchev and the military at Pitsunda in February, in March the General Staff formulated new plans for the Strategic Missile Force in an attempt to respond to the American program. On the basis of studies by NII-4 in Bolshevo, a plan was created to develop an integrated array of ICBMs. This would include at least four categories of missiles. A light, solid-fuel equivalent of the Minuteman was planned that would be cheap enough to be deployed in large numbers. It would be supplemented by smaller numbers of a heavy ICBM, equivalent to the American Titan, that would be more accurate and deliver heavier warheads. A super-heavy missile would also be built in modest numbers, designed to carry the new fifty-megaton warheads for attack of select command-and-control targets such as the Cheyenne Mountain command center. To deal with the possibility of an American antiballistic-missile system, a special category of "global" missile would be developed that could circumvent the northern-oriented ballistic-missile early-warning network (BMEWS) and destroy key American command-and-control networks as the vanguard to the main missile strike. In addition, the program halted all further work on future ICBM programs that were already under way, such as Yangel's new R-26 design, because they did not fit the new requirements. The Council of Ministers released the decrees on this program in April 1962. In July and August 1962 construction efforts on new missile launchers for the R-9 and R-16 were halted.

The Cuban Missile Crisis

The Cuban Missile Crisis occurred in the wake of the Soviet military-political debate over the future direction of the Soviet strategic forces. Most accounts of the Cuban Missile Crisis have shown little awareness of the military controversies preceding this critical confrontation, although recent studies do recognize that Khrushchev's problems in the Soviet strategic-missile program were one of the roots of the crisis.[38]

The reasons for the missile deployments on Cuba have long been confused by the autocratic and secretive nature of Soviet defense decision making and by obfuscation by Khrushchev. In his memoirs, Khrushchev stated that the Soviet deployment of intermediate-range missiles in Cuba was a response to U.S. support of anti-Castro forces and the basing of U.S. IRBMs in Italy, the United Kingdom, and Turkey. Due to the perception in the United States in the late 1950s that the Soviet Union was far ahead in deployed missiles, the United States had won approval from its NATO allies to station small numbers of intermediate-range missiles in the United Kingdom, Italy, and Turkey that could strike targets in the western Soviet Union.[39] When deployed in the early 1960s, these missiles were significantly outnumbered by the burgeoning Soviet force of R-12 missiles aimed at NATO. NATO's main advantage remained the substantial bomber force directed against the Soviet Union, which included not only forward-deployed U.S. aircraft, but British bombers as well.

While some Soviet action to bolster Castro's regime in Cuba was not unexpected, the type of deployment was surprising. A large-scale missile deployment was not Khrushchev's only option. Other possibilities, such as the basing of Soviet conventional forces in Cuba, would also have had a deterrent effect on U.S.-Cuban entanglements, particularly if it were publicly announced that those forces were armed with short-range tactical nuclear weapons. Furthermore, such a deployment would not have raised the stakes as high as a nuclear-missile deployment aimed at the United States, while having a high probability of achieving the ostensible goal of preventing an invasion of Cuba.

The Cuban crisis became the Cuban *Missile* Crisis largely due to Khrushchev's rash attempt to compensate for the shortcomings of his much delayed and poorly planned Strategic Missile Force. This bold and inexpensive shortcut would deploy several dozen intermediate-range missiles on Cuba as an immediate counterweight to America's intercontinental advantages. At the time of the Cuban crisis, the Soviet Union's missile force was substantially smaller than the American force. There were only six launch pads for the R-7A, two improvised launch pads for the unproven R-9A, and about twenty interim launchers for the R-16. The Soviet bomber force was a tenth the size of the U.S. force. The Russian missile gap formed the military roots of the Cuban operation, code-named Operation Anadyr.

The Cuban missile deployment was reckless, ill conceived, and poorly managed. Khrushchev was convinced by the Soviet military leadership that the missiles could be surreptitiously deployed without the United States being aware of the effort. He intended to hand the Kennedy administration a stunning fait accompli in November 1962. In fact, Soviet attempts at concealment were hopelessly inadequate and inept, and the missile sites were discovered long before they became operational.

The original order-of-battle for Operation Anadyr was significantly different from the force that was eventually deployed.[40] The main element was the reinforced 43rd Missile Division from Romny, with three R-12 regiments and two R-14 regiments, totaling forty ballistic-missile launchers. The navy was expected to deploy the 18th Submarine Missile Cruiser Division from the Northern Fleet, consisting of seven Project 629 (Golf) submarines, each armed with three R-13 nuclear-armed ballistic missiles. In addition, the navy was expected to contribute a significant force of other warships, including four attack submarines, two cruisers, two missile destroyers, and two escort destroyers, plus twelve missile boats.[41] The air force's contribution was a pair of cruise-missile regiments and a single nuclear-capable IL-28 bomber regiment.

The R-12 (SS-4) intermediate-range missile was at the heart of the Cuban Missile Crisis. The original plan to transfer the 43rd Missile Division to Cuba fell through. This unit was equipped with a single regiment with the R-12, and two regiments were being equipped with the new R-14 missile. Since the R-14 was not yet fully operational, it was decided to draw two R-12 regiments from other divisions. The resulting improvised unit was renamed the 51st Missile Division and placed under the command of Gen. Maj. Igor D. Statsenko.[42] The three R-12 regiments had a total of twenty-four launchers. The two R-14's (SS-5) never reached Cuba due to the blockade. In total, 7,956 missile troops were deployed with the division, along with forty-two missiles and thirty-six associated nuclear warheads.[43] As training for the Cuban deployment, RVSN troops conducted an exercise code-named Tyulpan on 1–8 September 1962, firing two R-14 missiles from the Aginsky proving ground toward nuclear impact sites on Novaya Zemlya, one armed with a normal nuclear warhead, and the other with a new experimental warhead (table 3.3).[44]

Although the R-12 missiles deployed on Cuba during the crisis were by far the best known, a number of other nuclear-capable missiles were also deployed. The Soviet Air Force deployed two FKR-1 Meteor land-attack cruise-missile units, the 561st and 584th Frontal Cruise-Missile (FKR) Regiments. This force has often been misunderstood in accounts of the Cuban crisis, since the Meteor missile was similar to the navy's S-2 Sopka conventional antiship missiles also deployed on Cuba.[45] U.S. intelligence at the time made the same mistake and was unaware that the Soviets had deployed a nuclear-armed land-attack cruise missile

Table 3.3

Soviet Missile Deployment on Cuba, October 1962 (51st Missile Division, RVSN)

Unit	Commander	Location	Operational Date	Launchers
79th Missile Regiment	Col. Sidorov	Citesito/Kalabazarde	20 Oct 1962	8 R-12
181st Missile Regiment	Col. Bandilovsky	Los Palasos	25 Oct 1962	8 R-12
664th Missile Regiment	Col. Yu. A. Solovyov	Santa Cruz de los Pinos	1 Nov 1962	8 R-12
665th Missile Regiment	Col. Kovalenko	Guanajay	7 Nov–1 Dec 1961	8 R-14
668th Missile Regiment	Col. Cherkesov	Remedios/Silueta	1 Jan 1963	8 R-14

in Cuba. Each Meteor launcher had a supply of five missiles, armed with a 50–120 kiloton nuclear warhead, totaling eighty nuclear warheads.[46] These warheads constituted the largest portion of the Soviet nuclear stockpile deployed on Cuba during the crisis, amounting to more than half of the 158 nuclear warheads on hand.[47] The cruise-missile regiments were by far the largest contribution of the Soviet Air Force to Operation Anadyr, the only other significant air force units being a squadron of IL-28 bombers with six nuclear free-fall bombs.[48] The role of the cruise-missile regiments was primarily to assist in the defense of Cuba from an American amphibious attack. They did not have sufficient range to pose a threat to the continental United States. What is unusual is the prominent role given these weapons. One of the FKR regiments was deployed in western Cuba in the area west of Havana near the port of Mariel. There was a major concentration of Soviet ballistic missiles in this area, and the mission of the regiment was to defeat any amphibious landings in the area.[49] The second FKR-1 regiment was deployed in eastern Cuba, near Mayari Arriba in the Sierra de Micaro hills, overlooking the U.S. base at Guantanamo Bay. The role of this regiment was the same as the other, to defeat any amphibious landings in the area, as well as to destroy U.S. forces operating from the Guantanamo Bay base. Normally, such regiments were deployed on a scale of only one per aviation army. Yet in Cuba there were two regiments. The cruise-missile regiments were a reflection of Khrushchev's "new look" approach to defense, stressing the economy of force possible with nuclear weapons compared to conventional forces.

Instead of deploying a large concentration of conventional forces, the Soviets deployed a modest force of only three motor rifle regiments, bolstered by a very substantial tactical nuclear force. Besides the eighty nuclear-armed cruise missiles, the motor rifle regiments were also supported by a dozen Luna (FROG, or free rocket over ground) tactical ballistic rockets. There is no evidence that Khrushchev deployed the tactical nuclear forces for their deterrent value. There

Cruise missiles were an early form of nuclear weapons delivery, and the first was the Mikoyan Kometa. A land-launched version, the FKR-1 Meteor, was the most widely deployed nuclear missile on Cuba during the 1962 crisis. This example of the air-launched version, known by NATO as the AS-1 Kennel, is preserved at the museum at Khodynka Field in Moscow.

were no known plans to disclose the presence of these units, and their existence was not revealed until the early 1990s, after the collapse of the Soviet Union. They were deployed to fight had the United States invaded Cuba, and U.S. intelligence at the time was not aware of them.[50] While U.S. intelligence had some suspicion that the Luna missiles might be present, they did not appreciate the very large number of Meteor nuclear cruise missiles.

The least-known element of the Soviet plans was the navy's missile submarine force. According to original plans, seven Project 629 (Golf) diesel submarines were to be deployed to Cuba, each carrying three R-13 (SS-N-4) ballistic missiles with a 1.5-megaton warhead, as well as nuclear torpedoes with 8–10 kiloton warheads.[51] Had these submarines been deployed, they would have nearly doubled the medium-range nuclear firepower of the Soviet forces in Cuba and could have struck targets in the United States to a range of 650 km (400 mi) from their launch site. In late September the navy's forces were changed, and the ballistic-missile submarines were dropped from the operation.[52] Although no explanation for the change has been revealed, the reason is fairly obvious. The submarines would have to have been loaded with fully fueled missiles prior to their departure from their base at Nerpicha, since there were no missile-handling facilities in Cuba. As was the case with all Soviet missiles during this period, the fuel could be left in the missiles for only about thirty days, at which point the missiles would become a hazard from corrosion, oxidizer leaks, and ensuing fires. Due to the lack of submarine facilities in Cuba, there would be no way to remove the fuel and replace the missiles. Furthermore, the standard Soviet method for removing missiles after their fuel-life expired was to fire them off. This was practical for unarmed training missiles, but not a reasonable solution for nuclear-armed missiles. In addition, the new submarines probably were not ready for deployment, because the R-13 missile system was not accepted for service until 1963.

The only submarines deployed into Cuban waters were four Project 641 diesel submarines from the 211th Submarine Brigade, equipped only with conventional torpedoes. The Soviet Navy also deployed a number of cruise-missile submarines into the northern Atlantic during the crisis, equipped with nuclear-armed P-5 and P-7 (SS-N-3 Shaddock) cruise missiles. It is not clear what role, if any, these submarines had in operational plans. During the Cuban crisis, Soviet submarines were hounded relentlessly by U.S. Navy antisubmarine forces, seriously devaluing their participation. Plans to deploy surface warships to Cuba were also dropped in September 1962.

As the crisis reached its peak around 24 October, the 51st Missile Division rushed to complete the launch sites and prepare their equipment. The FKR regiments prepared their weapon systems for action in their base areas. On 27 October one group from each of the cruise-missile regiments was deployed from the base camps to preselected launch sites in anticipation of combat orders.[53] U.S. intelligence assessed that all three ballistic-missile regiments would be fully operational by Sunday, 28 October 1962. The Russian plan had called for two regiments to be ready, but other Russian officials later stated that only six to eight missile launchers were operational when the dismantling order arrived on the afternoon of 28 October 1962.[54]

Although there has been some debate over whether the local commanders were given launch authority in advance by the Soviet government, recent documents released in Russia make it clear that Moscow informed the commander of the Group of Forces in Cuba that the nuclear warheads on the FKR, Luna tactical rockets, and IL-28 jet bombers were not to be employed without specific authorization from the Kremlin.[55] However, the evidence would suggest that Moscow did not have any actual negative technical control over the weapons, and that the local commanders could have used them without permission had war broken out, assuming the assent of the custody units.

While the crisis was brewing in Cuba, the Soviet Union's nascent strategic forces were placed on high alert for the first time in their history. The strategic-bomber divisions began to move from the bases to their forward-staging bases, and they were armed with nuclear free-fall bombs.[56] The R-7A launchers at Plesetsk were readied and their flight-control systems wired for strikes against New York, Washington, Chicago, and other major U.S. cities. At the time of the Cuban missile crisis, two R-9 missiles were made operational at the Tyuratam proving ground.[57] Several of the R-16 launch sites were also readied for launch.

In the end, better sense prevailed in Washington and Moscow, and the crisis was brought to a diplomatic conclusion. Faced with America's overwhelming strategic superiority, the Soviet Union was forced to back down. Khrushchev was obliged to remove the missiles, with a promise from Kennedy not to invade Cuba and a concession on the missiles in Turkey.

The Cuban Missile Crisis of 1962 had a more profound effect in Moscow than the Sputnik shock had on the White House in 1957. The Cuban crisis was regarded as unacceptable humiliation by Soviet political and military leaders. It ended the debate within the Soviet military over the primacy of strategic nuclear weapons. More traditional leaders in some of the military branches had been slow to embrace the priority afforded the new Strategic Missile Force, in part due to the distaste they felt toward Khrushchev and his "hare-brained schemes." The crisis ended once and for all any resistance within the military to strategic-missile weapons. It made clear the centrality of such weapons in contemporary great-power confrontations and sealed the debate in the favor of the RVSN. The future basis of Soviet military power would be parity or superiority in strategic nuclear arms. The Cuban humiliation was one of the underlying causes of the coup against Khrushchev in 1964.

Redeeming the First Generation

In spite of the April 1962 decision to proceed with all haste to field a second generation of strategic missiles, it would take at least five years to do so. As a result, efforts were made to improve the existing intermediate- and intercontinental-range missiles by basing them in silos. These silos were hardly ideal, and like the surface basing already in use, clustered the launchers around common fueling systems. Nevertheless, it provided an increase in survivability without forcing a complete redesign of the entire weapon system.

The R-12 intermediate-range missiles were the first to be tested from an experimental Mayak silo launcher on 31 August 1959 at the Kapustin Yar proving ground. The first silo-based R-12U missile regiment became operational on 1 January 1963, but continuing problems meant that the system was not accepted for service use until 9 January 1964.[58] Work on a silo-launched version of the R-16 ICBM began two years later, but the higher priority afforded this program meant that it reached service sooner. The first silo-based R-16U regiment became operational at Nizhny Tagil on 5 February 1963, and official government acceptance of the system came on 15 June 1963. A total of 128 R-16 surface launchers were deployed, compared to 69 silo launchers. These silos were a stopgap and were not as well hardened as comparable U.S. silos, nor separated to make them more difficult to target. Each complex consisted of three silos clustered together for economic reasons to enable them to use a common fueling system. The complex was about 150 m (500 ft) long, making all three silos vulnerable to a single U.S. missile.

Korolyov's cryogenically fueled R-9 missile continued to be a source of difficulty. The original Desna-N surface-launch complex was not sufficiently automated, and launch preparation time was about two hours. As a result, the RVSN refused to accept it for service. This was followed by an improved Dolina ground-launcher system that reduced the preparation time to twenty minutes, and the first test launch from the Dolina test site took place on 22 February 1963. The development of the R-9 was so prolonged and troubled that Khrushchev refused to accept it for service. Due to pressure from Dmitry Ustinov and Leonid Smirnov, the head of the missile industry, the R-9 was accepted for service use two months after the coup against Khrushchev in 1964. The first surface launchers became operational on 14–15 December 1964, when four regiments were activated at Kozelsk and Plesetsk. When first deployed in the soft sites, it took sixteen hours to prepare and fuel the R-9 and move it to the launcher, and twenty-one minutes to prepare it for launch once on the launcher. The first test of a R-9 missile from a Desna-V silo launcher took place on 27 September 1963, and the first silo-based regiment became operational at Kozelsk on 26 December 1964, only a few weeks after the first surface launch site. The silo-launched configuration was much more efficient than the surface launcher. R-9 deployment peaked in 1965, with only fourteen soft sites at Kozelsk and Plesetsk, and nine hard sites at Kozelsk, and the system was widely regarded as a failure. U.S. intelligence assessed the R-9A as having a relatively low force reliability, only 55 percent, due to its complicated fueling system.

Rocket Science, Russian Style

By the early 1960s the structure of the Soviet strategic-missile industry was beginning to mature. Besides the Korolyov OKB-1 and the Yangel SKB-586 design bureaus, two other major design centers had emerged by the later half of the Khrushchev years.[59] In the late 1950s Korolyov had established a branch office at Zlatoust to refine the R-11 (Scud) tactical ballistic missile and its associated submarine-launched version, the R-11FM. Under the direction of Viktor Makeyev, the SKB-385 bureau was relocated to Miass and became the center of Soviet submarine-launched ballistic-missile development. It would remain so to the present.

The other bureau to emerge in the early 1960s was Vladimir Chelomey's OKB-52 in Reutov in the Moscow suburbs. Chelomey's career provides an interesting insight into the dynamics of Soviet weapons development in the Khrushchev years.[60] Chelomey had been an early developer of pulse-jet engines in World War II, so when the Soviet Union obtained data on the German pulse-jet-powered V-1 "Buzz Bomb" cruise missile in 1944, Chelomey was assigned to develop a Soviet counterpart. His new OKB-51 design bureau was assigned the facilities of the Polikarpov fighter design bureau, the premier fighter developer in the 1930s, which had been crippled during Stalin's purges. In the early 1950s Chelomey ran afoul of the political intrigues of other design bureaus. The Mikoyan jet fighter design bureau, headed by the younger brother of Stalin's aide, Anastas Mikoyan, had teamed up with the KB-1 electronics design bureau, headed by Sergei Beria, the son of the head of the Soviet secret police, Lavrenty Beria. This team was itself working on jet-powered cruise missiles and in 1952 exercised their considerable political connections, shutting down Chelomey's design bureau as well as two others working on cruise missiles. From this experience, Chelomey learned an important lesson about the role of Kremlin politics in the upper reaches of weapons design. He managed to win the navy's favor with his cruise-missile designs, starting with the P-5 (SS-N-3 Shaddock). Because of his ban, he was not allowed to form a new design bureau until after Stalin's death, by which time Beria's son was out of favor after the execution of his father for high crimes. Chelomey hired Nikita Khrushchev's son, Sergei, to work in his missile-guidance department. This connection provided him with an important avenue to the senior Kremlin leadership. By the late 1950s Chelomey appreciated Khrushchev's fascination with space adventures and strategic missiles, and decided to escape the backwater of naval cruise-missile design in favor of the greater rewards of these high-priority fields.

By 1960 Khrushchev had become disenchanted with his former favorite, Korolyov. Both the military and party leadership had long complained that Korolyov had been given too much independence in the management of space and missile programs, and was ignoring the accepted guidelines. Khrushchev himself was under pressure to make good his promises about the Strategic Missile Force and was annoyed by Korolyov's recalcitrance on the issue of storable fuel for ICBMs. Although Khrushchev was still willing to support Korolyov on his space extravaganzas, he felt compelled to deepen the research base for ICBMs and military space programs. Khrushchev began to move several Korolyov supporters out of key positions in the military-industrial network.

Chelomey sensed his opportunity and pushed it to the fullest. He managed to persuade Khrushchev to turn over the facilities and design staffs of two senior aerospace firms, the Lavochkin and Myasishchev design bureaus. The Lavochkin design bureau had managed to incur Khrushchev's wrath by its failures with the Burya strategic cruise-missile program and its Dal strategic defense system. Myasishchev had also failed with the competitive Buran strategic cruise missile, but more importantly his M-50 strategic bomber had been a major disappointment. A deal was worked out under which Korolyov gained control of the Grabin artillery design bureau, and Chelomey took over parts of Lavochkin and Myasishchev. Lavochkin's design bureau would form the basis of Chelomey's new military space programs while Myasishchev's bureau in Fili was renamed OKB-52 Branch #1 and given the task of developing Chelomey's ballistic missiles.[61] Finally, Chelomey convinced Khrushchev to turn over control of the Fili aviation plant to him for conversion to missile production. The Fili plant was the largest aerospace plant in the Soviet Union and one of its oldest and most experienced centers. An engineer from a rival design bureau later wrote that giving Chelomey control of the plant was like "sewing a great coat to a lonely button."

With Khrushchev's support, Chelomey rather than Korolyov would challenge Yangel on the design of the R-16 follow-on, and Chelomey would challenge Korolyov in the development of a Soviet equivalent of the American Minuteman light ICBM. Chelomey's sudden rise to power caused considerable consternation within the missile industry. Chelomey had been associated with the rival aviation ministry, not Ustinov's defense industries, which had dominated the missile program. Not only did he manage to absorb two of the most prominent aviation design bureaus of his own ministry, but he schemed to take over others outside his ministry, including the Moscow KB-1 electronics bureau, as part of a ploy to take over the nascent antiballistic-missile program. Korolyov attempted to form an alliance of other senior military industrial leaders to petition Khrushchev over Chelomey but was unable to enlist the support of other general designers who realized that the tide of Khrushchev's favor had turned away from Korolyov and toward Chelomey. The infighting within the industry embittered the military, and a popular saying of the time was, "Korolyov works for TASS, Yangel works for us, and Chelomey works for the toilet."

The Missile-Design Process

By the mid-1960s the design process for strategic missiles had matured.[62] As in other defense industries, basic research was undertaken by institutions of the Academy of Sciences. Basic research consisted of the scientific investigation of phenomena, materials, and technologies with potential applications to the weapons development process. Advanced development, the further elaboration of this process, was generally undertaken by the NII (scientific research institutes). The NII were subordinated to the industrial ministries or to branches of the Ministry of Defense. The industrial institutes tended to specialize in a particular area of technology such as guidance or advanced materials. The Ministry of Defense's institutes were often think tanks that examined future requirements in their fields.

Two organizations played the most significant role in directing ICBM research: NII-88 and NII-4 MO. NII-88, in Kaliningrad in the Moscow suburbs, had originally been the administrative center of the missile industry.[63] However, by the early 1960s, with the rise of the design bureaus and the maturation of the ministries, its role returned to one more typical of other NII.[64] It became the main scientific research center for the missile industry rather than an administrative center. It was a direct counterpart to central organizations such as TsAGI in the aviation industry and TsIAM in the aerospace propulsion industry and was eventually renamed TsNIIMash (Central Scientific Research Institute of the Machine Building Industry). TsNIIMash was responsible for the conduct of advanced missile technology research. The second institute central in the missile design process was NII-4 MO (Scientific Research Institute-4 of the Ministry of Defense), in the Bolshevo suburb of Moscow. This was the think tank of the RVSN. Although it was responsible for the advanced development of strategic-weapons technology, its main function was to examine the technological needs and future requirements of the RVSN and coordinate research efforts to this end. The NII-4 and TsNIIMash were the primary agents in establishing the TTZ (technical-tactical requirements) document, which initiated all major ICBM engineering development programs.

The actual design and development of a weapon system was the responsibility of the design bureaus, variously called OKB, SKB, or simply KB.[65] The missile-design bureaus were industrial organizations, usually under the Ministry of General Machine Building (MOM) after the 1965 industrial reforms. The design bureaus acted as the prime contractors for the development program and coordinated their efforts with other design bureaus responsible for subsystems such as propulsion, guidance, launch systems, and so on, in conjunction with the ministries.[66]

Coordination of the design effort took place at two levels. At the technical level, coordination of design efforts between design bureaus from different ministries was accomplished through the Council of Chief Designers. This was once an informal collaborative effort started by Korolyov but eventually became formalized. From an industrial and production standpoint, the most important coordination organization was the Military Industrial Commission of the Council of Ministers, known by its Russian acronym, VPK. Dmitry Ustinov had been appointed chairman of the VPK Military Industrial Commission in December 1957.[67] The VPK was the Council of Ministers' administrative organization for managing the defense industries, and its centralized position enabled it to coordinate complex weapons programs that crossed ministerial lines. Missile programs were a particularly difficult example, since major subcomponents such as warheads, propulsion, fuels, guidance platforms, launcher systems, flight-control computers, and command-and-control systems were developed and manufactured by several different ministries. Not only did the design efforts have to be coordinated, but the plants of the different ministries had be to be coordinated for eventual production, and these efforts integrated into state economic plans. The design bureaus could not undertake this function, since they had little role in the manufacturing portion of the program. As a result, this process was significantly different from the subcontracting relationship in Western aerospace industries.

The design bureau was usually headed by a general designer.[68] This was a *nomenklatura* rank bestowed by the Central Committee of the Communist Party, and not simply a job title. Even after the ministries gained more independence in the Brezhnev years, the Communist Party continued to exert its influence in the industrial sphere by continued control over senior appointments. The general designer was supported by one or more chief designers, who were responsible for specific programs within the bureau when multiple programs were under way, or responsible for a particular aspect of a program.

The weapons design process usually began with a draft project.[69] Draft projects could be initiated by the design bureau itself based on promising technology. But more often, the draft project was a collaborative effort with the NII-4 and TsNIIMash to help define the technological potential of various design options and to better establish the requirements for a future system. Draft projects could result in experimental prototypes, but due to the cost of ballistic missiles, they usually resulted in subscale models or paper designs.

The system requirements were codified in the TTZ, the culmination of the earlier design studies and formulation of requirement process. The TTZ defined the basic technical parameters of the new weapon system. The issuance of the TTZ to the design bureau took part in conjunction with a decree from the Council of Ministers. This process had three functions. The TTZ itself initiated engineering development of the new weapon and established its schedule. The decree also established a state commission composed of specialists from industry and the military to oversee the progress of the program. Finally, the decree established a plan for the eventual production and deployment of the weapon, and so initiated the process on the industrial side of preparing to manufacture the weapon, on the military side of planning to deploy the system, and on the government side of integrating the new weapon into the budget and economic planning cycle.

As the design reached completion, fabrication of test missiles was undertaken in an experimental plant controlled by the design bureau. Tests were usually preceded by engine trials and other subsystem tests. The initial flight tests were not necessarily full-up tests, that is, they sometimes were intended to test only part of the systems, especially if the missile included radically new technology. Tests of ICBMs were conducted from two state proving grounds: Tyuratam (Baikonur) for liquid-fuel missiles, and Plesetsk for solid-fuel missiles.[70] SLBM tests were conducted from Nenoska, aviation missiles from Aktyubinsk, and tactical ballistic-missile trials from Kapustin Yar. The initial series of trials were called flight-design tests.[71] These were intended to validate the design and correct any design problems. Once the design was refined, the missile was subjected to a second round of tests, called state trials or joint trials.[72] These final trials were intended to establish whether the design had met the TTZ goals. If the requirements were met, the system would be accepted for service use by validation of the State Commission.

Due to the long lead time needed to prepare missile silos and start the process of manufacturing the missile and its subsystems, some discontinuity between the test and manufacture schedules was not unusual. Most often the missile design slipped in its schedule, and as a result, the deployment of the weapon system, such as the silo launcher, began before the State Commission accepted the missile for service. It was not uncommon for missile systems to go into operation before the official state acceptance. The Soviet process of parallel development and industrialization often led to a situation where the initial missile design still incorporated flaws that were being ironed out in the trials process. As a result it was not unusual to see a new subvariant appear in tests shortly afterward intended to clear up these defects.

The Soviet industrial system was fundamentally different from Western corporate organization, where the design office was part of the company that manufactured the weapon. In the Soviet system, the design bureau was a separate entity from the manufacturing plant. Some plants were closely associated with design bureaus, such as Korolyov's with the Progress plant in Kuibyshev, Yangel's with the Yuzhmash plant in Dnepropetrovsk, Chelomey with the Khrunichev plant in

Fili, Makeyev's with the Krasnoyarsk and Zlatoust plants, and the later Moscow Institute of Thermotechnology (MIT) with Votkinsk. Following the completion of the first series-production missiles, another set of test flights would be undertaken, called series control firings, which determined whether the series production missiles were acceptable.[73]

Beginning with the second generation of ICBMs, the Soviets began the practice of manufacturing ICBMs in transport-launch containers (TPK), a system pioneered by Chelomey. This led to a different maintenance practice than in the U.S. Air Force. Rather than repair defective components of an ICBM in the silo, the Soviet practice was to remove the entire transport-launch container and send it back to a depot on the base for minor repairs, or to the plant for major servicing. Repairs were not necessarily effected immediately, and in some cases waited until a scheduled servicing period. As a result, Soviet ICBMs tended to be built in larger numbers than U.S. ICBMs, since a portion of the missiles served as a maintenance float.

After a new missile type went into service, design work on improved versions continued at the design bureau. This often included new warhead designs but could also include new propulsion or other subsystems. The method of incorporation of these new features into the weapon system depended on the extent of the modification. Some discrete subcomponents, such as a new warhead or gyro platform, could be mounted into existing missile airframes during periodic servicing. However, more extensive modifications required new missile production. It should be noted that U.S./NATO code names such as SS-9 Mod 1 do not distinguish between modified missiles versus new construction. From the Russian perspective, missiles assigned new industrial codes by GURVO (Main Missile Directorate) were new production missiles.[74]

Soviet strategic weapons had a warranted life during which the manufacturing plant was responsible for ensuring a steady supply of parts for faulty subcomponents. The lives of ICBMs were usually warranted for about seven to ten years, though these service lives could be extended by special programs. This system was based in part on assessments of the degraded reliability of the missile after prolonged storage of corrosive liquid fuel and deterioration of electronic components. The warranted life span varied depending on whether the missile was deployed in a fueled alert state in a silo or simply left unfueled at a base warehouse as a backup.

Strategic Command and Control

One of the most significant changes in national security brought about by the revolution in military affairs of the Khrushchev years was the compression of time in which state leaders had to make decisions in time of crisis. With the advent of the missile, national leaders found that in a crisis, they might have to respond to news of a surprise attack in twenty minutes or less. This required sophisticated command-and-control systems to activate the strategic forces. Strategic command and control remained the Achilles' heel of the Soviet strategic forces. This weakness significantly undermined the survivability of the strategic forces, since the command-and-control network could not speedily identify a surprise nuclear attack, nor could it rapidly order the Soviet forces to respond.

During the late Stalin and early Khrushchev years, the strategic nuclear forces employed existing command-and-control networks and lacked dedicated facilities. This meant quite simply that orders were passed using telephone or telegraph landlines through the usual military district structure. The General Staff could also use enciphered radio transmissions. In the mid-1950s the only nationwide, secure communications network was a new one being created to coordinate the PVO-Strany Air Defense Command. In the late 1950s portions of this network were taken over by the General Staff to direct the strategic-bomber and strategic-missile force until a dedicated network could be created.

Radio transmission was vital in the 1950s due to the dispersion of strategic-missile units into remote areas of the Soviet Union that were poorly serviced by existing communication networks. While previous forms of strategic forces such as strategic-bomber bases were already integrated into existing military communication networks, the new missiles were in many cases deployed to new bases, usually away from population centers and established landlines. Development of the cryptologic systems to code the radio communications was undertaken by NII-2, near Moscow, now called NPO Avtomatika.[75] This was important, since the United States established signals-intelligence posts in neighboring countries such as Turkey, Iran, and Pakistan.

In the early 1960s it was not unusual for a message to take days to reach the RVSN commander.[76] To facilitate and centralize the decision-making process, on 6 June 1960 the Central Command Post of the General Staff (TsKP-GSh) became operational at Odintsovo-10, near Vlasikha in the suburbs southwest of Moscow.[77] This became the central node in the system to activate the strategic forces in the event of war. Besides the headquarters building itself, the RVSN also constructed its underground Central Command Post bunker nearby, which was already functional at the time of the 1962 Cuban crisis.[78]

As Soviet defense planners began to become aware of the archaic nature of the existing communications network, they were also becoming aware of the disruptive effect of electromagnetic pulse and other subsidiary effects of nuclear detonations on radio. A series of upper-atmospheric nuclear detonations, code-named Operation K, were conducted in the early 1960s to examine their effects on strategic offensive and defensive weapons as well as the command infrastructure. It quickly became apparent that the existing communication network was vulnerable.

This led to a crash program managed by the Ministry of Communications to assign landlines to the General Staff for strategic command and control. Many of the best long-distance communication lines emanating from Moscow were taken out of civilian service and assigned to the General Staff instead. However, even these did not prove adequate for the rapidly expanding forces, leading to the need for a major communications upgrade program. Even with the upgrade, during a national crisis, the system still required that existing military communication channels be closed and the regional communication centers be shifted manually to strategic control by means of passwords. As in the case of missiles and other technology of the day, it took some time before standardized equipment was fielded.

One of the most serious shortcomings of the early Soviet command-and-control network was the lack of an adequate early-warning network. In the early 1950s, under Stalin's massive strategic air defense program, the PVO-Strany Air Defense Command had started to create an early-warning network of air defense radars around the periphery of the Soviet Union. The sheer size of the Soviet Union made this very difficult, and the U.S. Air Force found numerous gaps, especially in the subarctic north, which defended against bombers coming over the North Pole. By the late 1950s the Soviet radar net was adequate for warning of a bomber attack. Missiles posed another problem since the radars deployed to detect bombers could not reliably detect missiles. Efforts to develop ballistic-missile early-warning radars began in the late 1950s as part of the Soviet Union's infant antiballistic-missile program. These did not enter service until the late 1960s.

Command and control of the strategic nuclear forces involve both positive and negative controls. *Positive control* refers to ensuring that a nuclear strike is launched as commanded by the General Staff. *Negative control* refers to preventing unauthorized use of nuclear forces.[79] The two requirements can conflict. Negative controls can inhibit and delay the execution of properly authorized actions, with serious consequences, given the short intervals for decision making and the execution of orders in the missile age. In general, the Soviet command-and-control style during the Cold War favored positive controls due to concerns that excessive negative controls would exacerbate existing shortcomings in the nuclear weapon systems, effectively preventing their use in time of war. Full details of Soviet command-and-control procedures through this forty-year period are far from clear, because such procedures are a closely held secret even today.

Positive control of the strategic nuclear forces was carried out by the General Staff. Under the initial Monolit system, the General Staff broadcast an encoded message to strategic nuclear force bases. Once authorization had been verified, the local units would open up special mission packets kept in safes and carry out the prescribed assignment. In the case of the RVSN missile crews, no targeting input was necessary, since first-generation strategic missiles were hardwired, with only a single target assigned to each missile. The crudity of the Monolit system became apparent during periodic training exercises. It was found that the simple act of opening the packet and decoding the message was needlessly time consuming, due to the nervousness of the crew in such a high-pressure situation.

Essentially the same system was used to control the strategic nuclear submarine force. Although the Soviet Navy controlled the basic day-to-day operations of the submarine force, the General Staff was in control of all launch operations. A set of coded messages was used to and from the submarine, providing basic status information and launch orders. The Soviet Navy operated its normal coastal communication sites of the Northern and Pacific Fleets for communications with the submarines on the surface.[80] Because the submarine was likely to be submerged, the messages were also transmitted from six land-based very-low-frequency (VLF) radio stations.[81] While the submarines could pick up these transmissions when submerged by using a trailing communications buoy, they could not respond unless near the surface. Surface radio transmissions were very dangerous, given the U.S. and Royal Navy practice of using radio direction finding to locate hostile submarines.[82] As a result, the submarines were issued with a chart for each voyage giving them a schedule of times when they could approach the surface and send a very brief coded message.

Command and control of the strategic-bomber force did not pose the same types of problems as for the other forces.[83] The Soviet Air Force did not rely on combat-alert flights, as did the USAF Strategic Air Command, due to the lower durability of its aircraft. As a result, bombers tended to be on the ground when the alert came from Moscow. In these circumstances, the crews were provided with target sets and unlocking codes for their weapons before takeoff. Communications with the bombers once airborne were conducted through the usual high-frequency radio channels. This was not a difficult problem until the Long-Range Aviation regiments were over the pole and approaching the United States, where interference and other effects disrupted the communication link.

It is not clear what type of negative controls existed in the Khrushchev period. Some details of Soviet nuclear weapons security are available for later years, but there is little data on when these innovations took place. The KGB was in physical control of early nuclear devices, and they were kept separate from their delivery system.[84] In 1959 the Twelfth Main Directorate of the Ministry of Defense (12GU-MO) was reorganized at the same time as the Strategic Missile Force to take control of nuclear weapons custody. There may have been some residual KGB control, such as the use of KGB signals officers to authorize warhead deliveries.

Antiballistic-Missile Defense

Khrushchev's conviction that bombers were obsolete was based on his assumption that defense against ballistic missiles was unlikely. Nonetheless, the Soviet Union began its first efforts to deploy a limited antiballistic-missile (ABM) system in the late 1950s.

Soviet research into antimissile defense had been conducted as early as 1948 but did not begin in earnest until 1955.[85] A test-bed antimissile system code-named System A began being developed by several institutes of the radio industry, notably Grigory Kisunko's SKB-30 office of the KB-1 design bureau.[86] In August 1956 a special antimissile proving grounds was established near Sary Shagan on Lake Balkash. An essential element in this work was the development of the Dunai-2 radar, the first Soviet radar designed for missile detection.[87] By 1960 System A's test-bed V-1000 antiballistic missile was ready for test.[88] Several interception tests in 1960 using the V-1000 missile against R-5 ballistic missiles were unsuccessful. The first successful interception of one missile by another occurred on 4 March 1961 at an altitude of 25 km (15 mi), and the target-missile warhead was destroyed by the fragmentation warhead of the missile interceptor. System A was not suitable for actual antimissile defense since the radar and missile could only deal with relatively slow targets like intermediate-range missiles. It served as a forerunner to the later A-35 (ABM-1) system.

Work at Sary Shagan involved not only the development of an ABM system, but also the development of countermeasures to defeat an American ABM system.[89] Starting in 1958 the Verba countermeasures program used inflatable balloons to create false targets and various types of chaff that would create a metallic cloud around the warhead, hiding its precise location. The Kaktus program, an early form of stealth technology, examined the use of special radar-absorbing materials (RAM) that would prevent the signal from ABM radars from returning to the receiver, making the warhead invisible to radar.[90] The Krot program examined the use of active electronic jammers to defeat American ABM radars. These three approaches were examined in flight tests in 1962–63. None of the methods were entirely satisfactory by themselves, and a new program code-named Kupol (Dome) developed a unified package for ICBM warheads. The first anti-ABM decoys were not ready for use on ICBMs until the late 1960s, about a decade after the start of their design.

With the System A test bed under way, the Kremlin authorized the start of the first actual anti-ICBM system, code-named A-35, on 8 April 1958. Like many late 1950s projects, the system requirements were not sufficiently examined, and the resulting weapon proved obsolete when it was finally fielded more than a decade later. The system was only designed to deal with an attack by six to eight ICBMs, a plausible enough scenario in 1959, but woefully inadequate in later years due to the much larger size of the U.S. ICBM force.[91] The preliminary design of the A-35 was completed in 1961 after designers studied the test results from the System A test bed. Early experiments with decoys and detection problems with the System A convinced the designers at SKB-30 that a conventional high-explosive warhead was not adequate. In 1961–62 the Ministry of Defense conducted nuclear tests in the upper atmosphere and in space over the Sary Shagan range under the code name Operation K to determine the effect of nuclear weapons on ABM radars as well as the likely effects on enemy missile warheads. As a result of these tests, in 1964 the A-35 system switched to nuclear warheads to defeat incoming ICBMs. Although the A-35 network was not ready for deployment for over a decade, the ballistic-missile early-warning radars reached fruition sooner.

The Khrushchev Era in Retrospect

In October 1964 Khrushchev was overthrown by a coalition of party officials headed by Leonid Brezhnev. While the military did not play a direct role in the coup, Khrushchev's overthrow was made possible by his alienation of the military commanders. Khrushchev's relentless efforts to trim the size of the military led to resentment, which was worsened by his impulsive and erratic efforts to reform the armed forces by substituting missiles for manpower. The final straw came in 1964, when Khrushchev began to talk about greatly reducing the army to a small, professional force, backed up by a territorial militia. None of the senior military leaders would back Khrushchev in a contest with Brezhnev and the other coup leaders.

On the industry side, Khrushchev had managed to alienate its most influential leaders. He removed Ustinov as head of the VPK and shifted him to a new post outside the military industry in charge of regional economic councils. The head of the Yuzhmash ICBM plant became the new head of VPK, but did not have Ustinov's experience or enormous influence. Khrushchev's constant meddling alienated other industrial leaders, particularly those in the aviation industry. Although the coup was carried out by party officials, there was enthusiastic support from most senior industrial leaders.

Khrushchev's reign saw the Soviet Union finally emerge as a true superpower rival to the United States. While the Soviet Union was still behind in many key areas of technology, it amassed enough nuclear weapons and plausible delivery systems to make American leaders wary of any international confrontation with the Kremlin. At the time, the United States was not fully aware of the many shortcomings of the Soviet nuclear forces. It was the Soviet recognition of the lack of survivability of their forces that prompted continued efforts to modernize the force, not American attempts to exploit their weaknesses.

The early Khrushchev period was the "era of the chief designers." Engineers like Korolyov and Tupolev dominated state decision making about strategic-weapons programs, since state and military organizations did not understand the new technologies. By the early 1960s this began to change as new state and military organizations were created to manage the nuclear weapons programs. The creation of the RVSN Strategic Missile Force in 1959 ensured that the military had a greater voice in establishing requirements for future weapons systems and force structure. Khrushchev's policy of "doubling" key design bureaus introduced a measure of competition into weapons development and allowed state institutions to take control back from the chief designers for major weapons decisions. This was most evident in the dispute over ICBM fuel options, where Korolyov was finally pushed aside due to his intransigence.

The autocratic style of state management continued to evolve but remained within the Stalinist mold. Although technocrats like Dmitry Ustinov had an important effect in shaping state defense policy, the ultimate arbiter of key weapons decisions remained the general secretary of the Communist Party. Khrushchev's enthusiasm for nuclear weapons helped carry out the revolution in military affairs, but his amateur dabblings into the many details of the programs was often distracting and ill conceived. The concentration of power was combined with the Stalinist proclivity toward information control, so that analysis of future requirements was left to a handful of senior officials, who were often intellectually unprepared to deal with such rapidly changing technology. Many of the key programs started in the late 1950s, such as the R-9/R-16 ICBM effort, were based on poorly conceived requirements that might have been avoided had a broader range of military and civilian experts been involved. Weapons decision making was often poor. The most egregious case was the Soviet Navy's submarine missile program, which fielded no fewer than three missile systems and five submarine types in a space of about five years, all based on hasty and poorly conceived requirements. Khrushchev's visceral dislike for heavy bombers deprived the Soviet Union of its only reliable nuclear delivery system in the early 1960s while the infant ICBM force was being deployed. Had the Soviet Air Force maintained a more robust bomber capability in the early 1960s, Khrushchev might not have felt compelled to attempt his risky and poorly conceived deployment of missiles on Cuba in 1962.

4.   The Race for Parity

1965–1973

The early Brezhnev years saw the most intense nuclear arms race of the Cold War. At the time of the coup against Khrushchev, the second-generation missile programs were coming to fruition. The new Soviet leadership decided to directly challenge the U.S. superiority in strategic nuclear weapons by reaching parity in the major types of intercontinental nuclear weapons. The precise size of the force was based largely on the size of the U.S. forces, more for its symbolic numerical equivalence than any formal doctrinal requirement.[1] Indeed, recent Russian accounts of Soviet strategic doctrine in the mid-1960s suggest that it was not refined enough to help determine force levels. This effort would prove to be one of the most expensive weapons programs in Soviet history. Paradoxically, the achievement of rough parity in the early 1970s also opened up the path for the first major strategic nuclear arms limitation treaties.

The New Leadership

The direction of Soviet defense policy in the immediate post-Khrushchev years was still in some turmoil in 1964–65 as Leonid Brezhnev and Nikolai Podgorny vied for primacy. Podgorny favored a more indulgent policy toward consumer goods at the expense of defense modernization. Brezhnev, long involved in the administration of the military industries, was more attuned to the concerns of both the military and the military industrial leadership. Brezhnev had been the Central Committee secretary for heavy industry, defense, and space in 1957–60 and again in 1963 in the wake of the Cuba fiasco. The big defense issue was not the modernization of the strategic forces, where a firm consensus had emerged after the ignominious Cuban debacle. Rather, the defense debate focused on conventional forces, which Khrushchev had kept in check during the later years of his regime. Brezhnev eventually agreed to a simultaneous modernization program of both the strategic forces and the conventional forces.

There was leadership turmoil in the military as well. The two most likely candidates to replace ailing defense minister Malinovsky were Dmitry Ustinov, the defense industry leader, and Gen. Andrei Grechko, the first deputy defense minister. Ustinov was the less likely candidate, because his background was primarily on the military-industrial side, and the defense minister was usually a soldier. Grechko was favored by the military, and Brezhnev selected him in April 1967,

The second-generation Soviet ICBMs, 1962–69.

with Ustinov maintaining an important role in military-industrial administration.[2] Up to that time, Grechko was not known as a particularly important player in Kremlin security politics. His advocacy of a surprise war against NATO in the early 1960s limited his influence with Khrushchev, who regarded him as a hothead. But he gradually adopted a more vocal role in Soviet defense policy making. Grechko put in place a counterrevolution to Khrushchev's military reforms, returning to a strong emphasis on conventional forces, or in the view of the Soviet military, a "balanced" force structure.

One of the first changes instituted by Brezhnev was a shake-up of the management of the defense industries. Khrushchev had abolished the traditional industrial ministries and replaced them with a combination of regional committees (the Sovnarkoms) and state technology committees.[3] Brezhnev quickly acceded to the demands of the industrial leaders that the ministries be restored. The enormous growth of the missile and space industries in the early 1960s necessitated the creation of a new ministry devoted exclusively to this growing branch of the aerospace industry, called the MOM (Ministry of General Industry).[4] This was pushed by the aviation industry's MAP (Ministry of Aviation Production), because they wished to be rid of the cannibalistic missile bureaus. During the Khrushchev years, the aviation industry had seen two of its premier bureaus, Lavochkin and Myasishchev, gobbled up by the upstarts in the missile industry, and their own industries had been diverted from their normal work to develop cruise missiles and other fantastic projects. This counterrevolution against Khrushchev's defense industrial reforms had significant effects on other aspects of policy, including a growing reluctance to follow Khrushchev's competitive development practices.

Red Minuteman

The government decrees of April 1962 initiated the development of the second generation of ICBMs. In contrast to the first generation, the new program envisioned several types of missiles to fulfill different roles. This included a new, light, solid-fuel ICBM as a counterpart to the American Minuteman, a new heavy ICBM to replace the R-9 and R-16 and serve as a counterpart to the American Titan II, a new class of super-heavy ICBMs to deliver a new generation of thermonuclear weapons with yields of over fifty megatons, and a new class of "global" missiles to deliver fractional orbital bombs to circumvent the emerging U.S. antiballistic-missile system. In addition, the plan included provisions to study more futuristic missile configurations, including mobile missiles.

The single most important element of the program was the light ICBM. This missile was intended to provide the bulk of the new force, matching the U.S. Air Force's Minuteman in role and numbers. Ideally, the Strategic Missile Force sought a direct counterpart, that is, a solid-fuel missile. Solid fuel held the attraction of greatly improving force readiness. Solid-fuel missiles did not require a lengthy fueling process and were ready for launch as soon as their flight-control system was ready. In the American case, the gyroscopes were kept operating continuously if the missile was on alert duty, so the missile could be launched about three minutes after receiving the launch command. In contrast to liquid-fuel rocket engines, solid-fuel engines could be deployed in a fully loaded state for many years. Existing Soviet storable liquid-fuel rocket engines as used with the R-16 could store their fuel no longer than six months, by which point the corrosive effects of the fuel reached the point where dangerous leaks could develop. To prevent this, the crews had to periodically remove the fuel, lift the missile out of the silo, and send it back to the plant for checks and rebuilding. In the interim, another missile would be loaded into the silo. As a result, the RVSN had to maintain a significant reserve pool of missiles to support this process, adding additional cost to operating the force. To further complicate matters, both elements of the propellants, the inhibited red fuming nitric acid oxidizer (IRFNA) and the heptyl fuel, were extremely toxic.[5] The IRFNA would consume human flesh, while the heptyl was almost as lethal as nerve gas if its fumes were inhaled. These factors led the U.S. Air Force to move away from liquid-fueled ICBMs as soon as possible. The U.S. Navy refused to field a submarine-launched missile with liquid-fuel rocket engines, waiting until the more desirable solid-fuel technology matured. Sergei Korolyov had been an ardent critic of hypergolic liquid-fuel rocket engines since his first experiences designing the early R-11. He initially preferred cryogenic liquid fuel using nontoxic liquid oxygen as the oxidizer. However, the R-9 program had proven this approach to be a failure. Korolyov then turned to solid fuel. Solid-fuel missiles promised to be much less expensive to operate than liquid-fuel types. U.S. experience had shown that solid-fuel ICBMs cost only about a tenth as much to operate per year as the first generation of cryogenically fueled ICBMs.

If solid fuel had many advantages, it also had substantial disadvantages. Early solid fuels were not as energetic as liquid rocket fuels, meaning that a greater weight of propellant was needed to propel a given payload. Solid propellant required a binder material to hold the powdered fuel and oxidant together. This added to the weight of the propellant, and every additional kilogram of weight was a kilogram less of payload. Casting large-diameter solid-fuel rocket engines proved to be a considerable engineering challenge. The cast engine had to be molded perfectly to ensure a uniform engine burn, otherwise uneven thrust would adversely affect accuracy. Solid-fuel-engine castings had the tendency to crack, especially as they aged. This could have catastrophic results after launch, and if the cracks were sufficiently large, the combustion would race through the crack, destroying the engine and the missile. There was no method other than actual launches to test whether the engines were suffering from cracking. In general, the Soviet Union had a far more difficult time developing solid-fuel rocket engines than did the United States. It had a far less mature chemical industry, and there was institutional resistance in the design bureaus, which were already comfortable with liquid-fuel rockets. The strongest advocate of solid-fuel missiles in the Soviet administration was Dmitry Ustinov, who continued to push forward these programs in spite of institutional foot-dragging.

Korolyov took the opportunity presented by the failure of the R-9 to shift his design bureau away from ICBM programs and more toward space programs. Nevertheless, his design bureau had been the first to start a serious effort to develop solid-fuel rocket engines for ICBMs.[6] Khrushchev's aversion to certain technologies, such as conventional artillery, led to a push to convert several of the key ordnance design bureaus into missile bureaus. The army's two primary artillery design bureaus, the Grabin bureau in Moscow and the Perm design bureau, were shifted to solid-fuel rocket research. Grabin's bureau was absorbed by Korolyov's neighboring facilities in Kaliningrad in 1959.[7] On the navy side, the Arsenal naval ordnance bureau in Leningrad was shifted to development of solid-fuel rocket engines for submarine ballistic missiles.

The first solid-fuel strategic-missile program at OKB-1 was authorized on 20 November 1959 as RT-1,[8] a relatively modest effort involving about five hundred engineers.[9] The RT-1 was intended to serve as a test bed for a future ICBM, the RT-2. Even though the RT-1 was larger and heavier than the American Minuteman missile, its range was only a fifth that of the Minuteman. Soviet plants could not yet manufacture large-diameter solid-fuel rocket engines, so the design was forced to rely on inefficient clusters of four small-diameter engines.[10] Flight tests of the RT-1 missiles began on 28 April 1962 but were plagued with problems, and the first successful launch didn't occur until 18 March 1963. Of the first nine missiles launched, only three were successful and displayed poor accuracy.[11] In contrast, the U.S. Minuteman was already entering service by this time.

The definitive RT-2 ICBM was officially authorized on 4 April 1961, but the February 1962 Gagra conference led to considerable rethinking about future requirements. As a result, a modified decree was issued on 29 June 1962, which called for the development of two different warhead types, added a highly automated launch system, and clarified the readiness requirements for the missile.[12] The launch time for the RT-2 missile was decreased to only three to five minutes, compared to the thirty minutes required with the first-generation missiles. The launch weight of the RT-2 was expected to be 46.1 tons, but this was viewed quite skeptically by many in Korolyov's OKB-1, since it was only about half the weight of the current R-9 ICBM, yet had similar range and payload. The problems experienced with the RT-1 test bed led to an interim design, the RT-1-1963, which was aimed at curing the fundamental problems in the solid-fuel engine designs. Three RT-1-1963 test missiles were launched from September to November 1965, and only one was successful.

The early failures of the RT-1 test bed led Khrushchev to authorize the start of parallel liquid-fuel missiles to serve as a backup in case the RT-2 failed. Yangel's SKB-586 began work on the R-38 light ICBM. Chelomey's rival OKB-52 had already done preliminary design studies of a light ICBM dating back to the late 1950s.[13] Chelomey began a political campaign against Korolyov's RT-2 in hopes of having his own proposed UR-100 substituted for it. He alleged that solid-fuel propulsion was inherently flawed, since cracks would develop with time and the missiles could not be checked for flaws. Therefore, there would be the risk that the missile would not fly in a predictable fashion and come crashing to earth on Soviet rather than American soil.[14] Chelomey also made the strong argument that the problems of the Soviet missile program were due to its dependence on the antiquated ordnance industry, which was not prepared to handle the manufacture of sophisticated weapons such as missiles. He contended that the work should be shifted to aviation bureaus like his that had experience in the mass production of large and sophisticated weapons. Furthermore, Chelomey argued that his effort would not disrupt the existing programs, since he would rely on new or underused subcomponent developers such as Kosberg's engine design bureau in Voronezh rather than the overworked Glushko bureau in Khimki.[15] Chelomey's arguments resonated with Khrushchev, who was having growing anxieties over Korolyov's failures. On 30 March 1963 Chelomey was authorized to begin development of the liquid-fueled UR-100 as a light ICBM, parallel to the RT-2.[16] Yangel's R-38 program was terminated to allow his bureau to concentrate on other programs, especially the R-36 heavy ICBM.

The problems with the RT-2 and Ustinov's insistence on the need for a solid-fuel ICBM led to at least two other efforts. Another ordnance bureau, Boris Shavyrin's mortar design bureau in Kolomna, was assigned the futuristic Gnom (Gnome) project. This was the first attempt to develop a road-mobile ICBM. In order to cut down weight, an unusual air-breathing ramjet engine was selected for the first stage.[17] While the engine reached the test stage, the program was far beyond the capabilities of such a small bureau, which had previously developed only relatively simple weapons. As a result, the Gnom never reached the flight-test stage. In 1964 Yangel's design bureau was also instructed to begin studying mobile solid-fuel missiles under the ambitious RT-20 (SS-X-15) program. Flight tests began in 1967, but the missile proved so flawed that it was canceled in 1969.

The UR-100 program quickly overtook the RT-2 program in its development. Chelomey's concept was to develop a system that was inexpensive to manufacture and inexpensive to deploy. Korolyov's RT-2 mandate had been for a highly sophisticated system using advanced basing concepts to pull even with American technology. For example, the RT-2's silo hardening was comparable to American standards through the use of shock mounting, while the other silo designs of this generation were designed to a lower hardness. To add yet another layer of difficulty, there was controversy over which guidance approach would be used for the missile, the archaic hybrid radio-inertial system or a pure inertial system.[18] These demands compromised an already troubled program.

The RT-2 launch complex included a SDUK (Remote Command-and-Control System). This automated the monitoring, management, and launch system of the silos, and had the dual benefit of reducing the manpower demands of the missile-silo regiments and improving their readiness rates. The development of the SDUK system caused a "minor civil war" between Korolyov, the military, the industrial ministries, and several design bureaus. In 1965 Korolyov selected the Avtomatika design bureau in Zaporozhye, headed by Konstantin Marks, to develop the SDUK system for the RT-2 missile system. However, in 1965 the RVSN had chosen the rival Leningrad Polytechnic Institute, headed by Taras Sokolov, to develop their new Signal strategic command-and-control system. The Signal system had to be interfaced with whatever SDUK command-and-control system was used in the silos, and Sokolov was already working on the integration of his design with the rival UR-100 silos. Marks complained that the Sokolov system was not compatible with his system. In the end a state commission had to be convened to resolve the issue. Marks was forced to resign, and the Sokolov approach was accepted, causing further delays in an already troubled program.

The UR-100 design proceeded quickly due to its simple and conservative design. The one major innovation in the design was a transport-launch container, which stemmed from Chelomey's earlier work on naval cruise missiles. The missile was shipped from the factory in a canister that had the necessary electrical connections for test equipment, launch connectors, and other fittings, reducing the need for time-consuming preparations. When in need of repair or refurbishing, the entire canister was removed from the silo. It contained the necessary rail for launching the missile, and the tube protected the missile during launch by diverting the exhaust gases to the outside of the launch tube into a void between the canister and the inner silo walls. Although a novel concept at the time, this type of canister later became typical of most Soviet ICBM designs. The UR-100 missile test flights began on 19 April 1965 at Tyuratam and concluded on 27 October 1966.[19] The rival RT-2 tests did not begin until nearly a year later, on 26 February 1966, beginning with a failure. The first successful RT-2 test launch occurred on 4 November 1966, a week after the UR-100 had completed its trials successfully, and even then its warhead disintegrated on reentry.

There was some lag time in any action from the main national leadership, which was preoccupied with the final deployments of the first-generation R-9 and R-16 divisions and the reorganization of MOM. The decision to proceed with the

UR-100 as the new light ICBM was made in July 1967.[20] The UR-100 proved more attractive than the RT-2 for several clear-cut reasons. There was a clear sense of urgency in the RVSN to reach parity with the United States, and the RT-2 had continued to slip behind schedule. The UR-100 was designed specifically to utilize the Soviet Union's aircraft industry infrastructure and did not require the substantial investment in new plants and handling equipment needed by the more radical RT-2 design. Since the light ICBM was intended to be procured in large numbers to match the U.S. Minuteman, an inexpensive missile like the UR-100 was preferable to an expensive design such as the RT-2. The UR-100 decision was backed by several key players in the military-industrial leadership, including MOM minister Sergei A. Afanasyev and Defense Minister Grechko. Ustinov continued to be a strong advocate of the need for Soviet solid-fuel technology, so the RT-2 program was allowed to continue even though its primary mission would be fulfilled by its rival.

The RT-2 program was plagued by technical difficulties during its trials. When the test program concluded on 3 October 1968, only sixteen of the twenty-five tests had been successful, and only four had been flown to the full range. While the tests had been going on, there were more disputes within the industry over the fate of the program. It had been Korolyov's intention prior to his premature death in 1966 to split off the solid-missile ICBM venture as an independent design bureau once it was successful, as he had done earlier with the submarine missile and the spy satellite programs. He planned to create a new bureau under Igor Sadovsky in Gorky, alongside the industrial plant, which would manufacture the missile.[21] The new head of OKB-1 after Korolyov's death, Vasily Mishin, did not share Korolyov's commitment to the solid-fuel missile program. Besides lacking enthusiasm for the program, he was in a major fight of his own with the MOM and the government leadership over the prestigious and troubled N-1 manned lunar program. Mishin was unwilling to fight for the program with Minister Afanasyev, because he knew the solid-fuel program had few supporters at the ministry. Sadovsky was further isolated due to disputes with Boris Zhukov, who led the design team on the solid-propellant engine.[22]

Zhukov began searching for another sponsor and found that the leadership of the old ordnance industry, now the Ministry of Defense Production (MOP), was more responsive to the notion of solid-fuel ballistic missiles. Dmitry Ustinov played an important role behind the scenes in this effort. MOM officials were aghast at the idea of transferring the solid-fuel ICBM program to another ministry, which they labeled as "seditious," since MOM had been organized specifically to manage all major strategic ballistic-missile programs.[23] Ustinov wanted to transfer the solid-fuel missile program to a new institute under MOP control, the MIT.[24] But the RT-2 ICBM effort was of a scope far beyond the experience of the new MIT. A compromise was reached. The RT-2 would stay with OKB-1 until completion, and any upgrade programs would be transferred to the Arsenal Plant in Leningrad, which was under MOM jurisdiction.[25] However, MIT would conduct the follow-on third-generation solid-fuel ICBM program.[26] As a result of all of these political machinations, the RVSN would receive a mixed force of a thousand UR-100's (SS-11 Sego) but only a token deployment of sixty RT-2's (SS-13 Savage).

Red Titan

While Korolyov and Chelomey were developing their light ICBMs, a vigorous contest was underway for the new heavy ICBM between Yangel and Chelomey. This contest reached its conclusion sooner than that for the light ICBM, because the technological challenges were far less.

Yangel's entry in the heavy ICBM contest was the R-36 (SS-9), a straight-forward evolution of the earlier R-16. The first stage was configured much like the R-16, but the enlarged second-stage fuselage diameter increased the fuel tankage, and more powerful engines allowed it to loft a much larger payload. Indeed, the original configuration was surprisingly archaic, including a hybrid radio-inertial guidance configuration shared with the UR-100.[27] As the design process continued, a debate began over the desirability of an all-inertial guidance system. Although designers connected with radio-inertial systems continued to argue that only their systems would give the missile sufficient accuracy, the RVSN preferred an all-inertial guidance system, not so much due to the possible jamming of the radio command link, as is widely believed, but due to the cost and inflexibility of the radio system. The hybrid guidance option required each silo to have one or more radio command stations erected down-range of the launch site to pass on the flight corrections.[28] Not only was this expensive, but the RVSN commanders had realized that this would make retargeting individual silos very difficult. The radio station had to be erected along the ballistic path to the target, which made it difficult to later switch a particular missile to another target. This was not as much of a problem with first-generation systems, which were very limited in their targeting flexibility because of the need to hardwire the flight controls. But the advent of transistors and early flight computers opened up the possibility that in the near future, missiles could be retargeted relatively quickly via software rather than hardware. As a result, the definitive configuration of the R-36 included an all-inertial guidance system, which offered an increase in accuracy from 2.7 km (1.7 mi) on the R-16U to 1.3 km (.8 mi) CEP on the R-36.[29]

The main innovation in the system design was the use of the new silos. After the fiasco with soft basing in the first-generation ICBMs, the RVSN preferred that the second generation follow the American pattern in individual silos, called OS in Russian.[30] These were not clustered together, as with the improvised Sheksna silos, used as a stopgap in the last batch of R-16U missiles. Instead, each missile regiment had a single launch command center and several silos separated from one another so than no single nuclear warhead could destroy more than one silo. The silo hardness was considerably better: only 28 psi with the interim first-generation silos, compared to about 170 psi with the second-generation OS silos.

The other innovation was in liquid-fuel storage. When the first-generation missiles were deployed in 1962, a missile could remain fueled for only two days before there was a risk of the oxidizer eating through the seals and pipes. By the mid-1960s, technologies were being introduced that extended this to six months, involving both the addition of chemical inhibitors to the oxidizer and new coatings to the fuel tanks. Even at six months, the fuel system durability was too low. This meant that the force could not regularly be left on alert duty fully fueled, since it would necessitate rebuilding two missiles per silo every year, a prohibitively expensive, dangerous, and time-consuming operation. The plans for the second generation expected a minimum storability of six months, but the program was to examine methods to extend this to three years at the earliest possible date. This process was called "ampulization," based on the notion that the oxidizer tanks could be lined with some sort of inert material like glass ampules that would minimize corrosion. In addition, a new oxidizer, nitric tetroxide, was used to enhance storability.

Chelomey's UR-200 competitor was similar in configuration to the R-36. The main difference was the relative inexperience of the design bureau in developing ICBMs, since this was their first ballistic missile. In contrast, Yangel's team had developed two successful intermediate-range missiles and one ICBM. The general configuration of the UR-200 was similar to that of the R-36 and also started out using a hybrid radio-inertial guidance system.[31] Problems with the flight-control system caused considerable strain between the guidance team and Chelomey's design bureau. During the first trials in 1963, fluctuations in the steering verniers shook the main exhaust chambers so severely that one of the initial test launches had to be halted. Chelomey blamed the problem on Pilyugin's flight-control system, which started a cycle of recriminations so bitter that Pilyugin attempted to have his institute excused from any further work with Chelomey.[32] The Central Committee of the Communist Party insisted that his institute remain on the project, but the feud spilled over to the UR-100 (SS-11) light ICBM program, where Chelomey again blamed Pilyugin's flight-control system for the problems with engine fluctuations. Another difference between the two designs was in the basing mode. Chelomey's missile used a clustered silo configuration similar to the Sheksna silos used with the R-16U, while Yangel's R-36 used the more advanced OS silos.

The first flight test of the R-36 took place from Tyuratam on 23 September 1963 and was a failure. The first successful launch was conducted on 3 December 1963. During 1964 a further sixteen launches were conducted, of which four were failures. Chelomey's UR-200 followed shortly after, with a first launch on 4 November 1963 and eight more launches through 20 October 1964.

The decision whether to adopt the R-36 or the rival Chelomey UR-200 became caught up in Kremlin politics shortly before the Khrushchev coup. In the summer of 1964, Chelomey managed to convince the Communist Party second secretary, Leonid Brezhnev, of the evident superiority of his design. Brezhnev's role at the time made him a supervisor of the defense industry and a key player in any major weapons procurement decision. However, by this time, Dmitry Ustinov and the military leadership had already come out firmly in favor of the Yangel design and convinced the pliable Brezhnev to reverse his position.[33] In October 1964 Nikita Khrushchev decided to select the R-36 design over the rival Chelomey UR-200 design for the new ICBM requirement, based largely on Ustinov's strong endorsement. The R-36 offered greater throw weight, and both its engine design and missile construction techniques were considerably more mature than the Chelomey design. The coup against Khrushchev in October 1964 delayed the official decision on the program, although it did not alter its ultimate course. The R-36 was not officially accepted for service until 21 July 1967. The R-36 was considerably more expensive than the UR-100 light ICBM. The program cost about as much as the UR-100 program, even though it involved only about a third the number of silos (table 4.1).[34]

The intended role of the R-36 in Soviet strategic planning has been the source of debate in the United States, both in the intelligence community at the time, and in academia ever since.[35] One of the schools of thought argued that it was intended to target the Launch Control Centers (LCC) of the U.S. Minuteman force, the presumption being that there were not enough R-36's deployed to attack the silos themselves.[36] An opposing view was that they were intended to attack cities, and the large warheads were intended to intimidate the U.S. leadership.

Neither of these views is supported by recent Russian accounts. The idea that the R-36 was specifically developed as a counterforce weapon capable of attacking hardened launch centers is undermined by the debate over guidance options and the uncertainties of all-inertial guidance even as late as 1966. This argument is further weakened by the late stage at which the RVSN was able to deploy surveillance and geodetic satellites capable of accurately locating the Minuteman command centers, suggesting that other roles were dominant when the requirements were first drawn up. The rationale for the R-36 was more political than tactical, and it was seen symbolically as a counterweight to the U.S. Titan force. Khrushchev had been aware of the massive new Titan II and wanted an analog for the Soviet forces. In the R-36's initial stages of development, the Kremlin desired

Table 4.1

Heavy ICBM Comparative Technical Data

Service Designation	R-36	UR-200	Titan II
Index number	8K67	8K81	LGM-25C
Developer	Yangel	Chelomey	Martin Marietta
Initial operational capability	1966	canceled	1963
Configuration (stages)	2	2	2
Length (m)	34.1	30	31.4
Diameter (m)	3.0	3.0	3.05
Launch weight (tons)	186.8	136.0	149.7
First-stage thrust (tons)	245.6	204	195
Second-stage thrust	95.2	62.5	45
Maximum range (km)	15,000	12,000	15,000
Payload (tons)	5.6	2.69	3.7
Warhead yield (megatons)	18	5+	5+

to have a missile like the Titan, capable of carrying the new, very large thermonuclear devices. From a technical standpoint, the R-36 was viewed from the outset as a multirole system.[37] The RVSN was unsure of exactly what it needed given the rapidly changing technology of the mid-1960s. Rather than be tied down with a medium ICBM such as the R-26, with very limited payload options, the requirements switched in 1962 to a multipurpose heavy ICBM that could be adapted to various payloads, including a heavy single warhead, fractional orbital bomb system (FOBS), depressed trajectory, or multiple independently targetable reentry vehicles (MIRV). Specific mission planning for the R-36 force followed, rather than preceded, the decision to develop the system.

Nuclear Weapons in Space

The FOBS was one of the most controversial weapons developed as part of the second-generation program. In the public mind, it was a modern sword of Damocles, a nuclear weapon orbiting the globe and able to drop down unexpectedly from the cold darkness of outer space. In fact, its requirement was more prosaic and its capabilities far more limited than the nightmarish popular image.

The FOBS system was called a "global missile" by the Soviets.[38] One of the first approaches to dealing with the threat of an American ABM system was to develop a missile capable of disabling the ABM network as the vanguard of the main nuclear strike. It was presumed that U.S. ballistic-missile early-warning radar coverage would be oriented toward the Arctic. Unlike a conventional ICBM, a FOBS missile put the warhead into orbit. So a FOBS missile warhead could approach from the south, where U.S. radar sensors had little or no coverage. The warhead could then be aimed at ABM radars or national command centers. Since they could not be reprogrammed when in flight, they could not be lofted indefinitely as blackmail weapons, as was often alleged in the U.S. press at the time.

A second, optional, launch mode was a depressed trajectory. Depressed trajectories were not normally practical for standard Soviet ICBMs, since they were not as efficient as normal trajectories and would require missiles with considerably greater range than normal. They were attractive from an anti-ABM standpoint, since their apogee of 500–600 km (310–370 mi) (rather than the usual 4,000–8,000 km [2,500–5,000 mi] of a normal ICBM) meant that even if they were fired over the North Pole, the ABM radar would have only two minutes to track the incoming reentry vehicles, versus the usual twelve to fifteen minutes.

The FOBS program was another competitive development effort, this time pitting Yangel against Korolyov. Yangel concluded that the requirement could be met by a version of the R-36 heavy ICBM with a new payload package, called the R-36-O, the "O" standing for orbital. Korolyov's entry was a new missile called the GR-1. Technically, it represented yet another attempt by Korolyov's OKB-1 to employ cryogenic fuel in spite of the RVSN's growing insistence on storable liquid fuels. Although two prototypes were constructed, the Korolyov GR-1 design was not seriously considered by the RVSN due to its use of cryogenic fuel. Indeed, there is some debate whether it was ever test launched. Chelomey attempted to muscle in on the competition with a FOBS version of his UR-500 Proton space booster, called the GR-2. Chelomey's ploy in this proposal was to offer a far heavier payload than was possible with Korolyov's smaller GR-1. However, Chelomey's proposal was not accepted.

The first flight tests of the R-36-O took place in December 1965, and twenty-four were conducted through August 1971. Seven of the tests were suborbital. While some of these were failures, most were intentional depressed-trajectory shots. The first R-36-O regiment became operational at Baikonur on 25 August 1966, and the FOBS system was officially accepted into service on 19 November 1968. U.S. intelligence did not credit the USSR with a FOBS system until 1971, when it was believed that about twenty missiles were operational.

The FOBS concept never proved entirely practical. Although such a weapon posed a particular set of challenges to the U.S. ABM network and to the early U.S. ballistic-missile early-warning system, the warhead was smaller and less accurate than comparable ICBM versions. It was further undermined by the advent of the Defense Support Program (DSP) satellite.[39] This ballistic-missile early-warning satellite entered development in 1969, and the first of a series of DSP satellites was launched in 1971. The DSP satellites used an infrared sensor to detect the hot exhaust plume of a ballistic-missile launch. This network offered an earlier warning than radars and had the capability of detecting a FOBS launch long before it would approach targets in the United States, thereby negating its surprise advantage. Although the DSP constellation did not reach full maturity until well into the 1970s, it largely undermined any advantage of the FOBS over more conventional ICBMs. This was recognized by the RVSN, and the FOBS remained more a curious technological footnote than a serious weapon. It was retired in 1983 with little fanfare.

Nuclear Rain

The fourth and least successful requirement of the second-generation program called for the development of a super-heavy ICBM capable of lofting very large thermonuclear warheads, with a payload on the order of thirty tons. The program was prompted by the development of very large nuclear devices like the RDS-220 150-megaton bomb, which weighed twenty-five tons. Such an enormous weapon could not be carried by normal heavy ICBMs like the R-36 or UR-200, which had a payload less than a sixth the size.

The super-heavy ICBM requirement was seized on with enthusiasm by all of the major design bureaus. This had less to do with the military requirement than with contemporary space efforts. With President John F. Kennedy's announcement of a planned manned lunar mission, the Soviet Union began a lunar program of its own. The Soviet lunar program was controversial, since if carried out, it would divert an enormous amount of funds and resources away from the second-generation ICBM program. Needless to say, it was viewed with considerable skepticism by the RVSN, which managed the Soviet civil space programs. The lead design bureau for the program was the Korolyov OKB-1, with its N-1 super-booster. In hopes of placating the military, Korolyov proposed military applications for the N-1. There had been a study conducted in the 1960s under the code name Raskat envisioning a missile that could carry seventy warheads and so be capable of destroying nearly every major U.S. city with a single missile. Korolyov offered a similar scheme, in which the N-1 could carry and deliver up to one hundred nuclear weapons against different cities. This system was never seriously considered, since it was doubtful that a guidance system could be developed with existing technology that would permit the weapon to accurately release such a large number of warheads.

The two other contenders were the Yangel R-46 design and the Chelomey UR-500. The R-46 design was pushed out of the competition quickly, because the military wanted the design bureau to concentrate on more sober requirements, such as the R-36 heavy ICBM. Chelomey's UR-500 actually reached the flight stage.

The program was tolerated by the RVSN, which recognized early on that such a rocket, even if not particularly suitable as a weapon, would be useful as a space booster for the increasingly heavy military satellites. The first test flight was conducted in July 1965. By this stage, the RVSN had largely given up on the need for a super-heavy ICBM, because the R-36 could loft a 25-megaton weapon. Furthermore, the basing for such a missile would be prohibitively expensive, especially if hardened. One of Chelomey's schemes was for an enormous underground revolver launcher that could fire six missiles in succession. The heavy-ICBM program officially ended in 1965, but a three-stage version of the UR-500 continued in development, later emerging as the highly successful Proton space booster, which remains one of the workhorses of the Russian space program to this day.

Red Polaris

The Soviet submarine ballistic-missile program did not receive the resources or priority of the land-based missiles. The early naval missiles were not impressive. The liquid fuel was so corrosive that the submarines were seldom loaded with live missiles. On the rare occasions when the submarines were loaded with missiles for combat patrols, the missiles were generally fired off at the end of the patrol rather than face the onerous task of removing them from the submarine tubes and returning them to the plant for rebuilding.[40] This problem had to be addressed to make missile submarines a practical weapon. Solid-fuel missiles seemed to offer the answer. As in the case of land-based missiles, the quest for a Soviet solid-fuel SLBM proved frustrating.

The solid-fuel SLBM program started on 5 September 1958. As in the case of the land-based missiles, Khrushchev encouraged the conversion of naval ordnance design bureaus to solid-fuel missiles. In this case, one of the oldest Russian naval arsenals, Pyotr Tyurin's bureau at the Arsenal plant in Leningrad, was converted.[41] The new solid-fuel missile system was called the D-6. Like the land-based programs, it was based around clusters of small-diameter, solid-fuel engines derived from the Luna tactical artillery rockets.[42] The design was further compromised by the decision to use a set of small rockets near the nose of the missile to extract it underwater from its launch tube, since there was some fear of an explosion if the main solid-fuel engines were ignited underwater. The program was so fraught with problems that on 4 June 1961 it was canceled. A second solid-fuel SLBM program was initiated in May 1960, which would have adapted the solid-fuel Temp (SS-12) tactical ballistic missile to submarines. Since the missile was not designed for underwater launch, it would be fitted inside watertight containers that would be released from the submarine, the missile engine igniting when the top of the canister breached the surface. This scheme never progressed beyond draft design. A related approach was considered in February 1959 under the D-7 program. Under this scheme, the missiles being developed for the liquid-fuel D-4 system would be mounted in special watertight containers. Instead of launching the missiles from the submarine, the containers would be separated from the submarine like moored mines floating immediately beneath the surface, and after two to four hours, they would launch themselves. This scheme was soon recognized as completely impractical, and it was canceled on 5 February 1960. In June 1961, following the cancellation of the D-6 and D-7 efforts, the D-7 designation was applied to a new scheme by Tyurin's Arsenal bureau to adapt the new land-based RT-15 solid-fuel missile for submarine launch.[43] The program was doomed by problems with the solid-fuel technology and by the lack of a nuclear warhead light and powerful enough to make the small missile practical.

While the solid-fuel program was stumbling badly, the Makeyev bureau, in Miass, was working on a new liquid-fuel missile. The D-5 program was authorized on 24 April 1962, using the compact new R-27 missile.[44] The R-27 missile was not envisioned as a strategic weapon to compete against Tyurin's RT-15M, but rather a tactical system to compete against Chelomey's P-6 antiship cruise missiles. The main targets of the R-27 were U.S. carrier battle groups, a bogeyman of Soviet security nightmares due to their ability to strike the Soviet Union from many different directions with nuclear weapons. While the U.S. Navy itself had envisioned carriers in such a fashion in the late 1940s during the debate with the U.S. Air Force over funding priorities, by the 1960s the ballistic-missile submarine had taken over the mantle of the naval strategic strike platform. The Soviet concerns may have been a belated echo of the late 1940s debates, a threat exaggeration by the GRU, or a combination of such factors. In the event, there was a perceived need to deal with the carrier threat by means other than conventional approaches alone.

Two versions of the R-27 missile were envisioned: the basic R-27, for use against stationary naval targets such as ports; and the R-27K, using a guided warhead section to attack ships at sea. The R-27 would be mounted in the small, highly automated Project 705B (Alfa) attack submarines, or on the conventional Project 605 (Golf).[45] Before this scheme proceeded much further, the navy leadership took stock of their hopelessly muddled efforts, comparing them to the U.S. Navy's Polaris submarine program. The first of the George Washington–class submarines went into operation in November 1960. These carried sixteen missiles, compared to the three on the most modern Soviet missile submarines. The U.S. Navy was planning on deploying more than forty of these submarines, vastly outpacing the Soviet program. Confronted with the glaring disparity in capability between the American and Soviet missile submarines, the Soviet Navy began shifting its attention from a new solid-fuel SLBM to a liquid-fuel SLBM, small enough to be carried in large numbers on a new submarine. In view of the long delays caused by the failure of the solid-fuel program, they decided to merge two existing programs in hopes of catching up with the Americans.

Design of a new nuclear-powered submarine, the Project 667, was already under way.[46] The original plan was to arm it with three of the large Beriev P-100 cruise missiles. This was quickly rejected, and the modified Project 667A Navaga (Yankee) was converted to use as a ballistic-missile submarine armed with Makeyev's small R-27 SLBM. The similarities between the Navaga and the American Polaris submarine led some Russian naval officers to sarcastically refer to it as the Vanya Vashington class. Development of the R-27 was aided by spinoffs from the ICBM program, especially the new nitric tetroxide oxidant and heptyl fuel, which were less aggressive than earlier storable liquid fuels. Development of the submarine proved relatively quick as well, and the lead boat of the class entered service in November 1967, seven years after its American analog.

The new missile submarine, though closer in capability to its American counterpart, was not as advanced. The R-27 missiles could not be quickly salvoed, like the American Polaris missiles.[47] The Navaga submarine lacked an integrated ship inertial navigation system, decreasing the accuracy of launch information and missile accuracy.[48] Compared to the American Polaris submarines, the Navaga's twin-propeller design and lack of sound dampening gave it a much higher acoustic signature underwater, making it more vulnerable to detection and attack. Although technically behind the U.S. Navy, the new class was a substantial improvement over all previous classes of Soviet missile submarines. The design was so sound that it served as the basis for most future submarine designs through the 1990s.

While the reorientation of the R-27 program in 1962–64 focused on the strategic land-attack mission, the Soviet Navy continued with plans to develop the R-27K version to attack naval targets.[49] This was prompted more by institutional concerns than by a real requirement. When Vladimir Chelomey learned of the R-27K scheme in 1962, he proposed that the navy instead acquire a version of his land-based UR-200 "universal missile" for this role. He offered this as a part of a broader program to develop a space strike system, in which a space-based radar station provided data on the location of U.S. naval battle groups.[50] The navy was not keen on sponsoring a shore-based missile, since there was some suspicion they would be taken over by the RVSN as part of Khrushchev's defense reforms. Instead, the navy continued its own efforts with the R-27K. The program had low priority and was finally brought to an end in the early 1970s following the signing of the SALT I treaty. Since the intended carrier for the R-27K, the Project 667V submarine, was externally identical to the normal Project 667A Navaga missile submarine, the tactical version would be counted against the Soviet Union's strategic-missile limit. This was unacceptable, and in 1974 the R-27K was accepted for experimental service for a few years on the modified Project 605 test submarine.[51]

Thirty-four boats of the Navaga class were built, the final one entering service in 1976. Regular submarine patrols toward the United States coast began in 1966 using the older Project 658M (Hotel II) class, but these tended to be limited to short sorties no further south than Newfoundland or off the Hawaiian islands. The Navaga was the first Soviet ballistic-missile submarine with enough endurance to conduct patrols close to the U.S. coast, and so was the first to begin to be considered as a factor in Soviet nuclear strike scenarios against the United States.[52] The Navaga class began patrolling within missile range of the United States coast in 1969.[53] By 1972 a stable pattern emerged, so that at any one time, the Soviet Navy deployed at least two submarines in the Atlantic in two "patrol boxes" within missile range of U.S. coastal targets, and two more submarines in the Pacific. Even though missile submarines began to figure in Soviet force planning, there was still some resistance within the General Staff to consider using them for high-priority missions. The main problem continued to be the lack of a secure and timely method of communication.

Deploying the Second Generation

As the second generation of missiles completed the test phase in the late 1960s, the RVSN faced the substantial challenge of deploying the force. The production program was the largest single weapons efforts in Soviet history and the most expensive, significantly outstripping the nuclear program of the late 1940s. While the missiles themselves represented a significant cost, the real expenses came in the necessary infrastructure. The late 1960s saw the RVSN consume a larger fraction of the Soviet defense budget than at any time in the postwar years, peaking in 1967 at about 18 percent of the budget.[54]

The second-generation missiles had sufficient range to reach targets in the United States from bases deep within the Soviet Union. This was an important feature, since the deep silos required the use of basing areas not affected by the permafrost conditions found in much of northern Russia. The new bases had to be near railroads to permit the shipment of the large missiles. As a result, the RVSN planned to deploy the new missile divisions in an arc from eastern Ukraine, through Kazakhstan, along the Trans-Siberian railway. While some of the older first-generation bases would be rebuilt, most of the missile sites were new. It was one of the largest construction projects in Soviet history. The first two years of silo construction alone involved excavating about 120 million cubic meters of earth, compared to only about 5 million cubic meters for the massive underground Krasnoyarsk nuclear processing facility.[55] At the height of construction, the labor force on the new missile bases totaled 650,000. This was in part due to the inefficiencies in the Soviet construction industry; the similar U.S. silo construction program involved a labor force less than a tenth the size.[56] The program also put enormous strain on the missile troops. Housing was appallingly poor for the first few years, often only tents or ramshackle barracks, and living conditions were very harsh.[57]

The first of the missiles to be deployed was the Yangel R-36 (SS-9), which entered service in 1966. It took eight years to deploy the entire complement of 308 missile silos in six locations. The Chelomey UR-100 (SS-11) followed quickly in spite of their later test program. The first regiments also became operational in 1966, and it took six years to deploy 950 silos at eleven locations. The sophisticated but troubled solid-fuel RT-2 (SS-13) was the last to be deployed, entering service in 1971.

The expansion of the missile bases necessitated a similar expansion of RVSN units. The RVSN's ICBM divisions increased fivefold in the decade from 1963 to 1972, from about 37,000 troops in 1963 to 154,000 in 1972. Total RVSN strength went from about 171,000 in 1963 to 273,000 in 1972.[58] The order of battle of the RVSN had already reached its peak of thirty-eight divisions in 1962, but at this stage they were largely paper divisions and only partly manned.[59] The last five new divisions were organized in October 1965, all intended for the new R-36 divisions. Through most of this period, the RVSN was organized into two missile armies responsible for the original intermediate-range R-12 and R-14 bases, along with seven missile corps responsible for the new ICBM divisions.[60] In April 1970 the organization was simplified by consolidating the ICBM corps into three new missile armies headquartered in Omsk, Chita, and Orenburg.

The new silo basing was also accompanied by the first comprehensive command-and-control system for the ICBM force, code-named Signal. Besides providing a more reliable means to control the force, it deprived the United States of a means of signals intelligence to determine the alert levels of the Soviet force due to lower reliance on open radio traffic to control remote silo bases (table 4.2).[61]

Table 4.2
Soviet Silo Hardness[62]

Silo Type	Plan	Actual
Sheksna (1960)	$2kg/cm^2$, 28 psi	$2kg/cm^2$, 28 psi
OS (1965)	$12 kg/cm^2$, 170 psi	$14-20 kg/cm^2$, 200–284 psi
OS-84 (1975)	$30 kg/cm^2$, 425 psi	$80-100 kg/cm^2$, 1,140–1,470 psi

The Intermediate Force Stagnates

In contrast to the extensive deployment of second-generation intercontinental missiles, the Soviet intermediate-range missile force stagnated in the late 1960s. While this was in part due to the technical failures of the missiles programs themselves, it also reflected the greater priority afforded the intercontinental strike mission.

By the mid-1960s, the R-12 and R-14 intermediate-range missiles were fully deployed in eighteen missile divisions, concentrated most heavily in the western Soviet Union and targeted on Europe. Both systems had been developed in sequence by the Yangel design bureau. Two major innovations were sought in the second-generation IRBMs: mobility and the use of solid fuel. Although the final batch of R-12 and R-14 missiles had been silo emplaced, increasing missile accuracy implied that even silos could be destroyed. Mobile basing would increase survivability. The desire for solid-fuel propulsion was linked to the mobility requirement, since mobile liquid-fuel missiles would be hazardous to move. The second-generation Yangel RT-15 IRBM program was envisioned by key decision makers, such as Dmitry Ustinov, as a pioneering effort, much as the R-12 and R-14 had pioneered the use of storable liquid rocket fuel. Experience with the less challenging IRBMs was expected to provide the technological groundwork for mobile solid-fuel ICBMs in the third generation.[63] The missile was mounted on a massive tracked chassis derived from the T-10 heavy tank.[64]

Flight tests began at Kapustin Yar in September 1965. There were a total of nineteen test launches through March 1970. The missile had some significant technical problems, and the minister of defense, Grechko, was not very keen on the expense of operating such a system. As a result, the state commission overseeing the program decided against recommending the missile for service use. However, pressure from Ustinov and the defense industry minister, S. A. Zverev, forced the army into accepting a small number of missiles for experimental use. Fifteen missiles were ordered, along with a single firing battery's complement of six launch vehicles. They were deployed on an experimental basis in Belorussia in the early 1970s.[65] Had there been a strong requirement for a new intermediate-range missile, the RVSN would have sponsored a parallel liquid-fuel missile program. Instead, the focus remained on fielding the second generation of ICBMs.

Much the same picture emerges from the parallel medium-bomber program. The Soviet Air Force had fielded the Tupolev Tu-22 (Blinder) bomber in the early 1960s in an effort to replace the old subsonic Tu-16 bomber.[66] The Tu-22 was an analog of the American B-58 Hustler, though considerably less sophisticated. The aircraft was one of Tupolev's least successful designs, suffering from a high accident rate and lingering technical problems. The majority of the aircraft were foisted on the navy's aviation branch for the anticarrier mission. This left a clear requirement for a new intermediate-range bomber. Khrushchev strongly opposed

The most ambitious Soviet bomber design of the 1960s was the Sukhoi T-4. Intended as an intermediate-range missile carrier, its cost was so enormous that it was dubbed the "hundred tons of gold." Although technologically brilliant, it gave way to the more conservative Tu-22M Backfire. One example still resides at the Monino museum.

bombers in general but was willing to consider an intermediate-range bomber for targets in Europe and Asia so long as it was armed with missiles. At the time, the air force was considering a new missile, the Kh-45 Molniya, an aeroballistic standoff missile akin to the U.S. Skybolt. The bomber program became mixed up in the political feuds that often distorted Soviet defense decision making. Khrushchev and the head of the aircraft ministry, Pyotr Dementyev, were frustrated by Tupolev's conservative design approach and his stubborn and independent manners when dealing with industry chiefs. Although Tupolev would have been the natural choice to manage the new bomber program, he was denied access to the requirements documents by Dementyev. Instead, the requirements were issued to two fighter-design bureaus, Yakovlev and Sukhoi. Sukhoi's T-4 design was selected in 1962, and plans were laid to build 250 of them in Kazan in 1970–75. The T-4 was the most advanced Soviet aircraft of its day, making extensive use of titanium construction to overcome heat buildup at high supersonic speeds. Although technically brilliant, the aircraft was soon dubbed the "100 tons of gold" aircraft, because that was roughly its unit cost. Khrushchev's ouster rebounded to Tupolev's favor, and in November 1967 the Council of Ministers authorized the start of a new Tupolev project which would emerge in the 1970s as the Tu-22M Backfire. The political intrigue around the medium-bomber program meant that most air force bomber regiments continued to fly the obsolete but dependable Tu-16 Badger through the early 1970s, almost twenty years after its debut.

Command and Control of the Second Generation

As discussed in a previous chapter, the Soviet tactical war-fighting doctrine for the ICBM force in the early 1960s was constrained by the poor survivability of the first-generation missile basing and by the lack of any means of early warning. Although the official policy of the Soviet government in the Khrushchev years was "no first use" and a launch-on-warning posture, this was not plausible given the shortcomings. With the U.S. side espousing a counterforce doctrine in the mid-1960s, there was a need to improve the force so that it could absorb a preemptive first strike and still carry out a response of such magnitude that the residual force alone would be a sufficient deterrent to the United States. The deployment of the second generation of ICBMs in OS silos was only a part of this effort. Improvements in command and control were equally important. This included two major elements: the establishment of a timely early-warning network to alert the Kremlin to the launch of an attack, and the improvement of the links between the major elements of the strategic nuclear forces to ensure that a retaliatory strike could be carried out in the event of a preemptive strike from the United States.

By 1965 the Soviet RVSN had accumulated several years of experience in operating the first generation of ICBMs. It was very evident from practice drills that the existing network based on conventional military communications systems was obsolete under the compressed decision-time cycle of missile warfare. Commands and routine administrative messages were sent from Moscow to missile bases using teletype by landline or encrypted radio, but this was too slow. In a worst-case scenario, with a U.S. attack beginning with a strike from Polaris submarines near the Soviet coast, the duration from launch to impact would be only thirteen minutes. An automated command system was needed to verify the attack, inform the supreme leadership, decide on a course of action, authorize the response, and communicate the response to the missile, bomber, and submarine bases. Two approaches could be taken: to create a system that was fast enough to permit the launch of the force before the impact of American missiles, or to design a system that could survive an attack and still control the residual RVSN force. The second option was viewed as being too demanding for the technology of the day, so the first approach became the basis for the new command-and-control system. The second approach was not completely ignored, since there was still some desire to consider the possibility of conducting follow-on strikes; but this received significantly less priority.[67] This was the major technological challenge posed to Soviet designers in the early Brezhnev years.

The initial hurdle in developing a command-and-control system to permit launch-on-attack was early missile warning. The Dnestr (Hen House) radar began construction at the Sary Shagan ABM test range in the late 1950s. It was so enormous that it took some time before American intelligence appreciated what it was.[68] The Dnestr was a major leap forward in Soviet radar technology, permitting detection of missiles at ranges of 3,000 km (1,900 mi), triple that of the earlier radars. Two prototypes were completed, and in 1961 work started on the definitive production version, the Dnestr-M. The Dnestr-M radars were intended to serve as the warning network for the Soviet strategic command-and-control system, and also to serve as the initial element of the new A-35 ABM system (ABM-1) being developed by Kisunko's design bureau. Construction of the first two Dnestr-M stations began in 1964. A total of eleven Dnestr-M radars were erected by the mid-1970s at five sites. Once these were completed, a second array was added at most sites to provide added azimuth coverage, and the double configuration was code-named Dnepr.[69] The Dnestr/Dnepr BMEWS had shortcomings typical of early radars of this type. The design sacrificed resolution for range, since their main priority was to extend Soviet early-warning time. Its structure was so large that nuclear hardening was almost inconceivable. Industrial rivalries between the design bureaus aggravated existing limitations of command-and-control technology.[70] In spite of their limitations, they accomplished their main task, to cue the Soviet strategic command-and-control system regarding the launch of a missile strike from the United States. They were less effective in their use of an ABM network due to their lack of resolution and vulnerability once a war began.

While work was progressing on missile warning, two competitive efforts were under way to develop an automated strategic command-and-control system. The first approach was pioneered by Vladimir Semenikhin of the Scientific Research Institute for Automated Devices (NII-AR), in Moscow, starting in 1963.[71] Semenikhin's team used microprocessors as the basis for the system. He argued that such an approach was more flexible, since changes to the system could be made by changes to the software rather than the hardware. The second approach was led by Taras Sokolov of the Leningrad Polytechnic Institute (LPI). Sokolov favored hardwired computing systems using ferrite-on-ferrite cells.[72] Prototypes of the command system were completed by 1965 and put through competitive trials.[73] The tests revealed that the hardwired systems offered substantially better reliability than the early microprocessors, and that the microprocessor designs were not yet mature enough. Ustinov was not happy about giving such an important development program to the small LPI team, but Sokolov was authorized to develop the RVSN command system. However, given the limitations of the LPI research team, the command system for both naval and air force strategic command and control went to Semenikhin.

Sokolov's first-generation command-and-control system, designated Signal, was deployed in 1967–68 with the second-generation ICBMs.[74] The system was deployed from the bottom up, the first systems going to the launch battalions' and launch regiments' launch-control centers.[75] The Signal system worked both to and from higher command levels. It enabled higher commands to pass down thirteen fixed commands to the launch units, including operating status, force readiness, the number of the operating plan, and operation start or abort. The Signal system also enabled the launch units to inform the higher command levels on status, missile readiness, delays, and mission completion or failure. The Signal system was intended to control the launch crews but had no direct control over the weapons themselves. The Signal system also contained the first elements of automated negative control over the silos. It included features that alerted senior commanders if attempts were made at a single silo or group of silos to bypass the coding systems and launch the missiles without authorization. Provisions were made to permit these renegade units to be cut off from the control system, and control of the silos would revert to neighboring launch-control centers.[76] Other negative controls were introduced into the missile system itself to prevent unauthorized use or premature detonation of the warhead. The safety and arming device on the nuclear weapons was integrated into the missile's inertial navigation system and flight-control system. The safety and arming system was armed only after a sequence of events occurred, including the high-G acceleration of lift-off, specified flight parameters, and specified reentry events. The Signal system was extensively used during command-post exercises during the 1970s, and these training activities helped to define the requirements for the next-generation system. The importance of the network led the RVSN to open a communications control center to support its central command post on 28 May 1974.[77]

The first automated command system for the strategic nuclear submarine fleet was developed at the same time.[78] The basic element of the new system was a Soviet equivalent of the American PAL (permissive action link), intended to prevent accidental or unauthorized launch. The submarine was provided with a code to sanction the launch, without which the launch was impossible. On board the submarine, it was necessary to insert three control keys to activate the missile system. These keys were controlled by the captain, the political officer, and the KGB security officer. The communication link between shore and submarine was improved at this time with the Dalnost semiautomated command system. Dalnost was deployed at the General Staff of the navy command post, with the fleet headquarters, and with the shore-based communication stations. The Dalnost systems basically allowed the commands from the national command authority to be passed on to the submarines with minimum delay. This system was first deployed on the Project 667A Navaga (Yankee) class.[79]

The automation of the command system for the strategic-bomber regiments of the air force followed lines similar to those of the RVSN missile divisions. The divisional headquarters were connected to the strategic communication system and provided with command links and displays.

By the 1960s the process of creating war plans for the use of the strategic nuclear forces had become more formal. The Soviet equivalent of the American SIOP (Single Integrated Operating Plan) was the Plan of Operation of the Strategic Nuclear Forces.[80] This plan was developed under the guidance of the Main Operations Department of the Soviet General Staff, which received input from the RVSN, navy, and air force, as well as from the GRU military intelligence branch and other government authorities. The General Staff was the primary agency in coordinating the war planning of the branches of the armed forces equipped with intercontinental nuclear weapons.

Strategic Defenses

While work was progressing on strategic offensive weapons, the Soviet Union continued its strategic air defense programs. The primary effort through the late 1950s and early 1960s was the development of an antibomber network. Following the deployment of the S-25 Berkut system (SA-1) in the late 1950s to protect Moscow, the S-75 Dvina (SA-2) was deployed nationwide. These early strategic defense efforts were the most expensive weapons program until the ICBM effort of the late 1960s, due to the sophistication of the equipment and the large scale of their deployment. The S-25 and S-75 cost about R 38 billion to deploy, about one and half times the cost of the strategic-bomber program.[81] The S-75 enjoyed its first success on 1 May 1960, when a battery near Sverdlovsk shot down the U-2 reconnaissance aircraft piloted by Francis Gary Powers. They were followed in the early 1960s by the S-125 (SA-3) network, to provide better low-altitude coverage, and the S-200 (SA-5), to provide high-altitude coverage. Besides surface-to-air missiles (SAM), the PVO-Strany Air Defense Command also had its own separate air force, equipped with jet interceptors and a large though obsolete force of radar-directed antiaircraft guns. The air defense command was quite substantial even after the Khrushchev reforms of the early 1960s, and in the decade of 1963–72 absorbed as much of the Soviet defense budget as the Strategic Missile Force.

A plan to deploy an antiballistic-missile system to defend Moscow, designated as the A-35, was authorized on 8 April 1958 and undertaken by Grigory Kisunko's SKB-31.[82] In 1962–63, the A-35 program was derailed by another of Vladimir Chelomey's schemes. Chelomey proposed to Khrushchev that his UR-100 ICBM could also be used to form a more economical basis for the ABM system, called Taran (Ram). Khrushchev was gulled into accepting this proposition, not realizing that the missile itself was only a very tiny fraction of the overall ABM effort. Furthermore, the UR-100 did not have the maneuvering capabilities needed in an ABM missile, and the ABM program became stymied as attempts were made to incorporate Chelomey's ill-conceived ambitions into the ABM effort. Chelomey's Taran scheme was finally abandoned in 1964 after Khrushchev was ousted. By this time the program was even further behind schedule. The initial deployment of the A-35 system began in 1967, several years behind schedule. When originally conceived in 1958, the ABM-1 was designed to deal with only six to eight ICBMs.[83] While this may have seemed sufficient in 1958, when it appeared that ICBMs would be extremely expensive and few in number, by the time the system was actually deployed, it was hopelessly inadequate.

Space and the Strategic-Weapons Programs

The Soviet space program was managed by the RVSN through most of its early years. Though civilian space spectaculars like the first Sputnik and the first man in space dominated the public perception of the Soviet space program, military space efforts dominated the Soviet space budget. The Central Directorate of Space Forces (TsUKOS) was formed in October 1964 to manage these programs, and the military space units eventually formed their own command, the VKS Military Space Force.[84]

Three of the early military space programs had a significant impact on the strategic-weapons program: strategic reconnaissance satellites, communications satellites, and geodetic satellites. The first Soviet reconnaissance program was started in 1957 by Korolyov's OKB-1 as part of a broader effort to develop a common family of manned and unmanned spacecraft. The first two Zenit-2 photographic reconnaissance satellites failed, and the first successful mission did not take place until 8 August 1962, about two years after the first successful American Corona photo reconnaissance mission.[85] The Zenit-2 was a wide-area survey satellite with cameras intended for the creation of accurate maps. This effort was central to Soviet targeting for both the missile and bomber force. However, the camera resolution was not sufficient for targeting of precise objects such as American missile launch-control centers, which were quite small and partially camouflaged. As a result, a related family of satellites for detailed surveillance photography were developed, the Zenit-4, which began operation on 16 November 1963. These were essential for Soviet efforts to accurately target ICBMs against military targets.

An important element in increasing the accuracy of strategic missiles was research into the variations in the earth's gravitational and magnetic fields, especially those along likely missile flight paths over the North Pole. That these natural and fluctuating fields could significantly affect overall accuracy led to the development of the Sfera geodetic satellites by the Reshetnev design bureau in Krasnoyarsk-26. The first test series of launches began on 20 February 1968 and lasted through 1972. Regular military missions began in 1973 and lasted through 1980.

The intercontinental strike mission necessitated a modernization of Soviet military communications networks. Radio communication with submarines and bombers on patrol could employ the Gorizont tropospheric radio system, but it was not entirely reliable. Satellite retransmitting stations were the obvious solution, and Korolyov's OKB-1 started such a program in 1960. The first two launches of the Molniya-1 communications satellite in 1964 failed, and the first successful flight was on 14 October 1965. The early systems had low reliability and endurance—only thirty hours' transmission on the first satellite. They were used primarily for military communications across the depth of the Soviet Union from Moscow to Vladivostok. Reliable, long-endurance satellite communications did not become common until 1968. The establishment of a satellite communications network enabled rapid communication between Moscow and the scattered missile bases. In addition, it allowed the command centers to communicate with bombers and submarines once they were fitted with appropriate antennas and radio systems.

The Chinese Crisis

The primary targets of the RVSN in the early Brezhnev years were the United States and its allies in Europe and Asia. In the late 1960s, another potential opponent emerged as relations between the Soviet Union and the People's Republic of China continued to deteriorate. In 1968 the RVSN was tasked with developing a war plan in the event of conflict with China.[86] Soviet ICBMs were not readily retargetable at this time, and even if their guidance systems were modified, many targets in China were below their minimum range. As a result, in July 1968 a series of special short-range tests of the UR-100 missiles were conducted at ranges of only 925 km (573 mi) to 1,100 km (682 mi), which covered the gaps between the ICBMs and IRBMs like the R-12 and R-14.[87] The two last divisions of UR-100 missiles deployed were targeted against China.

The China crisis reached a head in the summer of 1969 after a series of border skirmishes provoked by the Chinese. Several R-12 regiments stationed with the 8th Missile Army were put on a heightened state of alert, only the second time the RVSN was mobilized during the Cold War. The Kremlin wanted to use the threat of nuclear attack to force the Chinese to back down. In the middle of August 1969, word was deliberately leaked to Western intelligence agencies and to several Warsaw Pact countries that strikes were being considered against Chinese missile bases and the Lop Nor nuclear test site, in the expectation that China would be informed. Chinese intelligence did learn of the threat, but lack of a Chinese response forced premier Aleksei Kosygin to repeat it to Zhou Enlai when they met at Ho Chi Minh's funeral in Hanoi in September 1969. This led to negotiations in October 1969, which finally defused the crisis.

The 1969 crisis changed the future force requirements of the RVSN. China now became a significant factor in targeting plans and requirements for future systems. The crisis also heightened Soviet interest in modernizing missile-guidance systems to permit them to be more easily retargeted, avoiding the need to have specific missiles permanently targeted at specific objectives.

Refining the Second Generation

By the end of the 1960s, the second generation of ICBMs was well on its way to deployment. Due to the lag time between development and deployment, the design bureaus continued to work on improvements and modifications to the missile designs as initial models were being manufactured. In the case of the second-generation ICBMs, some of these improvements were quite significant.

The first major innovation adopted in the second-generation ICBMs was the use of decoys to overcome American ABM defenses. Tests of various types of decoys had been going on since the early 1960s, based on R-12 intermediate-range missiles. As an outcome of these studies, in July 1965 the Yangel design bureau began development of its List (Leaf) system for the R-36. This included inflatable balloons made of metallized plastic to create false radar returns during the exo-atmospheric midcourse phase of flight, as well as subscale heavy decoys for the terminal phase, when the warhead entered the atmosphere. The List system was accepted for service on 21 July 1967. The main problem with the decoy package was that it weighed so much that the missile was limited to a smaller warhead. The normal R-36 was armed with the 8F675 reentry vehicle, first fitted with a ten-megaton thermonuclear warhead, and later with an improved warhead with a selectable yield of eighteen to twenty-five megatons. The warhead with the List system could only carry a smaller five-megaton warhead.

The Chelomey bureau followed suit with its own anti-ABM package, but about two years behind the Yangel bureau. Tests of the warhead with decoys began on 20 September 1967. This package was developed as part of a broader modernization package for the UR-100 called the UR-100UTTKh (SS-11 Mod 2). The flight tests of the modernized UR-100UTTKh began on 23 July 1969, and thirty-four were conducted through October 1971.[88] U.S. intelligence assessments concluded that there were one or two penetration aids in the package, probably metallized balloons.[89] The improved warhead of this version had a higher ballistic coefficient with higher speed during the terminal atmospheric phase of the trajectory, which would give any U.S. ABM system less time to react than the reentry vehicle used with the earlier UR-100.

A second approach to overcoming ABM defenses was to use multiple warheads to attack multiple targets. Both the United States and the Soviet Union had played around with this concept in primitive forms since the 1950s. In the Soviet case, there had been schemes to mount multiple warheads even on the early R-5 (SS-3) missile in the 1950s. The Global Missile scheme of the Khrushchev years had also examined the possibility of lofting a massive rocket that would carry hundreds of warheads. None of these schemes came to fruition, because they required the development of a sophisticated guidance system to control the individual warheads. Such a system would eat up a significant fraction of the missile's payload, and as a result, the yield of the nuclear warheads would be significantly less. In addition, it was not until the mid-1960s that compact, high-yield thermonuclear warheads were developed that were suitable for such a design. For many years, Soviet planners felt that decoys would be a more effective and less expensive way to penetrate ABM defenses.

The United States began to study MIRV warheads more seriously in the mid-1960s as a means to overcome ABM defenses and increase the number of warheads.[90] Since ABM missiles and ICBMs were similar in size and cost, by fractionating the warhead, the exchange cost between the two would come down clearly in favor of the ICBMs. The MIRV program was approved in April 1965, and the necessary changes to the Minuteman III begun in 1966.

The Soviet program proceeded somewhat differently from the U.S. program. Some Russian accounts suggest that a MRV (multiple reentry vehicle) configuration was under study as early as 1962.[91] Instead of a single MIRV effort, three sep-

Early Soviet MIRV warheads differed from their American counterparts in their un-shielded configuration on the nose of the missile. Soviet studies had concluded that a cover over the warheads did not appreciably improve the aerodynamics of the missile. This Pioneer (SS-20) intermediate-range ballistic missile, with a three-warhead cluster, is currently preserved at the Smithsonian's National Air and Space Museum in Washington.

arate programs were initiated at the three main missile-design bureaus to examine different reentry vehicle technologies. Chelomey's design bureau was assigned the task of developing reentry vehicles using plastics, Yangel's bureau mixed plastic and metallic designs, and Makeyev's naval-missile bureau was to examine metallic alloy compositions.[92] The other significant difference was that the Soviet Union adopted a less sophisticated warhead package than the American ICBM programs, initially opting for a MRV configuration rather than a true MIRV. This approach paralleled that of the U.S. Navy, which used a MRV warhead with its Polaris A-3 submarine missile. The MRV warhead did not use a sophisticated guidance bus, but simply released all of its warheads (usually three) at the same time. The MRV was something akin to a shotgun firing multiple shots against a single target, while the MIRV was more akin to an automatic rifle capable of firing multiple shots at different targets. The MRV was useful in penetrating

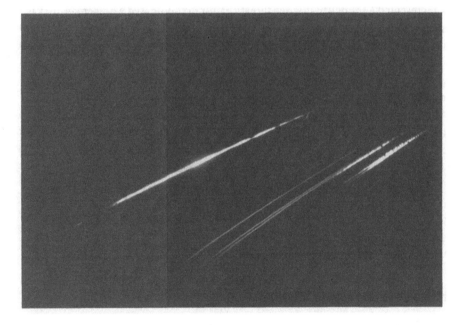

A glimpse of Armageddon. A Soviet R-36P (SS-9 Mod 4) ICBM reenters the atmosphere over the Pacific near the Kura impact area, off the Kamchatka Peninsula. The bright streak at the top is the missile body burning up, and the streaks below are from the glowing ablative coatings on the three multiple reentry vehicles carrying the missile's warheads. This photo was taken from one of the U.S. Air Force reconnaissance aircraft that regularly monitored Soviet tests during the Cold War. (Courtesy U.S. Air Force)

ABM defenses, but its unsophisticated guidance meant that its use was limited to area targets, not precision targets such as missile silos. The Soviet approach was to some extent forced on them by the lack of compact guidance systems for the reentry bus.

In early 1967 the Yangel design bureau began engineering development of a multiple reentry vehicle warhead section for the R-36 missile with three warheads, designated the R-36P (SS-9 Mod 4 "Triplet"). Unlike American MIRVs, the warheads were not mounted inside a protective nose cone but externally mounted around a central core. The three warheads, fitted to a rail, were usually released sequentially rather than simultaneously, as with the Polaris A-3 warhead. About twenty test launches of the R-36P took place from 23 August 1968 to 1971. It was accepted into service on 26 October 1970 and became operational in 1971. About 100 of the 288 deployed R-36 missiles were fitted with this warhead.

The American assessment of the Triplet became entangled with the American ABM controversy. Secretary of Defense Melvin Laird argued that the SS-9 Mod 4 represented a serious first-strike threat against the silo-based Minuteman, and as such would have to be countered by ABM deployment. His position was based on the highest estimates of SS-9 accuracy and deployment objectives. It presumed that the Triplet would eventually be capable of 450 m (1,500 ft) accuracy and that about 450 SS-9 Mod 4's would be deployed. The presumption was that an accuracy of 450 m (1,500 ft) CEP was needed for the R-36P to have capability against Minuteman silos. However, the U.S. intelligence community assessment was that the R-36P warheads had a CEP of about 900 m (0.5 nautical miles; 3,000 ft), or double the desired figure, and some argued that its CEP was never any better than 1.8 km (1.0 nautical miles; 1.1 mi). Recent Russian accounts have stated that its CEP was 1.34 to 1.97 km (.83 to 1.22 mi), on the low end of the U.S. estimates.[93]

The Chelomey design bureau began testing its own MRV warhead on the UR-100 two years later in August 1970.[94] Nineteen tests were conducted through late 1971.[95] This new warhead was intended for a new version of the UR-100, the UR-100K, which was accepted for service in December 1972.

Maturation of the Missile Industry

The late 1960s witnessed the most intense phase of the Cold War's nuclear arms race. One rough measure of this was the number of test launches from the proving ground at Baikonur, which totaled some eighty ICBM tests in 1966 alone.[96]

The failure of Korolyov's OKB-1 in the second-generation missile competitions led to its withdrawal from any further significant work on strategic missiles. This appears to have been Korolyov's intention, rather than the result of a state rebuke. The second-generation contests established the Yangel SKB-586 as the premier strategic-missile design center in the USSR. The Chelomey OKB-52 had a strained relationship with the new Brezhnev administration. Khrushchev's favoritism toward Chelomey in the early 1960s backfired, because many of the prominent military-industrial leaders in the Brezhnev administration had been marginalized in the late Khrushchev years. Chelomey's chief supporters in the early Brezhnev years were very important ones: S. A. Afanasyev, the head of the Ministry of General Machine Building, and Marshal Andrei Grechko, the defense minister. But his antagonists from the Khrushchev years continued to gain power. Among the most prominent of these was Dmitry Ustinov, who, upon becoming defense minister in 1976, would finally push Chelomey out of the ballistic-missile business.

The resurrection of the industrial ministries and their growing political power created a more complicated environment, in which decisions were not made solely by the military and party, but involved the industry in the debates as well. The 1970s were marked by a growing shift in the decision-making process for strategic weapons. The autocratic micromanagement of defense decision making, so characteristic of the Stalin and Khrushchev years, largely disappeared. Consensus of the major power centers was the Brezhnev style. The Communist Party continued to set broad goals. This was especially the case with arms-control policy, which came to play an increasingly contentious role in strategic-arms decision making. The Brezhnev administration gradually surrendered technological decision making to the industrial ministries and the military, which debated between themselves over weapons requirements. A provocative study suggests that the ministries were able to push the party apparatus out of a broad range of decision making, not limited to the military.[97] Indeed, there is evidence that the industry was able to use its growing power to occasionally overrule the military on some weapons decisions. Chelomey's continued survival as a general designer of ICBMs, in spite of his antagonistic relationship with some of the military branches and design bureaus, is a vivid case of the growing complexity of the Soviet defense establishment.

Defense-industrial practices continued to evolve, further reinforcing ministerial influence. The practice of presenting awards to design bureaus and industrial plants at the conclusion of a successful new weapons development program became a much more formal and important event. In the Stalin years, these honors were symbolic, and the material prizes offered were usually confined to a handful of the most senior engineers and directors. But by the late Brezhnev years, these award documents could approach the size of a book. They remained an important incentive to senior engineers and management since under the equalitarian Soviet salary scheme, they were one of the few ways to reward distinguished individuals. But in contrast to earlier periods, they also included significant benefits for the rank and file of the design bureaus and plants. The awards often included authorization to construct new housing for the bureaus and plants, and lack of adequate housing remained one of the most serious shortcomings of the entire Soviet period. This further enhanced the power of the industries over the Communist Party, since this housing was under plant or ministerial control. The industry, not the party, gradually came to control many of the day-to-day aspects of the lives of Soviet citizens in the aerospace industry, from food supply, to housing, to employment.

The entrenchment of this awards process in Soviet industrial culture also merged with other factors to reinforce the tendency to develop a new generation of weapons roughly every decade. The design bureau sought to produce a new design to keep its work force occupied and earn new awards. The plants sought a new design, since within a decade, it had completed construction of the previous generation of missiles. Soviet industrial culture in the Brezhnev years did not favor competitive weapons development, because the plant forced unwanted hard choices on the ministry. The clearest case of this was the upcoming SS-17/SS-19 controversy, one of the few attempts at competitive weapons design during the Brezhnev era. As a result of these factors, the Soviet military was saddled with far more missile designs than the U.S. armed forces during the same period, even though both countries enjoyed similar levels of technological innovation.

5.   Beyond Parity

1973–1985

With a rough parity in strategic nuclear forces reached by the early 1970s, Soviet military leaders prolonged the strategic-arms race through the 1970s by expanding their definition of strategic equivalence. "Deep parity" with the United States required that the Soviet Union not only match America's intercontinental capabilities, but block its advantages in projecting military power around the Soviet frontier. The growing assertiveness of the military leadership came in conflict with Brezhnev's foreign policy of détente, leading to a decade of tumultuous debate over Soviet defense policy. The excessive demands of the military continued to place great strain on the stagnating Soviet economy, laying the seeds for the crises of the 1980s. The leadership cohort, who had proven themselves as innovative and resourceful leaders in the Great Patriotic War, became old, tired, and complacent. Brezhnev's stroke in 1976 led to years of political and economic stagnation. After a decade of growth in the 1960s, the excessively militarized economy was beginning to shudder. Instead of pursuing reform, the Brezhnev generation tried to squeeze out even more military power from a faltering economy.[1] By the end of the decade, as the generation began to pass away, reform would become nearly impossible.

The Little Civil War

The Soviet weapons programs of the late 1960s aimed at reaching a rough numerical equivalence to American strength in strategic missiles. But at its core, the Soviet conception of nuclear parity with the United States differed from the American view. While the United States focused on intercontinental weapons capable of reaching American soil, the Soviets took a broader view due to their vulnerability to nuclear strikes conducted by American or allied forces based near the USSR. The availability of European air bases for American strike aircraft, the U.S. Navy's nuclear-armed carriers, and the British and French nuclear forces were all viewed as a part of the United States' strategic capability. This shaped the Soviet perception of the size of the forces needed to obtain deep parity with the United States. Also, the late 1960s saw a severe deterioration in relations with China, which forced Soviet planners to devote some of their strategic assets against China.

While these views were broadly accepted by the Soviet elite, there was no such consensus when it came to the critical details of defense policy. The strategic culture of the Soviet armed forces favored acquiring the capability for a preemptive strike against all possible opponents. Nevertheless, preemption was not endorsed by the national political leadership. This clash in views would be at the center of the debate over the third generation of strategic missiles.

Strategic superiority seemed far more obtainable to the Kremlin in the early 1970s than at any time since the beginning of the Cold War. The Vietnam War had a detrimental impact on U.S. strategic-weapons programs, draining them of funding during the war itself and leading to a strong antimilitary sentiment in the wake of the war, which led to declines in spending. Furthermore, the Vietnam War led to serious soul searching by the American political establishment, which raised serious questions about the morality of nuclear forces. This change was most noticeable in the Democratic Party, which lost its enthusiasm for strategic-force modernization, compared to what had been advocated in the Kennedy years. This diluted efforts to modernize the nuclear force and was a major incentive in the American interest in strategic-arms controls.

There was no such crisis of confidence in the Soviet Union. On the contrary, the "correlation of forces" seemed to be moving in the Soviet Union's favor. The size of the nuclear arsenal grew at a faster pace than in any other decade, increasing threefold from 1970 to 1980. The heavy investment in the industries supporting the strategic-missile forces created institutional pressures to continue the development and production of new generations of strategic weapons.

The decision to proceed with the third generation of ICBMs was made in 1969–70 with the issuance of a set of decrees authorizing the beginning of engineering development. This sparked one of the most heated debates to have occurred during the entire postwar period about the relationship between military doctrine and technological innovation in strategic weapons. It was dubbed the Little Civil War by the participants.[2]

By the late 1960s the style of Soviet defense decision making had changed from the authoritarian model that had been followed by Stalin and Khrushchev.

Brezhnev showed little interest in making key weapons decisions and instead sought consensus among the major state institutions. There were four major centers of power in decisions over strategic weapons. The party was represented by Dmitry Ustinov, the secretary of the Central Committee for Defense Affairs. Ustinov had been involved in the strategic programs since World War II and was the single most influential individual in these decisions during the Brezhnev years. The military was represented by the minister of defense, Andrei Grechko, and the chief of the General Staff. The missile industry was represented by the minister of general machine building, Sergei A. Afanasyev. Finally, the Military Industrial Committee (VPK) served as the surrogate for a number of state organizations, since its role was to coordinate weapons programs with the other industrial ministries, state economic planning organizations, and a host of other institutions.

A study to address the innovations needed in the third generation of ICBMs was undertaken jointly by Yangel's design bureau and the industry's main think tank, TsNII-Mash.[3] State policy in the late 1960s stated that the Soviet Union would not be the first to use nuclear weapons. While this was the official declaratory position, there was little unanimity about actual nuclear war–fighting tactics. Much of the leadership of the Soviet Army was inclined to consider the use of the missile force in a preemptive first strike, a lingering effect of the lack of survivability of the Soviet missile force since the late 1950s. The TsNII-Mash study dismissed the notion of a preemptive strike as being contrary to state policy and ultimately futile against an opponent such as the United States, which had its forces widely dispersed in silos, submarines, and bombers. As modeling of nuclear war became more possible, the uncertainties of little-understood physical phenomena related to nuclear explosions introduced complexities into the calculations that raised serious questions about the existing war plans. The study concluded that a preemptive strike was unlikely to be successful and would result in the destruction of both sides. Launch-on-warning was ruled out, because the Soviet early-warning network was not yet reliable enough, nor were its warnings prompt enough to launch the Soviet missile force before the first wave of American missiles impacted. The study found that the only durable doctrine was launch-on-attack. The RVSN would have to be able to survive an American first strike and retain enough force to ensure an unacceptable level of damage to the United States. They labeled this policy the Doctrine of Restraint.

The technical basis of this conclusion was both offensively and defensively driven. The study anticipated further American advances in accuracy, which would necessitate further silo hardening to survive a first strike. Ultimately, the land-based force would have to be made mobile. At the same time, improved missile readiness would eventually ensure force survivability in conjunction with new programs to improve early warning. Finally, automation of the command-and-control system would shorten the time needed to launch the retaliatory strike, so that a portion of the force might be launched before the impact of the first wave of an American preemptive strike.

From the offensive side, the advent of integrated circuits and new digital computers promised much more precise guidance systems, which could possibly provide counterforce capability for the first time, that is, the ability to target U.S. missile silos. Advances in the new integrated circuits permitted the development of guidance systems that were no longer hardwired against a single target, but could be more easily reprogrammed for other targets, thereby increasing force flexibility. This was an important consideration during this period due to the rise of the Chinese threat. Finally, improvements in electronics miniaturization also made possible the first generation of true MIRVs.

This study was met with little enthusiasm by the military. The RVSN was in the midst of one of the largest construction projects in Soviet history, and the study proposed yet another round of silo construction before the first was even finished. Likewise, the regimental launch commanders were only starting to become familiar with the new generation of ICBM launch complexes, and the industry was already starting to talk about replacing them with an entirely new generation of fundamentally different systems. The RVSN had been involved in two generations of missiles in less than a decade, and a third seemed too much of an imposition, even if it would not be ready until the mid-1970s. The complexity of the new ICBMs was far beyond that of any weapon ever deployed in the Soviet armed forces, and they were being deployed at rates far faster than more conventional weapons. This imposed a tremendous burden on the RVSN officers, who were barely managing to keep the conscript force adequately prepared to handle the existing systems. By way of comparison, Soviet tanks had shared the same engine design for over thirty years and the same transmission design for nearly twenty years. Strategic-missile systems were infinitely more complex, had very little commonality between generations, and were being replaced hardly a decade after their initial deployment. The Soviet dependence on short-duration conscripts, combined with the complexity of the new weapons, ensured a low level of readiness.[4] The day-to-day difficulties of running the new missile force was the major preoccupation of the leadership of the armed forces at this time. Conservative resistance by the military to technological innovation was not a new phenomenon, but this is seldom appreciated.[5]

In early 1968 opposition to the plan began to coalesce around Yangel's rival, Vladimir Chelomey. After Brezhnev's rise to power, Chelomey had been marginalized by many senior industrial and political leaders due to his position as the favored general designer in the Khrushchev years. Chelomey was astute enough to realize that he needed to curry favor with some element of the power structure for his bureau to survive the transition to the new Brezhnev regime. He was out of favor with the political leadership due to Ustinov's influence with Brezhnev, and the new ministries were not well enough established to ensure adequate political support. Chelomey was forced to turn to the military. In the late Khrushchev years, he had been despised by many military leaders, who viewed his profusion of fanciful schemes with contempt. Instead of proposing bold new visions, Chelomey completely shifted positions and became an ardent advocate of the conservative schemes favored by the military. In particular, he became closely attuned to the interests of the new defense minister, Andrei Grechko.

Chelomey began by suggesting that all that was needed was a modest upgrade to the widely deployed UR-100 light ICBM, his improved UR-100K. This added ABM decoys and modernized warhead options, and the UR-100K would be based in the existing silos. The proposal did little to address the broad issues raised by the TsNII-Mash study, so Chelomey began questioning the need to further harden the silos, a controversial point that especially angered the military. The military favored a launch-on-warning doctrine, which avoided the need to strengthen the silos, since in theory, at least, the missiles would be launched before the impact of American missiles. To add a patina of modernity to his scheme, Chelomey proposed that the silos be protected by a regional ABM network, which of course would be developed by his bureau. He was able to point to the U.S. deployment of the Sprint/Spartan ABM system to defend U.S. silos in the Dakotas as a rationale for such a system. Chelomey also claimed that a regional ABM network would be more cost effective than another round of silo construction. There were strong hints that the ABM network did not have to be too leakproof, since many military leaders leaned toward a preemptive strike against the United States in the event of a crisis, regardless of the Kremlin's official "no-first-use" doctrine. Chelomey also scorned the proposal to incorporate digital computers on the new missiles to improve accuracy, a view shared by more conservative elements in the military and industry about the dependability of this new technology. The need for MIRV warheads was also questioned, because some military leaders did not like the idea of replacing one very powerful warhead with three smaller warheads that did not equal the single warhead in total destructive yield or accuracy. Finally, Chelomey acted as the military's vanguard in attacking Ustinov's prized innovation, mobile, solid-fuel ICBMs. The military was skeptical of the mobile ICBMs due to the cost and complexity of the systems. Chelomey was able to challenge the concept on the basis of the vulnerabilities of the solid-fuel technology. This argument resonated in the Ministry of General Machine Building, which also opposed solid-fuel missiles as technologically risky.

Chelomey's position was welcomed by Grechko, a crusty commander of the old school who was particularly contemptuous of the civilian analysts and their irritating views. Grechko's position was soon echoed by the industrial minister in charge of the missile program, Afanasyev, who felt it prudent to support the views of his chief customer. The main supporters of the TsNII-Mash Doctrine of Restraint were Dmitry Ustinov, the secretary of the Central Committee for Defense Affairs; and Leonid V. Smirnov, former director of the Yuzhmash ICBM plant, then head of the military-industrial commission (VPK), and a longtime ally of both Yangel and Ustinov. As a result, the four main power centers in defense decision making were evenly split in the debate, creating a stalemate.

The debate continued through the summer of 1968, when TsNII-Mash tried to pin down the senior party and military leadership on their interpretation of Soviet strategic doctrine and its implications for the weapons program. A draft document attempting to establish the Doctrine of Restraint as the accepted interpretation of Soviet policy was prepared by the head of TsNII-Mash, Gen. Lt. Yury A. Mozzhorin, and approved by Gen. Lt. Anatoly Sokolov.[6] Sokolov was later forced to resign for siding with TsNII-Mash in the controversy. The draft document was submitted to Leonid Brezhnev in March 1969, who expressed his general support of the position to Ustinov. However, Brezhnev's opinions often changed depending upon who had his ear last, and the debate continued. To avoid having to make the decision himself, Brezhnev agreed that a special commission of distinguished experts would be set up, headed by the mathematician Mstislav Keldysh, who had been heavily involved in the early missile and space programs.

By the time the Keldysh commission had convened in the summer of 1969, the proposals for the next generation of ICBMs had become more refined. The Yangel design bureau was offering a new missile, the MR-UR-100 (SS-17), which could be placed within the existing UR-100 silos. The Chelomey design bureau was offering a two-phase upgrade: the modestly modernized UR-100K (SS-11 Mod 2), and an entirely new missile with a MIRV warhead capable of being launched from the UR-100 silo, deceptively labeled the UR-100N (SS-19). Chelomey advertised the new UR-100N missile as providing the capabilities of a heavy ICBM in the size of a light ICBM.

The Keldysh commission quickly devolved into two contrary factions and wasn't even able to release a report that all could agree upon. As a result, in July 1969 the major contenders were called to a special meeting of the Defense Council, held at Stalin's former resort in the Crimea and chaired by Brezhnev. Faced with an acrimonious deadlock, Brezhnev simply approved a little of everything. Chelomey was allowed to proceed with both the UR-100K and UR-100N, and Yangel was authorized to build the MR-UR-100 and an upgraded version of the R-36 heavy ICBM, the R-36M (SS-18). Ustinov was placated by approval for his quest for the Holy Grail, a mobile solid-fuel ICBM. The decision was typical of the management style of the Brezhnev years, when lavish funding of defense programs was typical, and central control was relaxed in favor of concessions to the industrial ministries. Indeed, Soviet planners coined a phrase to cover this tendency — *vedomstvennost* — a practice of the industry favoring its own interests against those of its ostensible customers, the military. The loser in this debate was the RVSN, which would find itself saddled with three entirely different missile systems for the same light ICBM role, with entirely different infrastructure, training requirements, and maintenance demands. Furthermore, new categories of mobile ICBMs were to be added to the existing categories of silo-based ICBMs, against the opposition of the military.

Arms Control

The Little Civil War raged alongside an equally contentious national security debate, the first serious attempt at arms control by the USSR and United States.[7] The notion of imposing some limits on the strategic nuclear arms race had emerged in the late 1950s. Soviet scientists working on the thermonuclear bomb had been among the first to question the unbridled expansion of weapons of such destructive power. Khrushchev had made a unilateral effort at a ban on nuclear weapons tests in 1959 but was pressured into ending the ban both by his own military advisers and the lack of reciprocal actions by the United States, France, and Britain. Arms control was impossible in the late 1950s, given the mutual suspicions of both the United States and Soviet Union over each other's intentions.

The first tentative steps toward superpower negotiations were taken during the final years of the Eisenhower administration, but these came to nothing in the wake of the shootdown of a U-2 reconnaissance aircraft in May 1960 before a planned Paris peace summit, and yet another crisis over Berlin. The sobering effect of the Cuban Missile Crisis convinced Khrushchev that more serious attention had to be paid to superpower relations, and the Partial Test Ban Treaty, eliminating atmospheric nuclear tests, was one sign of his program of "peaceful coexistence." The possibility for further strategic arms limitation agreements was enhanced by the growing capabilities of reconnaissance satellites like the American Corona and Soviet Zenit systems. These removed the high levels of uncertainties that plagued defense decision making in the late 1950s and early 1960s and which triggered the nuclear arms race of the 1960s.

Although the Soviet Union and the United States had begun to discuss strategic-arms limitations in the Kennedy administration, no serious discussion to control the delivery systems took place until January 1969, when Brezhnev accepted overtures from the new Nixon administration to begin talks.[8] The Strategic Arms Limitation Talks (SALT) began in Helsinki in November 1969. The delay in starting such discussions was due in no small measure to the resistance to arms control among the Soviet military while the USSR was still in a position of marked inferiority to the

United States. Until the late 1960s, the Soviet Union did not have a credible deterrent force. By the late 1960s the serious strategic instability that had existed in superpower relations was beginning to abate with the deployment of the second generation of strategic missiles. Foreign policy disagreements such as the Vietnam War and the Soviet invasion of Czechoslovakia in 1968 were further impediments to arms control. By the end of the decade, as the RVSN began to approach and reach parity with the United States, the prospects for arms control improved. Defense Minister Grechko remained very wary of arms control, which he regarded as an American plot. Grechko could not openly oppose the Brezhnev administration's efforts to reach détente with the United States, but he engaged in a behind-the-scenes guerrilla campaign against the SALT I treaty that helped to stall the process.[9] The SALT I discussion began nearly seven years after the start of development of the Soviet second-generation ICBMs and would not conclude until the development of the third generation of ICBMs was well under way.

The Kremlin's goals in this process were to end the uncertainty in the strategic-arms race, to rationalize and stabilize the strategic balance, and to secure the advantages that the Soviet Union had acquired in certain areas.[10] Brezhnev and senior party leadership looked more favorably on arms control in the late 1960s as a way to dampen down superpower hostilities that lay at the heart of both the nuclear and conventional arms race, a belated echo of Khrushchev's concerns from a decade earlier. The cost of this arms race was staggering, especially for the smaller and weaker Soviet economy. Although Brezhnev had acceded to the demands of the military to permit a simultaneous modernization of strategic and conventional forces in the mid-1960s, by the end of the decade, the cost of this decision was becoming more apparent. Many weapons designers look back on the late 1960s and early 1970s as the "golden age" of Soviet weapons design, when the Kremlin splurged on the most elaborate conventional-arms programs of the Cold War years.[11] The cost of these programs only became manifest when they reached the production stage in the early 1970s, and the huge expense forced some reconsideration by the Kremlin.

There was also some recognition that the nuclear arms race was getting dangerously out of control. The sheer size of the second generation of ICBMs, amplified by the new MIRV warheads, was leading to a force with thousands of nuclear warheads. By the mid-1960s, the Soviet defense think tanks began to use computer modeling and other analytic tools to study the effects of superpower nuclear war. The Soviet studies came a few years after the heyday of think tanks and McNamara's "whiz kids" in the United States. The investigations concluded that nuclear war between the superpowers would lead to catastrophic results for both sides. U.S. studies had concluded that in an all-out exchange in 1967, casualties would amount to 120 million dead in both countries; presumably the Soviet estimates were similar.[12] The Soviet studies ran against the conventional wisdom of the party and military. Conditioned by its ideology and the apparent shift of the correlation of forces in favor of the Soviet Union, the political leadership was inclined to believe that nuclear war would lead to the collapse of capitalism and the global victory of communism. There was the notion that Soviet society could survive a nuclear holocaust by the implementation of a massive civil defense effort. Nevertheless, the new studies planted the seeds of doubt in some leaders, even if the conclusions ran contrary to the accepted ideology. They helped create an atmosphere more conducive to arms control, even if their conclusions were not fully accepted. Another difference between the Soviet Union and the United States in the 1960s was the lack of a strong arms-control constituency within the Soviet foreign ministry, owing in no small measure to the success of the Soviet military in monopolizing information on the strategic balance.[13]

The military leadership was more resistant to the implications of the nuclear war studies. The commanders of the Soviet Army during this period were mostly older officers who had received command in the wake of the Purges of 1937–38, earned their rank in the war years, and reached senior command in the early decades of the Cold War. On the whole, they were poorly educated and provincial in outlook. Given the paranoid culture of the Soviet security system, few had experience of the world beyond the communist frontiers except for their wartime service. Their day-to-day experience was consumed by the Herculean task of melding the baffling new missile weapons into a force structure manned by poorly educated and poorly motivated conscripts. They had tasted war firsthand and were contemptuous of the civilian analysts, whose language and analytical style was alien to the traditional discourse of military tactics and doctrine. Those few who did stare into the nuclear abyss rationalized the genocidal potential of the new weapons with the Tolstoyan view that war should be made so horrific that it would not be started. The military solution to the dilemmas posed by the studies was to gradually purge the institutes of their senior civilian heads, replacing them with army commanders.[14]

Of the major institutional players in the arms-control debate, the political and industrial leadership was generally in favor, while the military remained the most vociferous opponent. The SALT I treaty was supported by the top party leadership, including General Secretary Leonid Brezhnev, Foreign Minister Andrei Gromyko, and the Central Committee secretary for defense, Dmitry Ustinov. It was opposed by Defense Minister Marshal Grechko and the chief of the General Staff, Gen. Viktor Kulikov, who viewed the whole process as an elaborate deception by the United States to win unilateral advantages.[15] Grechko's hard-line views were behind the Soviet refusal to release any actual numbers on the size and composition of the Soviet strategic forces, even though it was evident that the United States had reasonably accurate information from reconnaissance satellites.

The central aim of the SALT I agreement was to halt the arms race of the 1960s by freezing the number of delivery systems on both sides. This was difficult because the composition of the forces differed. The United States relied more heavily on aircraft and submarines, and the Soviets on land-based ICBMs. Several concessions had to be won from the United States before the Soviet military would accept the agreement. Due to U.S. advantages in submarine-launched ballistic missiles, the Soviets insisted on pushing out their limits on SLBM launchers by 210, trading the retirement of older R-9 and R-16 soft sites for additional SLBMs. The Soviet Navy opposed any limits on SLBMs and ballistic-missile submarines, but the U.S. concession giving the Soviet Union an advantage on the upper limit of submarines (sixty-two versus forty-four) helped win the support of navy commander Adm. Sergei F. Gorshkov. The main sticking point on land-based ICBMs was the issue of heavy versus light categories. Grechko adamantly refused such categorization, because it could be interpreted as placing the new SS-17 and SS-19 systems, still in development, into the heavy category, even though they were intended to replace the older "light" SS-11. In the end, the U.S. side made a unilateral declaration on the matter, which they hoped the Soviets would follow, while the Soviets felt that they were free to replace the SS-11 with new missiles. These ambiguities would cause problems in later years.

The Soviet position at the outset of the SALT I negotiations was that an overall agreement should include not only U.S. strategic forces based in the United States, but also forward-based U.S. systems that could strike the USSR, and British and French strategic forces. This notion that the strategic correlation of forces must compare the Soviet Union to the sum of its potential adversaries was a cornerstone of the Soviet "equal security" policy, the public name for the military's deep parity ideas. This viewpoint was strongly resisted by the United States, which regarded the forward-based systems as counterweights to Soviet conventional, not strategic, forces. The Soviet military, including Minister of Defense Grechko and the chief of the General Staff, remained adamant on this point.

Strong disagreements over many key issues within the Soviet government forced Brezhnev in May 1971 to appoint a special Politburo commission headed by his ally, Ustinov, in an attempt to break the impasse. The commission recommended significant changes to the Soviet negotiating position and considered acceding to the U.S. position that forward-based U.S. systems as well as British and French systems would not be considered under the SALT I talks. However, Soviet negotiators continued to insist on including U.S. forward-based systems and European strategic systems. During discussions leading up to the 1974 Vladivostok accord, Brezhnev finally removed the forward-based systems precondition. The Soviet concept of equal security would remain a contentious issue in later arms-control negotiations and sow the seed for the Euromissile controversy a decade later.

The second element of the SALT I negotiations was the attempt to limit anti-ballistic-missile systems. The Soviets did not initially share the American viewpoint of the destabilizing nature of ABMs, as exemplified by Premier Kosygin's outburst at the Glassboro summit: "Defense is moral, aggression is immoral!"[16] The United States argued that ABM systems were destabilizing even if not totally effective in repulsing a full-scale attack. In the event that one side launched a preemptive strike on the other, a limited ABM network would be capable of defeating the surviving strategic missiles of the victim, making a preemptive first strike more attractive. Whether or not the Soviet leadership agreed with the U.S. position, problems in developing a viable ABM system made them more inclined to accept ABM limits. The A-35 system had gone into operation around Moscow much behind schedule, and its capabilities were extremely limited even in the opinion of its designers. Studies of future requirements such as the Saturn project concluded that MIRVs and decoys would seriously undermine the viability of future ABM systems. Neither side was entirely willing to abandon research on ABM systems, and the military in both countries were pushing for some limited ABM capabilities, at a minimum to deal with the Chinese threat. As a result, rather than banning ABM systems, the treaty was aimed at limiting the ABM systems below a threshold at which they might undermine the deterrent value of the other superpower. This eventually translated into a single site limited to 100 ABM missile launchers.

The two interim agreements were signed in May 1972. Although the signing of the SALT I agreement was not viewed with enthusiasm by the military leaders in the Soviet Union at the time, it was a testament to the success of the RVSN in reaching parity with the United States. Had the Soviet Union not been close to parity, it is doubtful that the Kremlin could have won the acquiescence of hard-liners like Defense Minister Grechko.

Developing the Third Generation

The third generation of ICBMs largely paralleled the second, and most of the effort was concentrated in the light and heavy ICBM programs. A classic paradigm of technological innovation is the S curve, the notion that early in the technology, near the bottom of the S, progress is very slow. This is followed by a rapid rise in the rate of innovation as the technology becomes better understood and more widely employed, and finally, at the top of the S, when the mature technology plateaus, it slows down again.[17] The Soviet ICBM program is a good example of this pattern. By the third generation of ICBMs, liquid-fueled systems were becoming mature, and the extent of technological innovation was becoming less pronounced. The one technology that remained the most controversial and difficult was the mobile solid-fuel missile, which would not prove practical for another generation.

The deployment of the third generation of ICBMs also included significant improvements in the infrastructure of the missile force. This included a new level of hardening of the silos, improvements in storability of liquid rocket fuel, new command-and-control features, and greater automation of the launch sites. The plan was for an increase in silo hardness from the existing level of $14-20$ kg/cm^2 (200–285 psi) to 30 kg/cm^2 (425 psi). In fact, the program was more successful than original plans, leading to a silo hardness of $80-100$ kg/cm^2 (1,140–1,470 psi).[18] The second-generation missiles could remain fueled for about three years before the oxidant corroded the fittings and required the missile to be sent back to the factory for rebuilding. The third-generation missiles had fuel tank improvements that raised this at first to five years, then to seven years. The seven-year level was an important milestone, since this was the warranted life of the missile, that is, the point at which other components of the missile had a high probability of failure as well. Automation of the silos helped reduce the manpower demands of the missile regiments. Due to the large number of missile silos entering service, the RVSN experienced a 60-percent increase in personnel in the early Brezhnev years, the largest increase in any branch of the Soviet armed forces.[19]

The RVSN's order-of-battle remained steady through the Brezhnev years, averaging thirty-six missile divisions, split between thirteen to fourteen intermediate-range divisions and twenty-two to twenty-three ICBM divisions. The last major organization change of the Cold War years took place in April 1970, when three of the separate missile corps headquarters were converted into missile armies to better handle the administrative tasks of the burgeoning force.[20] This brought the total of higher headquarters to five missile armies.

The light ICBM effort to modernize the UR-100 remained contentious if only from lingering animosities and rivalry from the Little Civil War. The Yangel design bureau was authorized to begin work on their MR-UR-100 (SS-17) in September 1970.[21] This was a conventional liquid-fuel missile designed to fit within the confines of the existing UR-100 silos. It introduced many small innovations in ICBM design, including so-called mortar launch. With this method, the missile was ejected out of the silo using a gas generator at the bottom of the launcher, and the engines ignited once free of the silo. The advantage of this "cold-launch" system over a normal "hot-launch" system is that it allowed the engineers to make better use of the entire volume of the silo, including the space that ordinarily would be used to duct the hot exhaust gas of the missile during launch. This was

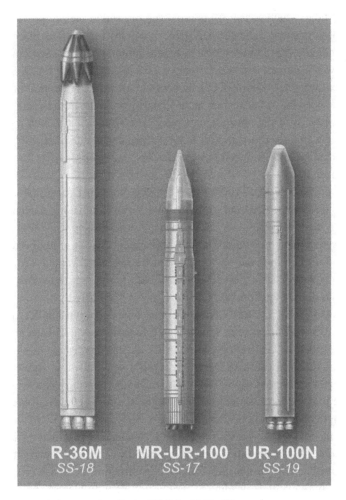

The third-generation Soviet ICBMs, 1968–75.

critical in the MR-UR-100 program for two reasons. To begin with, the missile, not really a light ICBM, was substantially larger and heavier to permit it to carry a big MIRV warhead. It was about half again as heavy as the UR-100, with a payload three times the weight, and correspondingly greater volume. In addition, the silo hardening was not primarily concerned about making the concrete silo structure hard, but rather in reducing the vulnerability of the silo to blast. Although some reinforcement of the concrete structure was undertaken, most of the effort was devoted to shock-mounting the missile's launch canister within the silo structure so that it would not be disabled by shock from nearby nuclear explosions. The shock-mounting of the launch container required the use of hydraulic buffers along the launch tube, which consumed internal volume within the silo previously used to vent hot exhaust gas. The MR-UR-100's initial test launch took place only two years after engineering development had been authorized, on 15 September 1972. This test was a failure, and the first successful test took place on 26 December 1972. There were only fourteen test launches by the time the program concluded on 17 December 1974, a testament to the maturity of Soviet liquid-fuel missile design. The new hardened silos weren't ready yet, so the first launch regiment at Bologoye became operational on 6 May 1975 in unhardened OS silos. The first regiment deployed in hardened OS-84 silos became operational at Bologoye on 11 November 1976.

The rival Chelomey UR-100N (SS-19) had a more checkered history. Unlike the Yangel design, the Chelomey missile used a conventional hot launch from the silo, which made silo hardening more difficult. The missile itself was an evolutionary improvement over the earlier UR-100, except that it was almost double the weight with three times the payload. Initial testing started about seven months later than the Yangel design, on 9 April 1973. The test program was also more protracted, with double the number of test flights—some thirty by the time the trials ended in 1975. The first UR-100N regiment became operational at Pervomaisk on 26 April 1975, and the system was accepted for service on 30 December 1975. The first regiment to become operational with the new hardened OS-84 silos was deployed at Tatishchevo on 18 December 1976. Eventually, four former UR-100 divisions were converted to the UR-100N, including Pervomaisk and Khmelnitsky in Ukraine and Kozelsk and Tatishchevo in Russia. The inventory reached its peak strength of 360 silo launchers in 1984.

During the test series, the missile showed a tendency to oscillate prior to first-stage burnout. These complaints were brushed off by Chelomey. However, in 1979, during routine testing of missiles from deployed regiments, these problems became even more manifest, leading to serious accuracy problems. The RVSN was extremely disturbed by the poor demonstrated accuracy of the missiles and forced the design team to adopt some quick fixes, which were applied to missiles in the silos in 1980–82. Concern over this issue accounts for the relatively sudden withdrawal of all UR-100N's by 1983, well in advance of their guaranteed shelf life of ten years. Problems with the UR-100N sealed Chelomey's fate as a ballistic-missile designer, and he would later be pushed out of the business.

The development of a new heavy R-36M (SS-18) ICBM was not particularly controversial, and it was viewed as simply an evolutionary extension of the earlier R-36 (SS-9). Preliminary design studies for this missile had begun in 1966, and the engineering development program was approved on 2 September 1969. Four different payloads were contemplated, including two different monoblock (single) warheads, a new MIRV warhead, and a maneuverable reentry vehicle. The role of the new missile has not been extensively discussed in Russian accounts, but like the earlier R-36, it was viewed as a versatile system that could be used in a counterforce role when armed with an accurate single warhead, and a countervalue weapon against cities or nonhardened military targets such as air bases when armed with a MIRV warhead. American assessments have tended to focus on its counterforce role, even though Soviet heavy ICBMs were being deployed with both single-warhead and MIRV-warhead versions. Flight tests of the R-36M began in October 1972, and the first successful test occurred on 21 February 1973. The missile tests proceeded with few problems, and the first R-36M missile regiment became operational at Dombarovsky on 25 December 1974 using existing R-36 silos.

The initial version of the R-36M (SS-18 Mod 1) was armed with a single 24-megaton nuclear warhead. This was followed by development of the first heavy MIRV, armed with eight 600-kiloton warheads. The first test flight of the 15F143 MIRV warhead took place in August 1973, and the test flight program concluded in October 1975. By this time the new hardened OS-84 silos at Dombarovsky were finally ready, so the first regiment armed with the R-36M with the MIRV warhead was the first unit deployed with them, in November 1975.

The Quest for Mobility

The studies conducted in the late 1960s recognized the growing trend toward precision in missile guidance, which implied that U.S. missiles would become accurate enough to destroy any silo. If a warhead landed close enough to a silo, the structure would actually fall into the crater, no matter how hard the silo structure might be. This led to the term "crater lethal" when referring to highly accurate warheads.

The Soviet General Staff still preferred land-based strategic forces over naval strategic forces due to lingering anxieties over the Soviet missile-submarine force. This meant new approaches to increasing the survivability of the land-based missile force. The idea of mobile basing for missiles was not new, but efforts to date had been premature. The earliest Soviet missile brigade in 1948–49 had some of its missile launchers based on a train. In the early 1960s the Yangel design bureau had studied train-basing for the R-16 missile, partly in response to a similar effort by the U.S. Air Force with its Minuteman force. The Soviet Union had over 160,000 km (99,000 mi) of suitable rail lines, so in theory, at least, the missile train could traverse great distances, making it impossible to find. The R-16 rail-mobile effort was discarded quickly due to the problems of deploying a liquid-fueled missile on a mobile platform. The vibration from the train was liable to crack open seams and joints, leaking the volatile fuel and oxidizer and leading to a serious accident.

This was followed by a number of efforts to develop ICBMs based on tracked vehicles, including the ill-fated Gnom and RT-20 (SS-15). The tracked programs proved difficult, since they placed a limit of about forty tons on the missile — near the limits of what was possible with Soviet missile technology of the time. Furthermore, the tracked vehicles induced vibrations in the missile launcher, leading to fears that the missile's cast engine or electronics could be damaged. This experience revived interest in rail-basing, since a larger missile could be accommodated. There was also some interest in the possibility of basing a mobile missile on a large truck, which might reduce the vibration problems. As a result, two programs were carried out in parallel, a rail-mobile system and a road-mobile system.

On 13 January 1969 the Ministry of General Machine Building issued the Yangel and Chelomey design bureaus an order for the design of a mobile military railway missile complex called a BZhRK.[22] The Yangel system employed the new solid-fueled RT-23 missile.[23] The Chelomey program did not progress very far before being rejected, in large measure because it depended on a liquid-fuel missile, which Ustinov opposed. The rail-mobile missile program proved extremely difficult and prolonged. The draft project at the Yangel design bureau, which normally would have taken only a few years, dragged out for over a decade and was not concluded until June 1980.[24] This was in part due to the technological challenge posed by solid-fuel technology, as well as by continued resistance to the mobile basing by Grechko and the military. Ustinov's strong advocacy of solid-fuel missiles led the Yangel bureau to establish a new plant at Pavlograd to specialize in the new technology rather than attempt to convert the existing plant at Dnepropetrovsk to the role.

The military's objections to the mobile basing were many. To begin with, such a system would invariably be more expensive and complicated to operate than a static, silo-based missile. The military was having more than enough problems with static basing and didn't want the added challenge of training the conscript force to employ a mobile system. In addition, the military's proclivity toward a launch-on-warning war-fighting doctrine undermined the rationale for a mobile missile, since survivability depended on launching before the impact of American missiles, not riding out an attack. Finally, mobile missiles raised considerable anxiety over command-and-control issues and nuclear custody. Once away from their base, the mobile missiles might have the same type of control problems as the navy's submarines. Furthermore, the deployment of mobile missiles would mean that large thermonuclear warheads would be wandering around the countryside, where they might be subject to accidents or hijacking. As a result, the rail-based missile program slid from the third generation until the fourth generation, not emerging until the late 1980s.

The road-mobile program started earlier than the rail-mobile effort, on 4 March 1966, at the new Moscow Institute of Thermotechnology (MIT).[25] In its early stages, the program was not a full-fledged engineering development effort but a proof-of-concept study to examine the suitability of road-mobile, solid-fuel missiles for both the IRBM and ICBM roles.[26] The program was undertaken by the Ministry of Defense Production (MOP), not the Ministry of General Industry (MOM), due to the continued resistance in MOM to solid-fuel programs.

Not only was it necessary for the new solid-fuel missiles to have a high degree of reliability, but it was also necessary to reduce their weight. At the time, the Soviet solid-fuel ICBMs such as the RT-2 (SS-13) weighed about fifty tons, and there were hopes that innovations in solid-fuel technology would reduce it to about thirty-five to forty tons. This was critical to the success of the mobile program, since anything larger would be unmanageable on the Soviet road network. To do this, it would be necessary for the Soviet chemical-propulsion industry to shift from clusters of small-diameter, solid-fuel engines to the production of more efficient, large-diameter engines using a new generation of solid fuel. The initial design studies examined different vehicle configurations, including various types of tracked chassis and articulated chassis. By 1968 the results of trials on earlier solid-fuel mobile missiles such as Yangel's troubled RT-20 (SS-15) were beginning to suggest the flaws of using a tank chassis.[27] The truck chassis was selected because it offered better road speeds, ease of maintenance, and fewer vibration problems. The new missile system, called the Temp-2S (SS-16), was approved for engineering development in November 1969, several months after the start of the rail-mobile program.[28] The Temp-2S was the first Soviet missile to use a large-diameter, cast, solid-fuel engine, nearly a decade after comparable American designs.

The first missile flight tests began on 14 March 1972 at Plesetsk, and there were thirty-five test flights of the Temp-2S through December 1974. The Soviet military insisted on an extremely rigorous camouflage program to prevent the discovery of the mobile-basing mode by U.S. intelligence, at first to enhance the survivability of the missile when deployed. During the SALT negotiations, the United States had firmly opposed deployment of land-mobile missiles, a position covered in an American unilateral statement, which added further incentive for camouflage. The CIA at the time reported that the SS-X-16 program "had been marked by an unprecedented concealment effort."[29] This effort was largely successful, and through the 1974 test, U.S. intelligence agencies were unable to conclusively determine whether the SS-X-16 was being tested with an associated mobile launcher. U.S. accounts of the program suggest that the Temp-2S had significant problems and was "a dog of a missile."[30] There were also problems with the new Uran launch truck. In spite of the difficulties, in 1971 the Votkinsk missile plant began a major expansion effort to begin manufacturing the Temp-2S.

The fate of the Temp-2S became embroiled in superpower negotiations. The United States had a negative view of land-mobile ICBMs due to the verification problem they posed. It was one thing to count static missile silos from space, but another thing to try to count truck-based missiles that could hide in the vast expanses of the Soviet Union. During the SALT I negotiations, the U.S. delegation sought to have them banned. In 1970 the chief Soviet SALT negotiator made clear that the Soviet Union viewed land-mobile ICBMs no differently from other mobile strategic systems such as missile submarines or missile-armed bombers. In May 1971 the Special Politburo Commission, headed by Ustinov, had concluded that the Soviet negotiation position up to that point had been too rigid.[31] The commission decided that ratifying SALT I served Soviet interests and that reconsideration of specific positions would be needed. During the Moscow summit in May 1972, General Secretary Brezhnev agreed to a ban on land-mobile ICBMs during the discussions leading to the so-called Interim Agreement. However, the Soviet government subsequently retracted Brezhnev's offer. It remains unclear what transpired in the Soviet government over this issue. There is some evidence to suggest that Brezhnev was willing to sacrifice land-mobile ICBMs to maintain the momentum of his détente policy with the United States. In his memoirs, President Richard Nixon concluded that Brezhnev had decided "to go all out for détente" at the meeting, and the concession may have been spontaneous and without discussions with other key Kremlin players. However, influential military industrial leaders, especially Dmitry Ustinov, resisted the concession, and Brezhnev reversed himself.

The U.S. position continued to harden in 1974 following the beginning of the flight trials of the mobile Pioner (SS-20) IRBM. As the tests continued, the close relation of the SS-16 ICBM and the SS-20 IRBM became increasingly evident to U.S. intelligence. The similarity of the missiles caused considerable anxiety in the United States over the risk of "breakout" from the new SALT II arms treaty, which was under negotiation. The SS-20 would not be limited under the treaty due to its shorter range. But the system was so close to the SS-16 missile and launcher that it could be rapidly modified in time of crisis into an ICBM by simply adding the appropriate third-stage section.[32] These concerns were voiced to the Soviet negotiators in 1976. In March 1977 Foreign Minister Andrei Gromyko offered to cancel any Soviet plans to deploy the mobile version of the SS-16. The U.S. negotiators considered this a nonoffer, since it left open the possibility that the USSR could continue to manufacture the SS-16 third stage for a possible treaty breakout. In October 1977, during negotiations in Geneva, the head of the Soviet team,

Vladimir Semyonov, agreed that the USSR would not produce, test, or deploy the SS-16 or any component unique to it, namely, the third stage. This remained a part of the SALT II agreement once it was signed.

One of the lingering mysteries of the Temp-2S was whether or not it had ever been operationally deployed. In 1976 the CIA's National Intelligence Estimate concluded that SS-X-16 had been deferred.[33] U.S. analysts concluded that about 200 missiles had been constructed, leaving an inventory of 165 beyond those expended in the test flight program. For a time the CIA thought that some might have been deployed in RT-2 (SS-13) silos, because they had not spotted the mobile launchers in overhead satellite imagery.[34] According to recent Russian accounts, two Temp-2S regiments became operational at Plesetsk on 21 February 1976, prior to Soviet agreements to ban the system.[35] Russian accounts suggest that the mobile launchers were used, contrary to CIA assessments. The Plesetsk regiments were well aware of the U.S. spy satellites and kept the equipment in service hangers when they knew that satellites were passing overhead.[36] In the event, the Temp-2S was never deployed in large numbers—under fifty launchers. This was in part due to the SALT treaty, but also to lack of enthusiasm for mobile solid-fuel missiles in the armed forces.[37]

Reinvigorating the Submarine Force

Of all the Soviet commanders to come to power in the 1960s, by far the most dynamic was Adm. Sergei Gorshkov. He began as a skeptic of the missile submarine, but by the Brezhnev years had adopted this cause as his own. Gorshkov's most important impact on Soviet defense affairs was his reassertion of the navy's demand for a blue-water navy. This was a repudiation of Khrushchev's far more circumscribed view of the navy's role and led to a massive shipbuilding program in the 1960s and early 1970s, the "golden age" of Soviet ship construction. It began in the 1960s as a response to the American Polaris missile submarines, with a strong accent on the antisubmarine mission. By the 1970s the navy's mission had expanded into global power projection, with efforts under way to develop aircraft carriers, amphibious assault ships, and a full range of surface warships to challenge the primacy of the U.S. Navy at sea.

The Soviet missile-submarine program did not proceed in parallel to the ICBM program, though they often shared common trends in technological innovation. The major program of the early Brezhnev years, the Project 667A Navaga (Yankee) nuclear missile submarine, finished construction in 1972 with the completion of the thirty-fourth submarine of its class. The Navaga was a substantial advance over previous Soviet missile submarines. Nevertheless, it suffered from some substantial operational liabilities. The short range of its R-27 (SS-N-6) missile meant that it had to patrol close to American shores to put its weapon system in range of its targets. To transit from Soviet ports on the Kola Peninsula to their Atlantic patrol box, the submarines had to pass through the U.S. Navy's SOSUS (sound surveillance system) acoustic sensor barrier in the Greenland-Iceland gap and through the densest concentration of NATO antisubmarine forces. Likewise, the exits from Soviet Pacific bases through the sea of Okhotsk were ringed with sensors and U.S. Navy submarine patrols.

To make matters worse, Soviet submarine design in the late 1960s was a generation behind the most advanced American designs, especially in terms of acoustic signature, which was key to the submarine's ability to survive by avoiding detection. This difference was in part due to a traditional Soviet preference for double-hull submarine designs and twin propellers, both the result of a 1959 program to standardize submarine development. While the double hull contributed to protection against conventional attack, the outer hull was a natural resonator for the noises emitted from the machinery in the inner hull and amplified hydrodynamic noises.[38] Twin-propeller configurations, combined with mediocre machining standards, led to further sound problems. As a result the Navaga was a particularly noisy submarine, with sound levels significantly worse than typical World War II submarines.[39] The Soviet submarine commanders were aware of this problem, but their complaints resulted in little action.[40] U.S. attack submarines patrolling off the coast detected the initial deployment of the first Navaga submarines in 1969 and were able to regularly track them on their patrol runs.[41] At first, the navy leadership was reluctant to admit the vulnerability of their new submarines. Acceptance of the submarine's vulnerability was forced on them by the revelations of the Walker spy ring in the late 1960s and early 1970s.

The Soviet General Staff remained dismissive of the navy's role in the strategic nuclear balance, in part due to lingering command-and-control problems, but also due to recognition of the vulnerability of the submarines to NATO naval forces. Another significant operational problem was posed by the limited patrol pattern of the submarine force. At any one time, there were usually only two missile submarines operating in the Atlantic patrol box and two more in the Pacific. In the event of a surprise attack, this meant that a large portion of the force would be caught in port, where the short range of their missiles prevented them from responding. Their use in a preemptive strike against the United States was undermined by the regularity of the patrols, since it would become readily apparent that something was amiss if a large number of Soviet missile submarines suddenly made a sortie out of the Kola Peninsula toward the United States. The Navaga class averaged a little more than one combat patrol per submarine annually during its career.[42] The low sortie and patrol rate of the Soviet submarine force was due to a fundamentally different approach to training and exercises. The Soviet submarines were less durable than American submarines, and the conscript force required longer periods of elementary dockside training prior to long missions. There was no practice of "blue and gold" crews as in the U.S. Navy, where a second crew takes the boat back out to sea while the first crew recuperates from the sortie and conducts training in port.

For the navy to assume a more important role in the strategic program, the survivability of the submarines had to be improved. The most obvious way to do so was to increase the range of the submarine missiles so that the submarines did not have to patrol so deeply in the Atlantic and Pacific. In April 1963 Chelomey attempted to broaden his influence even further by offering to develop a navalized

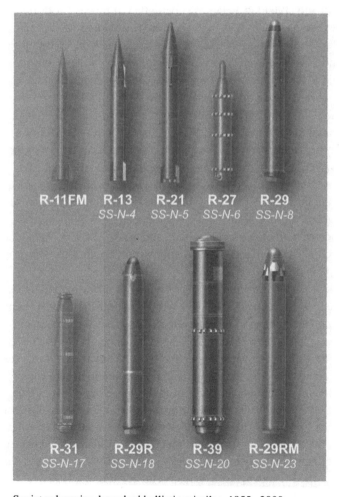

Soviet submarine-launched ballistic missiles, 1955–2000.

version of his UR-100 ICBM, called the UR-100M.[43] He argued that such a system could be launched from near Soviet coastal waters, where the submarine would not be at risk. He also proposed basing the UR-100M on ships camouflaged as Arctic coastal transports, providing a quick and cheap alternative to submarine basing.[44] The navy responded by authorizing the start of competitive designs of Chelomey's D-8 system and Makeyev's D-9 system on 3 July 1963. The preliminary design showed the serious flaws in Chelomey's concept. The submarine could carry only four missiles, compared to twelve for the Makeyev design, and it depended on shore-based radio correction for its guidance, which could be subjected to interference in wartime. In contrast, the Makeyev R-29 (SS-N-8) missile was the first to use an astro-correction guidance system, providing much superior accuracy. In July 1964 Chelomey was permitted to proceed with further design work on exotic applications for the UR-100M, including its concealed deployment in lakes, on islands, in remote mountains, and on transport ships. But authorization for actual engineering development of a new submarine missile was granted to the Makeyev design bureau on 28 September 1964 for its far more conventional D-9 system and its associated R-29 missile.

The R-29 was a two-stage design with an effective range of 8,000 km (5,000 mi), compared to only 2,500 km (1,500 mi) for the older R-27 (SS-N-6). In addition to its novel stellar navigation feature for improve accuracy, it was the first Soviet SLBM to use lightweight decoys to penetrate U.S. ABM defenses. The new D-9 launch system permitted salvo firing, in which the missiles were launched at seven-second intervals.[45] The innovations complicated the development, and the first test launch did not occur until 25 December 1971. Nineteen test launches were conducted with only a single failure, and the R-29 was accepted for service on 12 March 1973. The basic R-29 was followed by the R-29D, with an extended range of 9,000 km (5,600 mi), in 1977.

A number of submarine designs were studied for use with the D-9 system, including the diesel-powered Project 601 and the nuclear Project 701, based on the old Golf and Hotel classes. Ultimately, the D-9 system was incorporated into an evolved version of the Project 667A Navaga submarine, the Project 667B Murena (Delta I). The Murena was yet another effort by S. N. Kovalyov's team at the Rubin Central Design Bureau in Leningrad, the primary development center for Soviet nuclear ballistic-missile submarines. Due to the larger size of the missile, the missile compartments had to be raised aft the sail, and the number of missiles was reduced from sixteen to twelve. In spite of the smaller number of missiles on each submarine, the Soviet Navy concluded that the D-9 system offered two and a half times the effectiveness of the older D-6 system (SS-N-6). The lead submarine went to sea in 1972, and eighteen were constructed through 1977.

The navy was not entirely happy with the reduction in the number of missiles, so an extended-hull version, the Project 667BD Murena M (Delta II), was designed. This returned the number of missiles from twelve to sixteen. Four submarines of this class were deployed through 1977. Some improvements to submarine silencing were introduced, and in 1980 one of the submarines, K-182, was sent on a special mission through the U.S. Navy's Atlantic SOSUS barrier to determine the vulnerability of the class to detection.[46] The advent of the extended-range R-29D in 1977 allowed the Murena force to try new tactics to avoid the NATO antisubmarine forces. In 1979 the submarines began exploring the fringes of the Arctic ice pack. Operations under the ice were hazardous, but the peculiarities of the ocean conditions near the ice also helped mask the acoustic signature of the submarines. In 1981 a Murena commanded by Capt. Leonid Kuversky managed to find a gap in the ice and conduct a simulated missile launch. With evidence that Arctic launches were possible, further missions were conducted. In 1983 a Murena was ordered north and conducted the world's first launch of an SLBM from the vicinity of the North Pole. This tactic led to technical changes in future Soviet submarine designs to permit them to operate from the ice, such as reinforcement of the sail to allow the submarine to penetrate through thin ice.

There was some hope that the value of the older Navaga submarines could be redeemed by the substitution of a new, longer-range missile. Largely at the urging of Dmitry Ustinov, the design bureau at the Arsenal plant in St. Petersburg began its third attempt at a solid-fuel submarine missile, the D-11 system with the R-31 missile. The R-31 missile was intended to be a counterpart to the U.S. Navy's Poseidon missile, with a range of 5,000 km (3,100 mi) and a MIRV warhead.[47] The program turned out to be a flop. Test launches began in 1976, but the performance was inferior to that of the obsolete American Polaris A-3 missile, which had gone into service a decade earlier. The range of the R-31 was 3,900 km (2,400 mi), not enough to justify the conversion cost of the large Navaga fleet. As a result, no Navaga submarines were converted to the system beyond the single test bed deployed in 1980.

In light of the difficulties with the R-31 missile, the Soviet Navy continued to support the gradual evolution of the liquid-fueled R-29 missile family. The next effort, started in February 1973, was to develop a version of the R-29 with a MRV warhead, the R-29R (SS-N-18 Mod 1). This missile carried three nuclear warheads and was accepted for service in 1977. It was carried on yet another evolution of the Murena, the Project 667BDR Kalmar. The lead boat was commissioned in December 1976, and fourteen were deployed through 1981. The main shortcoming of the R-29R missile was that the range decreased from the 8,000 km (5,000 mi) of the R-29 to only 6,500 km (4,000 mi). As a short-term solution, a single-warhead version was developed as an alternative, the R-29RL (SS-N-18 Mod 2), with the range returning to 8,000 km. The final major evolution of the R-29 family was the R-29K (SS-N-18 mod 3) in 1979, which was the first Soviet SLBM with a true MIRV warhead. Although the range again decreased to

The guidance platform of an intercontinental ballistic missile is its brain. This 4A73 guidance platform was used on the D-9 and D-9R (SS-N-8) submarine missiles. It was the first Soviet naval missile system to use an integrated inertial guidance platform with stellar update features.

6,500 km, the new guidance system offered such an improvement in accuracy that this model became the standard version deployed.[48] The main drawback of the new submarines was the significant increase in cost compared to the earlier missile submarines, about R 35 million for the Navaga, but over R 150 million for the Kalmar.[49] This increase was due to the growing sophistication of the onboard electronics, including a much-superior shipboard inertial navigation system and enhanced communication systems, including satellite navigation and satellite communication systems.

The development of the R-29 missile family and the later models of the Project 667 submarine led to a shift in Soviet naval tactics in the late 1970s and early 1980s, called the "bastion strategy" in the West. Instead of facing NATO antisubmarine forces, the Soviet submarines began to conduct their patrols in waters closer to home, where they could be protected by Soviet attack submarines, surface warships, and naval patrol aircraft. Ideally, the Soviet Navy desired a missile that could be launched from near the submarine bases, leading to the most expensive and controversial Soviet submarine design of the Cold War, the Project 941 Akula and its associated Taifun weapon system.[50] Development of this massive submarine began in 1972, but the first submarine of its class did not emerge until 1980 (table 5.1).

Table 5.1

Soviet Ballistic Missile Submarine Order-of-Battle, 1980

Unit	Base	Type
Northern Fleet		
1st Submarine Flotilla	*Zapadnaya Litsa*	
11th Submarine Missile Cruiser Division	Gremicha	Delta I
18th Submarine Missile Cruiser Division	Nerpichye	Golf, Hotel (Typhoon)
31st Submarine Missile Cruiser Division	Yagelnaya	Hotel, Yankee
41st Submarine Missile Cruiser Division	Gremicha	Delta I
3rd Submarine Missile Cruiser Flotilla	*Gadziyevo, Olenya Bay*	
13th Submarine Missile Cruiser Division	Olenya Bay	Yankee, Delta II, Delta IV
19th Submarine Missile Cruiser Division	Skalisty	Yankee
32nd Submarine Missile Cruiser Division	Skalisty	Golf II, Hotel, Yankee, Delta I, II, III
Pacific Fleet		
4th Submarine Missile Cruiser Flotilla	*Rybachy*	
21st Submarine Missile Cruiser Division	Rybachy	Delta II
25th Submarine Missile Cruiser Division	Rybachy	Delta I
45th Submarine Missile Cruiser Division	Rybachy	Hotel II

Strategic Command-and-Control Improvements

One of the most important improvements accompanying the deployment of the third generation of ICBMs was the modernization of the strategic command-and-control network. This included the use of hardened launch centers, new space-based communications, the establishment of a more secure and centralized command system, and significant innovations in ballistic-missile early warning.

Accompanying the new generation of hardened OS-84 silos was a new type of launch-control center (LCC). Under the previous configuration, each regiment of ten silos was controlled by a single buried LCC. The location of the LCC was predictable, and in theory, at least, the entire regiment of ten launchers could be put out of action by destroying the LCC. Two steps were taken to avoid this: a semimobile LCC, and remote activation of the missile silos. The new LCC was configured like the missile transport-launch container emplaced in the silo.[51] Some of each regiment's silos were wired so that the LCC could be periodically moved between silos. Since this shift could be camouflaged as periodic maintenance of the silo, U.S. intelligence would never know which silo contained the LCC and which contained the normal missiles. To further address the problem, each silo was fitted with a small surface-mounted radio antenna. The silo could be activated remotely from divisional headquarters and the missiles launched without the intervention of the regimental launch-control center.

The vast distances separating Moscow from the scattered missile and submarine bases favored the development of a space-based communication system. The first communications satellite system, the 11F67 Molniya-1, was developed by Korolyov's design bureau starting in October 1960. This system was viewed as a test bed for a more refined space communications system, but it did provide some limited capability. Flights began in January 1964, and by 1965 there were enough satellites in orbit to establish regular radio contact between Moscow and the military headquarters in Vladivostok on the Pacific Ocean. Thirty-one Molniya-1 satellites were orbited through 1975, and the associated Korund and Ruchei radio systems were deployed at key strategic-missile and bomber bases starting in the late 1960s. The Molniya-1 was followed by the second-generation Unified Space-Communication System (ESSS) in the early 1970s. The Molniya-2 was an improved evolution of the Molniya-1, supplemented by the Raduga satellites in geosynchronous orbit. Test flights began in 1971, and the system became operational in 1974.

The advent of dependable radio communications via satellite enabled improvements to be made in the existing Strategic Missile Force command network. The Soviet General Staff favored a highly centralized command system, epitomized by the new Signal-M system, introduced in the mid-1970s with the hardened

OS-84 silos.[52] Under the original Signal system, launch commands were passed to individual regimental launch-control centers, which typically directed six to ten missile silos, depending on the missile type. As mentioned earlier, the new silo design, coupled with the Signal-M system, enabled the missile-division command post to remotely launch from all of its silos, with the divisions controlling six to eight regiments and as many as eighty silos. The Signal-M system also made it possible to conduct launching from missile army or even national command posts, though this does not appear to have been the standard practice. In 1976–78 the Signal-M system introduced a new feature to permit simultaneous status reporting between all levels of the RVSN, using landlines, radio, radio relay, and the new satellite communications links via the Vyuga communication network. The system was accepted for service in 1982 and later extended to include other elements of the strategic nuclear forces, including bomber and submarine bases.

The new satellite communications system was linked to the new Poetika long-range communication system for the bomber force.[53] Under the old system, the bomber crews were issued a set of packets containing a limited number of attack options. The new system provided more flexibility, since the instructions could be modified after the bombers took off on their mission. As a means of further control and to prevent the unauthorized use of nuclear weapons on Soviet soil, design efforts were begun to develop a negative control system integrated into the bomber's inertial navigation platform. Under this scheme, a nuclear bomb or cruise missile could not be armed unless the aircraft traveled a certain distance from base and in the appropriate direction.[54]

The new space-based systems were an important innovation for the submarine missile force as well. For the first time, it provided reliable communications while at sea. The first integrated space communications system was introduced on the Project 667B Murena (Delta) submarines in 1976.[55] The Parus system was an integrated system allowing communication back to the Soviet Union via the new network of Tsikada-M navigation satellites.[56] A reserve system was also developed, based on a pair of IL-22 radio-transponder aircraft under the code name Okean (Ocean).[57] A lingering problem with this system was that it required the submarine to trail an uplink antenna buoy on the surface, which could lead to detection of the submarine by antisubmarine forces. The problem of reliably communicating with submarines operating in deep water remained a vexing problem for the Soviet Navy throughout the Brezhnev years. Toward the end of the 1970s, the navy requested the aid of the Soviet Academy of Sciences to help solve this problem.[58] This led to studies of long-frequency radio for increasing the depth of penetration of the radio beams into the water. The problem with such radio systems was that the data transfer was extremely slow, and only very short alert messages could be passed. A special extremely low-frequency (ELF) station, code-named Zevs, was built on the Kola Peninsula near Severomorsk in the early 1980s, specifically designed to alert submarines to come near the surface for more detailed instructions. This required the use of the new Lastochka and Paravan towed antenna arrays, which trailed behind the submarine for several kilometers.

While the weapons control systems were being developed, a parallel effort was under way to ensure communication links among the political and military leaders and between the national command authority and the strategic nuclear forces. At the pinnacle of the network was the new Kazbek sanctioning system. Kazbek was a network of several systems, including the Cheget "nuclear briefcase," the Kavkaz communications transmission system, and the Baksan sanctioning receiver system.

The Cheget was a Soviet equivalent of the American "nuclear football."[59] Three of these were issued: to the national leader, the minister of defense, and the head of the General Staff.[60] The method used to coordinate the three suitcases in the authorization of nuclear strike has not been officially described.[61] It would appear that the national leader provided the first sanction, which was then verified by the minister of defense or chief of the General Staff (or both), presumably with some provisions if any of the members of the nuclear triumvirate are disabled. The Cheget was linked via the Kavkaz communications system. The Kavkaz was a series of redundant command links, including landlines, radio, radio relay, and satellite systems, used to ensure connection between the upper echelons of state officials to make the sanctioning decision. Once the decision was made, the Kavkaz served as the transmission network to pass the sanctioning instructions to lower levels of command.

The sanctioning commands arrived at RVSN and other strategic nuclear forces bases via the Baksan system. The Baksan was deployed at each General Staff command post and the central command posts of the Strategic Missile Force, air force, navy, and air defense command. In the case of the missile force, the commands were then passed down to the missile silos via the Signal-M system. The Kazbek and Kavkaz systems were developed in 1979–83 and fielded in 1985, roughly parallel to the Signal-M system. Although these systems represented a significant advance over previous systems, a 1997 CIA report suggested that the links to the silos were only slightly better than Russia's archaic and unreliable telephone system.[62]

To extend the decision time of the Supreme Leadership, key defense posts were placed in deep bunkers to make them survivable against the first wave of relatively inaccurate submarine-launched missiles. The General Staff concluded that an unanticipated "bolt from the blue" strike was unlikely, and that nuclear wars would occur only after extended periods of international crisis, providing time to evacuate the Supreme Leadership either to nearby command bunkers in Moscow and the Moscow suburbs, or to distant command bunkers. The existence of several such sites would make it very difficult for any enemy missile strike to decapitate the Supreme Leadership before it acted.

The effort to put a large fraction of key decision centers in deep underground bunkers built upon an already extensive network of such facilities started under Stalin. Soviet command-and-control facilities in the Moscow area have relied on deep reinforced bunker complexes since the 1930s, connected by a secret subway unofficially dubbed Metro-2. The first General Staff bunker was built beneath the staff headquarters at 37 Myasnitskaya Street in 1933–36, and the air defense command under Tver Square in 1940.[63] Through the Cold War years, additional complexes were constructed to house the national command authority and government officials, and to serve as backups for other military command facilities. A major strategic command-and-control center for use by the General Staff was created in the southern Moscow suburbs near Chekov, and a redundant command center in case of evacuation of the capitol was created near Penza. In the event of a sudden crisis, a major underground command post was created within the capitol in the Ramenki district near Moscow State University.[64] In the late 1980s, a new deep wartime relocation center for the Supreme Leadership was created near Sharapovo, south of Gorky.[65]

As an alternative to the fixed command bunkers and to permit continued command and control to be exercised during any evacuations from Moscow, mobile command posts were developed. The earliest form of these were mounted on trains, and they were regularly exercised in peacetime between Moscow and the Urals. These were decommissioned in the 1980s, because more useful methods were in place.[66] Special airborne command posts began to be developed in the 1960s for the party leadership and senior military leaders under the Zveno program. A portion of the Metro-2 subway led to Vnukovo airfield, where the special Zveno aircraft were located. Although painted in Aeroflot markings, these aircraft were controlled by the military and KGB. The first specialized aircraft for this role was the Tupolev Tu-135, a derivative of the normal Tu-134 jet airliner. This aircraft was fitted with the Baikal communications system, linking it with the strategic command-and-control system.[67]

Ballistic-Missile Early Warning

In the early 1970s the Soviet strategic-command network depended on a network of eleven Dnestr-M ballistic-missile early-warning system (BMEWS) radars around the periphery of the Soviet frontier. The early radars had significant reliability and resolution problems, which undermined their ability to provide continuous, reliable warning. Furthermore, radars could only detect incoming missiles after they had passed over the horizon. As a result, the radars would begin to detect the incoming missiles only about ten minutes before impact, making it very difficult for the Kremlin to decide whether the alarm was real and what action to take. This was a substantial problem in view of the Soviet doctrine, which favored a launch-on-warning posture. To extend the decision cycle to its fullest possible extent, it would be necessary to develop new detection technologies to warn of missile launches as soon as they took place. The upgrade of the early-warning network in the late Brezhnev years took the form of a new network of more powerful BMEWS radars, a first generation of over-the-horizon radars, and the first early-warning satellites.

As in the case of the first generation of Dnestr-M radars, the second-generation Daryal BMEWS radars were closely tied to the development of a new antiballistic-missile network. Since the BMEWS served the needs of both the ABM system and the national command-and-control system, its development started in 1968, before the associated A-135 (ABM-3) system. The Daryal was intended to be a piece of a larger early-warning network, so its technical characteristics shifted compared to the first-generation Dnestr-M system, from range to greater resolution, to provide more accurate information for the new ABM system. Other key requirements of the new Daryal program were to provide total perimeter coverage and close gaps in the existing BMEWS line. A test bed of the Daryal entered construction near Pechora in northern Russia in 1978.[68] Like the earlier BMEWS radars, these were enormous structures, costing about $300 to $400 million each. They were one of the largest construction projects of the late Cold War years, employing some 100,000 construction workers through most of the 1970s.[69] The high cost and complexity of these radars would lead to one of the most bitter controversies of the late Cold War years, the Krasnoyarsk radar debate.

Early-warning radars can only detect incoming missiles once they are within line of sight of the radar station. Ideally, missile warning should occur as soon as the missile is launched to give national leaders as much time as possible to make their decisions. The late 1950s saw the first experiments with over-the-horizon (OTH) radars. Unlike conventional radars, OTH radars work by bouncing the radar waves off the ionosphere, which then detect missile launches by sensing the atmospheric disturbances caused by the missile exhaust plume. Over-the-horizon radars held out the theoretical possibility of detecting an ICBM launch at ranges as great as 12,000 km (7,400 mi), nearly double the range offered by more conventional early-warning radars.

The experimental Duga-2 OTH radar was erected near Gomel in Ukraine in the late 1960s. The trials were promising enough that development of a full-scale radar was authorized in 1971.[70] Construction of the first definitive Duga radar began in 1975 at Balshy Kartel, near Komsomolsk-na-Amur in the Pacific. The

Western code name for these radars was Steel Works, due to their large, intricate girder structure. The work was delayed when 1976 experiments with the modified Duga-2 test-bed radar near Gomel revealed serious shortcomings in the radar's design. The early Soviet efforts were plagued by a number of problems that delayed their introduction a decade behind similar U.S. programs. Soviet limitations in computer technology inhibited processing techniques that could have overcome the inherent OTH problems of low reliability and resolution due to ionospheric instability. This matter was further complicated by the Soviet need to use the OTH radars over the North Pole, with the resultant problems associated with auroral disturbances in the ionosphere. A second Duga radar was erected starting in 1979 at Nikolayev, near the Black Sea, to keep an eye on Chinese missile fields.

Trials of the Duga at Komsomolsk in 1980 against Minuteman missiles launched by the United States from Vandenberg Air Force Base, California, toward the U.S. monitoring station on Kwajalein Atoll revealed that it could not reliably detect single missiles, though it could detect multiple near-simultaneous launches. Gen. Col. Yury Votintsev, the commander of the ABM force of the national air defense command, concluded that the system was unacceptable. The radar's designer argued that the system was adequate for the task, since its main mission was to detect a massive U.S. ICBM or SLBM attack, not a single missile. Having already spent so much money, the Council of Ministers agreed. The Duga station at Komsomolsk was accepted for conditional service on 30 June 1982.[71] The performance of the radar remained poor, and so the design bureau was obliged to begin an extensive upgrade effort on the Duga network, called the Polar Program. The OTH program ended in scandal due to the hundreds of millions of rubles spent on a system that never provided any significant benefits.[72]

The other method of detecting a missile launch in its first moments is from early-warning satellites in orbit over the missile launch sites. The United States launched its first early-warning satellites, the Midas, in 1960. This was followed by launches of the far more successful Defense Support Program (DSP) series, beginning in 1968. In the Soviet Union, basic research was undertaken in the detection of rocket-engine plumes from space only in the 1960s. In 1973 the Council of Ministers authorized the start of engineering development of a missile early-warning satellite under the code name Oko (Eyes), with deployment to take place by 1978.[73] The aim was to deploy a low-orbit network by 1978 and follow this with a high-orbit or geosynchronous network called Prognoz by the 1980s. The test flights of the Oko satellite began on 9 September 1972, but the sensor was not yet ready.[74] In late 1976 a prototype Oko satellite had managed to detect a missile launch from Soviet territory. Continued space trials in 1977 were unable to overcome lingering problems with the sensor, forcing the test of a different type of sensor in 1978. The Oko satellite design was plagued by technical problems, satellite disintegrations, and orbital drifting. A total of three series-production Oko satellites were in orbit by 1978, and the system was accepted for conditional service.[75] In fact, the early Oko network was still focused on experimental work on missile detection and could not provide an actual early-warning capability. However, 1978 did mark the first time when the Oko system detected a U.S. ballistic-missile launch. A full constellation of nine satellites was not in place until 1982, four years behind schedule.

Strategic Defense

The Soviet Union remained committed to strategic defensive systems to a far greater extent than the United States in the 1970s. These efforts were focused primarily on antibomber defense rather than antiballistic-missile defense. The PVO-Strany Air Defense Command had roles beyond the bomber defense mission, though these were diminishing with time. The PVO-Strany guarded the Soviet frontiers against intrusions by U.S. reconnaissance aircraft. After the May 1960 shootdown of the CIA U-2, the United States ceased further penetration flights of the Soviet Union as too provocative, and by the mid-1960s this mission had been completely taken over by reconnaissance satellites. Nevertheless, enormous resources were committed to the PVO-Strany, about 15 percent of total defense expenditures in the late 1960s and early 1970s, on a scale of that devoted to the navy. The cost of the these efforts did not correspond to the threat posed by U.S. strategic bombers, which were declining in importance through this period, nor to the spy-plane threat, which had disappeared entirely. This situation was a reflection of the institutional inertia in the Soviet armed forces, and the lax control over military policy in the late Brezhnev years.

In contrast, the United States continued to trim back its own strategic-defense forces as a waste of resources. In the United States, the bomber-defense mission became marginal by 1970 due to the widespread recognition that missiles had become the primary weapon of Soviet offensive strategic forces. The number of U.S. interceptor squadrons fell from 40 in 1964 to 11 in 1972, and the number of army strategic SAM batteries fell from 107 to 21. In the Soviet Union, the picture was quite different. Although the size of the U.S. strategic-bomber force fell by more than half, the Soviet SAM force continued to grow.[76] By the mid-1960s, the PVO-Strany had deployed 3,800 S-75 (SA-2) and 320 S-125 (SA-3) surface-to-air missile launchers to defend against American strategic bombers.[77] A new high-altitude SAM, the S-200 Angara (SA-5), entered service in 1967, and by 1980 about two thousand launchers had been added. This missile was justified partly by its ability to defeat newer generations of U.S. spy planes like the SR-71. But the proliferation of SAMs in the 1960s led the U.S. bomber force to shift to low-altitude tactics, which substantially undermined the effectiveness of the new high-altitude SAMs.

The PVO-Strany also deployed its own air interceptor regiments, separate from the air force, for the antibomber mission. In the 1970s a new generation of interceptors was fielded, including the Mikoyan MiG-25 and Sukhoi Su-15. The total number of PVO-Strany interceptors fell from 3,200 to 2,500 as obsolete subsonic interceptors were retired, but the force remained out of all proportion to the threat.[78] Furthermore, the PVO-Strany remained a heavy drain on the Soviet defense budget, because the missiles and interceptors were developed specifically for this force, while the air force and army developed and procured a separate line of fighters and missiles. The large network of air defense radars, missile bases, and interceptor squadrons also represented a substantial drain on manpower, averaging about 635,000 troops through the 1970s. In comparison, U.S. personnel in similar units totaled only 77,000 in 1970, and this figure had fallen to 30,000 by 1980. By the late 1970s the U.S. bomber force had atrophied to only 316 subsonic B-52 bombers. Some of the more cynical U.S. planners argued that the United States should continue to field a new generation of bombers such as the B-1A simply to encourage the Soviet Union to continue to waste so many of its defense rubles on this dubious force.

The PVO-Strany formed the new Antiballistic-Missile Defense command (PRO) on 30 March 1967 to manage its new A-35 ABM system around Moscow. In the early 1970s Soviet planners estimated that Moscow would be targeted by at least sixty warheads of one megaton each, nearly ten times the planned capability of the A-35 system. With the advent of MIRVs in the early 1970s, the threat increased by a further order of magnitude. In spite of its obvious shortcomings, the system was accepted for experimental use on 10 June 1971.[79] Even before it entered service, a substantial upgrade program called A-35M Aldan (ABM-1B) was in the works to bring the system up to minimal standards, such as an ability to cope with decoys. The modified version went into service in 1978. The failure of the A-35 program was a major reason for the Kremlin's willingness to sign the ABM treaty in 1972.

The problems with the Moscow ABM system were addressed in a special Defense Council meeting chaired by Brezhnev in 1965, when it considered several alternatives. Two new ABM systems, code-named Avrora and S-225, were on the drawing boards in the late 1960s, aimed at providing territorial defense rather than the limited site defense possible with the A-35. These systems were not intended to provide total national defense, but coverage of key strategic objectives, including missile fields and key cities. The technical objectives of the programs were to develop ABM missiles that could repel a massed ICBM attack that would be masked by as many as seven decoys per missile.

In the late 1960s, a series of studies were conducted to examine future ABM requirements in light of new developments, particularly the advent of decoys and MIRVs. Offensive technology was quickly outstripping defensive technology. The MIRV warheads radically changed the economies of defense, since the massive ABM missiles cost as much as if not more than the ICBMs. Since two or more ABM missiles were needed to have a good chance of shooting down a single ICBM warhead, the price tag for a defensive system became astronomical. At the time, the senior Soviet leadership had not given much thought to the linkage between offensive and defensive strategic systems except in the narrow technical sense.[80] Studies of future ABM requirements and the consequences of MIRV under programs such as Saturn began to undermine support for the ABM effort. The Saturn study examined ways of dealing with the MIRV, without much success.

In September 1967 another state commission was formed to examine future ABM configurations. The Avrora territorial ABM system was rejected at this time, because it was felt that it could not deal with future targets and could not offer sufficient reliability. Debates over the role of ABM defenses of ICBM sites was a significant controversy during the Little Civil War of the late 1960s on the future of Soviet offensive strategic weapons. This debate ended without any firm commitment to a new ABM system for defense of the ICBM fields. Although research on new ABM systems continued into the early 1970s, none of the proposals appeared promising enough to justify full-scale engineering development. The work of the various competing design bureaus was consolidated into a new organization, the Vympel Central Scientific Production Association, on 31 December 1970, in hopes of avoiding the destructive infighting that had crippled the earlier A-35 program.[81] In the wake of the 1972 ABM treaty, work on the territorial ABM programs was gradually brought to a halt.

The American decision to press ahead with its own new ABM system, the Safeguard, helped provide a rationale for a revived Soviet ABM effort. Vympel proposed its own analog of Safeguard, called the A-135, to replace the obviously flawed A-35 system around Moscow. The basic outline of the new A-135 ABM system was approved in June 1975. The ABM treaty limited the USSR to only 100 ABM launchers. As a result, the A-135 system was intended to provide so-called adequate defense, as opposed to optimum defense. It was evident that any system limited to 100 launchers could be overwhelmed by a full-scale U.S. attack. The nominal justification for the A-135 was the defense of Moscow against a renegade U.S. ballistic-missile submarine armed with sixteen missiles, a "limited, provocative" attack from the United States with a small number of ICBMs, or a full-fledged attack from China with up to 100 DF-4 IRBMs. As in the case of its predecessor, the A-35, the A-135 program became mired in technical problems and controversy and was not finally declared operational until 12 February 1995, twenty years after its start.

The possible applications of revolutionary new weapons technologies for ballistic-missile defense were of considerable interest in the Soviet scientific and defense community in the late 1960s. The initiative in this area came mainly from the Ministry for Radio Industry (Minradioprom), which had managed the development of the ABM program since the late 1950s. In the late 1960s and early 1970s, a series of discussions were held among representatives of the Academy of Science, the military scientific-research institutes, design bureaus, and the Soviet General Staff on the issue of space weapons. The consensus that emerged was that a program should be undertaken in two phases, code-named Fon-1 (Background-1) and Fon-2. Fon-1 represented advanced concept and technology development, including directed-energy weapons (which use nonkinetic techniques such as high-energy laser, neutron beam, particle beam, and high-energy microwave), electromagnetic rail guns, novel warhead technologies, new ABM missiles, and space platforms for applications of these weapons. Fon-2 was intended to transition these technologies into the engineering development phase in order to field actual systems.

The Fon-1 program formally began in 1976, although work on basic research of many of the novel directed-energy technologies had begun earlier. This program was not unanimously supported, and it was vigorously opposed by some segments of the defense and industrial communities as a waste of funding. Among its opponents was Grigory Kisunko, the general designer of the initial Moscow ABM system. In 1976 a research study connected with Fon-1 began at OKB Kometa, the design bureau that had developed the first Soviet antisatellite system in the 1960s. Kometa was given the task of designing a system that could destroy ten thousand reentry vehicles and cruise missiles in five to twenty-five minutes with a 99.9-percent probability of destruction. Kometa concluded that such a system was not practical for both technological and economic reasons. Nevertheless, Fon-1 continued to be funded, and much of the effort was devoted to antisatellite missions rather than ballistic-missile defense. The rapid expansion of development work on space-based weapons reached the point in the 1970s that the Ministry of Defense Production was obliged to set up a new Eighth Main Directorate specifically to manage these programs and coordinate the various research institutes.

Building Deep Parity

The importance of reaching strategic parity with the United States in the late 1960s led the Kremlin to put modernization of intermediate regional forces on hold. There were a number of halfhearted attempts to develop a new generation of intermediate-range missiles and intermediate-range bombers, but these were not given significant priority. As a result, by the late 1960s the existing intermediate-range nuclear forces were approaching retirement. The R-12 and R-14 missile forces were a decade old, and the Tupolev Tu-22 bomber had been a technical disappointment with lingering problems.

The desire to modernize the intermediate-range forces was based on several factors besides the age of the weapons. U.S. refusal to include its regional nuclear forces in the SALT I talks did not dissuade the Soviet military leadership from pressing forward with its concept of deep parity. It is not clear if Marshal Grechko won an explicit promise from Brezhnev to support these initiatives in return for acquiescence to the SALT I treaty, though this seems likely. A second consequence of the SALT I talks was that it placed a premium on all missiles dubbed "strategic" by the United States. While the RVSN controlled strategic missiles of both continental and intercontinental range, the U.S. arms-control initiatives were concerned only with the intercontinental missiles able to reach the United States. There was no hard distinction in the first two generations of Soviet strategic missiles in this regard. In particular, the UR-100 (SS-11) was targeted both at intercontinental targets in the United States and intermediate-range targets in Europe, China, and Japan.[82] The SALT I treaty had the unintended consequence of pushing the USSR into an expansion of its intermediate missile force. By expanding its intermediate-range force to take over targets previously assigned to the UR-100, the RVSN could free up all of its ICBMs for targeting against the United States.

Another catalyst was the modernization of weapons aimed at the Soviet Union in the late 1960s by countries other than the United States. China, Britain, and France all maintained modest nuclear bomber forces through the 1960s, and they were all beginning to modernize their deterrent forces with modern missile weapons, prompted in no small measure by the advent of the Soviet R-12 and R-14 IRBM force in the early 1960s. The Soviet missiles made the British "V" bomber force obsolete, shifting the British deterrent force toward missiles.[83] By the late 1960s Britain was in the process of deploying the new HMS *Resolution*-class of ballistic-missile submarine, armed with sixteen Polaris A3 missiles. The first submarine was deployed in June 1968, and four submarines of this class were operational by September 1970, with sixty-four ballistic missiles.[84] France followed suit, deploying a land-based strategic ballistic missile, the SSBS S2, beginning in July 1968, and eventually, eighteen hardened silo launchers.[85] France also deployed its first ballistic-missile submarine, *Le Redoutable,* in January 1972, armed with the indigenous MSBS M1 missile. By May 1971 China had begun to deploy the first of about fifty DF-3 ballistic missiles, the first Chinese systems capable of striking major population centers in central Russia.

There were two principal weapons initiatives for the regional strategic forces: the Pioner (SS-20) mobile missile, and the Tu-22M (Backfire) medium bomber. Both programs would prove to be extremely controversial.

Developing the Pioner

As was usually the case with Soviet strategic missiles, the development of a new generation of weapons started as the previous generation was completing deployment. The Yangel R-12 had entered service in 1959, and the R-14 in 1962. The life expectancy of such weapons was about a decade. As mentioned in the previous discussion of the Temp-2S (SS-16), a new study program by the MIT design bureau was authorized on 4 March 1966.[86] In the wake of the failure of Yangel's RT-20P, in 1969 the MIT study effort split into two programs, the Temp-2S ICBM (SS-16), and the Pioner IRBM (SS-20).[87]

The technical characteristics of the Pioner were based in large measure on threat assessments undertaken by the GRU military intelligence branch as well as various military research institutes. Most of the previous generation of IRBMs had been based at inexpensive, but vulnerable, surface sites. The final batch of R-12 and R-14 missiles had been deployed in an early type of silo that was not well hardened compared to current Soviet ICBM silos. The U.S. Army had been deploying its medium-range Pershing I missile from mobile launchers, and Soviet threat studies concluded that it would continue to face the threat of mobile ballistic missiles.[88] With the increasing accuracy of modern ballistic missiles, a mobile system would be less vulnerable than a silo-based missile. The Pioner was essentially the first two stages of the Temp-2S ICBM, but with a new postboost vehicle. Like the Temp-2S, it could be armed with MIRVs, carrying three warheads. Testing of the Pioner began in the autumn of 1974, about two and a half years after the initial Temp-2S flight test, and concluded on 9 January 1976. The Pioner system was accepted for service on 11 March 1976.

The decision to deploy the Pioner (SS-20) came shortly before Marshal Grechko's death in April 1976. Although Grechko was not fond of mobile missiles, the mobile-IRBM option had several important advantages. A silo-based IRBM might have caused significant problems in the arms-control realm, since it would be impossible to verify whether the silo contained a Pioner or its larger brother, the Temp-2S. In addition, Grechko was one of strongest advocates of deep parity, and the Pioner was an important element of any such effort. At the time, the RVSN had thirteen IRBM divisions deployed, armed with 543 old R-12 and R-14 missiles. The intention of the Pioner program was to replace them on a nearly one-for-one basis. This could triple the firepower of the IRBM divisions, since the Pioner could be

At the heart of the intermediate nuclear forces (INF) controversy was the Pioner (SS-20) mobile intermediate-range missile, the culmination of a long series of attempts to deploy a mobile, solid-fuel missile, and a precursor of today's Topol missile system. The missile is deployed on a MAZ-7916 heavy truck, which contains all the equipment necessary to launch it. All Pioner systems were destroyed after 1986 as a result of the INF treaty, but a handful of demilitarized examples were permitted at museums, including this one at the Central Armed Forces Museum in Moscow.

armed with a three-warhead MIRV payload. Two developments helped to ensure a large production run for the Pioner.

The Pioner entered production shortly after the Temp-2S ICBM at the Votkinsk plant. The Votkinsk plant was an established ballistic-missile plant that previously manufactured small tactical ballistic missiles such as the R-17 (Scud). In anticipation of the production of the new solid-fuel missiles, an elaborate extension of the plant was added at considerable cost. With the premature curtailment of production of the Temp-2S due to SALT treaty obligations, the facility would have been underutilized under the existing five-year plan. This also affected the plant's manufacturing the associated launch vehicle.[89] The essential similarity between the Pioner and Temp-2S made it tempting to simply have the Pioner fill in for the shortfall in Temp-2S production.

An added factor was the development of new U.S. theater missiles. In 1972 the U.S. Navy began development of a new cruise missile, the Tomahawk. This small missile was a revolutionary change in warship and submarine armament. In could be fitted to a wide range of warships due to its small size and give them the capability to strike targets thousands of miles away with a nuclear warhead. Prior to this, surface warships and attack submarines had no long-range land-attack capability.[90] From the Soviet perspective, this added yet another weapon to the U.S. arsenal capable of striking the Soviet Union. Tomahawks could be launched from submarines or warships in the seas around the Soviet Union. The flight path of the cruise missile was designed to allow it to skirt under existing air defense radar networks, seriously undermining the Soviet Union's marginal ballistic-missile early-warning capability. While the Pioner could not remove the Tomahawk threat, some Soviet military leaders saw it as a response. The United States was essentially sneaking under the launcher limits imposed by SALT by deploying a new category of weapon not in the strategic basket. The sheer size and expense of the Pioner program led many leaders of the European NATO countries to consider it a provocative move to threaten and dominate Western Europe.[91]

The U.S. military was worried about the SS-20 in connection with strategic arms limitation talks. Since the Pioner consisted basically of the first two stages of the SS-16 ICBM, there was some concern that it represented a clandestine breakout system. In peacetime, it would be deployed in its two-stage intermediate-range configuration; in the event of a crisis, the upper bus would be replaced by the SS-16 third stage and bus, making it a potent, mobile ICBM.[92]

Developing the Backfire

The second major element of the modernization of Soviet continental strike forces was the Tupolev Tu-22M, better known in the West as the Backfire. The Soviet intermediate-range bomber force was getting long in the tooth. The Tu-16, which had been developed in the late Stalin years, was a dependable but obsolete analog of the long-retired American B-47. An earlier attempt to replace it in the Khrushchev years, the Tu-22 Blinder, was a flop, and it was deployed mainly with the navy's anticarrier force. Tupolev had lost favor with Khrushchev, and the development of a new supersonic medium bomber had been turned over to the Sukhoi design bureau. Sukhoi's brilliant but extravagant T-4 was still in development in the mid-1960s. It was one of the most sophisticated aircraft in Soviet history, and a technological accomplishment somewhat on the order of the American SR-71 Blackbird reconnaissance aircraft. Shunned by Khrushchev, Tupolev was once again in favor with the new Brezhnev regime. The Soviet Air Force wanted a new bomber, and after the failure of the ambitious Tu-22 Blinder, it was skeptical of the even more futuristic Sukhoi T-4. The air force commander, Gen. Pavel Kutakhov, supported a more conservative design, and Tupolev was given the go-ahead in late 1964.

The requirements for the new bomber were a range of at least 5,000 km (3,000 mi), a speed of at least Mach 2 at high altitude and near Mach 1 during low-altitude penetration missions, a payload of at least twenty tons to include missiles and bombs, and the ability to operate from forward air bases.[93] The Tu-22M was promoted by Tupolev as a low-cost alternative to the rival high-tech T-4. The weapon system was based around the same Kh-22 standoff cruise missile as that of the older, and failed, Tu-22 Blinder, instead of the new Kh-45 Molniya aero-ballistic missile arming the T-4. To further accent the point, Tupolev called the design the Tu-22M, implying that it was simply a modernized version of the earlier Tu-22. This was not true, and aside from the weapon system, the two air-craft were almost completely different. As a result of this marketing ploy, the Soviet Air Force ended up with an advanced aircraft design armed with an old and marginally adequate weapon system.

In November 1967 the Council of Ministers decided to proceed with engineering development of the Tu-22M and to abandon Sukhoi's T-4 program. The Tu-22M appeared to be a more reasonable compromise in terms of performance and cost

One focus of the INF controversy was the Tupolev Tu-22M Backfire bomber. Although U.S. intelligence originally believed that it had intercontinental range, later assessments recognized its inadequate performance for this mission. This Tupolev Tu-22M3 is on display at the Zhukovsky air force test facility, on the outskirts of Moscow.

than the T-4. The first test of the Tu-22M flight took place on 30 August 1969. The early production aircraft proved troublesome in service, and only nine aircraft were manufactured in 1971–72. The difficulties with the initial Tu-22M1 version prevented it from being accepted for series production. After significant improvements to the flight-control and navigation system, the modified Tu-22M2 (Backfire B) was accepted for service in 1976.[94]

The international controversy over the role of the Backfire bomber had already begun by 1975, when the bombers began entering service. At the time, negotiations were under way between the United States and USSR on SALT II. Hardline American critics of the arms-control efforts argued that the Backfire was a strategic-weapons system capable of reaching the United States with refueling, a point echoed in later years in the Department of Defense's annual booklets, *Soviet Military Power.* Contemporary U.S. Air Force intelligence assessments estimated that the Backfire B had an unrefueled combat range of 9,075 km (5,625 mi), which could be extended to 12,775 km (7,925 mi) with a single prestrike refueling.[95] The Soviets argued equally vehemently that it was not intended for the intercontinental role and therefore should not be classified as a "heavy bomber" in SALT treaty terminology. The U.S. evaluated the Backfire in terms of American aviation technology. In reality, the conservative design approach of the Tupolev bureau and the inefficiency of its propulsion meant that it did not have the range and performance of a comparable American aircraft of its size and weight. The high estimates were in part due to overestimates of fuel stowage, which U.S. Air Force and Defense Intelligence Agency (DIA) analysts put at 150,000 lbs. Recent Russian documents indicate hat the combat range of the Tu-22M-0 was 5,000 km (3,000 mi) unrefueled, with a three-ton payload, and that of the Tu-22M2 was 5,100 km (3,200 mi).[96] There was a long-standing controversy between the U.S. CIA and DIA over the range and payload capabilities of the Backfire B. The DIA pushed the argument that the aircraft was a true intercontinental bomber. In 1985 the DIA finally conceded that the CIA's lower estimate of 3,000 miles (4,800 km) was substantially correct.[97]

During the course of negotiations on the SALT II treaty in 1979, an accommodation on the Backfire controversy was made when Leonid Brezhnev wrote a formal letter to President Jimmy Carter. It stated that any significant increase in the range or payload of the Backfire would be inconsistent with the terms of the SALT II treaty, and that production would be frozen at the annual rate of thirty. The Soviet side also agreed to remove the nose refueling probe from the Backfire, intending to put to rest the allegation that the bomber could reach intercontinental ranges if refueled. Since it was recognized that the aircraft could be easily retro-fitted with the refueling probes, the Soviets assured the Americans that the size of the Soviet tanker force would not be enlarged sufficiently for the large-scale use of tankers to support the use of the Backfire in an intercontinental role.

Beyond Parity?

What was most striking about the strategic balance in the 1970s was the enormous effort by the Soviet Union and the relatively modest scale of comparable U.S. efforts. The Soviet Union finally began to surpass the United States both in numbers of missiles and numbers of nuclear warheads. The third generation of Soviet ICBMs were deployed from 1975 to 1981, while the U.S. ICBM force did not deploy any new type of ICBM. The modernization of the United States land-based arsenal concentrated instead on new guidance and warhead technology, represented most notably by the deployment of the Minuteman III in 1970 with a triple MIRV warhead, a feature matched by the Soviet third-generation systems. Force modernization in the United States was limited to the submarine leg of the triad, with the deployment of the Poseidon C-3 and a ten-warhead MIRV beginning in 1973. Attempts to modernize the U.S. Strategic Air Command were minimal, and the Carter administration canceled the supersonic Rockwell B-1A.

By the end of the 1970s, the technological dominance of the U.S. strategic force was heavily eroded compared to a decade earlier. While the U.S. forces continued to enjoy many narrow technological advantages, especially in the new MIRVs, the Soviet forces began to enjoy overall advantages due to the sheer size and power of their land-based force. The short-term U.S. advantage in MIRVs was illusory, since the larger Soviet missiles permitted the Soviets to field improved variants with their own MIRV technology, exceeding the U.S. MIRV count by a large margin as the third-generation deployment progressed. The Soviet ICBM force began exceeding the U.S. force in the number of warheads in 1975 and within a decade was three times larger. In addition, the third-generation missiles enjoyed a substantial increase in accuracy, which began to threaten U.S. ICBM silos. The rapid increase in MIRV warheads undermined the balance that was supposed to be achieved by SALT I. Furthermore, U.S. concern about the growing accuracy of Soviet ICBMs when used in a counterforce role against U.S. missile silos created the impression of a "window of vulnerability" to U.S. critics of American arms-control and strategic-weapons policy.[98] To arms-control advocates in the United States, these developments further reinforced the need for the SALT II treaty and more explicit restrictions. To U.S. arms-control critics, the third-generation improvements represented clear evidence of Soviet duplicity and the futility of arms control.

The Soviet Navy exceeded the U.S. Navy in total number of SLBMs in 1972–73, though the U.S. Navy maintained a substantial edge in the number of warheads deployed, especially once it began deploying MIRVs in the early 1970s. More importantly, U.S. submarine silencing ensured a higher degree of survivability than in the Soviet submarine force, especially in light of the vigorous U.S. Navy anti-submarine-warfare effort. The more robust patrol rate of the U.S. submarine force also added to its survivability and its competence in carrying out its mission. The only area of clear U.S. numerical dominance was in the intercontinental bomber force, though its relevance was diminishing in U.S. war plans.

In spite of the Soviet Union's success in reaching parity with the United States in the 1970s, the Soviet Union still did not have the capability to launch a pre-emptive strike against the U.S. strategic forces that would eliminate U.S. retaliatory capability. While the Soviet Union continued to rely on land-based ICBM forces, the U.S. force structure was turning increasingly toward the naval leg of the strategic triad. Even if the U.S. ICBM force was becoming more vulnerable to Soviet counterforce capabilities, the submarine force remained relatively invulnerable to Soviet antisubmarine forces. Furthermore, the U.S. submarine missile force remained the most worrisome element of the U.S. force to Soviet strategic planners due to the continued shortcomings of its strategic command and control. U.S. SLBMs could be launched closer to the Soviet Union than ICBMs, thereby reducing their flight time to under fifteen minutes, too little time for the Soviet command-and-control system to fully activate its own forces.

While seldom openly discussed in Soviet or current Russian accounts, the actual capability to launch a surprise preemptive strike was doubtful through most of the Brezhnev years. In the early 1970s there was considerable turmoil in the RVSN as new generations of missiles came on line, upgrades were introduced, and new cadres of officers and enlisted men were brought into service. As the new systems became more familiar to their operating crews, they also came closer to the end of their life expectancy. Preparations began yet again for another wave of modernization, along with all the uncertainties and turmoil it involved. There have been no candid memoirs by former RVSN officers on the realities of service in the missile force in these years. But there are many reasons to believe that the day-to-day capabilities of the missile force were nowhere near the idealized portrait painted both by Soviet propaganda and the shriller American polemics. Indeed, some Russian accounts suggest that the deployment of some of the new missile systems, especially the UR-100N (SS-19), was especially troubled.

6.

To the Brink of Collapse

1985–1991

The last decade of the Soviet Union was the most contentious and turbulent since the Khrushchev years. In the wake of Brezhnev's growing debilitation, the Soviet military began to assert their claims to a greater role in Soviet defense policy making, leading to tensions with the political leadership over state policy and relations with the United States. The massive and unconstrained buildup of the 1970s led to an American backlash. After a decade of relative American quiescence, the "New Cold War" of the early 1980s threatened to restart the arms race. With the passing of the wartime generation by 1984, the Soviet leadership confronted a lack of consensus on defense needs. The Soviet military insisted on broad, unrestrained force modernization, while the new political leadership of Mikhail Gorbachev insisted on reforms that would inevitably include heavy cutbacks in military funding. Gorbachev attempted to tame the military by installing new senior commanders, and his radical foreign policy initiatives alienated the military. The demoralization of the Soviet elite, ongoing since the late Brezhnev years, led to the corrosion and collapse of the Soviet state in 1991.

What Is to Be Done?

The institutional inertia of the military industries led to continued modernization of the strategic forces during the final decade of the Soviet Union. Development of the fourth generation of Soviet ICBMs began in 1976 and was preordained. Soviet missiles had a finite warranty life, and so there was a built-in rationale to field a new generation roughly every decade.[1] The increasing accuracy of American missiles, especially the advent of counterforce capability in the new Trident submarine force, implied that silo hardening would no longer be an adequate method to defend against an American preemptive strike. The obvious solution to this dilemma was missile mobility. The United States was considering mobile missiles such as the rail-mobile MX and the road-mobile Midgetman, but the U.S. preference was to place greater emphasis on the submarine force. In the Soviet case, mobility of the land-based ICBM force became the primary innovation of the new generation. Improvements in Soviet solid-fuel engine technology raised the hopes of improving force readiness and reducing the maintenance burden posed by liquid-fuel rocket engines. Given the size of the Soviet missile force, it was not possible to completely replace the entire land-based missile force with mobile, solid-fuel missiles in one generation. There-fore, the fourth generation consisted of two parallel efforts: a pair of new mobile missiles, the Molodets (SS-24) and Topol (SS-25); and the evolution of the three most modern silo-based ICBMs with more accurate warheads: the MR-UR-100 (SS-17), R-36M (SS-18), and UR-100N (SS-19).

From a command-and-control standpoint, the requirements for the fourth gen-eration were to shorten the time between initial warning and launch, prompted by improvements in the U.S. submarine missile force. While the earlier generation of U.S. SLBMs was intended to attack urban and industrial targets, by the early 1970s, the U.S. Navy was giving serious consideration to adding counterforce capability to the new Trident I missile.[2] This was worrisome from several standpoints. To begin with, the Trident could be launched from positions nearer the Soviet Union than the fixed-site ICBMs, thereby reducing warning time. The navy could theo-retically launch the missiles from as little as ten minutes away from Moscow, not providing enough warning time for the existing Soviet command-and-control net-work to activate the force. This posed a dual threat: the decapitation of the Soviet national command authority, and the loss of the ICBM force. The Soviet RVSN Strategic Missile Force estimated that the later D-5 Trident II had fifteen times the combat effectiveness of the Poseidon. The RVSN concluded that by the year 2000, the U.S. ICBM and SLBM force would triple its counterforce capability and in-crease its soft-target destruction capabilities by one and a half times. Its capabili-ties in cruise missiles and aircraft would increase fourfold, and the number of British and French deliverable nuclear warheads would increase to about 1,500.[3]

The 1980s saw yet another attempt by the two other services, the Soviet Navy and Air Force, to wrest away a larger portion of the strategic nuclear mission from the RVSN. The navy's program to deploy its latest submarine missiles was the culmination of its bastion doctrine.[4] The new missiles had sufficient range to per-mit the submarines to remain within the secure bastion of Soviet home waters, protected against marauding U.S. attack submarines by the Soviet fleet. The navy contrasted the superior survivability of its submarine force to the dubious survivability of the land-based force, a point that was not accepted by the General Staff. The air force had long been the weakest element of the Soviet strategic forces and by the early 1980s had almost evaporated. The advent of a new generation of cruise missiles revived hopes that the air force could reassert their role in the Soviet strategic programs.

The 1980s saw a continued heavy level of expenditure on strategic defense in the Soviet Union. While this period is better known for Ronald Reagan's Star Wars program, the Soviet Union continued to spend a significant portion of its defense budget on both traditional and revolutionary strategic defenses. While pursuing a foreign policy that would limit the U.S. Strategic Defense Initiative (SDI), the Soviet armed forces pursued their own secret SDI program, code-named Fon-2. This program was on the verge of testing space-based weapons in the years preceding the Soviet collapse and began a limited program of testing ground-based weapons in the late 1980s. At the same time, more conventional modernization occurred to deal with the new cruise-missile threat.

The American Star Wars program had unexpected consequences for Soviet strategic force modernization. The Soviet program of the 1980s was designed to ensure the survivability of the Soviet missile force by preventing its destruction on the ground by means of mobile launchers. The SDI program brought this into question, since it implied that Soviet missiles could also be defeated after they had been launched. This led to a crash program in the mid-1980s to develop countermeasures to SDI, which at the same time undermined commitment to the weapons that were on the verge of deployment. As a result of this technical issue, as well as the uncertainties imposed by ongoing arms-control negotiations, the deployment of the fourth-generation ICBMs was extremely ragged compared to the previous two generations.

Industrial Restructuring

Debate over the shape of the new generation of strategic weapons was avoided due to important changes in the senior leadership. Minister of Defense Andrei Grechko died on 26 April 1976. Brezhnev's preference for consensus on security issues led him to appoint Dmitry Ustinov as the new defense minister to avoid the steady string of confrontations that had been going on for a decade with Grechko. Ustinov has actively supported Brezhnev's détente policy. Ustinov's appointment concentrated unparalleled power in his hands. His traditional role as the Communist Party's top defense expert, his new role as military commander, and his longstanding influence in the industrial ministries assured broad support for his ideas.

To avoid a repeat of the Little Civil War, Ustinov instituted a number of reforms in the early 1970s that finally took hold by the early 1980s. Reforms started in 1974 ensured that major weapons programs would be preceded by a series of scientific investigative studies (NIR) to examine the likely impact of new technologies as well as the likely threat fifteen years in the future. It was hoped that these studies would raise major doctrine and technology issues years before the start of engineering development, avoiding a messy debate, as occurred in 1968–69. In turn, these NIR would serve as the basis for a preliminary weapons development study that would be initiated ten years before the intended deployment of the new systems. By the time that a weapons program had to be incorporated into the five-year planning cycle, its general requirements would already be well understood. The 1974 reforms were not a radical departure from existing practices, but codified a process that at times had been poorly managed.

Ustinov's new role as defense minister also allowed him to rein in the industry. Exasperated by Vladimir Chelomey's disruptive behavior in the past, Ustinov set about to severely curb his powers. He had been at loggerheads with Chelomey since the mid-1960s over his attempts to circumvent the normal ministerial authorities to promote his various schemes. His disruptive role in the Little Civil War had infuriated Ustinov, because it had thrown the third-generation program into chaos and led to the detrimental decision to deploy three different types of missile to replace the old UR-100. Chelomey had alienated other influential leaders in the industry, especially Valentin Glushko, who now headed the expanded version of Korolyov's old bureau, now called NPO Energia.

Ustinov, with his power as the head of the Ministry of Defense, with the MOM under his thumb, and allies in charge of the VPK, decided to settle the issue once and for all. Beginning in 1976, he blocked nearly all of Chelomey's attempts to gain new contracts. Chelomey's efforts in the fields of space and strategic missiles were based around his control of the old Myasishchev OKB-23 design bureau at Fili. In 1981 Ustinov removed the Branch No. 1 design bureau at Fili, the ICBM portion of Chelomey's organization, from his control. Initially, it was reassigned to the NPO Energia space conglomerate for work on the recently started Fon-1 strategic-defense program.[5] This effectively eliminated Chelomey's ballistic-missile design team, pushing him out of the ICBM business and back into the bush leagues of naval antiship missile design.[6]

Chelomey's demotion occurred during a period of reorganization in the Soviet defense industry. In the Soviet Union, the design bureaus were a separate entity from the production plant, following the assumption that if a design bureau proved unusually successful, its designs could be manufactured at plants other than its associated plants. Likewise, if it was unsuccessful, its associated plants could produce the weapon designed by another bureau. In fact, this advantage proved illusory, and the separation between the design bureau and production plant proved to be inefficient.

This organizational configuration favored the development of new weapons designs rather than the steady evolution of existing designs due to the nature of the incentives. As a result, the Soviet military industry fielded a significantly larger number of different missile types than did the United States during the Cold War. This proliferation took place in spite of the fact that the Soviet military preferred a smaller number of new designs to make it easier to train its conscript-based force. In the 1970s a program began to convert the Soviet defense industry to a pattern more like that of Western companies. Design bureaus and production plants were amalgamated into a new structure called the Research Production Association, or NPO. Although the NPO concept was first authorized in 1968, by 1975 there were only ninety-seven NPOs in the entire USSR, including civilian and defense firms. This number had doubled by 1985, but the biggest jump came in the late 1980s, by which time over five hundred NPOs had been formed. The missile and space industry was led by the amalgamation of Korolyov's OKB-1 and associated plants into NPO Energia. Yangel's SKB-586 was already intimately tied to the associated Southern Machine Building (Yuzhmash) plant in Dnepropetrovsk, so the resulting change was mostly cosmetic.

Upgrading the Third Generation

The first element of the fourth generation to reach fruition was the evolutionary development of the three existing silo-based missiles. These programs were relatively straightforward and took only about three years from the start of development until initial deployment. The three upgrade programs shared a number of features in common. Liquid-fuel technology had developed to the point where the oxidizer could be left stored in the missile virtually indefinitely, so that the missile did not have to be periodically removed and rebuilt during its usual seven-year lifetime. New advances in computer technology and flight-control systems promised greater accuracy for MIRV systems, making them capable of destroying U.S. missile silos.

Modernization of the R-36M (SS-18) began on 16 August 1976. The new R-36MU variant had two warhead options, the 15B86 single warhead (SS-18 Mod 3) and the 15F183 MIRV warhead (SS-18 Mod 4).[7] The single-warhead version was developed for better accuracy.[8] Flight tests began on 31 October 1977 and concluded on 27 November 1979. The first three regiments with the new missile became operational in September 1978, and the type was officially accepted for service on 17 December 1980. All 308 silos were converted to the new type by 1983. This version of the R-36M caused the most consternation in the United

States. The system was assessed as having an accuracy of 250 m (825 ft) CEP with its ten warheads, suggesting it was intended mainly for the counterforce role, that is, to destroy U.S. missile silos. Assuming that two warheads were targeted against each silo, the R-36MU force was viewed as being capable of destroying 60–80 percent of the U.S. ICBM force while still keeping one thousand warheads in reserve. This would give rise to the contentious "window of vulnerability" that prompted U.S. strategic-force modernization in the 1980s.

An upgrade of the MR-UR-100 (SS-17) was also initiated on 16 August 1976.[9] The main aim of the program was the development of the new 15F161 MIRV warhead, with significantly improved accuracy. The testing began on 25 October 1977 and concluded on 15 December 1979. The first regiment with the new MR-UR-100U became operational at Bologoye on 17 October 1978, and the missile was accepted into service on 17 December 1980. All 150 silos were converted to the new missile by 1983.

The rationale for improving Chelomey's UR-100N (SS-19) was somewhat different from that of the other third-generation missiles. There had been recurring problems with the UR-100N since it was first deployed. The problems were serious enough that a series of quick fixes were developed to modify the existing missiles in the silos. As a long-term solution, the new UR-100NU was developed with a redesigned flight-control system. The first test flights of this missile began on 26 October 1977 and concluded on 26 June 1979. The first UR-100NU regiment became operational at Khmelnitsky on 6 November 1979 and completely replaced the flawed UR-100N version by 1983.

Moving the Missiles

By the 1980s missile accuracy had reached the point where newer warheads were crater-lethal. No matter how hard the silo construction, these improved warheads signaled the eventual doom of static, land-based ICBMs. As a solution, Dmitry Ustinov had been pressing for the development of mobile, land-based ICBMs. He had been stymied by Grechko, but with Grechko gone, mobile missiles took center stage in the new programs.

The two new fourth-generation missiles were the Topol (SS-25), a light ICBM with a single warhead; and the Molodets (SS-24), a medium ICBM with a MIRV warhead. Neither program was entirely new, and both were in fact evolutions of failed missiles of the third generation. The Topol was a reincarnation of the canceled Temp-2S (SS-16) with numerous technical improvements. Design of the Topol program began at the Moscow Institute of Thermotechnology on 19 July 1977.[10] The first test flight of the Topol took place on 27 October 1982 from Plesetsk but was a failure. The first successful test took place on 8 February 1983, and

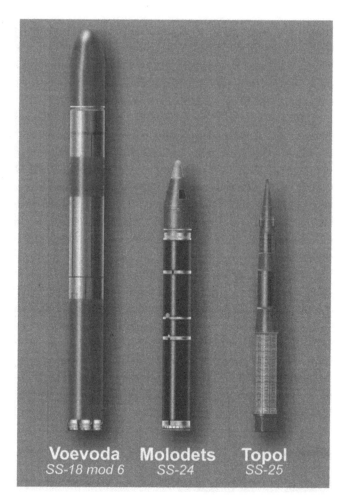

Voevoda   Molodets   Topol
SS-18 mod 6   SS-24   SS-25

The fourth-generation Russian ICBMs, 1980–2000.

fifteen tests were made through April 1985. Although most of the tests involved a warhead design with a single reentry vehicle, a version of the MIRV with four warheads was tested at least once. The truck-based launcher system for the Topol was similar to that of both its relatives, the Temp-2S (SS-16) and the Pioner (SS-20). The launcher truck was deployed in a Krona hanger, which sheltered the vehicle when not in use. In the event of a surprise attack, the roof could be opened to permit the missile to be launched without leaving the shelter. However, the intended pattern of deployment was to have a portion of the Topol force on the move around its base area on a daily basis to prevent the launcher from being targeted. In its original version, the launch would take place from a presurveyed location to ensure its accuracy.

The first two Topol bases entered construction in 1984 at Yoshkar Ola and Yurya. These were not as complicated to construct as silo missile bases, and the first Topol regiment became operational on 23 July 1985.[11] This regiment was a trials unit, because some elements of the new Topol system were not yet ready. The first regiment with the full support equipment became operational on 28 April 1987 at Nizhni Tagil. A more complete system with mobile berthing was fielded in April 1987, a new mobile command post in May 1988, and an improved launcher vehicle with improved land-navigation features in December 1988.[12]

Development of the new medium Molodets ICBM was far more protracted than that of the Topol. Ustinov had won government permission to begin development of a solid-fuel rail-mobile missile, designated the RT-23, on 13 January 1969. The program was delayed due to resistance by the military and concerns over the arms treaty negotiations, which sought to ban mobile ICBMs. The program was restarted on 23 July 1976, and the Yangel/Yuzhmash design bureau was also instructed to add a silo-based version intended to replace the earlier Yangel MR-UR-100 (SS-17).[13] The initial testing of the RT-23 missile began at Plesetsk on 26 October 1982, but the first-stage engine failed. A successful launch followed in December 1982, but the third test, in May 1983, was also a failure.[14] Of the eleven test flights, seven failed. The problems with the RT-23 design were so severe that Yuzhmash was forced to consider an upgraded version, the RT-23UTTKh, in November 1982.[15] The problems with the RT-23 missile led the government to reject it on 10 February 1983. However, the rail-mobile launcher system was accepted for experimental use to familiarize the troops with its operational features.[16] The program was reorganized in August 1983, with consideration given to three launchers for the RT-23U missile: the rail-mobile Molodets system, the road-mobile Tselina-2, and the silo-based version.[17] Of these three configurations, the road-mobile was the first discarded due to the awkwardness of the enormous launcher trucks.[18] The first test flights of the rail-based RT-23U took place on 27 February 1985, followed by the first flight tests of the silo-based missile on 31 July 1986.[19]

Due to the protracted development time of the RT-23U, it was the last of the new generation to be deployed. The final test launch of the rail-based version took place on 22 December 1987, and the first regiment became operational at Kostroma the same month. About ten trains were operational within a year's time.[20] The program was quite costly, because it was necessary to renovate the tracks near the operating bases.[21] Each rail-mobile missile division consisted of twelve launch cars organized into four trains, with three launch cars per train. The final test launch of the silo-based version took place on 23 September 1988, and the first regiment became operational at Pervomaisk on 19 August 1988.[22] Eventually, six former MR-UR-100 (SS-17) divisions at Pervomaisk and Tatischevo were converted to the new type, totaling sixty launch silos. The program suffered a further setback when a blast and major fire took place on 12 May 1988 at the Pavlograd plant, which manufactured its solid-fuel engines.[23] The RT-23U Molodets was accepted for service on 28 November 1989, twenty years after the start of its development.

Naval Modernization

Ustinov's plan to convert the Soviet missile force to solid fuel extended to the navy as well. In view of the failure of the first solid-fuel SLBM, the R-31 (SS-N-17) missile, by the Arsenal design bureau in Leningrad, Ustinov pressured the main submarine-missile bureau, the Makeyev bureau in Miass, to develop a solid-fuel missile. The bureau was resistant to the demand, arguing that a solid-fuel missile would be considerably heavier than a comparable liquid-fuel missile. To simplify the process, Ustinov ordered that the new R-39 solid-fuel missile would share a common first stage with the new RT-23 (SS-24) ICBM. This led to the most expensive and controversial ballistic-missile submarine in Soviet history.

The problem with using the RT-23 first stage was that it was massive, weighing about fifty-five tons. Furthermore, submarine missiles are generally stubby compared to land-based missiles. There is a premium on missile height since it must fit within the confines of a submarine hull. While it might have been possible to design a submarine with deeper than ordinary draft, the navy was unwilling to spend the sums necessary to dredge the main submarine harbors on the Kola Peninsula. As a result, the new submarine armed with the R-39 missile had to be large enough to accommodate the massive missile within its hull, while at the same time having a draft shallow enough to permit it to use existing submarine bases. The most experienced Soviet missile-submarine designer, Sergei Kovalev of the TsKB-18 Rubin design bureau, began development of the Project 941 Akula with the D-19 Taifun (Typhoon) missile system in December 1972.[24] This submarine is better known by its NATO name, Typhoon, due to a misunderstanding in Western intelligence, which associated its weapon-system name for its actual class name. Due to the unique problems posed by the design, Kovalev chose a very unusual configuration for the submarine, mounting all twenty missile tubes forward of the sail. The internal configuration was equally novel, with five pressure hulls within the design. The Akula class was substantially larger than any ballistic-missile submarine of the period, with a submerged displacement of 33,800 tons. Indeed, the unique hull configuration required the use of such large ballast tanks that the submarine was derisively referred to as the "water carrier" by its critics.[25]

The Soviet Navy's most impressive and controversial missile submarine was the Project 941 Akula class, better known in the west as the Typhoon. This unusual design placed all twenty of its enormous R-39 solid-fuel missiles in the hull, in front of the sail, instead of the traditional location, aft the sail. It proved so expensive that only six were built. (Courtesy U.S. Department of Defense)

The design was intended to offer a variety of new features, including the ability to surface through Arctic ice packs to launch its missiles. This feature was a reflection of growing interest by the Soviet Navy in operating its missile submarines in nearby Arctic waters, based on their expectation that this would counteract efforts by U.S. submarines to track and attack missile submarines. In addition, the new missile system had such long range that the Akula could actually carry out its launch mission from within the security of its base in northern Russia. This could significantly increase the contribution of the submarine missile force to the Soviet balance. Due to the shorter range of earlier missiles, previous submarine types had to leave port to reach their firing zones. Since only a small fraction of the submarine force was on patrol at any one time, the submarines in harbor contributed nothing to a Soviet retaliatory strike in the event of an American attack. The Akula was also the first submarine designed to have its missiles reloaded at sea from the new Project 11570 (Sadko) submarine tender. This feature was part of a Soviet program to enhance its ability to conduct a prolonged nuclear war if necessary.

Design of the associated R-39 missile proved to be protracted and troublesome. Test flights began in January 1980, and the first four were failures. The first successful flight didn't occur until December 1981, when the lead Akula submarine entered service. A majority of the seventeen missile test flights in this series were unsuccessful. A crash program to overcome the problems was begun, and a final set of test flights was conducted from the first completed Akula submarine. This corrective effort succeeded, and eleven of the thirteen test flights were successful. As a result, the D-19 Taifun weapon system with its R-39 missile (SS-N-20) were accepted for service in May 1983.

The main problem of the Akula submarine was not its difficult development, but its cost. The contemporary Kalmar (Delta III) cost about R 150 million, while the Akula cost about three times that, making it the most expensive submarine ever built for the Soviet Navy. By the late 1980s, when the construction program was under way, a bitter debate had begun about the scope of the program. Although many elements of the navy wanted to continue the program, both the main staff of the navy and the General Staff recommended that the program be limited to a single division of six submarines. Critics of the program argued that the size of the Akula limited its basing, and that its enormous missiles were a major problem in the fleet due to the need to move them by rail and special cranes. In the end, the critics won the argument, and the seventh Akula was broken up before completion.[26]

The high cost of the Akula had already prompted a parallel program in the late 1970s to develop a more economical submarine missile system based on the current Kalmar submarine. The new submarine, the Project 667BDRM Delfin (Delta IV), was a modest evolution of the existing design and posed little engineering challenge. However, the improved missile was a greater challenge, since it had to fit

The final evolution of the Navaga class was the Project 667BDRM Delfin (Delta IV), armed with the D-9RM (SS-N-23) missile system. The increasing height of the newer missiles obliged the submarine designers to continue raising the height of the missile compartment aft the sail. (Courtesy U.S. Department of Defense)

within the volume of the existing submarine design, yet have range capabilities similar to those of the massive ninety-ton R-39 on the Akula submarine. Makeyev's design team did this by increasing the volume of the first two stages and adding an unusually compact and clever third stage. Unlike conventional designs, in which the postboost vehicle separates from the final stage, the warheads were built around the third-stage engine. The R-29RM (SS-N-23) design began in January 1979, and the first flight test took place in 1984. Although the missile was accepted for service in February 1986, lingering reliability problems prevented widespread deployment until 1988. The design bureau has boasted that it was the most accurate Soviet submarine missile ever deployed.[27]

During the debates over a possible response to the U.S. Star Wars program, the navy offered some possible asymmetric responses should the U.S. field the system. One of the proposals was to substantially increase the number of SLBMs by converting existing cruise-missile submarines into ballistic-missile launchers.[28] This proposal involved substituting a dozen R-29RM missiles on the massive Project 949A Antei (Oscar II) for the existing Granit (SS-N-19) antiship missiles. This program never transpired, though it was examined again in the 1990s due to continuing concern over U.S. strategic defense programs.

In spite of the growing capabilities of the Soviet submarine force, the General Staff remained concerned about the vulnerability of the command links to the submarine. The various shore-based radio sites were unhardened and vulnerable to destruction in the early phase of a nuclear war. An alternative was the development of airborne radio-relay systems, patterned after the American TACAMO system. The Tu-142MR (Bear-J) maritime patrol aircraft was modified with the Orel system and first deployed in 1986.[29] Russian accounts suggest that the resulting aircraft had parameters generally inferior to those of the U.S. TACAMO. Even after these upgrades, many General Staff planners were unhappy with the command-link system in the mid-1980s. Other technologies were studied, including lasers and seismic signaling, but no entirely satisfactory system was found prior to the Soviet collapse.

The Cruise-Missile Revolution

Of the three legs of the Soviet strategic triad, the Soviet bomber force was by far the weakest and least important through the 1960s and 1970s. The force never entirely recovered from Khrushchev's opposition to bomber development. By the late 1960s most of the Myasishchev 3M (Bison) bombers had been converted to the tanker role. The worn-out Tu-95M (Bear A) bombers were the only active portion of the force, and their armament and avionics were obsolete. In hopes of extending their life, the air force modified the Tu-95 with the K-22 (AS-4) air-to-surface missile starting in 1973.[30] The first modified Tu-95K-22 (Bear-G) flew on 30 October 1975. Conversion of the remaining force of Tu-95Ks was given a very low priority, and the type was not accepted for service until 1987.[31] Furthermore, the converted bombers were earmarked for the anticarrier role, not for intercontinental missions.

The Soviet Air Force had a requirement for a new bomber since the early Brezhnev years, but the program had a low priority and little funding. A new bomber program began in 1967 with proposals that included the futuristic Sukhoi T-4MS and Myasishchev M-20.[32] Nothing came of the program, and it was revived yet again in 1970, this time pitting Myasishchev against Tupolev. Myasishchev's design was judged superior, but given his old bureau's poor track record and the lack of experience of his newly reconstituted design bureau, the contract was awarded to Tupolev in 1975 for the Tu-160 bomber.[33] The Tu-160 was very similar in appearance to the American B-1A bomber, though significantly larger and heavier. The armament for the Tu-160 was intended to be the same Kh-45 Molniya aeroballistic missiles planned for Sukhoi's ill-fated T-4 medium bomber a decade earlier. However, new trends in aircraft armament eventually upset these plans.

In 1968 the main avionics research institute, GosNIIAS, conducted a study code-named Ekho to examine future trends in strategic-aircraft weapons.[34] While the trend in Soviet aircraft armament had been toward supersonic or even hypersonic missiles, the Ekho study instead recommended the development of small, subsonic cruise missiles. The study argued that the hypersonic missiles were so large that only a few could be carried, and that they remained vulnerable to contemporary air defenses in spite of their speed. The advantage of small subsonic cruise missiles was that a bomber could carry a dozen or more, somewhat akin to a MIRV capability for bombers. Furthermore, advances in flight controls suggested that the missiles could be designed to fly a "nap-of-the-earth" profile, bringing them under radar detection and thereby avoiding air defenses. The recommendation was viewed with considerable skepticism by both the air force and the ministry of aviation production.

The U.S. Air Force arrived at the same conclusion, though by a different route.[35] The U.S. studies resulted in the AGM-86 ALCM (air-launched cruise-missile) program, which started in 1974. In view of the reluctance of the Carter administration to fund the new B-1A bomber, the ALCM took on new importance, since it could extend the life of the B-52 bomber force. The attraction of the ALCM for the U.S. Air Force was that it could be launched at standoff ranges outside the heaviest Soviet air defenses, significantly improving the survivability of the B-52 while at the same time increasing the number of targets a single aircraft could attack. The U.S. Navy had also been examining the idea of cruise missiles, though for another reason. A small cruise missile could be launched from the torpedo tube of attack submarines, or from canisters on surface warships. Up to this point, such warships had no significant capability to attack land targets. The navy started its Tomahawk SLCM (sea-launched cruise missile) program in 1974.

The Soviet Ministry of Defense became aware of these programs and began to reconsider its attitudes. However, there was still no consensus on whether future cruise missiles should follow the traditional pattern of large supersonic missiles, or the type proposed by the 1968 Ekho study. As a result, a trio of parallel programs was undertaken: Chelomey's supersonic Meteorit, the Raduga design bureau's subsonic Kh-55 ALCM, and the Novator's subsonic naval Granat SLCM. While Vladimir Chelomey was now being shunned by the Strategic Missile Force, his antiship missiles remained popular with the navy. Chelomey's chief rival in the naval cruise-missile business was the Raduga design bureau in Dubna, which had been responsible for closing his first design bureau in 1953. Raduga was also the main design bureau for bomber-launched cruise missiles. When the air force announced plans for a new missile competition in 1976, Chelomey came forward with another of his grand schemes, a "universal strategic cruise missile," which could be launched from land, from bombers, and from submarines or surface warships. Chelomey's strong connections with the navy ensured their support, and there was still considerable interest in supersonic missiles within the air force. Chelomey enticed the air force further by promoting his Meteorit missile as the world's first multiple-warhead cruise missile. Instead of a single warhead, the Meteorit had two separate warheads, each with its own rocket engine for the terminal phase of the attack.

Development of all three missiles proved troublesome. The main challenge facing the Raduga Kh-55 ALCM (AS-15) was its sophisticated Sprut (Octopus) guidance system, which, like its American counterparts, used an inertial guidance system combined with a terrain reference system relying on an onboard computer, which stored radar maps of the approach to the target area. This was especially difficult due to the size constraints imposed by such a small missile and the limitations of Soviet digital computers. The first test flights of the Kh-55 began in 1978, but it took a decade to iron out all the problems.

Chelomey's Meteorit (AS-19/SS-N-24) program was a complete fiasco. The first system launch took place two years after that of the Kh-55, on 20 May 1980, and all of the first four launches were unsuccessful. The program was complicated by Chelomey's obsession to develop a missile equally suitable for air and naval launch. The first submarine launch took place on 26 December 1983 in the Barents Sea. Of the twenty-two test launches of the Meteorit through the end of 1984, only one reached the required 5,000 km (3,000 mi) range. By this time the multiple-warhead feature had become less attractive, because the Soviet Union had agreed to ban such schemes under the 1978 SALT II treaty. In light of its technical problems,

The cruise-missile revolution began in the closing years of the Soviet Union. An air-launched cruise missile, the Kh-55 (AS-15), was deployed on newer bombers, including the Tu-95MS and Tu-160. This is a Kh-65SE, a conventional export version of the nuclear Kh-55SM, displayed at Zhukovsky Air Force Base.

and Defense Minister Ustinov's hostility to Chelomey, the program was canceled in 1984.

At first the Soviet Air Force considered following the American lead and using its Kh-55 ALCM to rearm its old Tu-95M bombers, called the Tu-95M55. These would have required an expensive avionics refit and other improvements to airframes that were worn out after more than two decades of service. Instead the air force decided to restart Tu-95 bomber production. Even though the last Tu-95 bomber had been built in the early 1960s, the Tu-95 production line had remained open at Kazan to supply the navy with its maritime patrol-aircraft version, the Tu-142. The new Tu-95MS was based on a modified Tu-142 airframe, with the Obzor attack radar and avionics of the new Tu-160 bomber. Production of the Tu-95MS began in 1984, and through 1992, about ninety had been manufactured.[36]

The Tu-95MS was regarded as a low-cost stopgap until the more advanced Tu-160 (Blackjack) was ready. The Tu-160's first test flight occurred on 19 December 1981, and it was ready for service in 1987. Production of 100 Tu-160's was authorized, exactly paralleling the number of B-1B Lancer bombers being built for the U.S. Air Force. However, the collapse of the Soviet Union prevented them from being built, and the Tu-160 became the last Soviet strategic bomber, with hardly a dozen in service.

The last of the Soviet Cold War heavy bombers was the Tupolev Tu-160 Blackjack. Although it is very similar to the American B-1B Lancer bomber in shape, it is significantly larger and heavier. Only a handful were deployed prior to the collapse of the Soviet Union. This example, one of the surviving Russian Air Force examples, is displayed at the Zhukovsky Air Force Base, where most Russian aircraft are tested.

The Soviet naval cruise missile paralleled that of the air force. In view of the failure of the R-31 (SS-N-17) solid-fuel ballistic-missile program, which was intended to rearm the old Navaga (Yankee) submarines, it was instead decided to arm them with cruise missiles. A modified Navaga could carry twelve Chelomey Grom (SS-NX-24) or forty Novator Granat (SS-N-21) cruise missiles. The cancellation of the Chelomey missile made the Granat the winner by default. A program to convert seven Navaga submarines into the Project 667AT Grusha (Yankee Notch) began in 1982, but only one was completed in 1988. Aside from these special cruise-missile submarines, several classes of standard nuclear attack submarines were also configured for the cruise missile, including the Project 971 Bars (Akula), Project 945 Barracuda (Sierra I), and Project 945B Mars (Sierra II). The new missile required a sophisticated targeting system on board the submarine to input navigational data before launch.

The Soviet cruise-missile programs ended up having a marginal impact on the strategic balance. Their development was more prolonged and less successful than that of their American counterparts, and they were deployed in much smaller numbers. In contrast, the American cruise-missile programs, especially the naval Tomahawk, caused considerable anxiety to Soviet military planners, becoming a major factor in the acrimonious intermediate nuclear forces (INF) debate.

Arms Control Stumbles

During the development of the fourth generation of ICBMs, the Soviet Union and the United States were involved in negotiations on a second arms-control treaty, SALT II. The aim of the negotiations was to set an outer limit on the number of delivery vehicles and warheads acceptable to both sides. The United States attempted to leave itself open to field new cruise missiles outside the treaty, while the Soviet Union attempted to protect its flexibility in modernizing its missile force by resisting U.S. efforts to limit the development of new missiles. After protracted and difficult negotiations, the SALT II treaty was finally signed in Vienna on 18 June 1978. The subsequent fate of the treaty in the United States was a barometer of the worsening relations between the two superpowers. The U.S. Senate refused to ratify the treaty. The problem was not so much the details of the treaty itself. Indeed, subsequent presidents, including Reagan, agreed to abide by its terms. It was the international context in which the debate took place.

Ultimately, arms-control treaties were intended by both sides to stalemate the arms race. The problem from the perspective of American critics of SALT II was that the arms race had slowed down in the United States but was continuing at a vigorous pace in the Soviet Union.[37] The United States had not deployed a new ICBM since the Minuteman, and new programs such as the MX were controversial and a decade away from deployment. The Carter administration had canceled the new B-1A bomber but approved the modernization of the old B-52 with cruise missiles. The only area where there was significant modernization was in the naval arena, where the U.S. Navy continued a steady program of evolution from the Poseidon to the Trident missile. Yet these American programs paled in comparison to the scale of Soviet efforts. From 1972, when SALT I was signed, to 1978, when SALT II was signed, the Soviet Union had already fielded an entire new generation of missiles and was working on yet another. These trends are also evident when examining the relative scale of missile production during this period. In the last decade of the Brezhnev administration, from 1972 to 1981, Soviet strategic-missile production was about four times larger than the American programs. The Soviet Union manufactured 2,250 ICBMs, compared to 510 by the United States, and 1,875 SLBMs, compared to 415.[38] In the view of conservative critics, the arms-control treaties had stalemated American strategic modernization, while the Carter administration was ignoring the scope and intent of the vigorous Soviet program.

Détente was collapsing in the international arena as well. The Soviet Union had expanded its arms transfers into the developing world and was playing a far more active role in regional conflicts in Africa and Central America.[39] In Europe the massive scale of deployment of the new Pioner (SS-20) shocked NATO and in December 1979 led to a resolution agreeing to the employment of new U.S. tactical nuclear systems in Europe, including the Pershing II missile and ground-launched cruise missile (GLCM). The Soviet Union's ill-considered invasion of Afghanistan in December 1979 sounded the death knell of détente and ushered in the period of the New Cold War. In one of the Carter administration's last major acts on U.S. military policy, in the summer of 1980, it adopted Presidential Directive 59, a new war-fighting doctrine that placed more emphasis on striking at the Soviet national command authority in the event of war. Strategic command and control remained the Achilles' heel of the Soviet strategic forces, and the combination of technological innovations and doctrinal changes caused serious anxiety to Soviet force planners. The failure of Carter's foreign policy with the Soviet Union helped to elect Reagan president in 1980 and led to the most confrontational and tumultuous decade in superpower relations since the early 1960s.

Decapitation and the Doomsday Machine

The Kremlin leadership had longstanding concerns over the possibility of a decapitation strike by U.S. strategic-missile submarines.[40] The problem posed by submarines was that their proximity to Moscow from launch sites in the North Sea would reduce Soviet warning time to about thirteen minutes, less than the command-and-control system would require to initiate a retaliatory strike. A variety of technological fixes were proposed, the most intriguing of which was code-named Perimetr. The Perimetr has sometimes been called a "doomsday machine," an allusion to the film *Dr. Strangelove*, Stanley Kubrick's black comedy about nuclear brinkmanship. The motivation behind Perimetr was to ensure that the Soviet strategic forces would launch a retaliatory strike even if the national leadership had been killed in a surprise nuclear attack. The government decree authorizing the design of the Perimetr system was signed on 30 August 1974.[41]

Perimetr was intended to be a stabilizing influence on the Soviet leadership, acting as a safety valve so that the national leadership was not forced by the tyranny of time to make a hasty decision to launch a nuclear war. Instead of being forced to issue hasty launch orders on the first sensor reports of American missile launches, reports that could very well be erroneous, the top national leadership could wait until there was adequate evidence that a full-scale attack actually was under way.[42] In the event of an ambiguous threat warning, the leadership knew that the Perimetr system would trigger a retaliatory blow even if the normal command-and-control system was disabled. The Russian nickname for the system was The Dead Hand.

The Perimetr system would sanction the strike if the national command authority was disabled, but only after an actual strike had occurred. The Perimetr system was a complex combination of sensors, command posts, and communication systems netted into the existing strategic command-and-control system. To activate the system, the General Staff would release a portion of the sanctioning codes to the Perimetr network during an international crisis or on first warning. At the heart of the Perimetr was a new sensor system that would detect the evidence of a nuclear attack. This system was a Soviet equivalent of the U.S. Integrated Operational Nuclear Detonation Detection System (IONDS), which was deployed in the early 1980s.[43] This sensor system was linked to a computer network that determined whether a war had broken out by means of an algorithm that required certain events to happen, presumably a given number of nuclear strikes against an array of specific targets. Russian officials have hinted that the system could not be triggered by a French, British, or Chinese strike, which presumably means that the system was only triggered by a fairly large number of nuclear detonations, as would be expected in an American nuclear attack.[44] The second criteria for authorizing the activation of the Perimetr system was interruption of command links to key Soviet leadership. There was a certain measure of human intervention in this system. The sensor data was fed to a central command center, and officers had to approve the decision to activate the Perimetr satellite based on a third criteria: a preliminary sanction for attack from the General Staff, which provided the first portion of the missile sanctioning codes. Once the three criteria had been met, the central command system activated a buried low-frequency radio antenna net that triggered the Perimetr launch system.

The Perimetr system, rather than using the existing Signal command-and-control system to remotely launch the ICBM force, introduced a new missile communication system. The command activated special missile sites, which would launch ballistic missiles with a special electronic payload. Instead of a nuclear warhead, these missiles contained a UHF radio transmitter, which broadcast special sanctioning codes to ICBM launch complexes. These signals made it possible to launch the ICBMs remotely, since the Signal-M system had introduced a radio receiver in the regimental launch complexes permitting remote launch. This satellite transmitter was somewhat similar to the U.S. Emergency Rocket Communication System (ERCS), except that the ERCS passes authorization codes to launch-control centers and does not actually launch the missiles without intervention by the crew. This novel communication system was incorporated because of the recognition that nuclear strikes would probably severely disrupt conventional communication due to electromagnetic pulse and damage to key elements of the command-and-control network.

Draft studies of the Perimetr system were undertaken in the early 1970s.[45] The final configuration consisted of the 15A11 command missile, derived from the MR-UR-100 (SS-17) fitted with the 15B99 communications package. This missile was designed to fly over selected ICBM sites, transmitting a series of launch signals to R-36M (SS-18 Satan) and MR-UR-100 (SS-17 Spanker) ICBM bases, automatically launching the ICBMs.[46] The first test flights of the Perimetr system took place in December 1979 and concluded in March 1982.[47] An operational test was conducted on 13 November 1984, when a missile launched from Kapustin Yar broadcast the launch order and activated and launched a selected R-36M ICBM from a silo in Kazakhstan. This test was part of a major Soviet nuclear exercise and served as the final stage of operational testing of the system. The Perimetr system became operational in January 1985. Curiously enough, the U.S. intelligence community was unaware of the existence of the Perimetr system until after the end of the Cold War.[48]

Soviet interest in the Perimetr system increased considerably in the early 1980s due to worsening superpower relations. As a result of the Pioner deployment, the United States and its NATO partners agreed to enhance theater nuclear forces with the addition of ground-launched cruise missiles and the Pershing II tactical ballistic missile. Of the two systems, the Pershing II posed the greatest dilemma for the Soviet General Staff. Based in Germany, it had the range to reach targets deep inside the Soviet Union with a precise terminal guidance system and earth-penetrator warhead.[49] To Soviet eyes, the intention of such a system would be to attack the command bunkers of the Soviet national command authority in the Moscow area. Due to its proximity and speed, the Pershing II represented a potent decapitation weapon, and the Soviets feared that it could destroy the national command authority before it had time to activate the strategic nuclear forces.[50]

This dilemma was symptomatic of the extremism of Soviet military thinking in the early 1980s. The Pershing II was not part of U.S. strategic-force planning, and it is by no means clear that it could actually reach Moscow. The controversy was the result of the Soviet tendency to exaggerate the American threat. Exaggeration or not, it was seriously believed by senior Soviet military officials. A variety of actions were taken to counter the Pershing II threat. Tests were ordered to determine whether the existing ballistic-missile early-warning network could be used to detect Pershing II launches. Deployment began of the Antei S-300V (SA-12), a tactical antiballistic-missile system designed to shoot down ballistic missiles like the Pershing II.[51] Other countermeasures followed traditional Soviet lines. The Communist Party attempted to stir up political opposition to the NATO countermoves in Western Europe among sympathetic disarmament groups. Eventually, the Gorbachev administration reconsidered the issue as part of their rethinking of Soviet security policy, prompting negotiations on the INF treaty.

The vulnerability of the national command authority to preemptive strikes was exacerbated by continuing delays of the ballistic-missile early-warning network, the most critical element of which was the new Oko early-warning satellite. The Oko was vital, since it could detect the initial launch of U.S. ICBMs more than ten minutes sooner than the missile-warning radars in the Soviet Union. The network was supposed to be up by the late 1970s but was delayed due to lingering technical problems. By 1980 the Oko network had been built up to four satellites, and by 1981, eight of nine orbital planes were filled. However, durability problems continued, and only five of the nine orbital planes were filled at year's end. From the inception of the operational program in 1976 through 1981, ten of nineteen Oko early-warning satellites had broken up, and two failed to reach orbit. In 1982, all nine orbital planes of the full system had been attempted, but by year's end, it had fallen to seven. A specialized command post was set up in the Moscow area to receive and disseminate the Oko data.[52] This marked the first time when the system could be viewed as operational to a significant degree. The initial configuration still could not cover U.S. SLBM launches from the Pacific. Nevertheless, the full system was accepted for service in 1982. Lingering technical problems with the Oko were one of the reasons for the KGB's peculiar high alert in the early 1980s.[53] Prompted by the aged and increasingly paranoid Yury Andropov, the KGB instructed its agents overseas to begin a heightened alert, code-named VRYAN (the Russian acronym for "warning of nuclear missile attack"), for any signs of an impending U.S. strike.

The initial Oko system differed markedly from the American DSP system,[54] which is in a high, geosynchronous orbit, while the Soviets settled on a low-altitude, semisynchronous orbit. This meant that the Soviets required nine satel-

Space is an essential element in strategic nuclear command-and-control systems. The Oko satellite played an especially vital role as part of the missile early-warning system, detecting missiles on launch, which activated the Soviet strategic network. This example is preserved at the museum of the Lavochkin design bureau, where it was designed. (Courtesy David Woods)

lites to maintain coverage over potential U.S. launch sites, while the United States required only three. The Soviet selection of this approach was due to difficulties in developing infrared detectors sensitive enough to operate from geosynchronous orbit. The geosynchronous satellites must be able to distinguish a missile plume against the active infrared background of the earth itself and sun-reflecting clouds. The low-altitude system can be oriented to detect the missile plumes in the direction of the horizon, omitting most of the active background. The situation gradually improved, and from 1984 to 1991, at least eight orbital planes were usually operational. The Oko satellites were finally supplemented by the new Prognoz geosynchronous orbit satellites starting on 29 March 1984.[55]

Problems with the Oko triggered one of the most serious incidents of the Cold War. This little-known episode was one of the few occasions that came close to activating the Soviet strategic forces and starting a nuclear war.[56] Through most of the Cold War, it was exceedingly unlikely that either side would seriously contemplate initiating a nuclear war. War was far more likely to start due to an error or misperception during a time of crisis, precisely the combination that occurred in 1983. In the weeks after the shoot-down of the KAL-007 airliner on 1 September 1983, Soviet-American relations were at one of their lowest ebbs, and Reagan denounced the Soviet action in the harshest terms. In the midst of this controversy, on 26 September 1983, an Oko satellite reported that a massive U.S. ICBM launch had taken place.[57] The alarm was repeated three times. In view of the past problems with Oko, the duty officer at the air defense early-warning center at Serpukhov-15, Lt. Col. Stanislav Petrov, believed it was a false alarm and decided against passing on the warning and triggering a nuclear alert.[58] Had Petrov passed on the warning, the Soviet nuclear strategic forces may have gone to full-alert footing, with dangerous and unpredictable consequences. This incident occurred in the midst of heightened international tensions and the paranoid KGB VRYAN scare. Given Soviet launch-on-warning doctrine and the international tensions, it is quite possible that the Kremlin would have launched a nuclear-missile strike based on the false Oko alert. When Petrov's action was later discovered, he was ousted from his post and forced into early retirement. A special emergency commission was created by the Ministry of Defense under the first deputy chief of the General Staff, Col. Gen. Valentin Varennikov, due to this worrisome shortcoming. It was discovered that the alarm had been triggered by increased solar activity that had not been anticipated in the system software.[59]

Lingering problems with the Oko network forced the Soviet early-warning system to rely on the ballistic-missile early-warning radars, in spite of their limitations. By 1983 the first five of the new Daryal radars were under construction.[60] Radars were needed to close gaps facing to the northeast in the Pacific region to keep track of U.S. submarine-launched Trident missiles. The initial recommendation called for two new radars at Norilsk and Yakutsk to comply with the 1972 ABM treaty, which insisted that the radars be located near the state border so that they could not serve as part of a nationwide ABM system. Yakutsk was ruled out due to a shortage of energy generation near the site. Other sites were also ruled out due to the expense and difficulty of constructing and operating such massive facilities in the remote wilderness of the Soviet Pacific coast, where there were no rail lines or roads to support construction. The chief of the General Staff, Nikolai Ogarkov, with the concurrence of Defense Minister Ustinov, decided to position a single radar 3,000 km (1,900 mi) from the Soviet frontier near Krasnoyarsk, in spite of its obvious violation of the 1972 ABM treaty.[61] This decision was primarily an economic one, because the Krasnoyarsk site offered the coverage of two radars closer to the coast and would be much easier to construct due to its proximity to the Siberian industrial region. If the installation were challenged by the United States on the issue, the official position was that the new radar was a space-tracking system and not part of the BMEWS network. The Krasnoyarsk radar was one of the most contentious issues of arms control in the 1980s and a serious roadblock to any further agreements.

To further speed the activation of the Soviet strategic force, a third version of the Signal strategic command-and-control system was deployed in the mid-1980s, called Signal-A. This system was designed to make it possible for the national command authorities in Moscow to launch the land-based ICBMs and IRBMs directly without having to pass the authorization commands to the missile divisions. The Signal-A system was accompanied by upgrades to the missile-guidance systems. With the advent of microprocessors in the flight-control systems of the later third-generation missiles, new targets could be quickly loaded into the on-board memory from a computer system colocated in the missile silo. The Signal-A system allowed the RVSN command center to change the targeting remotely from Moscow in ten to fifteen seconds. In the event of a preemptive U.S. strike, it would enable the General Staff to reconfigure its response even if some of its silos were destroyed by the first strike. In the event of prolonged nuclear war, it gave the General Staff greater flexibility in its targeting decisions. Even with the advent of the Signal-A and the improved Perimetr system, Soviet ICBM silos continued to be manned to provide a manual launch capability in the event that the automated system failed and to monitor the maintenance status of the missiles. The usual duty cycle was for a team of officers to remain in the silo for three to four days, with a two-man team occupying the launch consoles in twelve-hour shifts.[62]

Concern over the vulnerability of the national command posts in the immediate Moscow area led to the construction of yet another layer of redundant hardened-bunker construction in the late 1980s. These measures included a strategic command post constructed in Kosvinsky Mountain in the Urals, 850 miles east of Moscow, and a massive new government relocation bunker in Yamantau Mountain in the Bakshir republic.[63] As in the past, the command bunkers were supported by airborne command posts. To supplement the older Tu-135 aircraft, in the 1970s a pair of Ilyushin IL-82 were built as strategic airborne command posts.[64]

The Era of Stagnation Ends

Leonid Brezhnev's death after prolonged illness in November 1982 led to three years of government instability. Yury Andropov succeeded him, but the disagreements over the future course of defense policy and relations with the United States between the party and military leadership went unabated.[65] Andropov had not been active in defense decision making, leaving it to Ustinov and the military. The young and dynamic head of the General Staff, Gen. Nikolai Ogarkov, insisted that the military retain its preeminent position in setting state defense policy, as it had in Brezhnev's later years. The aged and infirm Soviet leaders were haunted by the specter of a slow coup by a dynamic new crop of military commanders. In neighboring Poland, the collapse of the local Communist Party in the face of the Solidarity movement had led to the imposition of martial law in 1980 and the accession to power of a military dictatorship. Andropov dubbed Ogarkov a "Napoleonchik" and began efforts to have him demoted rather than risk his taking over the defense minister's post from the ailing Ustinov.

Andropov himself died in February 1984, having been in power for hardly a year, and was succeeded by a geriatric Brezhnev crony, Konstantin Chernenko. Chernenko's reign was even shorter, and he died in March 1985 after hardly a year in office. Long the party's main defense authority, Dmitry Ustinov died in December 1984. The wartime generation had clung to power far too long, leaving the country in the hands of younger men who in many cases had not been properly prepared to handle their responsibilities.

Mikhail Gorbachev, the first Soviet leader of the post–World War II generation, was selected in March 1985. Gorbachev was very different from every previous Soviet leader in his complete lack of affiliation with either the military or the military industries.[66] Not only had he been too young to have served in the war, his party positions were remote from state defense policy. This was both a blessing and a curse. On the one hand, it allowed him to look at the vexatious debates on defense from a new and fresh perspective. On the other hand, he was untutored in the complexities of defense decision making, undermining his credibility with the military commanders and industrial leaders, and he was left without a strong vision for the future of state defense policy. Unlike Khrushchev, he was not particularly interested in the arcane details of defense technology, and his grasp of the fundamentals of defense policy was weak at best. Nor did he have a strong team of defense advisers, since the military tended to monopolize defense expertise as a means to control defense policy.[67] There was no tradition of civilian defense analysis comparable to that in the United States to offer alternative visions to those of the General Staff or the defense industries.[68] There were some efforts by foreign policy think tanks to shape defense policy, but the military's monopoly of even the most elementary data on strategic weapons undermined the credibility of their proposals.

By the mid-1980s relations between the military and civilian leaders had come to their lowest ebb since the Khrushchev years.[69] During the "era of stagnation" in the late Brezhnev years, the military had gradually usurped more and more power over defense policy, both in terms of defining state security interests and in shaping expenditures on the armed forces. A prominent Soviet official recalled: "The leadership made the [defense] decisions, but the military and the military-industrial agencies prompted those decisions and even managed to 'pre-program' the political leadership. Shaped and executed under the cloak of secrecy, military policy ceased being an instrument of our foreign policy and acquired a life of its own."[70]

Ogarkov had insisted that the Soviet Union respond to NATO modernization with a major modernization of its own. He argued that the advent of a revolutionary new generation of smart weapons would undermine the Soviet Army's numerical superiority over NATO. Ogarkov foresaw the new age of "information warfare" that would become so manifest during the 1991 Gulf War. Prior to Ogarkov the Soviet Army had measured combat power by World War II indices such as tank strength and artillery firepower. Insufficient attention had been paid to new technologies. While NATO could derive a significant portion of these technologies from their vibrant civil economy, the Soviet commercial sector had become emaciated in the 1970s by the drain of research and development funding into the predominantly military economy. Although Ogarkov understood the problem, he remained wedded to the panacea of higher defense expenditures and lacked an understanding of the need for profound economic reform to support modernization.

The military-party debate occurred within a broader context of industrial and technological stagnation.[71] Since the mid-1970s the rate of growth in the Soviet economy had continued to decline, while the Soviet armed forces had continued to insist on increases in defense expenditures. Gorbachev and his advisers believed that stimulating and reforming the economy would have to take place at the expense of the military, who were a disproportionate drain on the economy.[72] Reform could only take place if international tensions were reduced from the strident levels of the early 1980s. This meant a reinvigoration of the arms-control effort that had been abandoned by both sides after the invasion of Afghanistan in 1978. Ogarkov's replacement, Marshal Sergei Akhromeyev, took a more cooperative position on arms control, though other commanders of the armed forces continued to bristle at talk of defense reform.[73] Akhromeyev had been a representative of the General Staff at previous arms-control negotiations and was more attuned to the foreign policy implications of Soviet defense policy than most Soviet commanders.[74] As a first step in paving the way to arms-control talks, Gorbachev replaced the head of the RVSN, Marshal Vladimir Tolubko, with a younger officer without strong links to the missile force, Gen. Col. Yury Maksimov.

Party control had been eroded in the economic sector, as well, as ambitious ministers and plant directors in the defense industry took a larger part in running the economy. In the past, the party had exercised broad control of the lives of workers through the monopoly over housing assignments, salaries, and other essentials. In the 1970s the party gradually ceded control of many of these matters to the industry. In turn, the defense industry depended upon the award of state prizes at the conclusion of successful weapons program to add new plant housing, new cafeterias, and other inducements for both the skilled and unskilled labor force. The new relationship of party and industry introduced a greater rigidity in defense planning, since the failure or cancellation of large weapons programs had dire consequences for local economies. There was a tendency to accept unsatisfactory weapons into service, even if in small numbers, rather than suffer the social consequences of outright cancellation. Previous state industrial policy had focused on the creation of major defense enterprises in smaller and more remote cities to help industrialize the country. Cities like Dnepropetrovsk, Miass, Zlatoust, Krasnoyarsk-26, and Votkinsk were one-industry towns, almost wholly dependent on the missile business. There was little labor mobility due to the chronic lack of housing. As a result, weapons were built as much to keep up employment as to satisfy any particular defense need. This led to many absurdities, such as the production of large quantities of older technologies rather than their replacement by smaller numbers of new, more reliable systems. For example, vacuum tubes remained a staple of Soviet defense electronics long after they had been abandoned in the West for transistors and integrated circuits. As a consequence, modernization of the electronics industry suffered. Plants were rewarded by meeting their centrally planned quotas and would lose rewards for producing smaller quantities of better products. The defense industry was woefully inefficient, employing far larger engineering and production staffs than comparable Western industries and having very low labor productivity.

Although inefficient, the Soviet defense industry had succeeded in matching the United States in the strategic-arms race. Could it still do so after reform? Gorbachev began by suggesting that reform would actually enhance Soviet national security, since it would eventually make the industry more efficient. But he soon began to question whether competing in the arms race was really necessary.

At the center of new arms-control controversies was the American Strategic Defense Initiative (SDI). Both the United States and the Soviet Union, under its Fon-1 program, had been involved in a broad range of research efforts on novel directed-energy weapons in the late 1970s.[75] However, Reagan accelerated the process by insisting that the development programs transition from lab research to engineering development of deployable weapons. The initial Soviet reaction was predictable. The party leaders began a propaganda campaign decrying the Star Wars program, while keeping the Soviet Union's own extensive activities a closely guarded secret. The military industries promoted two new weapons programs. The head of the missile industry at the time, Oleg Baklanov, pushed to transition the Soviet Star Wars program from the Fon-1 research stage to the Fon-2 engineering development stage. The transition was authorized by Andropov in 1983.[76] A separate effort, code-named Protivodeistviye (Counteraction), started in 1985 as an asymmetric response to SDI, aimed at improving the ability of ICBMs to survive against space-based weapons.

The first ground-based test of the Fon-1 program took place at the insistence of Defense Minister Ustinov in 1984. The Soviet military was convinced that the new U.S. Space Shuttle was a thinly disguised attempt to acquire a dominant position in space. The Shuttle was variously assessed as having the capability to drop nuclear weapons from space and a unique space-reconnaissance role. The Fon program was not simply about stopping a missile attack but also included research on destroying U.S. satellites. Ustinov ordered the program managers to test out the system to see if they could accurately aim at the Shuttle. On 10 October 1984 the Terra-3 high-energy laser facility at Sary Shagan was used to track the U.S. space shuttle *Challenger* in conjunction with the neighboring Argun phased-array radar.[77] This exercise allegedly caused malfunctions on the Space Shuttle and distress to the crew.

Earlier Soviet studies of space-based weapons had concluded that they were outside the reach of Soviet technology. Whether they were within the reach of U.S. technology was another matter. Soviet military intelligence had habitually exaggerated the capabilities of U.S. military technology, and their SDI assessments were probably no exception. Soviet contacts with the U.S. aerospace industry such as the joint Apollo-Soyuz space missions in the 1970s had made it clear that the United States continued to enjoy some significant advantages in technologies directly applicable to advanced space-based weapons. Even if the Soviet Union could catch up to the United States in critical areas of electronics, sensors, and computer processing, the economic hurdles appeared formidable. The Soviet Union had exhausted its economic resources in the Brezhnev years trying to catch up in tactical and conventional weapons, even though the U.S. defense budget was in decline during this period. If past experiences were any indication, the prospects for Soviet success in a new arms race with the United States were far from assured. When the United States had joined the technology race in earnest, such as during the arms race and space race of the 1960s, the Soviet Union had not been able to keep pace. The Reagan program presented a challenge more like those of the Kennedy-Johnson years of the 1960s than the Ford and Carter years of the 1970s.

The accident at the Chernobyl nuclear power plant in April 1986 had a profound effect on Gorbachev and the new Soviet leadership. It undermined confidence in the abilities of Soviet technology and suggested that other problems might be lurking unseen and unrecognized. The enormous consequences of even a small nuclear accident provided a potent reminder of the dangers of nuclear war. Chernobyl helped to ensure that strategic-arms control would become the central element of Gorbachev's defense agenda.

Because there were no ongoing talks on strategic defensive weapons, Gorbachev attempted to tie SDI to the discussions on limiting intermediate nuclear forces (INF). Talks on INF had been held since late 1980 but had made little progress. From the Soviet perspective of the mid-1980s, the modernization of their own intermediate forces in the late 1970s, especially the Pioner (SS-20), had proven to be a mixed blessing.[78] The strong reaction of the European NATO members, especially Britain and Germany, had reinvigorated the alliance and led to an unanticipated American response. Soviet intelligence exaggerated the role and capabilities of the Pershing II and created a bogeyman that in the end would cost the Soviet military dearly. Furthermore, the deployment of the Pioner had given the United States more incentive to deploy new nuclear Tomahawk cruise missiles on ship and submarines to act as a counterweight to the new Soviet missiles. Launched from the oceans around the Soviet Union, the cruise missiles added yet another worry to Soviet strategic defense planners. The Pioner deployment did little to enhance Soviet security but was a catalyst for the deployment of new weapons that posed a novel threat to the Soviet Union.

The knee-jerk reaction of the Soviet military was to respond tit for tat by increasing the number of weapons aimed at the United States. Since the size of the Soviet Strategic Missile Force was constrained by the SALT treaties, the only way to do this was to increase the tempo of submarine patrols and bomber missions near the U.S. coast. The sortie rate of the new Tu-95MS (Bear-H) bombers was increased in the Arctic approaches to the United States.[79] Patrols by the old Navaga (Yankee) missile submarines had decreased substantially in the late 1970s owing to the arrival of more modern submarines with long-range missiles, and the new bastion defense doctrine.[80] Instead of the usual routine of two submarines on patrol at any one time, in 1979 the navy ordered the tempo increased to as many as six or seven submarines on patrol off the U.S. coast. The increased operational tempo placed great strain on the old submarines and was accomplished at the expense of maintenance and crew preparation. In early October 1986, a week before the planned Reykjavik summit, one of the old submarines, *K-219,* suffered a catastrophic explosion in one of its missile tubes and a near failure in its nuclear reactor, sinking off the coast of Bermuda along with its load of nuclear-armed missiles.[81] Coming only a few months after Chernobyl, the prospect of a nuclear explosion or serious nuclear accident so close to the American coast had a sobering affect on Gorbachev. The loss of *K-219* was symptomatic of the hidden decay in many branches of the Soviet military and emphasized the need to ratchet down the tension between the superpowers.

Reagan and Gorbachev met at Reykjavik in October 1986 to discuss progress on INF. Gorbachev tried to drive a wedge between the United States and Europe but failed when his attempt to link an INF treaty with a limit on SDI was rejected outright by Reagan.[82] This proved to be a temporary setback, because Gorbachev was desperate for an agreement. The exaggerated threat of the Pershings gave Gorbachev ammunition in his debates with the military over the INF negotiations, since it created a threat serious enough to warrant concessions to the Americans.

The first successful Soviet missile submarine was the Project 667A Navaga class, better known to NATO as the Yankee. Although similar to the U.S. George Washington class, it used the liquid-fuel R-27 (SS-N-6) missile. Liquid fuel was a persistent problem. On 3 October 1986 a fuel leak on this submarine, *K-219,* led to an explosion that finally sank the boat off the Bermuda coast a few days later. (Courtesy U.S. Navy)

Relations between the military and the Kremlin were at their lowest ebb. Gorbachev responded to the resistance in the military by further purges of senior commanders. When a German light plane landed in Red Square in May 1987, Gorbachev used it as the pretext to remove the minister of defense, Marshal Sergei Sokolov, along with a number of other old-guard commanders. He replaced him with a young unknown from the provinces, Gen. Dmitry Yazov.

With the military commanders temporarily battered into submission, Gorbachev made most of the concessions that made the INF treaty possible. Not only did the treaty specify total elimination of all Soviet INF weapons in exchange for elimination of their U.S. counterparts, but there was no tie to SDI, no tie to forward-deployed U.S. aircraft, and no tie to sea-based cruise missiles. Verification would include on-site inspections inside the USSR itself for the first time. Details of the treaty, which Gorbachev signed with Reagan on 7 December 1987, infuriated military commanders. The USSR was obliged to destroy far more weapons than the United States, including the new Oka (SS-23) tactical ballistic missile, which did not even fall within the treaty's range restrictions. The thought of American inspectors poking around Soviet missile bases was anathema to most Soviet commanders, who had been brought up in a paranoid culture of secrecy.

From past experience with other treaties, the senior commanders at least hoped to gain some concessions from the Kremlin in exchange for the acquiescence to the treaty. The Politburo, with Chief of Staff Akhromeyev's consent, was inclined to disband all fourteen RVSN missile divisions formerly equipped with the INF missiles, both as a matter of economy and as a prudent foreign relations gesture. However, the RVSN staff urged the disbanding of only five of the divisions, those equipped with the obsolete, fixed-site R-12 missiles, and the retention of the Pioner divisions, which were to be gradually reequipped with mobile ICBMs. This position was supported by Defense Minister Yazov, who was able to persuade Akhromeyev to change his mind. In April 1988 a decision was reached with General Staff support to add a further 135 Topol (SS-25) mobile launchers to the 180 Topols already planned to be deployed by 1989.[83] However, the matter was far from closed, and to save money, Gorbachev's Defense Council recommended that additional rail-mobile Molodets (SS-24) missiles be acquired instead, with an equivalent number of warheads. Since the Molodets had MIRV warheads, this meant acquiring only 14 additional Molodets launchers instead of 135 Topols. The chief of the RVSN, Maksimov, opposed this move, because it failed to take into account the large number of RVSN officers who would have to be demobilized and added little to RVSN force survivability. Eventually the RVSN position prevailed when a Council of Minister's decree in January 1991 authorized the manufacture of a further 135 Topol launchers.[84] The Topol decision helped the military save face in an otherwise one-sided encounter with the Kremlin over the latest round of arms control.

Relations with the military remained testy. In the light of American refusal to abandon Star Wars, the military wanted to begin testing elements of the Fon-2 program, even though the tests would undermine Gorbachev's attempts to portray the SDI effort as a unilateral abrogation of the ABM treaty. The first space-based test of the Fon-2 program was the Polyus space station, scheduled for launch in 1987.[85] The station included a number of experiments to test ground-based directed-energy weapons and disrupt U.S. SDI efforts, such as a system to disperse a barium cloud intended to interfere with American directed-energy weapons. On being shown the satellite on a visit to the Baikonur launch facility in early 1987, Gorbachev insisted that the space experiments not be carried out for fear that they would derail Soviet efforts to limit SDI. It became a moot point when the station, launched on the new Energia booster on 15 May 1987, failed to reach orbit and fell into the Pacific Ocean.

The START I Treaty

The INF treaty was only the first step in a broader effort by Gorbachev to reduce international tensions. Discussions had started at Reykjavik over substantial reductions in strategic offensive forces. Previous treaties, such as SALT I and SALT II, had placed caps on force growth but had not led to any actual reductions. The new talks were aimed at cutting back the size of the forces for the first time. Reagan and Gorbachev had toyed with the idea of totally eliminating strategic nuclear weapons during private discussions at Reykjavik, but this was too utopian a scheme, and it foundered over Reagan's attachment to SDI.

From the perspective of most Soviet military analysts, cutbacks were acceptable if accompanied by a Kremlin commitment to force modernization. The RVSN was still equipped with a large number of obsolete missiles that were beyond their service life, including several hundred old UR-100 (SS-11), and old naval missiles like the R-27 (SS-N-6), which had been responsible for the loss of the submarine off Bermuda in 1986.

By 1987 the Soviet military leadership had formulated three force options for the year 2000. The first and preferred option presumed another strategic-arms agreement, with continued U.S. acceptance of the ABM treaty.[86] It envisioned a force of 1,398 ICBM launchers consisting of half MIRV types (308 R-36M/SS-18's, 280 RT-23/SS-24's in silos, and 96 RT-23/SS-24's on rails), and 700 single-warhead missiles (Topol and the new Kuryer). This position was attractive to the RVSN, since it got rid of the older types and consolidated the force entirely on new missiles. The RVSN concluded that such a force structure would have a combat value 200–300 percent greater in terms of throw weight and accuracy, while at the same time enhancing the survivability of the force by increasing the share of mobile launchers from about 20 to 50 percent.

The second force structure presumed a cut of the heavy-ICBM force based on a tentative agreement at the December 1987 Washington summit. Under this scheme, the MIRV missiles would take the most serious cuts, down to only 25 percent of the number of permitted launchers (154 R-36M/SS-18's, 56 RT-23/SS-24's in silos, and 36 RT-23/SS-24's on rails), while the single-warhead types would remain the same (500 mobile Topol/Kuryers and 200 silo-based Topol/Kuryers).

The third position presumed a failure of the START negotiations or a U.S. abandonment of the ABM treaty in favor of Star Wars deployment. Under this later condition, the RVSN was proposing a rapid expansion. This would be based around two efforts. One was the new Kuryer (Courier) light ICBM, which the

RVSN planned to rapidly deploy in extremely large numbers. The second effort was an acceleration of the Protivodeistviye program, which aimed at improving the ability of heavy and light ICBMs to survive Star Wars. This program included acceleration of the Soviet Fon-2 ABM program and of active defenses such as antisatellite weapons aimed at Star Wars satellites.

Ultimately, none of these positions emerged intact, because both sides traded off concessions to win an agreement.[87] The final START I treaty, signed on 31 July 1991, envisioned major cuts in the Soviet heavy-missile and MIRV force, with the aim of creating a force less well suited to a preemptive counterforce strike. The former head of the RVSN estimated that the shift in emphasis between the RVSN and the Russian Navy and other force-level changes inherent in START I would decrease the counterforce capability of the RVSN by 8 times, the overall counterforce capability of all Russian strategic forces by 2.2 times, and the retaliatory capabilities of the force by 1.5 times.[88] The START treaty set overall force limits in terms of missiles and warheads but left it up to both sides to determine for themselves the exact composition of their forces.

A fifth generation of Soviet ICBMs was in development in the final years of the Soviet Union. These are the least known of the Soviet programs, since many of the programs collapsed along with the Soviet Union. The MIT began work on the Kuryer program in 1981 as a centerpiece of the Soviet Union's asymmetric response to SDI. It was designed as a very low-cost solid-fuel missile that could be built in extremely large numbers. It was a very small missile, weighing only about fifteen tons, and somewhat similar to the U.S. MGM-134 "Midgetman." The draft project was finished in 1984 and helped form the basis for the Protivodeystvie anti-SDI effort. However, the flight-test program did not begin until 1992, by which time any rationale for the program had collapsed.[89] The MIT also sponsored several other studies of asymmetric responses to SDI, including an improved version of the existing Topol light ICBM. The proposed Topol-M used a fast-burn first stage, which would limit the amount of time that the missile remained exposed to space-based SDI directed-energy weapons during the boost phase. The Topol-M also included other anti-SDI techniques, such as a maneuvering warhead bus to complicate interception in the midcourse and terminal phase of flight. Topol-M had low priority during most of the 1980s but was restarted after the Soviet collapse. The MIT was also examining a new missile code-named Skorost (Speed) as a successor to the Pioner intermediate-range missile. A single test was conducted at Kapustin Yar on 1 March 1987, but the program was canceled a week later, on 7 March 1987, due to the INF treaty.[90]

The main ICBM bureau at the Yuzhnoye plant in Dnepropetrovsk had two major ICBM programs in the 1980s. The Ikar was planned as a follow-on to the R-36M2 Voevoda (SS-18) heavy ICBM. Work on this program did not progress to the flight-test stage prior to the Soviet collapse. It was also heavily involved in improving the Molodets (SS-24) and examining possible successors.

Ustinov's death in 1984 prompted Chelomey's NPO Mashinostroyeniye design bureau to try to break back into the ICBM business, even though the main design team at the Fili plant had been taken away. The new director since Chelomey's death, Gerbert Yefremov, won government permission to start the Albatros missile program on 9 February 1987. This was planned to be another asymmetric response to SDI, but had not reached the test-flight stage by 1991–92, at which time funding collapsed.

The Soviet Strategic Forces in Retrospect

By the late 1980s Gorbachev's attempts at reform and rejuvenation had begun to fail. Faith in Marxist dreams had become exhausted, giving way to cynicism and demoralization. If Chernobyl had shaken confidence in the omnipotence of Soviet science, the rise of the Solidarity movement in Poland and the collapse of the communist governments in the Warsaw Pact countries in 1989 had shaken confidence in the omnipotence and legitimacy of the Communist Party. As the Soviet Empire slipped away, Gorbachev's fate was sealed.

To preempt a communist collapse in the Soviet Union, senior government and military leaders began to plan a coup patterned on the one against Khrushchev in 1964. The coup was supported by the senior leaders of the army, KGB, and military industries. One of the key plotters was the former head of the missile industry, O. D. Baklanov. Defense Minister Yazov and the chief of the General Staff, Akhromeyev, were involved. Many of the plot leaders were mediocrities typical of senior party leaders in the Brezhnev days, with little charisma and no broad support within the Soviet elite. The August 1991 coup collapsed within hours of being staged, leaving Gorbachev nominally in power. But in reality the coup had sapped any legitimacy from the government, and alternative power centers emerged in the form of republic governments, especially the Russian federation, headed by Boris Yeltsin. To sweep away the remains of the Soviet government, in December 1991 the republic leaders signed a joint declaration declaring their independence and marking the end of the Soviet Union.

If wars are won by will, Russia's loss of the Cold War cannot be attributed to a loss of will on the part of the Soviet military leadership. The generals remained imbued with the sacred cause to the end. The collapse of the Soviet Union was due to a loss of will on the part of Russia's political elite, weakened by the impossible demands of the military and the resultant failures of the bankrupt economy.[91]

The Soviet military system proved to be remarkably resistant to reform.[92] The gangrenous legacies of the Stalin years and the horrors of World War II left a tragic legacy for the postwar generations. The Stalinist inheritance of paranoia and xenophobia became intertwined with the bloody memories of the sacrifices and triumphs of the war years. The defense of the Soviet homeland became a sacred cause demanding unquestioned sacrifice. Discussion of major defense issues, even by the senior leadership, was made difficult and often impossible by the stranglehold of secrecy of the Stalinist military culture. A decade after the end of the Cold War, former Soviet leaders admit they had no firm idea of the actual cost of Russia's defense burden.

Soviet strategic policy was a victim of the manic-depressive contradictions of traditional Russian security strategy and Marxist ideology. Steeped in the painful memories of centuries of humiliating defeats at the hands of smaller but more advanced opponents, Russia's traditional security anxieties were an uneasy match for the triumphalist Marxist expectations of the inevitable triumph of socialism over capitalism. The dark dreams of past military disasters could not be banished from memory, even if the "correlation of forces" seemed pointing to the Soviet Union's bright future. For the Soviet commander, the propaganda image of the omnipotent Soviet military clashed with the daily realities of poorly trained troops, low readiness rates, and frequent equipment failures.

The Stalinist legacy of a hypermilitarized economy was one of the principal roots of the Soviet failure, draining the vitality of the Soviet economy.[93] While the Soviet Strategic Missile Force had some role in this process, the nuclear arms race was not the principal or even most significant element of Soviet defense expenditures. Total Soviet spending on its intercontinental nuclear forces amounted to about 7 percent of its total defense spending in 1951–90, plus another 4 percent devoted to intermediate-range nuclear forces.[94] The sheer size of Soviet conventional forces caused a far greater drain on the Soviet economy. Other branches of the armed forces, such as the PVO-Strany strategic air defense force, absorbed budgets comparable to those of the strategic-missile forces while at the same time offering only marginal contributions to Soviet security.[95] Brezhnev's counter-revolution to Khrushchev's defense reforms made the Soviet armed forces resistant to any attempts at reorganization and rationalization.

Even if the Soviet strategic nuclear forces were not a significant cause of the Soviet collapse, their inefficiencies were part of a broader pattern of military extravagance that corroded the Soviet economy. During the Cold War years, the Soviet Union fielded no fewer than eleven ICBMs types in no fewer than twenty variants. In contrast, the United States fielded only four types in six major variants. The excessive number of missiles developed in the Soviet Union were due to the institutional rigidities of the defense industries. There were similar trends in the manufacture of the missiles as well. From 1975 to 1989, Soviet missile plants manufactured 2,490 ICBMs, compared to only about 280 in the United States.[96]

The Soviet missiles had far shorter service lives than their American counterparts, and the advent of new types every decade or so meant that they were replaced more often than their U.S. counterparts. A similar pattern is evident in the naval realm. A Russian naval officer concluded that the Soviet Union spent about 70 percent more on its ballistic-missile submarines than the U.S. Navy during the Cold War, yet they failed to provide a comparable contribution to the Soviet strategic forces. The Soviet Navy fielded eight types of submarine ballistic missiles, compared to three U.S. types. From 1975 to 1989, Soviet naval ballistic-missile plants manufactured 2,195 missiles, compared to 651 U.S. missiles.

Even if inefficient, the Soviet Union's strategic nuclear forces had accomplished their mission of deterring attack against the Soviet state. As a counterfactual history, it is easy enough to imagine the likelihood of a major war between the United States and the Soviet Union had the nuclear deterrent forces never existed. The level of suspicion and a string of crises in Berlin, Cuba, and the Mideast provided ample tinder for global conventional war. From the end of the Stalin years, major war between the superpowers had become unthinkable.

From a Russian perspective, the creation of the Soviet nuclear deterrent force was a remarkable technological achievement. In spite of the technological weakness of the Soviet Union in 1945 and the impoverished state of the economy well into the 1960s, Soviet engineers had managed to create a force rivaling that of its far richer nemesis, the United States. The Soviet Union was able to assert its position as one of the world's two superpowers due primarily to its powerful nuclear-missile force.

7.   Soviet Becomes Russian

1991–2000

The disintegration of the Soviet Union in December 1991 affected the RVSN more profoundly than it did any other branch of the Soviet armed forces. The newly formed Russian republic took over the control of the strategic nuclear forces, most of which were on Russian soil. But a significant fraction of the missile and bomber forces were at bases in the newly independent republics.[1] As a result, Russia lost control of nearly a quarter of the ICBM force—23.9 percent of all launchers, including some of the most recent fourth-generation systems. The submarine missile force remained intact, since the force was based entirely in Russian waters. The losses of the air force bomber fleet were the most serious of any leg of the triad, and Russia lost almost half of its aircraft to the other republics. Russian and American pressure led to the speedy denuclearization of all of the other republics. Besides the loss of much of its equipment, the new Russian RVSN suffered major setbacks in terms of its industrial base, its command-and-control facilities, and its testing facilities. There was no immediate rethinking of nuclear strategy, if only because of the turmoil caused by the effects of Soviet disintegration and the impact of new arms-control agreements.

Denuclearizing the Republics

The Soviet armed forces did not dissolve immediately after December 1991. To maintain a measure of centralized control, Russian authorities created a new administrative entity, the Confederation of Independent States (CIS), with an associated high command. There was some hope that the other republics would acquiesce to CIS control of the strategic forces remaining on their soil, which would have permitted the strategic nuclear forces to remain mostly intact. However, the CIS concept did not take hold, and Russia was obliged to deal with the varying demands of the successor republics, most of whom preferred denuclearization to retaining nuclear forces under Russian control. The Lisbon Protocol of 31 July 1991 recognized all four republics of the former USSR as the designated successor states of the USSR in terms of past treaty commitments, notably the START I arms-control treaty.

Behind the discussions of nuclear weapons was the specter of civil war. Armed clashes had already broken out in the Caucasus and central Asia, and there was some fear that a general civil war could break out on a scale comparable to that of 1917–21. One of the most immediate issues was the control over nuclear weapons, especially the smaller tactical nuclear weapons.[2] Such weapons held the greatest potential for trouble, since they might by seized by extremist groups or used in any potential conflict between the newly created republics. They had far less elaborate controls, and their small size made them susceptible to pilferage. The tactical nuclear weapons were more numerous and more widely dispersed than the strategic nuclear weapons in potential hotspots such as the Caucasus and Armenia. They included nuclear artillery projectiles, tactical missile warheads, and a variety of naval weapons, including torpedoes, mines, depth charges, and missile warheads.[3] The republics quickly appreciated that any attempts to take over control of nuclear weapons would provide Russia with a pretext to invade. Since the allegiance of former Soviet forces on republic soil was far from evident, this would probably mean a quick end to independence. The United States made it quite clear that it preferred nuclear weapons to remain under centralized control and encouraged the new republics' leadership to allow Russia to withdraw tactical nuclear weapons. In 1992 Russia began a speedy and largely secret effort to withdraw all tactical nuclear weapons from the other republics. About three thousand tactical nuclear warheads were withdrawn from Ukraine alone.[4] This process progressed smoothly and was largely accomplished by May 1992.[5] Although the weapons themselves were removed, several republics retained fragments of the nuclear industry, including processing facilities.[6]

The withdrawal of strategic nuclear weapons, including missile warheads, aircraft free-fall nuclear bombs, and aircraft-launched nuclear cruise missiles, did not begin immediately. The missile warheads represented the least threat, since the missiles could not be readily retargeted on Russia. Most of these missiles had a substantial minimum range, on the order of 3,000 km (1,900 mi), which would prevent them from being targeted against most of central Russia. In addition, it was by no means certain that the independent republics could recruit engineers familiar enough with the guidance systems to actually carry out the reprogramming.

Russia proposed that the CIS control a broad range of "strategic" forces, including not only the strategic nuclear offensive and defensive forces, but also a significant portion of the navy and air force, as well as specialized army units, such as paratroopers that could be deployed beyond the borders of the Soviet Union. The attitude of the other republics to the CIS initiative was less than enthusiastic. The Russian definition of "strategic" was too broadly defined and included warships, transport aircraft, bombers, and other systems that were previously considered tactical weapons. In the eyes of the republics, the CIS represented a Russian attempt to retain control of many of the best elements of the former Soviet armed forces under the pretext of centralized control of the strategic nuclear forces. Nevertheless, there was no immediate resistance when control over the ICBM force was nominally assumed by the CIS high command starting in December 1991. The United States began to apply pressure for the other republics to denuclearize, with the lure of receiving cash assistance. Russian authorities began to reconsider the desirability of leaving strategic nuclear weapons outside of their borders, especially after Ukraine began to discuss the possibility of retaining an independent nuclear force.

There was far less debate over these issues in Belarus and Kazakstan (the names of the independent republics) than in Ukraine. Both Belarus and Kazakstan agreed in principal to allow Russia to retain control over these forces, and to transfer the weapons back to Russia, where feasible, or permit their demilitarization. Belarus never asserted its control over the strategic nuclear forces on its soil, and they remained under central Russian control. The denuclearization of Belarus was somewhat simpler than in Ukraine, since the two missile divisions stationed there were equipped only with fifty-four mobile Topol (SS-25) ICBMs. The first three regiments were returned to Russia in the spring of 1994.[7] The Belarus government temporarily halted the return of the last two regiments in August 1995, but this was mainly a bargaining ploy to gain additional Russian concessions. The final regiment of the 49th Strategic Missile Division departed for Russia in November 1996.[8]

Kazakstan presented a somewhat similar picture. Kazakstan "nationalized" Soviet units in April 1992 but never asserted control over the strategic nuclear forces. In July 1993 Russia and Kazakstan agreed to a military program under which Russia would provide a quarter of the forces stationed in Kazakstan in return for a program to train Kazak officers for the future armed forces. The 79th Heavy Bomber Division of 49 Tu-95MS Bear heavy bombers at Semipalatinsk was flown back to Russia in 1993 in exchange for the transfer of a number of fighter aircraft to Kazak control. The 104 R-36M (SS-18) ICBMs stationed at Derzhavinsk and Zhangiz-Tobe had their warheads removed by April 1995, and the last silo was dismantled in September 1997.

The Ukrainian government had not reached consensus on the nuclear issue in early 1992, and some nationalist politicians advocated a retention of some nuclear capability.[9] There were proposals to retain the most modern ICBMs, such as the 176 Molodets (SS-24), and some bomber-launched cruise missiles. However, in 1992 the government of Leonid Kravchuk informed the United States that it would eliminate all nuclear weapons within seven years. The details of this process took years of negotiations to work out. Ukraine finally adopted its own military doctrine following a parliamentary vote in October 1993. The doctrine supported earlier assurances of the elimination of nuclear weapons but made them conditional on Western security assurances.

The issue of the control of strategic nuclear weapons on Ukrainian soil continued to plague Russia-Ukrainian relations. In April 1992 Ukraine began steps to take over control of the RVSN bases on its soil. Although the Ukrainian government had no means of actually controlling the launch of the missiles, it began to take steps to ensure that it could prevent the launch of the missiles. In September 1992 Russia insisted that the forces should revert to Russian control rather than CIS control, a position that Ukraine rejected. As a result, in November 1992 Ukraine declared that it owned the strategic nuclear forces on its soil. The 43rd Missile Army, the higher headquarters of the strategic-missile units in Ukraine, was reorganized by the Ukrainian government with troops who had sworn an oath of loyalty to Ukraine. To ensure the gradual assimilation of the RVSN units into the Ukrainian armed forces, Kiev agreed to take over financing of the missile bases. This was not a minor issue, since the payrolls of the troops at the missile bases had been erratic since 1991, and Kiev hoped to ensure the loyalty of the missile troops by promising them both pay and housing. Soviet practice had been to allow retired officers to retain their apartments on base, so the housing provisions were intended to encourage officers to shift their loyalty to Ukraine. In the spring of 1993, Moscow complained that Ukraine was attempting to retarget the missiles and defeat the existing control systems. Since one of the Soviet Union's manufacturers of the permissive-action links (PAL) was the Ukrainian Monolit plant, this was plausible. In July 1993 the nuclear-custody units were placed under Ukrainian control, and officers who refused to take the loyalty pledge were sent back to Russia. On 21 January 1994 the head of RVSN forces in Ukraine, Gen. Lt. Vladimir Mikhtiuk, took the oath of allegiance to Ukraine, as did 1,400 of 2,300 RVSN officers. Those who did not were removed from command and replaced. Ukraine turned increasingly to the United States to act as a broker after a string of unfruitful discussions with Moscow. The United States tied aid and good relations to gradual denuclearization and pledged an aid package of $700 million. With promises of U.S. support, the Ukrainian parliament ratified the START I treaty

The end of the Cold War has seen a dismantling of the strategic nuclear forces outside of Russia. Here, on 18 April 1995, a UR-100NU (SS-19) missile at the Pervomaisk base of the 43rd Missile Army in Ukraine is being taken out of its silo. The silo cover is barely evident to the left of the missile under a camouflage net, and the silo opening can be seen behind the missile. (Courtesy U.S. Department of Defense)

and the Nuclear Nonproliferation Treaty (NPT) in November 1993.[10] This was a critical step in the dismantlement of the strategic-missile force in Ukraine.

The 43rd Missile Army began taking the missiles off alert duty in the summer of 1993, when two regiments (20 UR-100NU/SS-19) at Pervomaysk were taken off line. The regiments were finally deactivated in January 1994. In December 1993 the first seventeen Molodets (SS-24) at Pervomaysk were deactivated. The first sixty ICBM warheads were transferred from Pervomaysk to Russia in March 1994. The United States provided $175 million for this effort. By 1 June 1996, all nuclear warheads from the Ukrainian missiles had been returned to Russia, completing the denuclearization of Ukraine. The removal of the actual missiles and the formal demilitarization of the launch silos was completed in 1999. The Russians eventually removed about two thousand nuclear warheads and twenty thousand tons of missile fuel from Ukraine from 1992 to 1997.[11]

The other significant nuclear force on Ukrainian soil was the 106th Heavy Bomber Division, based at Priluki. This included twenty-seven Tu-95MS (Bear H) bombers, two obsolete Tu-95M (Bear A) and nineteen new Tu-160 Blackjack bombers, and twenty associated IL-78 Midas aerial tankers. The nuclear armament of this force included 564 Kh-22 (AS-4) and Kh-55 (AS-15) air-launched nuclear cruise missiles. Ukraine showed far less interest in returning these aircraft to Russia, since they could be used in roles other than nuclear attack. However, the Ukrainian Air Force soon found that the bombers were expensive to operate and difficult to support since Russia refused to sell spare parts. As a result, Ukraine began a protracted series of discussions over the possible sale of the aircraft back to Russia. The talks dragged on so long that the condition of the aircraft seriously deteriorated. In November 1998 some of the older aircraft began to be scrapped under a program funded by the U.S. government. In October 1999 Ukraine finally agreed to transfer the aircraft in adequate condition back to Russia in return for debt forgiveness for previous oil shipments. This included eight Tu-160's, three Tu-95MS's, and all of the nuclear cruise missiles that were delivered to Russia in early 2000.[12]

Reorganizing the Russian Force

The sudden and unexpected collapse of the Soviet Union disrupted all previous planning for the future of the Russian strategic-missile force. The missile industry was disrupted even more than the armed forces, and some claimed that 75 percent of the industry was outside Russia.[13] The large number of plants in the Ukraine were the most critical loss. The largest and most important development and production center for Soviet ICBMs, the Yuzhmash complex in Dnepropetrovsk, was in Ukraine. Furthermore, this plant's new solid rocket fuel plant at Pavlograd was also in Ukraine, as was the main Soviet ICBM inertial guidance development center and manufacturing plant, in Kharkov.[14] This plant produced 90 percent of the ICBM guidance systems. Other facilities lost in Ukraine were the Monolit plant, which manufactured PALs used for nuclear security systems. Due to the 1976 shutdown of the Chelomey design bureau's ICBM branch, Russia was left with only one ICBM design bureau, MIT, in Moscow, compared to three bureaus at the peak, in the early 1970s. There was a loss of other facilities in other republics, such as the Sigma onboard computer plant in Moldova, but nothing to compare to the massive hemorrhage of development talent and manufacturing capability in Ukraine.

The plants in Ukraine were confused about the future, hoping to remain in business through interrepublic agreements. The Yuzhmash plant offered to continue developing and manufacturing missiles for Russia.[15] The offer was rejected by Russian officials, due in part to the testy relations between Moscow and Kiev, and also due to pressure from Russian industry, which was having a hard time getting funding from Moscow for their own programs.

The loss of the Ukrainian facilities affected not only future production possibilities, but also the maintenance of the existing ICBM force. Certain expendable items such as inertial guidance platforms were manufactured in Ukraine, and Ukraine was the center for many other spare parts vital to future upgrade. For example, the certified life of the inertial guidance platform on the Molodets (SS-24) missile was 30,000 operating hours (1,250 days, or three years and three months). The inertial measurement unit must be kept running when the missile is on combat-alert duty, otherwise the system takes about twenty minutes to warm up from a cold start. At the time, about two-thirds of the ICBM force was kept on combat alert at any time, implying that the inertial platforms had to be replaced at least every five years, twice within the life expectancy of a missile.[16] The RVSN faced the prospect of limiting the number of missiles on alert duty or seeing a large fraction of the force become inoperable due to parts shortages. Due to these factors and the drastic decline in the Russian defense budget, by March 1997 about half of the ICBMs in Russian service were beyond their certified life.[17] While missiles could be operated beyond their certified life, their reliability declined significantly. The situation was ameliorated somewhat by the return of missiles from Kazakstan and the existence of a large maintenance float of spare missiles, which could be cannibalized or used as replacements. Nevertheless, this was a finite resource. By 1998, 60 percent of the deployed ICBMs had been in use for double their certified life.[18]

The situation was exacerbated by the decline in the Russian defense budget. In contrast to the former Warsaw Pact states, such as Poland, Hungary, and the Czech Republic, the Russian economy suffered from a catastrophic decline in the years following the end of communist rule. Corrosive inflation, mismanagement, and massive corruption crippled the economy. The Russian government proved to be unable to collect adequate taxes. At first, the military industries and armed forces continued to act as though nothing had happened. Plants continued to turn out missiles even though they were not paid. A clear example of this comes from the Votkinsk plant, the last functioning ICBM plant in Russia. Production at Votkinsk in the late 1980s averaged sixty-three Topol (SS-25) missiles annually but fell to fifty-six in 1990, twenty in 1993, nine in 1994, and six in 2000.[19] By the mid-1990s it was not unusual for RVSN missile troops to be owed six months or more of wages. In 1998 the governor of one region considered taking over the missile bases in his area owing to the payroll problems.[20] On several occasions RVSN troops were obliged to take control of local power stations when local authorities shut off electricity to the missile bases due to lack of payment.

The situation with SLBMs was not as bleak. The one and only SLBM design center, Makeyev's bureau in Miass, remained in Russia. The same applied to both naval missile production plants: the R-39 (SS-N-20) plant at Zlatoust, and the R-29R plant at Krasnoyarsk-26. In addition, the main inertial guidance system manufacturer for SLBMs was in Russia, in Omsk. The main Soviet heavy-bomber design bureau also remained in Russia, as did the main bomber plant in Kazan. However, production at all these plants ground to a halt by the mid-1990s due to a lack of funds.

Kazakstan inherited the Baikonur proving ground, one of two in the former Soviet Union, and its main space-launch center. While Kazakstan continued to permit Russian activity at the center, the political and economic turmoil that gripped Russia in the mid-1990s led to a serious deterioration in the facility. This did not affect missile tests, since most could be conducted from the second test range at Plesetsk. But it did have a particularly serious effect on the military space program. The other key facility lost in the early 1990s was the strategic-defense proving ground at Sary Shagan in Kazakstan. By the mid-1990s, the site had been largely abandoned and its mission partly reconstituted at test facilities in Russia.[21] This loss was the death knell of the Red Star Wars program, Fon-2.

Arms Control and Modernization

Mikhail Gorbachev signed the START I accord on 31 July 1991. This arms-control treaty was the first to codify an actual reduction in the size of the nuclear arsenals on both sides, down to 1,600 delivery systems and 6,000 warheads. Implementation of the treaty was complicated by the collapse of the Soviet Union and the need to win the acquiescence of the republics. A second phase of the discussion continued through the early 1990s, resulting in the START II treaty, which was signed by Boris Yeltsin in 1993. This treaty aimed to eliminate land-based missiles with MIRV warheads and specified a further reduction of warheads to 3,500. The two treaties aimed at eliminating about two-thirds of the nuclear firepower that existed at the end of the Cold War. The START II treaty ran into unexpected difficulty due to the need to obtain approval of the new Russian parliament. The Duma was dominated by communists and nationalists who were deeply resentful of the decline of Russia's power. The expansion of NATO into the former Warsaw Pact countries of Poland, Hungary, and the Czech Republic was most often cited as the reason for rejecting the treaty, though there were a variety of other complaints. Opponents of the treaty were critical of the provisions to remove the R-36M (SS-18) heavy ICBMs, which they saw as Russia's most potent strategic weapon. In contrast to previous arms-control treaties, the START accords were generally supported by the Russian military leadership, since there was a widespread recognition that the Russian missile force was going to shrink anyway due to budget and maintenance problems. The START II treaty was finally ratified by the parliament on 14 April 2000, after Yeltsin's retirement, and even then with revisions.

The modernization of the Russian strategic-missile force took a back seat to efforts simply to keep the force operational. The inertia in the military industries meant that new missiles continued to roll off the production lines at least until 1994–95, by which time the budget arrears had halted most production. As in the case of the assembly lines, the engineers working in the design bureaus continued to show up at their facilities even after funding evaporated.[22] Testing on some missiles started in the final Soviet years, such as the lightweight Kuryer, were conducted in 1991–92 but eventually ground to a halt. In spite of the budget problems, the Yeltsin government favored continued modernization of the strategic force. In view of the decline of Russian power in the wake of the Soviet collapse, there was recognition that the nuclear arsenal was the only guarantor of Russia's great-power status.

The only ICBM design bureau left in Russia was the MIT. The new director suggested that an upgraded version of the Topol, still in production at Votkinsk, would be the most likely candidate for the future Russian force. This missile, called Topol-M (SS-27), was an evolutionary upgrade of the Topol, and its single-warhead configuration made it suitable under the START II treaty. Formal authorization to begin engineering development of the Topol-M came in February 1993.[23] Due to the lack of funds, the RVSN decided to deploy the first regiments of the new Topol-M in silos rather than on the mobile launchers used with the earlier Topol (SS-25). This avoided the cost of creating new equipment and bases for the mobile launchers and promised to reduce life-cycle costs due to the lower operating costs of silo missiles versus mobile missiles. On the other hand, it significantly decreased the survivability of the Topol-M force, undermining efforts to shift from a launch-on-warning posture to a more stable launch-on-attack posture. Plans called for fielding the Topol-M in 1995, but funding was completely inadequate, and the program was delayed three years. The appointment of Igor Sergeyev, the former head of the RVSN, as the new minister of defense in 1997 helped to give the program greater priority. Even after the number of test flights was trimmed back to cut development costs to the bone, it still took two more years to deploy the first regiment in December 1997. This deployment was mostly for show, and the system was not accepted for service until April 2000.[24] The RVSN had hopes of acquiring about thirty-five to forty missiles a year to enable the force to retire older missiles while still maintaining the size envisioned under the arms-control treaties. Budget realities limited annual production to ten missiles a year in the late 1990s, and to six a year in 2000. By the late 1990s, the RVSN was receiving less than half of the funding needed to maintain the force.[25]

The loss of the missile bases in the independent republics, combined with the disbanding of the intermediate-range missile divisions in the wake of the INF treaty, led to a sizable decline in the size of the RVSN even before the START-related cuts took effect. The INF force reductions alone cost fourteen divisions. By early 1997 it was down to 112,000 troops, about 10 percent of the total Russian armed forces—less than half the size of the RVSN at its peak strength during the Soviet period.[26] In 2000 the RVSN was organized into four missile armies, with nineteen missile divisions. In terms of launchers, the RVSN had a total of 1,398 ICBM launchers in 1991; by 1997 this had been reduced to 756 launchers as the force adapted to the START treaty cutbacks. In 1997 the RVSN accounted for 5–6 percent of the Russian defense budget.[27] A tentative decision was made by Yeltsin in the mid-1990s to eventually absorb the RVSN into the air force, but this issue remained controversial through 2000.

The navy's modernization program proved much more difficult than that of the RVSN. In 1991–95 the navy received less than a third of its budget requirements.[28] The navy's primary strategic-missile effort was the long-delayed D-31 system, which used an improved version of the solid-fuel R-39, the 3M91 Bark (SS-NX-28). Russia laid down the first of its new class of Borei nuclear-powered ballistic-missile submarines in November 1996.[29] The missile was intended for retrofit of the existing Typhoon submarine class as well. The new missile program fell behind schedule due to sharp funding cuts. The Bark program was the responsibility of the Makeyev bureau, in Miass, which faced a significant challenge, since the first stage of the missile was designed by Yuzhmash and manufactured at Pavlograd, both facilities in Ukraine. The first three tests of the missile, in 1996–97, were failures, leading to a controversial decision to cancel the program. The cancellation threw the entire submarine program into chaos, since the new Borei submarine construction could not proceed without a mature missile-system design. Given the Makeyev design bureau's lack of experience with solid-fuel rocket-engine design, in 1998 the Russian government decided to start a new missile program in conjunction with the MIT bureau called Bulava-30. The Bulava is intended to take advantage of the propulsion technology of the Topol-M. The Makeyev bureau was not happy about this decision and offered an evolutionary improvement of their liquid-fuel R-29RM (SS-N-23) called the Sineva.[30] In either case, the cancellation of the Bark program set back the Russian naval strategic-missile program by a decade.

The Russian Air Force continued to be the weakest partner in the strategic triad. With little success in retrieving the Tu-160 bomber regiment from Ukraine, the force was entirely dependent on the Tu-95MS bombers and a handful of Tu-160 Blackjacks. Although there were occasional promises to initiate a new bomber program, the intercontinental mission atrophied due to a lack of funding for new aircraft.[31] Funding limits constrained air force modernization plans to a modest upgrade of the existing force. Raduga was assigned the development of a new stealth cruise missile (i.e., one with reduced visibility to radar detection), the Kh-101, as well as upgraded versions of the existing Kh-55 (AS-15) air-launched cruise missile.

The collapse of the Soviet Union in 1991 adversely impacted the Russian strategic command-and-control system. The most immediate impact was the loss of many early-warning radars, which created many blind spots. Work was still under way on the new generation Daryal system, and not all of its radars were complète. U.S. complaints about the illegal Krasnoyarsk radar led to a halt in its construction in 1987 and its eventual dismantlement. Most of the other Daryal radars were outside of Russia in the now-independent republics: Skrunda in Latvia; Mukhachevo, Sevastopol, and Nikolayev in Ukraine; Lyaki in Azerbaizhan; and the main Sary Shagan test range in Kazakstan. Concern over environmental hazards put an early end to further work on the Skrunda station. Other Daryal stations still under construction in the other republics were not completed, and in some cases, the operational stations ceased operation or saw operations cut back. A major problem of the Russian stations was their high power consumption. Electrical power for the radar at Pechora cost R 40 billion in 1994.[32] An upgraded version of the Daryal radar, code-named Volga, entered construction in Belarus in the mid-1990s as an attempt to fill the gap created by the Latvian Skrunda radar dismantlement.

The space-based network of Oko and Prognoz satellites continued to decline through the 1990s due to lack of funding for new satellites and space boosters.[33] The last of the geosynchronous Prognoz satellites failed in 1998, and no replacement was available.[34] An attempt was made to improve the Oko network with the test launch of a new version of the early-warning satellite in 1993.[35] The constellation of Oko satellites was seldom kept at its full configuration of nine satellites, and four was the norm. While the Oko and Prognoz space-based early-warning systems might have made up for the gaps in the land-based radar network, the collapse of the Russian defense budget crippled this effort.

There were plans to deploy a new national command-and-control system in the early 1990s, code-named Tsentr (Center). Tsentr was intended to provide an integrated network for the command and control of both conventional and nuclear forces, linked to the RVSN's Signal-A network. The Kazbek system, used by the national command authorities, was to be replaced by a new system called Vershina. This upgrade was considerably slowed down by the collapse of the Soviet Union in 1991. As a result, many elements of the Kazbek system exceeded their expected life, and their reliability became questionable. Some elements of the new system were fielded, including a new airborne command post, the Ilyushin IL-86VKP (NATO: Maxdome). This aircraft was specifically developed for the General Staff and is a Russian analog of the U.S. Air Force E-4B National Emergency Airborne Command Post (NEACP).

Efforts to modernize the command and control of other branches of the Russian deterrent forces were hampered by a lack of funds and the technical challenge. The naval element of the Tsentr system, known appropriately enough as More (Sea), was intended to extend the Perimetr "dead hand" system to sea. Since the radio signals used for the existing Perimetr system would not penetrate water, the More relied on transferring the signals to a land-based relay station and then on to the submarine via very-low-frequency (VLF) or extremely-low-frequency (ELF) signals. The U.S. Navy had a parallel ELF program in the 1980s.[36] Portions of the More system were deployed in the early 1990s, but the system as a whole was never completed. The Tsentr's airborne element was designated Krylo (Wing). As in the case of More, the Krylo system was intended to extend the Perimetr concept to the Tu-160 and Tu-95MS strategic bombers and upgrade the existing communications network. The later portion of the effort was analogous to the U.S. Air Force's Strategic Air Command Digital Network (SACDIN) program of the 1980s.[37] Through the 1990s Krylo progressed only as far as experimental design work.

The budget problems that prevented the full deployment of the Tsentr system also made it difficult to maintain the existing command-and-control network. Power cutoffs to RVSN bases and command centers, disruption of the cabling to RVSN sites by thieves pilfering the copper wiring, and other difficulties led the worried minister of defense, Igor Rodionov, to state in 1997 that control over the Russian strategic nuclear forces was on the verge of collapse.[38] In February 1998, the head of the RVSN, Gen. Col. Vladimir Yakovlev, indicated that 71 percent of the systems in the strategic command-and-control network were beyond their warranty period.[39] In 1997 it was reported that on several occasions, the command-and-control network had inadvertently been switched to the "combat mode," presumably a reference to an initial warning order sent out to alert the chain of command to a possible transmission of actual orders.[40]

The incident that has caused the most concern about the status of the Russian strategic command-and-control network occurred on 25 January 1995, when Norwegian scientists launched a scientific rocket from Andoya Island, in the Arctic, to study the aurora borealis. Although Russia had been alerted through official channels of the planned launch, this information was apparently not sent to appropriate elements in the command-and-control network. As a result, when the rocket was detected by early-warning radars, it was interpreted as a possible

American submarine missile launch. The strategic command-and-control network was activated—the only time in the existence of the Kazbek system.[41] The early-warning radar system sent a signal, which led the duty general at the General Staff headquarters to activate Kazbek. President Yeltsin was informed by the officers operating his Cheget briefcase, and a conference call was held between Yeltsin and Defense Minister Pavel Grachev. By this time Russia's early-warning radars had determined that the flight path of the missile was not into Russia, and as a result, the duty general at the General Staff headquarters switched the Kazbek system back into normal operating mode and ended the alert. Given the near collapse of the former Soviet early-warning system, the incident raised real questions of the resilience of the Russian strategic command-and-control system.

The Andoya incident was especially worrisome due to the traditional launch-on-warning posture of the Soviet and Russian missile force. In an effort to reduce the risk of future misunderstandings, the United States government began to take steps to give the Kremlin access to the U.S. early-warning network. In September 1998 Presidents Clinton and Yeltsin agreed to establish a joint center to share early-warning information. The first joint operation took place in late 1999 due to concerns over the possible effect of a Y2K computer glitch on 1 January 2000. Russian officers were stationed at a special facility at the American early-warning center at Cheyenne Mountain. Steps were begun afterwards to open a permanent U.S.-Russian joint facility in 2001.

Attention in the United States has been focused mainly on the threat of a local Russian unit accidentally launching a strategic missile against the United States. From a Russian perspective, the opposite is more likely. Through the 1990s the command-and-control network has deteriorated to the point where the Kremlin now has to wonder whether instructions to launch a missile strike would be transmitted, received, and carried out.

Doctrine and Missions

The decline of Russian military strength in the wake of the Soviet disintegration led to considerable debate over future doctrine.[42] The first published statement on the defense doctrine of the Russian federation in 1993 marked a reversal in declaratory policy on the first use of nuclear weapons. While a "no-first-use" doctrine had been publicly stated by the Soviet Union for several decades, the 1993 doctrine stated that Russia would consider using nuclear weapons first for self-defense. However, the Foreign Ministry went to great pains to reaffirm that Russia's policy was one of deterrence. The end of the no-first-use doctrine was more a reflection of the decline of Russian conventional military strength than a major shift in strategic-forces policy. Russian planners recognized that the threat of global nuclear conflict had substantially diminished, while the risk of regional conflict had increased. With the Russian Army growing weaker by the day, the threat of the use of tactical nuclear weapons was viewed as a prudent shift in policy. This policy was reaffirmed in other formal policy statements in 1997 and 1999.[43]

The trend toward reducing the threat of strategic nuclear weapons continued in spite of the policy pronouncements. In January 1994 the United States and Russia signed a declaration in Moscow to "detarget" strategic missiles aimed at each other. This agreement has been more of symbolic value than anything, because the Signal-A system can retarget the missiles in ten to twenty seconds.[44]

The START treaties favored weapons less likely to be used in a surprise attack, such as aircraft and submarines. Since the late 1980s both the Russian Air Force and Navy have argued that their nuclear forces should be given a greater share of the strategic-deterrence mission. Nevertheless, the RVSN still retained a disproportionate share of the strategic nuclear missions, being responsible for about 90 percent of the strategic missions, even though it possessed only about 60 percent of the missile and warheads of the strategic nuclear force.[45] This was due both to the traditional biases of the General Staff and the serious decline in readiness of the submarine missile force due to a lack of operations and maintenance funding. Land-based silos are cheaper to keep in operation than submarines, and the training of Russian submarine crews declined drastically due to a lack of funding to conduct patrols away from the harbor. Of the sixty-two ballistic-missile submarines in operation in 1990, only twenty-three were operational in 1998, and this number has continued to decline. The lack of maintenance funding had a far more adverse effect on the navy due to the difficulties of operating liquid-fueled missiles at sea. The number of Russian submarine patrols, including missile and attack submarines, declined from fifty-five in 1991 to twenty-six in 1996.[46] At least one more missile-fuel accident occurred at sea in May 1998, which provided further incentive to retire the older submarines.[47]

The performance of the land-based force declined as well, and only 63 percent of the missile divisions received an evaluation of "good" in 1998.[48] However, this was a higher readiness level than that earned by the navy or air force. The air force role in the strategic mission continued to decline if for no other reason than the miniscule size of the force. In 1998 the separate Long-Range Aviation branch of the air force was abolished and the strategic-bomber units consolidated under the 37th Air Army headquarters.

In an effort to create a centralized authority for the deterrent forces, in 1998 the Ministry of Defense began to take steps to create a Joint Supreme Command of the Strategic Deterrence Forces.[49] This organization was intended to replace the General Staff as the primary director of the strategic forces in hopes of providing a more balanced and independent view of force requirements. The General Staff had traditionally favored the RVSN over the other two branches of the strategic forces, and there was some concern in the Russian government that the navy in particular was not being afforded a proper role in force planning.[50] However, the effort was stymied in April 1999 by the General Staff, which argued that a unified command already existed within the General Staff.[51]

While there was no consensus on unification of the deterrent forces, there was widespread agreement over the need to rationalize the organization of the Russian armed forces to reduce the redundant and expensive bureaucracy. On 18 July 1997 President Yeltsin signed a decree on organizational reforms in the armed forces. Under the terms of the decree, the RVSN Strategic Missile Force absorbed the Military Space Forces (VKS), the Missile Space Defense Forces, the early-warning elements of the PVO-Strany Air Defense Command, and the nuclear-custody units of the 12th GUMO (a main directorate of the Ministry of Defense).[52] As a consequence of these reforms, the RVSN had direct control over several key elements of the command-and-control network, namely early-warning satellites and radars. The reform had little effect, and in early 2001 the space force split off again after arguments that the RVSN was neglecting its needs.

Russia's strategic nuclear forces are likely to decline over the next decade in both size and efficiency due to the industrial problems associated with the Soviet collapse and Russia's harsh economic decline.[53] Although the Russian Ministry of Defense has asserted that the strategic programs will receive the top priority of all of its procurement programs, it has never received even the minimum acceptable level of funding in recent years. Starved of funds, and entangled in the contradictions between the superpower pretensions of Russian nationalists and the painful realities of Russia's faltering economy, the strategic nuclear forces are likely to decay in an uncontrolled and unpredictable fashion.

Appendix 1   Missile Technical Data

Legend

Abbreviations

AI	astroinertial
IOC	initial operational capability
IRFNA	inhibited red fuming nitric acid
LOX	liquid oxygen
Mt	megatons
PBV	postboost vehicle
Penaids	penetration aids (countermeasure decoys)
SL	sea level
T	metric tons
Ts	tons per second
UDMH	unsymmetric dimethylhydrazine
vac	in a vacuum

Design Bureaus

Avtomatika	NPO Avtomatika, Moscow
Barmin	KSKB Spetsmash
Chelomey	OKB-52 GKAT, TsKBM, Reutov
Glushko	OKB-456, Energomash, Khimki
Iskra	Tsurilnikov KB, OKB-172, Perm KBM
Khartron	NPO Khartron, Kharkov
Klimov	OKB-117
Korolyov	OKB-1, TsKBEM, Kaliningrad
Kosberg	KBKhA, OKB-154

Kuznetsov	NII-692
MIT	NII-1 MOP, Moscow Institute of Thermotechnology
Pilyugin	NIIAP
Rudyak	KBSM, TsKB-34, Leningrad
Soyuz	V. P. Zhukov KB, NPO Soyuz, Lyubertsy
Titan	TsKB Titan at PO Barrikady, Volgograd
Tyurin	TsKB-7, Leningrad
Vympel	Filial No. 2, OKB-52, now NPO Vympel
Yangel	OKB-586, KB Yuzhnoye, Dnepropetrovsk

Manufacturing Plants

Arsenal	Arsenal Plant, Leningrad
Khrunichev	Khrunichev Plant, Khimki
Pavlograd	Pavlograd MZ, filial plant of Yuzhmash
Perm	Perm Machine Building Plant No. 172
Polyot	Omsk Polyot Aviation Plant No. 166
Progress	Progress Plant No. 1, Kuibyshev
Strela	Orenburg Aviation Plant No. 47 Strela
Votkinsk	Votkinsk MZ
Yuzhmash	Yuzhnoe MZ No. 586, Dnepropetrovsk

First-Generation ICBMs

Soviet designation	R-7	R-7A	R-16	R-16U	R-9A
GURVO designation	8K71	8K74, 8K710	8K64	8K64U	8K75
System designation	n/a	n/a	Sheksna-N	Sheksna-V	Desna-N
U.S. designation	SS-6	SS-6	SS-7 Mod 1, 2	SS-7 Mod 3	SS-8
NATO code name	Sapwood	Sapwood	Saddler	Saddler	Sasin
Design bureau	Korolyov	Korolyov	Yangel	Yangel	Korolyov
Production	Progress	Progress	Polyot, Yuzhmash	Polyot, Yuzhmash	Progress
Design start	20 May 54	2 Jul 58	17 Dec 56	Mar 60	Apr 58
First flight	15 May 57	23 Dec 59	2 Feb 61	10 Oct 61	9 Apr 61
Initial operational capability	9 Feb 59	1 Jan 60	1 Nov 61	5 Feb 63	14 Dec 64
Service acceptance	20 Jan 60	12 Sep 60	20 Oct 61	15 Jul 63	21 Jul 65
Retirement	mid-1960s	1968	1974	1978	1978
Missile stages	cluster	cluster	2	2	2
Missile length (m)	31.07	31.07	30.4–34.3	30.4–34.3	24.1–26.5
Missile diameter (m)	11.2	11.2	3.0	3.0	2.68
Launch weight (T)	280.0	280.0	141.2	141.2	80.5-82
Fuel weight (T)	253.0	253.0	130.0	130.0	71.1
Payload (T)	5.5	2.2–3.7	1.4–2.2	1.4–2.2	1.7–2.2
Empty weight (T)	27.0	27.0	10.6–11.2	10.6–11.2	9.4
Max. range, light warhead (km)	n/a	9,500	13,000	13,000	12,500
Max. range, heavy warhead (km)	7,900	9,000	11,000	11,000	10,300
CEP (km)	2.5–5.0	>5.0	2.7	2.7	8
Warhead	RDS-37	RDS-46A	8F17, 8F115, 8F116	8F17, 8F115, 8F116	
Light-warhead yield (Mt)	n/a	3	3	3	1.65
Heavy-warhead yield (Mt)	3–5	5	5–6	5–6	2.5
Guidance	inertial, radio	inertial, radio	inertial	inertial	inertial, radio
Guidance design bureau	Pilyugin	Pilyugin	Khartron	Khartron	Pilyugin
Fuel	Kerosene	Kerosene	UDMH	UDMH	Kerosene
Oxidizer	LOX	LOX	IRFNA	IRFNA	LOX
First-stage engine	RD-108	RD-108	RD-218	RD-218	RD-111
Vernier	S1.35800	S1.35800	RD-68	RD-68	n/a
Thrust (SL, Ts)	75.9	75.9	380	380	141.2
Engine design bureau	Glushko	Glushko	Glushko	Glushko	Glushko
Second-stage engine	4 x RD-107	4 x RD-107	RD-219	RD-219	RD-0106
Vernier	S1.35800	S1.35800	RD-69	RD-69	n/a
Engine design bureau	Glushko	Glushko	Glushko	Glushko	Kosberg
Thrust (vac, Ts)	83.7	83.7	45	45	31.5
Launch type	Hot	Hot	Hot	Hot	Hot
Launcher	8U215 Tyulpan	8U215 Tyulpan	8P864	8P764	Desna-N
Launch-system design	Barmin	Barmin	Kaputinsky	Rudyak	Barmin

Second-Generation ICBMs

Soviet designation	R-36	R-36O	R-36P	UR-100	UR-100U	UR-100K	RT-2	RT-2P
GURVO designation	8K67	8K69	8K67P	8K84	8K84M	15A20	8K98	8K98P
U.S. designation	SS-9 M 1, 2	SS-9 Mod 3	SS-9 Mod 4	SS-11	SS-11 Mod 2	SS-11 Mod 3	SS-13	SS-13 M 2
NATO code name	Scarp	Scarp	Scarp	Sego	Sego	Sego	Savage	Savage
Treaty pseudonym	n/a	n/a	n/a	RS-10	RS-10	RS-10M	RS-12	RS-12
Design bureau	Yangel	Yangel	Yangel	Chelomey	Chelomey	Chelomey	Korolyov	Arsenal
Production	Yuzhmash	Yuzhmash	Yuzhmash	Khrunichev, Strela, Polyot	Khrunichev, Polyot	Khrunichev	Perm, Arsenal	Perm
Development start	16 Apr 62	16 Apr 62	1967	30 Mar 63			4 Apr 61	18 Dec 68
First flight	23 Sep 63	Dec 65	Aug 68	19 Apr 65	23 Jul 69	12 Sep 69	26 Feb 66	16 Jan 70
IOC	9 Nov 66	25 Aug 66	1971	24 Nov 66	1 Mar 70	1973	8 Dec 71	1973
Service acceptance	21 Jul 67	19 Nov 68	26 Oct 70	21 Jul 67	1 Mar 70	28 Dec 72	12 Dec 68	28 Dec 72
Retirement	1970s	Jan 1983	1979	1988	1986	1996	1976	1995
Missile stages	2	2	2	2	2	2	3	3
Missile length (m)	32.2	34.5	32.2	16.97	19.0	18.9	21.3	21.3
Missile diameter (m)	3.05	3.05	3.05	2.0	2.0	2.0	1.84	1.84
Launch weight (T)	183.9	180.0	183.0	39.4	50.1	50.1	46.1–51.0	51.9
Empty weight (T)	17.7	17.7	17.7	4.5	4.8	4.8	7.7	7.7
Max. range, light warhead (km)	15,500	40,000	n/a	12,000	n/a	n/a	9,600	10,200
Max. range, heavy warhead (km)	10,200	n/a	n/a	5,000	13,000	12,000	5,000	n/a
Max. range, MIRV (km)	n/a	n/a	12,000	n/a	n/a	10,600	n/a	n/a
CEP (km)	1.3	1.1	1.34	1.4	1.1	0.9	1.8	1.5
Standard warhead	8F675 (Mod 2)		8F021		15F842			15F1
Light warhead yield (Mt)	5	5	n/a	0.5	n/a	n/a	0.6	0.75
Heavy warhead yield (Mt)	10, 18–25	n/a	n/a	1.0	1.2	1.3	n/a	n/a
MIRV yield (Mt)	n/a	n/a	3 x 2 or 5	n/a	n/a	3 x 0.35	n/a	n/a

Continued on next page

Second-Generation ICBMs continued

Soviet designation	R-36	R-36O	R-36P	UR-100	UR-100U	UR-100K	RT-2	RT-2P
Payload (T)	3.9–5.8		6.0	0.76–0.8	0.9–1.2	1.2	1.4	0.47
Penaids	List	n/a	List	n/a	Palma	Palma	No	Bereza
Guidance	inertial	inertial	inertial	inertial	inertial	inertial	inertial	inertial
Guidance design bureau				Pilyugin	Pilyugin	Pilyugin	Pilyugin	Pilyugin
Fuel	UDMH	UDMH	UDMH	UDMH	UDMH	UDMH	solid	solid
Fuel weight (T)	48.5	48.5	48.5	10.7	13.0	13.0	44.0	44.2
Oxidizer	IRFNA	IRFNA	IRFNA	IRFNA	IRFNA	IRFNA	n/a	n/a
Oxidizer weight (T)	121.7	121.7	121.7	27.4	30.0	30.0	n/a	n/a
Shelf life (years)	5–7.5	5–7.5	5–7.5	17	17	17	20	15
First-stage engine	RD-251	RD-251	RD-251	RD-0216	RD-0216	RD-0216	15D23	15D23P
Vernier	RD-68M	RD-68M	RD-68M	RD-0217	RD-0217	RD-0217	n/a	n/a
Thrust (SL, Ts)	241	241	241	86.2	86.2	86.2	91	100
Engine design bureau	Glushko	Glushko	Glushko	Kosberg	Kosberg	Kosberg	Iskra	Iskra
Second-stage engine	RD-252	RD-252	RD-252	15D13	15D13	15D13	15D24	15D24P1
Vernier	RD-69M	RD-69M	RD-69M	15D14	15D14	15D14	n/a	n/a
Engine design bureau	Glushko	Glushko	Glushko	Klimov	Klimov	Klimov	Tyurin	Tyurin
Thrust (vac, Ts)	120	120	120	13.6	14.1	14.1	44	44.6
Third-stage engine	n/a	RD-854	n/a	n/a	n/a	n/a	15D25	15D94
Launch type	Hot	Hot	Hot	Hot	Hot	Hot	Hot	Hot
Missile system	15P067	15P069	15P067	15P084	15P084	15P020	15P098	15P098
Silo	OS-67	OS-67O	OS-67P	15P784	15P784	15P884	15P798	15P798
Launch-system design	Rudyak	Rudyak	Rudyak	Barmin	Barmin	Barmin	Rudyak	Rudyak

Third-Generation ICBMs

Soviet designation	Temp-2S	MR-UR-100	MR-UR-100U	UR-100N	UR-100NU	R-36M	R-36MU
GURVO designation	15Zh42	15A15	15A16	15A30	15A35	15A14	15A18
U.S. designation	SS-16	SS-17 M 1, 2	SS-17 Mod 3	SS-19 M 1, 2	SS-19 Mod 3	SS-18 M 1, 2, 3	SS-18 Mod 4
NATO code name	Sinner	Spanker	Spanker	Stiletto	Stiletto	Satan	Satan
Treaty pseudonym	RS-14	RS-16A	RS-16B	RS-18A	RS-18B	RS-20A	RS-20B
Design bureau	MIT	Yangel	Yangel	Chelomey	Chelomey	Yangel	Yangel
Production	Votkinsk	Yuzhmash	Yuzhmash	Khrunichev	Khrunichev	Yuzhmash	Yuzhmash
Design start	6 Mar 66	Sep 69	16 Aug 76	19 Aug 70	16 Aug 76	2 Sep 69	16 Aug 76
First flight	14 Mar 72	15 Sep 72	25 Oct 77	9 Apr 73	26 Oct 77	21 Feb 73	31 Oct 77
Initial operational capability	21 Feb 76	6 May 75	17 Oct 78	26 Apr 75	6 Nov 79	25 Dec 74	Sep 79
Service acceptance	1976	30 Dec 75	17 Dec 80	30 Dec 75	15 Nov 79	30 Dec 75	17 Dec 80
Retirement	1970s	1984	1994	1980s	n/a	1983	n/a
Missile stages	3	2	2	2	2	2	2
Missile length (m)	18.5	23.9	23.9	24.0	24.3	33.6–36.8	34.3
Missile diameter (m)	1.79	2.25	2.25	2.5	2.5	3.05	3.0
Launch weight (T)	44.2	71.1	72.0	105.6	105.6	209.6–210	211.1
Fuel weight (T)		63.2	63.2	93.1	93.1	188	188
Empty weight (T)		7.9	8.8	12.5	12.5	21.6	21.6
Max. range, monoblock, (km)	10,500	10,320	n/a	9,650	n/a	11,200–16,000	n/a
Max. range, MIRV (km)	n/a	10,200	11,000	9,650	10,000	10,200	11,500
CEP (km)	0.45–1.64	<1.08	0.92		0.92	1.0	0.92
Monoblock warhead yield (Mt)	0.65–1.5	3.6, 4–6	n/a	2.5–5	n/a	18–20; 20–25	n/a
MIRV yield (Mt)	n/a	3 x 0.3–0.75	4 x 0.55–0.75	6 x 0.55	6 x 0.55–0.75	8 x 0.5–1.3	8–10 x 0.5–0.55
Payload (T)	0.94	2.55	2.55	4.3	4.3	7.2	8.8
Penaids	yes	yes	yes	yes	yes	yes	yes
Guidance design bureau	Pilyugin	Pilyugin	Pilyugin	Khartron	Khartron	Khartron	Khartron
Fuel	solid	UDMH	UDMH	UDMH	UDMH	UDMH	UDMH

Continued on next page

Third-Generation ICBMs continued

Soviet designation	Temp-2S	MR-UR-100	MR-UR-100U	UR-100N	UR-100NU	R-36M	R-36MU
Oxidizer		IRFNA	IRFNA	IRFNA	IRFNA	IRFNA	IRFNA
Shelf life (years)		10	10	10	10	10	10
First-stage engine		RD-268	RD-268	RD-0233	RD-0233	RD-264	RD-264
Vernier		n/a	n/a	RD-0234	RD-0234		
Thrust (SL, Ts)		117.0	117.0			425	425
Engine design bureau	Soyuz	Glushko	Glushko	Kosberg	Kosberg	Glushko	Glushko
Second-stage engine		RD-862	RD-862	RD-0235	RD-0235	RD-0229	RD-0229
Vernier		RD-863	RD-863	RD-0236	RD-0236	RD-0230	RD-0257
Engine design bureau	Soyuz	Yangel	Yangel	Kosberg	Kosberg	Kosberg	Kosberg
Third- (or PBV) stage engine		n/a	n/a	RD-0237	RD-0237		RD-864
Engine design bureau	Soyuz	n/a	n/a	Kosberg	Kosberg		Yangel
Launch type		Cold	Cold	Hot	Hot	Cold	Cold
Launch-system design	Titan	Rudyak	Rudyak	Vympel	Vympel	Rudyak	Rudyak

Fourth- and Fifth-Generation ICBMs

Soviet designation	R-36M2, R-36N	RT-23 UTTKh	RT-23 UTTKh	RT-2PM	RT-2PM2
GURVO designation	15A18M	15Zh60	15Zh61	15Zh58	
Missile system	Voevoda	Molodets	Molodets	Topol	Topol-M
U.S. designation	SS-18 Mod 5, 6	SS-24 Mod 1	SS-24 Mod 2	SS-25	SS-27
NATO code name	Satan	Scalpel	Scalpel	Sickle	
Treaty pseudonym	RS-20V	RS-22A	RS-22B	RS-12M	RS-12M2
Design bureau	Yangel	Yangel	Yangel	MIT	MIT
Production	Yuzhmash	Pavlograd	Pavlograd	Votkinsk	Votkinsk
Design start	9 Aug 83	9 Aug 83	Jun 80	19 Jul 76	Feb 86; Feb 93
First flight	21 Mar 86	31 Jul 86	27 Feb 85	27 Oct 82	20 Dec 94
Initial operational capability	30 Jul 88	19 Aug 88	Dec 87	23 Jul 85; 28 Apr 87	27 Dec 97
Service acceptance	11 Aug 88; 23 Aug 90	28 Nov 89	28 Nov 89	1 Dec 88	Jan 00
Missile stages	2	3	3	3	3
Missile length (m)	34.3	23.8	23.8	21.5	22.7
Missile diameter (m)	3.0	2.4	2.4	1.8	1.95
Launch weight (T)	211.1	104.5	104.5	45.1	47.2
Payload (T)	8.8	4.05	4.05	1.0	1.2
Max. range, monobloc (km)	16,000	n/a	n/a	11,000	11,000
Max. range, MIRV (km)	11,000	11,000	11,000	n/a	n/a
CEP (km)	0.5	0.5	0.5	0.5	>0.3
Warhead yield; monoblock (Mt)	0.55–0.75; 20	0.3–0.55	0.3–0.55	n/a	n/a
Penaids	Yes	Yes	Yes	Yes	Yes
Guidance design bureau	Khartron	Khartron	Khartron	Avtomatika	Avtomatika
Fuel	UDMH	solid	solid	solid	solid
Oxidizer	IRFNA	solid	solid	solid	solid
Shelf life (years)	10	10	10	10	15
First-stage engine	RD-264	15D305	15D305		
Engine design bureau	Glushko	Iskra	Iskra	Soyuz	Soyuz
Second-stage engine	RD-0256	15D339	15D339		
Engine design bureau	Kosberg	Iskra	Iskra	Soyuz	Soyuz
Third-stage engine	RD-869	RD-866	RD-866		
Engine design bureau	Yangel	Yangel	Yangel	Soyuz	Soyuz
Launch type	Cold	Cold	Cold	Cold	Cold
Launch-system design	Rudyak	Rudyak	Rudyak	Titan	Rudyak

Intermediate-Range Ballistic Missiles

Soviet designation	R-5M	R-12	R-14	Pioner
GURVO designation	8K51	8K63	8K65	15Zh45
U.S. designation	SS-3	SS-4	SS-5	SS-20
NATO code name	Shyster	Sandal	Skean	Saber
Treaty pseudonym	none	none	none	RSD-10
Design bureau	Korolyov	Yangel	Yangel	MIT
Production	Yuzhmash	Yuzhmash, Polyot	Yuzhmash, Polyot	Votkinsk
Design start	Oct 51	13 Aug 55	2 Jul 58	28 Apr 73
First flight	2 Apr 54	22 Jun 57	Jul 60	21 Sep 74
Initial operational capability	10 May 56	15 May 60	1 Jan 62	30 Aug 76
Service acceptance	21 Jun 56	4 Mar 59	24 Apr 61	11 Mar 76
Retirement	1966	1989	1982	1989
Missile stages	1	1	1	2
Missile length (m)	20.75	22.77	24.3	16.5
Missile diameter (m)	1.66	1.65	1.65	1.79
Launch weight (T)	28.6	27.0	87.0	37.0
Empty weight (T)	4.39	3.35	8.57	n/a
Max. range (km)	1,200	2,080	4,500	5,550
CEP (km)	3.7	1.1–2.4	1.25–1.9	0.55
Warhead yield (Mt)	0.3	1–1.3	1.0–2.0	3 x 0.15
Payload (T)	1.49	1.36	1.58	1.74
Guidance	inertial	inertial	inertial	inertial
Fuel	alcohol	TM-185	UDMH	solid
Fuel weight (T)	10.0	7.3	15.9	
Oxidizer	LOX	AK-27I	AK-27I	solid
Oxidizer weight (T)	13.9	29.1	63.3	
First-stage engine	RD-103	RD-214	RD-216	
Thrust (SL, Ts)	43.8	64.8	163.3	
Engine design bureau	Glushko	Glushko	Glushko	Soyuz
Launch type	hot	hot	hot	cold
Silo	n/a	Dvina	Chusovaya	n/a

Submarine-Launched Ballistic Missiles

Soviet designation	R-11FM	R-13	R-21	R-27	R-29	R-31	R-29R	R-39	R-29RM
GURVO designation	8A61FM	4K50	4K55	4K10	4K75	3M17	4K75R	3M65	3M37
System	D-1	D-2	D-4	D-5	D-9	D-11	D-9R	D-19	D-9RM
U.S. designation	none	SS-N-4	SS-N-5	SS-N-6	SS-N-8	SS-N-17	SS-N-18	SS-N-20	SS-N-23
NATO code name	Scud	none	Sark	Serb	Sawfly	Snipe	Stingray	Sturgeon	Skiff
Treaty pseudonym	none	none	none	RSM-25	RSM-40	RSM-45	RSM-50	RSM-52	RSM-54
Design bureau	Korolyov	Makeyev	Makeyev	Makeyev	Makeyev	Arsenal	Makeyev	Makeyev	Makeyev
Production	Votkinsk	Zlatoust	Zlatoust	Zlatoust	Krasnoyarsk	Arsenal	Krasnoyarsk	Zlatoust	Krasnoyarsk
Design start	26 Jan 54	25 Aug 55	17 Mar 59	24 Apr 62	28 Sep 64	10 Jun 71	Feb 73	Sep 73	Jan 79
First flight	26 Sep 54	Jun 59	14 Aug 60	Jun 66	Mar 69	24 Dec 74	Nov 76	Jan 80	Jun 83
Service acceptance	20 Feb 59	16 Oct 61	15 May 63	13 Mar 68	12 Mar 74	28 Aug 80	25 Aug 77	25 May 83	2 Jul 86
Retirement	1967	1979	1989	1995	1996	1989	–	–	–
Missile stages	1	1	1	1	2	2	2	1	3
Missile length (m)	10.34	11.83	14.21	8.89	13.0	10.6	14.1	16.0	14.8
Missile diameter (m)	0.88	1.3	1.3	1.5	1.8	1.54	1.8	2.4	1.9
Launch weight (T)	5,466	13,745	18,653	14,200	33,300	26,900	35,300	84,000	40,300
Max. range (km)	150	600	1,420	2,500	9,100	3,900	6,500	8,300	8,300
CEP (km)	8.0	4.0	3.0	1.9	0.9	1.4	0.9–1.4	1.4	0.5–0.6
Number of warheads	1	1	1	1	1	1	3	4 or 10	10
Warhead yield (Mt)	0.1	0.5–1	1.8, 2.5	0.6–1.2	1.0	0.5–1.0	0.2	0.1	0.1
Payload (T)	0.975	1.59	1.18	0.68	1.1	0.45	1.65	2.55	2.8
Penaids	no	no	no	no	yes	yes	yes	yes	yes

Continued on next page

Submarine-Launched Ballistic Missiles continued

Soviet designation	R-11FM	R-13	R-21	R-27	R-29	R-31	R-29R	R-39	R-29RM
Guidance	inertial	inertial	inertial	inertial	AI	AI	AI	AI	AI
Fuel	AK-20I	AK-27I	Amine	UDMH	UDMH	solid	UDMH	solid	UDMH
Oxidizer	T-1	TG-02	IRFNA	N2O4	N2O4	solid	N204	solid	N2O4
First-stage engine	S2.253	S2.713	S5.38	4D10		3D17A		3D65	RD-0243
Thrust (SL, Ts)	8.26	25.7	33.6	26.8	48.9	59.0			
Engine design bureau	Isayev	Isayev	Isayev	Isayev	Isayev	Arsenal	Kosberg	Pavlograd	Kosberg
Launch type	surface	surface	submerged	submerged	submerged	submerged	submerged	submerged	submerged

Appendix 2   Soviet Strategic Forces, 1960–Present

Intercontinental Ballistic Missiles

	1960	1961	1962	1963	1964	1965	1966	1967	1968	1969
R-7A (SS-6)	2	6	6	6	6	6	6	3	0	0
R-16 (SS-7)	0	10	50	114	172	202	202	197	196	196
R-9A (SS-8)	0	0	0	2	11	26	29	26	26	26
R-36 (SS-9)	0	0	0	0	0	0	72	120	168	222
R-36-O (SS-9M3)	0	0	0	0	0	0	0	0	0	6
UR-100 (SS-11)	0	0	0	0	0	0	160	420	620	770
Subtotal	2	16	56	122	189	234	469	769	1,010	1,220

	1970	1971	1972	1973	1974	1975	1976	1977	1978	1979
R-16 (SS-7)	195	169	165	161	161	137	69	0	0	0
R-9 (SS-8)	26	21	21	21	21	19	0	0	0	0
R-36 (SS-9)	258	282	288	288	288	288	272	232	132	68
R-36-O (SS-9M3)	12	18	18	18	18	18	18	18	18	18
UR-100 (SS-11)	930	950	950	850	640	429	350	270	190	130
UR-100K (SS-11M3/4)	0	20	24	120	310	420	420	420	420	420
RT-2P (SS-13)	0	30	60	60	60	60	60	60	60	60
MR-UR-100 (SS-17)	0	0	0	0	0	20	50	80	120	150
R-36M (SS-18)	0	0	0	0	4	21	36	76	176	240
UR-100N (SS-19)	0	0	0	0	80	120	120	120	100	100
UR-100NU (SS-19M3)	0	0	0	0	0	40	90	140	180	230
Subtotal	1,299	1,511	1,531	1,527	1,582	1,572	1,485	1,416	1,396	1,416

Intercontinental Ballistic Missiles continued

	1980	1981	1982	1983	1984	1985	1986	1987	1988	1989
R-36-O (SS-9M3)	18	18	16	0	0	0	0	0	0	0
UR-100 (SS-11)	100	100	100	100	82	28	17	0	0	0
UR-100K (SS-11M3/4)	420	420	420	420	420	420	420	419	380	345
RT-2P (SS-13)	60	60	60	60	60	60	60	60	60	59
MR-UR-100 (SS-17)	150	150	150	150	150	150	149	135	110	69
R-36M (SS-18)	308	308	308	308	308	308	308	308	290	272
R-36M2 (SS-18M5)	0	0	0	0	0	0	0	0	18	36
UR-100N (SS-19)	60	40	30	20	0	0	0	0	0	0
UR-100NU (SS-19M3)	300	300	330	340	360	360	360	360	340	306
RT-23U (SS-24M2)	0	0	0	0	0	0	3	9	18	27
RT-23U (SS-24M1)	0	0	0	0	0	0	0	0	20	50
RT-2PM (SS-25)	0	0	0	0	18	72	81	99	162	234
Subtotal	1,416	1,396	1,414	1,398	1,398	1,398	1,398	1,390	1,398	1,398

	1990	1991	1992	1993	1994	1995	1996	1997	1998	1999
UR-100K (SS-11M3/4)	308	208	180	70	10	0	0	0	0	0
RT-2P (SS-13)	40	40	40	20	0	0	0	0	0	0
MR-UR-100 (SS-17)	44	40	40	20	10	0	0	0	0	0
R-36M (SS-18)	250	244	214	196	164	128	122	122	122	122
R-36M2 (SS-18M5)	58	76	88	82	79	70	58	58	58	58
UR-100NU (SS-19M3)	300	300	300	280	260	220	200	160	160	150
RT-23U (SS-24M2)	36	36	36	36	36	36	36	36	36	36
RT-23U (SS-24M1)	56	56	56	56	56	56	56	10	10	10
RT-2PM (SS-25)	306	333	351	369	360	360	360	360	360	360
RT-2PMU (SS-27)	0	0	0	0	0	0	0	2	10	20
Subtotal	1,398	1,333	1,305	1,129	975	870	832	748	756	756

Intermediate-Range Ballistic Missiles

	1960	1961	1962	1963	1964	1965	1966	1967	1968	1969
R-5M (SS-3)	32	36	36	36	36	36	4	0	0	0
R-12 (SS-4)	172	373	458	564	568	572	572	572	556	532
R-14 (SS-5)	0	17	28	54	82	101	101	101	100	96
Subtotal	208	426	522	654	686	693	677	673	656	628

	1970	1971	1972	1973	1974	1975	1976	1977	1978	1979
R-12 (SS-4)	504	480	480	480	480	480	456	448	404	372
R-14 (SS-5)	89	87	87	87	87	87	87	79	73	45
15Zh45 (SS-20)	0	0	0	0	0	0	18	51	99	138
15Zh53 (SS-20)	0	0	0	0	0	0	0	0	0	18
Subtotal	593	567	567	567	567	567	561	578	576	573

	1980	1981	1982	1983	1984	1985	1986	1987	1988	1989
R-12 (SS-4)	316	264	224	112	112	112	112	48	18	6
R-14 (SS-5)	35	25	16	0	0	0	0	0	0	0
15Zh45 (SS-20)	180	216	216	216	171	153	153	153	111	42
15Zh53 (SS-20)	36	81	135	162	225	252	252	252	207	153
Subtotal	1,983	1,982	2,005	1,888	1,906	1,915	517	453	336	201

Submarine-Launched Ballistic Missiles

	1960	1961	1962	1963	1964	1965	1966	1967	1968	1969
SS-N-4	30	57	66	66	66	66	66	54	48	45
SS-N-5	0	0	6	6	6	9	12	33	39	42
SS-N-6	0	0	0	0	0	0	0	0	48	128
Subtotal	30	57	72	72	72	75	78	87	135	215

	1970	1971	1972	1973	1974	1975	1976	1977	1978	1979
SS-N-4	42	21	21	21	21	21	15	12	9	3
SS-N-5	45	60	60	60	60	60	60	60	60	57
SS-N-6	224	320	416	480	512	578	548	532	500	484
SS-N-8	0	0	0	28	80	156	220	286	286	292
SS-N-17	0	0	0	0	0	0	0	12	12	12
SS-N-18	0	0	0	0	0	0	0	64	128	144
Subtotal	311	401	497	589	673	815	843	966	995	992

	1980	1981	1982	1983	1984	1985	1986	1987	1988	1989
SS-N-5	57	57	57	45	45	42	39	39	33	24
SS-N-6	468	448	384	384	368	336	304	272	240	192
SS-N-8	292	292	292	292	292	292	292	292	292	286
SS-N-17	12	12	12	12	12	12	12	12	12	12
SS-N-18	150	208	224	224	224	224	224	224	224	224
SS-N-20	0	20	20	20	40	60	80	100	100	120
SS-N-23	0	0	0	0	0	0	48	48	64	96
Subtotal	979	1,037	989	977	981	966	999	987	965	954

	1990	1991	1992	1993	1994	1995	1996	1997	1998	1999
SS-N-6	192	176	128	32	32	16	0	0	0	0
SS-N-8	280	280	268	232	160	172	60	0	0	0
SS-N-17	12	0	0	0	0	0	0	0	0	0
SS-N-18	224	224	224	224	224	208	208	208	192	192
SS-N-20	120	120	120	120	120	120	120	120	80	60
SS-N-23	96	112	112	112	112	112	112	112	112	112
Subtotal	924	912	852	720	648	628	500	440	384	384

Ballistic-Missile Submarines

	1960	1961	1962	1963	1964	1965	1966	1967	1968	1969
Golf I	10	19	22	22	22	22	22	18	16	15
Golf II	0	0	1	1	1	1	1	5	6	7
Hotel	0	0	1	1	1	2	3	6	8	7
Hotel III	0	0	0	0	0	0	0	0	0	1
Yankee	0	0	0	0	0	0	0	0	3	8
Subtotal	10	19	24	24	24	25	26	29	33	38

	1970	1971	1972	1973	1974	1975	1976	1977	1978	1979
Golf I	14	7	7	7	7	7	5	4	3	1
Golf II	8	13	13	13	13	13	13	13	13	13
Golf III	0	0	0	0	0	0	0	1	1	1
Golf IV	0	0	0	0	0	0	0	1	1	1
Golf V	0	0	0	0	0	0	1	1	1	1
Hotel	7	7	7	7	7	7	7	7	7	7
Hotel III	6	6	6	6	6	6	6	6	6	6
Yankee	14	20	26	30	32	33	34	33	31	30
Yankee II	0	0	0	0	0	0	0	1	1	1
Delta I	0	0	0	1	4	9	13	18	18	18
Delta II	0	0	0	1	2	3	4	4	4	4
Delta III	0	0	0	0	0	0	0	4	8	9
Subtotal	49	53	59	65	65	78	83	93	94	92

	1980	1981	1982	1983	1984	1985	1986	1987	1988	1989
Golf II	13	13	13	13	13	13	13	13	12	8
Golf III	1	1	1	1	1	1	1	0	0	0
Golf IV	1	1	0	0	0	0	0	0	0	0
Golf V	1	0	0	0	0	0	0	0	0	0
Hotel	6	6	6	2	2	0	0	0	0	0
Hotel III	1	1	1	1	1	1	1	1	1	1
Yankee	29	28	24	24	23	21	18	17	16	12
Yankee II	1	1	1	1	1	1	1	1	1	1
Delta I	18	18	18	18	18	18	18	18	18	18
Delta II	4	4	4	4	4	4	4	4	4	4
Delta III	13	13	14	14	14	14	14	14	14	14
Delta IV	0	0	0	0	0	1	2	3	4	6
Typhoon	0	1	1	1	2	3	3	4	5	6
Subtotal	88	87	83	79	79	77	75	75	75	70

Ballistic-Missile Submarines continued

	1990	1991	1992	1993	1994	1995	1996	1997	1998	1999
Yankee	12	10	6	4	2	1	0	0	0	0
Yankee II	1	0	0	0	0	0	0	0	0	0
Delta I	18	18	17	14	8	7	5	0	0	0
Delta II	4	4	4	4	4	4	0	0	0	0
Delta III	14	14	14	14	14	13	13	13	12	12
Delta IV	6	6	7	7	7	7	7	7	7	7
Typhoon	6	6	6	6	6	6	6	6	4	3
Subtotal	61	58	55	53	51	38	31	26	23	23

Strategic Bombers

	1960	1961	1962	1963	1964	1965	1966	1967	1968	1969
Tu-95M	48	48	47	47	46	46	45	45	44	44
Tu-95K	37	46	55	62	65	67	66	66	66	66
3M	56	57	57	57	57	56	54	54	54	52
Subtotal	141	151	159	166	168	169	165	165	164	162

	1970	1971	1972	1973	1974	1975	1976	1977	1978	1979
Tu-95M	43	42	41	40	39	38	37	36	35	34
Tu-95K	65	65	65	65	65	65	65	65	65	65
3M	50	50	49	48	47	46	46	45	44	43
Subtotal	158	157	155	153	151	149	148	146	144	142

	1980	1981	1982	1983	1984	1985	1986	1987	1988	1989
Tu-95M	34	33	33	28	25	0*	0	0	0	0
Tu-95K	65	65	65	64	63	60	60	55	55	50
Tu-95MS	0	0	0	0	0	25	50	60	65	65
3M	39	37	35	32	31	30	15	0**	0	0
Tu-160	0	0	0	0	2	3	4	8	13	16
Subtotal	138	135	133	124	121	118	129	123	133	131

	1990	1991	1992	1993	1994	1995	1996	1997	1998	1999
Tu-95K	45	45	40	38	38	24	10	0	0	0
Tu-95MS	70	75	85	65	63	65	63	63	63	63
Tu-160	21	24	24	5	5	6	6	6	6	6
Subtotal	136	144	149	108	106	95	79	69	69	69

* The Tu-95M converted to trainers in the early 1980s.
** The surviving Bisons converted to tankers in 1985.

Strategic Nuclear Warheads

	1960	1961	1962	1963	1964	1965	1966	1967	1968	1969
ICBM	2	16	56	122	189	234	469	769	1,010	1,220
SLBM	63	87	104	104	104	104	104	143	196	288
Bomber	245	256	263	270	271	271	264	264	262	258
Total	310	359	423	496	564	609	837	1,176	1,468	1,766

	1970	1971	1972	1973	1974	1975	1976	1977	1978	1979
ICBM	1,421	1,490	1,526	1,518	1,982	2,332	2,385	2,696	3,136	4,210
SLBM	400	591	633	658	734	858	937	1,051	1,192	1,282
Bomber	251	249	245	241	237	233	231	227	223	219
Total	2,072	2,330	2,404	2,417	2,953	3,423	3,553	3,974	4,551	5,711

	1980	1981	1982	1983	1984	1985	1986	1987	1988	1989
ICBM	5,122	5,142	6,406	6,420	6,420	6,420	6,444	6,448	6,542	6,600
SLBM	1,373	1,617	1,617	1,801	1,985	2,217	2,262	2,396	2,430	2,698
Bomber	172	168	166	152	168	276	673	861	1,001	1,032
Total	6,667	6,927	8,189	8,373	8,573	8,913	9,379	9,705	9,973	10,330

	1990	1991	1992	1993	1994	1995	1996	1997	1998	1999
ICBM	6,630	6,661	6,471	5,919	5,320	4,580	4,280	3,582	3,590	3,540
Submarine	2,740	2,776	2,716	2,584	2,512	2,460	2,332	2,272	1,824	1,624
Bomber	1,127	1,243	1,398	818	794	816	780	790	790	790
Total	10,497	10,680	10,585	9,321	8,626	7,856	7,392	6,644	6,204	5,954

Appendix 3   Guide to Soviet and
                               Western Designations

With an increasing amount of archival and reference material becoming available from Russia, it is important to understand the proper Russian designations for their weapons. Until the mid-1990s, the actual Russian names for most strategic-weapon systems was not publicly disclosed. As a result, Western intelligence agencies applied their own designations to these weapons. The oldest system was applied by NATO's Air Standards Coordinating Committee (ASCC) to aircraft and stemmed from a similar system used in World War II to identify Japanese aircraft. So Soviet bombers received a name beginning in B (Bear, Blinder, Backfire, etc.), and fighters with F (Fishbed, Flanker, etc.). Variants of the basic design received a letter suffix, such as Bear-B for the second version of the Bear bomber. A similar system was applied to submarines, except that initially, the names were issued in alphabetical order such as Echo, Foxtrot, Golf, Hotel. When Zulu was finally reached, the system changed to use of Russian-sounding names such as Akula, which further confused matters, since the Western name did not correspond with the actual Russian name. So, NATO navies call the Project 971 Shchuka class "Akula," while the Russian Project 941 Akula class is called "Typhoon" by NATO. Hence, the need for these charts!

In the case of missiles, two separate sets of designations were used, and NATO decided to apply the same sort of naming system used with other weapons. Ballistic missiles, considered "surface-to-surface," received names beginning in S such as Scunner, Serb, etc. The NATO rule was that a name wasn't applied until a photo of the missile was available. As a result, there was a lag between the time the missile was first identified by radar or telemetry and the time it was actually seen. So the U.S. intelligence agencies adopted its own alphanumeric system, for example, SS-11. The alphabetical prefix indicated the missile role (SS = surface-to-surface, SS-N = surface-to-surface-naval), while the numerical suffixes were issued in sequence. While the missile was still experimental, an X was inserted in the middle, as in SS-X-10. Variants of a missile received a "Mod" suffix such as SS-11 Mod 1, sometimes abbreviated SS-11M1.

To further confuse matters, U.S. intelligence in the 1980s adopted a practice of initially identifying a missile with a temporary designator when it was first picked up on radar or noticed from telemetry. It was often not clear whether this was a new missile or simply a variation of an existing type, hence the temporary designator. These temporary designators used a two-letter prefix identifying the Soviet test range, followed by a sequential numerical suffix. So PL-08 was the eight missile spotted at the Plesetsk test range; NE-08 (later SS-N-20) was the eighth type identified from the navy's Nenoska test range. This system is not widely known outside the U.S. intelligence community, although it will be encountered by scholars in declassified documents such as CIA studies.

The Soviet Union initially had two parallel designation systems. The design bureaus began using designations beginning in R for "raketa" (missile) such as R-1. There were some variations in this pattern, such as Chelomey's practice of calling his missiles UR- (the U standing for universal), and other bureaus used RT- (the T indicating solid fuel). Various suffixes were added, including U or UTTKh (improved technical-tactical characteristics), D (extended range), M (modified), OS (silo variant), and BZhRK (rail mobile). When adopted by the armed forces, the missile usually retained this designation, and it is used most commonly in this book.

This service designation was regarded as top secret, so the GRAU (later GURVO) development agency decided to use the usual Russian industrial parts designation system to identify the missile and its various components for production and logistics applications. This follows a complicated alphanumeric system of number/letter/number. The pattern follows certain guidelines, but these have changed through time, so no further elaboration is given here, although patterns are evident in the chart below. As in the American case, different designations were given for the missile system versus the missile itself. So for example, the 15P016 missile system consisted of the 15A16 missile, armed with the 15F161 MIRV warhead, and launched from the 15P176 silo. This system is very difficult to keep straight, and after numerous complaints from policy makers in the 1970s, Dmitry Ustinov instituted a practice of giving names to various weapons systems for their convenience. These are listed here as well.

To further complicate matters, in the 1970s U.S. officials insisted that the Soviet Union provide designations of their weapons for use in arms-control treaties instead of relying on the Western intelligence designations. The defense minister, Andrei Grechko, adamantly refused to use either of the official, top-secret names, so treaty pseudonyms were invented expressly for arms-control purposes. These phony names are not used internally by either the military or the aerospace industry, although they are widely mistaken in the West as actual Russian designations.

Ballistic-Missile Designations

U.S. Number	NATO Name	GURVO Index	Bureau/Service Designation	Treaty Pseudonym
SS-1a	Scunner	8A11	R-1	none
SS-2	Sibling	8Zh38	R-2	none
–	–	8A67, 8A63	R-3, R-3A	none
SS-3	Shyster	8K38,8A62	R-5	none
SS-3	Shyster	8K51, 8A62M	R-5M	none
SS-4	Sandal	8K63, 8K63U	R-12, R-12U (silo)	none
SS-5	Skean	8K65, 8K65U, 8A63	R-14, R-14U (silo)	none
SS-6	Sapwood	8K71	R-7	none
SS-6	Sapwood	8K74, 8K710	R-7A	none
SS-7	Saddler	8K64, 8K64U	R-16, R-16U with 8F96	none
Pseudo SS-8		8K66	R-26	none
SS-8	Sasin	8K75, 8K75A	R-9A	none
–	–	8K95	RT-1	none
SS-LX		8K82	UR-500	none
SS-LX		8K68	R-56	none
SS-9 Mod 1	Scarp	8K67; 8U64	R-36	none
SS-9 Mod 2	Scarp	8K67; 8U64	R-36	none
SS-9 Mod 3	Scarp FOBS	8K69, 11K69	R-36-O, OR-36	none
SS-9 Mod 4	Scarp	8K67V; 8U64V	R-36P with 8F675	none
SS-X-10	Scrag	8K81	UR-200	none
Pseudo SS-10		8K713, 11A513	GR-1	none
SS-11 Mod 1	Sego	8K84, 15A10	UR-100	RS-10
SS-11 Mod 2	Sego	8K84UTTKh	UR-100UTTKh	RS-10M
SS-11 Mod 3	Sego	8K84K, 15A20	UR-100K	RS-10M
SS-11 Mod 4	Sego	15A20U	UR-100U	none
SS-13 Mod 1	Savage	8K98	RT-2	RS-12
SS-13 Mod 2	Savage	8K98P	RT-2P	RS-12
SS-14	Scamp/ Scapegoat	8K96	RT-15	none
SS-15	Scrooge	8K99, 8K99P	RT-20, RT-20P	none
–	–	15Zh41	RT-21	none
–	–	8K97	RT-25	none
SS-16	Sinner	15Zh42	Temp-2S	RS-14
SS-17 Mod 1, 2	Spanker	15A15	MR-UR-100	RS-16A
SS-17 Mod 3	Spanker	15A16	MR-UR-100UTTKh with 15F161	RS-16B
SS-17	Spanker	15A11	Perimetr	none
SS-18 Mod 1	Satan	15A14	R-36M with 15B86	RS-20A
SS-18 Mod 2a	Satan	15A14	R-36M with 15F143	RS-20B
SS-18 Mod 2b	Satan	15A14	R-36M with 15F143U	RS-20B

Continued on next page

Ballistic-Missile Designations continued

U.S. Number	NATO Name	GURVO Index	Bureau/Service Designation	Treaty Pseudonym
SS-18 Mod 3	Satan	15A18	R-36MUTTKh with 15B86	RS-20A UTTKh
SS-18 Mod 4	Satan	15A18	R-36MUTTKh with 15F183	RS-20B UTTKh
SS-18 Mod 5	Satan	15A18M	R-36M2 with 15F173	RS-20V
SS-18 Mod 6	Satan	15A18M	R-36N with 15F178	RS-20V
SS-19 Mod 1	Stiletto	15A30	UR-100N (monoblock)	RS-18
SS-19 Mod 2	Stiletto	15A30	UR-100N (MIRV)	RS-18
SS-19 Mod 3	Stiletto	15A35	UR-100NU, UR-100NUTTKh	RS-18B
SS-20 Mod 1	Saber	15Zh45	Pioner	RSD-10
SS-20 Mod 2	Saber	15Zh53	Pioner-UTTKh	RSD-10
SS-20	Saber	15Zh55	Pioner-3, Skorost	none
SS-24 Mod 0	Scalpel	15Zh44 (silo); 15Zh53 (rail)	RT-23	RS-22
SS-24 Mod 1	Scalpel	15Zh61	RT-23-OS- UTTKh Molodets	RS-22
SS-24 Mod 2	Scalpel	15Zh60	RT-23-BZhRK- UTTKh Molodets	RS-22
SS-25	Sickle	15Zh58, 15Zh62	RT-2PM Topol	RS-12M
Pseudo SS-X-26	–		Kuryer	none
SS-27			Topol-M	RS-12M1, RS-12M2

Submarine-Launched Ballistic Missiles

U.S. Number	NATO Name	GURVO Index	Service Designation	Treaty Pseudonym	System
none	Scud	8A61FM	R-11FM	none	D-1
SS-N-4	none	4K50, 3M50	R-13	none	D-2
none	none	R-15	none		D-3
SS-N-5 Mod 1	Sark	4K55	R-21	none	D-4
SS-N-5 Mod 2	Sark	4K55A	R-21A	none	D-4A
SS-N-6 Mod 1	Serb	4K10	R-27	RSM-25	D-5
SS-N-6 Mod 2	Serb	4K10A	R-27A	RSM-25	D-5A
SS-N-6 Mod 3	Serb	4K10U	R-27U	RSM-25	D-5U
none	none		Tip P, Izd. D-6	none	D-6
none	none	4K22	RT-15M	none	D-7
none	none		UR-100M	none	D-8
SS-N-8 Mod 1	Sawfly	4K75	R-29	RSM-40	D-9
SS-N-8 Mod 2	Sawfly	4K75D	R-29D	RSM-40	D-9D
SS-NX-13	none	4K18	R-27K	none	D-5K
SS-N-17	Snipe	3M17	R-31	RSM-45	D-11
SS-N-18 Mod 1	Stingray	4K75R, 3M40	R-29R/R-29DU	RSM-50	D-9R
SS-N-18 Mod 2	Stingray	4K75RL, 3M40L	R-29RL	RSM-50	D-9RL
SS-N-18 Mod 3	Stingray	4K75K, 3M40K	R-29K	RSM-50	D-9RK
SS-N-20	Sturgeon	3M65, 3M91	R-39	RSM-52	D-19 Taifun
SS-N-23	Skiff	3M37	R-29RM	RSM-54	D-9RM
SS-NX-28	none	3M81	R-39UTTKh Bulava-30	RSM-52B	D-31 Bark

Missile Submarines

NATO	Soviet/Russian	Russian Name	Missile System	Missile
Zulu V	Project 611AV	none	D-1	R-11FM
Golf I	Project 629	none	D-2	R-13
Golf II	Project 629M	none	D-4	R-21
Hotel I	Project 658	none	D-2	R-13
Hotel II	Project 658M	none	D-4	R-21
Yankee	Project 667A	Navaga, Nalim	D-5	R-27
Yankee	Project 667AU	Navaga-U	D-5U	R-27U
Yankee II	Project 667AM	Navaga-M	D-11	R-31
Delta I	Project 667B	Murena	D-9	R-29
Delta II	Project 667BD	Murena-M	D-9D	R-29D
Delta III	Project 667BDR	Kalmar	D-9R	R-29R
Delta IV	Project 667BDRM	Delfin	D-9RM	R-29RM
Typhoon	Project 941	Akula	D-19 Taifun	R-31
	Project 955	Borei		Bulava-30

Strategic Bombers

NATO	Soviet Air Force	Design Bureau
Bull	Tu-4	B-4
Badger-A	Tu-16A	Samolyot 88, Project N
Bear-A	Tu-95M	Samolyot 95, Obyekt V
Bear-B	Tu-95K-20, Tu-95KD	Obyekt VK
Bear-C	Tu-95KM	Obyekt VKM
Bear-G	Tu-95K-22	Obyekt VK-22
Bear-H6	Tu-95MS6	Obyekt VP-021
Bear-H16	Tu-95MS16	Obyekt VP-021
Bison-A	M-4	2M, Izdeliye 25
Bison-B	M-6	3M
Bison-C	M-6	3MD
Bounder	none	M-50
Blinder-A	Tu-22B	Samolyot 105
Blinder-B	Tu-22K	Samolyot 105A
Backfire-A	Tu-22M1	Samolyot 145, Project YuM
Backfire-B	Tu-22M2	Izdeliye 45-02, Project A
Backfire-C	Tu-22M3	Izdeliye 45-03, Project AM
Blackjack	Tu-160	Izdeliye 70, Project K

Notes

Two U.S. government organizations translate foreign publications for use by the intelligence and policy community: JPRS (Joint Publication Research Service) and FBIS (Foreign Broadcast Information Service). I have provided the JPRS or FBIS citation in the following notes when I know they are available, because they may be more useful to those who do not read Russian. Publications are available on a subscription basis from the NTIC (National Technical Information Service) and at federal document repositories at some larger universities.

Chapter 1. Revolution in Military Affairs: 1946–1953

1. *Boyevoi sostav sovetskoi armii,* pt. 5 (Moscow: Military Academic Directorate of the General Staff of the Soviet Army, 1990), 170.
2. G. F. Krivosheyev, *Grif sekretnosti snyat* (Moscow: Voyenizdat, 1993), 355–60.
3. These comments were from the British ambassador to Moscow. *Foreign Relations of the United States, 1945,* vol. 2 (Washington, D.C.: Government Printing Office, 1967), 83.
4. Alexander Werth, *Russia at War, 1941–45* (New York: Carrol & Graf, 1964), 1037.
5. A. Kruglov, quoted in P. V. Oleinikov, "German Scientists in the Soviet Atomic Project," *Nonproliferation Review,* summer 2000, 10.
6. Mark Harrison, ed., *The Economics of World War II* (Cambridge: Cambridge University Press, 1998), 292–93.
7. Vojtech Mastny, *The Cold War and Soviet Insecurity: The Stalin Years* (Oxford: Oxford University Press, 1996).
8. On the roots of the military economy, see David Stone, *Hammer and Rifle: The Militarization of the Soviet Union, 1926–33* (Lawrence: University·of Kansas Press, 2000).
9. Andrei Kokoshin, *Soviet Strategic Thought* (Cambridge: MIT Press, 1998), 112–13.
10. In 1946 the U.S. Air Force had only 9 combat-ready atomic bombs, only 45 in 1948, and only 298 in 1950.

11. Tad Szulc, "The Untold Story of How Russia Got the Bomb," *Los Angeles Times Opinion Magazine,* 26 August 1984, 3.
12. Col. Gen. Yu. V. Votintsev, "Neizvestniye voiska ischeznuvshei sverkhderzhavy," *Voyenno-Istorichesky zhurnal* 8 (1993): 58.
13. Steven Zaloga, "Soviet Air Defense Radar in the Second World War," *Journal of Soviet Military Studies* 2, no. 1 (March 1989): 104–16.
14. By way of comparison, the solid fuel for the Katyusha contained about 3 kg of binder material per 1 kg of propellant. On the most archaic solid-fuel missile of the 1960s, the RT-1, there was only 0.15 kg of binder per 1 kg of propellant.
15. The most thorough history of the Soviet atomic bomb program is David Holloway, *Stalin and the Bomb* (New Haven: Yale University Press, 1994). One of several official Russian accounts from the perspective of the KB-11 design bureau is E. A. Negin, ed., *Sovetsky atomny proyekt* (Nizhny-Novgorod: Arzamas-16, 1995). For an overview of archival revelations about the bomb program, see *Cold War International History Project Bulletin,* especially 4 (fall 1994); N. E. Zavoiskaya et al., "Atomnaya problema i otechestvennaya nauka v predvoyennye gody," *Istoria atomnovo proyekta* 1 (1995): 36–51.
16. K. Smirnov, interview with A. P. Aleksandrov, "How We Made the Bomb," *Izvestia,* 23 July 1988 (trans. JPRS-UMA-88-029, 55–56); A. S. Sonin, "Soveshchaniye, kotoroye ne sostoyalos," *Priroda,* March 1990, 91–102; April 1990, 91–98; May 1990, 93–99.
17. D. Holloway, "Entering the Nuclear Arms Race: The Soviet Decision to Build the Atomic Bomb, 1939–45," *Social Studies of Science* 11 (1981), 159–97.
18. This material came from John Cairncross, private secretary to Lord Hankey, who chaired the British Scientific Advisory Council. C. Andrew and O. Gordievskiy, *KGB: The Inside Story* (New York: Harper Collins, 1990), 311–12.
19. R. C. Williams, *Klaus Fuchs, Atom Spy* (Cambridge: Harvard University Press, 1987).
20. T. M. Chernoshchekov and V. Ya. Frenkel, *Lyudi nauki: I. V. Kurchatov* (Moscow: Prosveshcheniye, 1989), 100–101.
21. This was a fairly modest amount, the equivalent of buying a hundred T-34 medium tanks, or roughly $3 million.
22. V. N. Mikhailov, ed., *Sozdaniye pervoi sovetskoi bomby* (Moscow: Energoatomizdat, 1995).
23. H. M. Hyde, *The Atom Bomb Spies* (New York: Ballantine Books, 1981); J. Albright and M. Kunstel, *Bombshell: The Secret Story of America's Unknown Atomic Spy Conspiracy* (New York: Time Books, 1997); R. Radosh and Joyce Milton, *The Rosenburg File* (New York: Vintage Books, 1984); Verne Newton, *The Cambridge Spies: The Untold Story of Maclean, Philby, and Burgess in America* (Lanham, Md.: Madison Books, 1991).
24. The relative importance of espionage in the Soviet bomb program has been a controversial subject between the Russian scientists and former spies. For a more elaborate discussion of the controversy, see the Kurchatov Institute's journal, *Istoria atomnovo proyekta* 2 (1995), which was devoted to this theme.
25. Holloway, "Entering," 41.
26. This organization can be traced to the short-lived Special Committee of the State Defense Council of the USSR, formed on 20 August 1945 under Stalin's directive. The name later changed to the First Chief Administration of the Council of Ministers (PGU pri SM).
27. Costs associated with the atomic bomb program were estimated by the CIA to be R 270 million in 1946, rising to R 7.5 billion in 1950. The latter figure indicates that the program absorbed over 2 percent of the Soviet gross national product. CIA, *National Intelligence*

Survey: USSR, no. 26 (January 1951), section 73, "Atomic Energy." On the Soviet industrial infrastructure, see V. N. Mikhailov, *Yaderniye ispytania SSSR* (Moscow: Izdat, 1997), 49.

28. David Irving, *The German Atomic Bomb* (London: Wm. Kimber, 1967). For an illuminating debate on why the German program failed, see "The Nazis and the Atom Bomb: An Exchange," *New York Review of Books,* 27 June 1991, 62–64.

29. N. S. Simonov, "New Postwar Branches: The Nuclear Industry," in *The Soviet Defence-Industry Complex from Stalin to Khrushchev,* ed. John Barber et al. (New York: St. Martin's Press, 1999), 157. Unless otherwise noted, "tons" refers to metric tons throughout.

30. CIA, *The Problem of Uranium Isotope Separation by Means of Ultracentrifuge in the USSR,* CIA Report EG-1802, 22 May 1957, 6.

31. N. Riehl and F. Seitz, *Stalin's Captive: Nikolaus Riehl and the Soviet Race for the Bomb* (Washington, D.C.: American Chemical Society, 1993).

32. Oleinikov, "German Scientists," 26.

33. GHQ, Far East Command, "Monazite Production in North Korea," *Far East Command Intelligence Digest* 12 (2 December 1951): 12–16.

34. An important source of information on the U.S. program was the so-called Smyth report, the first official unclassified report of the Manhattan Project published in the United States. Henry DeWolf Smyth, *Atomic Energy for Military Purposes, 1940–45* (Princeton: Princeton University Press, 1945).

35. CIA, *National Intelligence Survey,* 73-19.

36. Jonathan Helmreich, *Gathering Rare Ores: The Diplomacy of Uranium Acquisition, 1943–54* (Princeton: Princeton University Press, 1986).

37. A. K. Kruglov, *Kak sozdavalas atomnaya promyshlennost v SSSR* (Moscow: TsNIIAtom-MinForm, 1995), 263.

38. A. P. Aleksandrov, ed., *I. V. Kurchatov,* vol. 3, *Yadernaya energia* (Moscow: Izd. Nauka, 1984), 73.

39. L. Nechayuk, "V gorode, u kotorogo net imeni," *Krasnaya zvezda,* 19 October 1990. The most thorough account of the infrastructure of the Soviet nuclear industry is T. B. Cochran et al., *Making the Russian Bomb: From Stalin to Yeltsin* (Boulder: Westview Press, 1995).

40. Zh. Medvedev, *The Legacy of Chernobyl* (New York: Norton, 1990), 227.

41. Yu. A. Shirmanov, *Otchizny shchit* (Krasnoyarsk-26: Muzeino-Vystavochny Tsentr, 1994), 4. Its first reactor went on line on 25 August 1958.

42. A. Tarasov and D. Khrupov, "Spy Satellites Are Made Here: Report from a Closed City," *Izvestia,* 11 January 1992 (trans. in JPRS-UMA-92-005, 12 February 1992, 71–72).

43. It is currently known by its Russian acronym, VNIIEF (Vsesoyuzny nauchno-issledovatelsky institut eksperimentalnoi fiziki: All-Union Scientific Research Institute for Experimental Physics).

44. Yu. B. Khariton and A. A. Brish, "Yadernoye vooruzheniye," in *Sovetskaya voyennaya moshch ot Stalina do Gorbacheva* (Moscow: Voyenny Parad, 1999).

45. Yu. Chernyshev, "Nam dali vsego 5 let, k istorii sozdaniya pervoi sovetskoi atomnoi bomby," *Inzhener* 12 (1991): 35.

46. The test site was formed in August 1947 under the code name of Mountain Seismic Station Object 905, reorganized in 1948 as the Training Proving Ground No. 2 of the Defense Ministry. It is more often called the SIP (Semipalatinsky ispytatelny poligon: Semipalatinsk Experimental Proving Ground).

47. Mikhailov, *Yaderniye ispytaniye SSSR.*

48. This was followed in December 1949 by a decree permitting the construction of the first series of ten RDS-1 bombs. Yu. Zavalishin, *Atomniy Avangard* (Saransk: Krasny Oktyabr, 1999), 106.

49. Yaroslav Golovanov, "The Portrait Gallery," *Poisk* 7 (1990) (trans. in JPRS-UST-90-006, 31 May 1990, 90). Many Russian accounts claim that the first failure was the 19 October 1954 test, but they may refer only to experimental trials.

50. V. N. Mikhailov et al., *Atomnaya otrasl Rossii* (Moscow: IzdAT, 1997), 169.

51. CIA, *Problem of Uranium Isotope Separation.*

52. N. M. Sinev, *Obogashchenny uran dlya atomnovo oruzhia i energetiki: K istorii sozdaniya v SSSR promyshlennoi tekhnologii i proizvodstva vysokobogashchennogo urana, 1945–52* (Moscow: MAEP SSSR, 1991).

53. CIA, *Problem of Uranium Isotope Separation,* 32.

54. Simonov, "New Postwar Branches," 168.

55. CIA, *Status of the Soviet Atomic Energy Program,* CIA Report SI 13-52, 8 January 1953, 11.

56. Mikhailov, *Atomnaya otrasl Rossii,* 146.

57. Khariton and Brish, "Yadernoye vooruzheniye," 171; S. Moroz, "Sdelano v SSSR," *Aviatsionnoye obozreniye* 5 (July 1996): 10.

58. Peter Korrell, *TB-3: Die Geschichte eines Bombers* (Berlin: Transpress, 1987).

59. This consisted of four TB-3 regiments. There was also a single partially formed Pe-8 regiment. Vladimir Ratkin, "Boevoi schet TB-3," *Mir aviatsii* 2 (1997).

60. "Pe-8: Last of a Generation," *Air International,* August 1980, 76–83.

61. The Soviet Air Force lost fifty-five Pe-8 bombers during the war and reached a strength of thirty bombers only in the summer of 1944. M. Maslov, "Drednout," *M-Khobbi* 5/6 (1996).

62. Vladimir Ratkin, "Pe-8: Ispytaniye boyevoye," *Mir aviatsii,* pt. 1, no. 1 (1996); pt. 2, no. 2 (1996); pts. 3 and 4, no. 1, 1997.

63. Howard Moon, *Soviet SST: The Techno-Politics of the Tupolev-144* (New York: Orion Books, 1989), 24; Joan Beaumont, *Comrades in Arms: British Aid to Russia, 1941–1945* (London: Davis-Poynter, 1980), 190.

64. In 1947 the strategic-aviation branch of the Soviet Air Force had 1,839 aircraft. However, only 32 were Pe-8 heavy bombers, and the rest were medium Il-4 bombers, lend-lease medium bombers like the American B-25, and converted transport aircraft like the Li-2/C-47. L. M. Sandalov, "Grif sekretnosti snyat-otkuda ugroza," *Voyenno-Istorichesky zhurnal* 2 (1989): 24.

65. It was then called Dalnyaya Aviatsia (DA-VVS), which also roughly translates as Long-Range Aviation.

66. Otis Hays, *Home from Siberia: The Secret Odysseys of Interned American Airmen in World War II* (College Station: Texas A&M Press, 1990).

67. L. Kerber and M. Saukke, "Ne kopiya, a analog: O samolyote Tu-4," *Krylya rodiny,* January 1989, 24–25, and February 1989, 33–34; A. M. Khorobrukh, *Glavny marshal aviatsii A. A. Novikov* (Moscow: Voyenizdat, 1989), 267–68.

68. A. N. Ponomaryov, *Sovetskiye aviatsionniye konstruktory* (Moscow: Voyenizdat, 1977), 36.

69. The plants were GAZ No. 18 in Kuibyshev in February 1949, and GAZ No. 23 in Moscow in early 1950. "Prikazano-Skopirovat!" *Aviatsia i kosmonavtika* 17 (June 1996): 59.

70. Reports to Stalin on the air operations can be found in "Uchastiye SSSR v koreiskoi voine (noviye dokumenty)," *Voprosy istorii* 12 (1994).

71. L. Krylov and Yu. Tepsurkayev, "Chornaya nedelya bombardirovochnovo komandovania," *Mir aviatsii* 2 (1999).

72. G. Lobov, "V nebe severnoi Korei," *Aviatsia i kosmonavtika* 11 (1990): 31.

73. CIA, *Soviet Capabilities for Attack on the U.S. through 1957,* CIA Report SNIE-11-2-54, 24 February 1954, 3.

74. C. L. Grant, *The Development of Continental Air Defense to 1 September 1954* (Maxwell Air Force Base: USAF Historical Division, 1956), 7.

75. The combat radius of a B-29 with a normal five-ton bomb load was 3,150 km (1,953 mi), compared to 1,460 km (905 mi) for the Tu-4. The Tu-4's radius would have been only 875 km (542 mi) with a twelve-ton payload. U.S. sources tended to credit the Tu-4 with performance identical to the B-29's, for example, *Soviet Capabilities for Attack on the United States through 1955,* CIA Report SE-36/1, 31 July 1953, 3. The formerly secret Soviet Air Force technical manual indicates otherwise. *Lyotno-tekhnicheskiye danniye i boyevyie svoistva samolyotov Tu-4* (Moscow: Voroshilov Academy, 1952), 19.

76. Piotr Butowski, "Russian Flight Refueling," *Air International,* August 1998, 100–105.

77. "Prikazano-Skopirovat!" 67.

78. Rostislav Angelsky, "Smertonosnaya chaika," *Tekhnika i oruzhie* 1 (1996).

79. On the war-scare atmosphere of the early 1950s, see the memoirs of Beria's son. Sergei Beria, *Beria mon père: Au coeur du pouvoir stalinien* (Paris: Plon, 1999), 316–28.

80. Gen. Lt. N. N. Ostroumov, "Armada, kotoraya ne vzletela," *Voyennno-Istorichessky zhurnal* 10 (1992): 39–40.

81. Aleksandr Shirokorad, "Tankovy desant na polyuse," *Tekhnika molodezhi* 12 (1996): 9.

82. A. V. Platanov, *Sovetskiye boeviye korabli, 1941–1945 gg.,* vol. 3, *Podvodniye lodki* (St. Petersburg: Tsitadel, 1996), 140–41.

83. D. E. Hillman and R. C. Hall, "Overflight: Strategic Reconnaissance of the USSR," *Air Power History,* spring 1996, 30.

84. Paul Lashmar, *Spy Flights of the Cold War* (Annapolis: U.S. Naval Institute, 1997), 176–77.

85. "Prikazano-Skopirovat!" 63.

86. I. V. Bystrova, *Voyenno-Promyshlenny kompleks SSSR v gody kholodnoi voiny* (Moscow: IRI-RAN, 2000), 124–52.

87. J. E. Loftus and A. W. Marshall, *Forecasting Soviet Force Structure: The Importance of Bureaucratic and Budgetary Constraints* (Santa Monica: Rand Corporation, 1963), 47.

88. Votintsev, "Neizvestniye voiska ischeznuvshei sverkhderzhavy," 58. This replaced the earlier Committee No. 3, formed on 10 July 1946 and disbanded on 15 August 1949, which had focused mainly on radar development.

89. Radar funding went from R 1.1 billion in 1950 to R 13.2 billion in 1955. Bystrova, *Voyenno-Promyshlenny kompleks SSSR,* 132; Nikolai Simonov, *Voyenno-Promyshlenny kompleks SSSR v 1920–1950e gody* (Moscow: ROSSPEN, 1996), 257–63.

90. About 60 percent of the jet fighter production went to the air defense regiments, and the remainder to frontal aviation. E. Arseneyev and L. Krylov, *Istrebitel MiG-15* (Moscow: Armada, 1999).

91. A. Shirokorad, *Entsiklopedia otechesvennoi artillerii* (Minsk: Kharvest, 2000), 863–85.

92. Of thirty-six new models of radar in development in 1947–48, fifteen were based on Soviet designs, and twenty-one were based on U.S. or other foreign technology. Bystrova, *Voyenno-Promyshlenny kompleks SSSR,* 128.

93. Loftus and Marshall, *Forecasting Soviet Force Structure,* 53.

94. G. Dyakonov and K. Kuznetsov, "Zenitniye upravlyayemiye rakety tretyego reikha,"

Tekhnika i vooruzheniye 5–6 (1997): 11–23; "Soviet AA Guided Missile Research at
Buro 11," *Intelligence Review* 135 (23 September 1948): 56–57.

95. Lt. Col. Anatoly Dokuchayev, "Rasskazyvayem vpreviye: Gordaya taina 'Almaza,'" *Krasnaya zvezda*, 12 September 1992, 5.

96. Boris Ye. Chertok, *Rakety i lyudi: Goryachiye dni kholodnoi voiny* (Moscow: Mashinostroyeniye, 1997), 273.

97. Votintsev, "Neizvestniye voiska yscheznuvshei sverkhderzhavy," 39; Pascal L'Ebrellec,
"La naissance de la defense antiaerienne sovietique," in *L'histoire du complexe militaro
industriel de l'ex-Union Sovietique, Enjeux atlantiques* 12 (February 1996): 39–40;
Soviet Surface-to-Air Missile Systems, Department of the Army Intelligence Research
Report A-566, 20 July 1958.

98. J. C. Hopkins and S. Goldberg, *The Development of Strategic Air Command, 1946–1986*
(Offutt Air Force Base: Office of the Historian, SAC HQ, 1986), 42.

99. T. Cochran, W. Arkin, and M. Hoenig, *U.S. Nuclear Forces and Capabilities*, vol. 1
(Cambridge, Mass.: Ballinger Publishing, 1984), 15.

Chapter 2. Bomber vs. Missile: 1953–1959

1. General Zhigarev's letter is quoted in N. V. Yakubovich and V. N. Lavrov, *Samolyoty V. M.
Myasishcheva* (Moscow: Rusavia, 1999), 45.

2. Yefim Gordon, "Tupolew kontra Miasiszczew," *Skrzydlata polska* 4 (1996): 48–49.

3. Yevgeny Podolny, "Bizon ne vyshel na tropu voiny," *Krylya rodiny* 1 (1996): 15.

4. The 3M was fitted with the SPS-2 EW system. S. Moroz, "Odnazhdy vospariv . . . ," *Avio*
2 (1992): 9.

5. A History of the Strategic Arms Competition, 1945–1972, vol. 3, *A Handbook of Selected
Soviet Weapon and Space Systems* (U.S. Air Force Supporting Studies, June 1976), 61–62.

6. Myasishchev proponents claim that the 3M, at a cost of R 12.1 million, was R 2.9 million
cheaper than its rival, the Tu-95. However, other budget data suggests that the Tu-95K was
significantly less expensive, costing about R 8.5 million in 1959. Yakubovich and Lavrov,
Samolyoty, 73.

7. Vladimir Rigmant and Yefim Gordon, "Tsel-Amerika," *Aviatsia i vremya* 5 (1996): 2.

8. M. S. Knaak, *Encyclopedia of U.S. Air Force Aircraft and Missile Systems*, vol. 2, *Post-
World War II Bombers, 1945–1973* (Washington, D.C.: Office of U.S. Air Force History,
1988), 208–9.

9. The prototype was powered by the TV-2FS 12,000 hp engines until the design of the more
powerful NK-12 was completed.

10. N. Kirsanov and V. Rigmant, "Ne imeyushchy analagov," *Aviatsia i kosmonavtika* 11
(1992).

11. It was also called the Tu-95LAL (LAL = *letayushchno-atomnaya laboratoria*, flying
atomic laboratory). Mikhail Rebrov, "Legendy i byli o 'Lastochke,'" *Krasnaya zvezda*, 7
July 1993.

12. S. Moroz, *Myasishchev M-4/3M* (Kiev: Arkhiv-Press, 1999), 14. By way of comparison,
Soviet tactical air force pilots at the height of the Cold War seldom received more than 250
flight hours annually, and in 2000 the annual flight time was down to a dangerous level of
only 25 hours a year.

13. In contrast, the United States had a third of the bomber force on fifteen-minute ground
alert in October 1957, increasing this to half the force in July 1961.

14. For example, the Shkval automatic antiaircraft gun was presumed to have a 65-percent probability of kill against a B-47, and a battery of six had a 95-percent probability of kill. The figure for contemporary cruise missiles, presumably the Snark, was 40–90 percent. Given actual antiaircraft-gun performance in wars of this period, these estimates were wildly optimistic, but they affected policy anyway. Col. Ye. A. Klimchuk, "Parity Is Coming to Grief," *Zavtra* 48 (November–December 1995): 4 (trans. FBIS-UMA-95-248-S, 27 December 1995, 28).
15. German Goncharov, "Beginnings of the Soviet H-Bomb Program," *Physics Today,* November 1996, 50. Sakharov himself noted the role of espionage in the program. Andrei Sakharov, *Memoirs* (Knopf: New York, 1990), 94; G. E. Gorelik, "S chego nachinalas sovetskaya vodorodnaya bomba?" *Voprosy istorii yestestvoznania i tekhniki* 1 (1993): 85–95.
16. The American counterpart to this idea was Edward Teller's Alarm Clock design of August 1946. In August 1990 the Soviet science journal *Priroda* published a special issue devoted to Andrei Sakharov, which contained more detailed notes on the early fusion bomb than Sakharov's own memoirs, especially the articles by V. E. Ritus and Yu. A. Romanov.
17. Goncharov, "Beginnings," 50–54.
18. The Super Oralloy bomb was developed in Los Alamos and tested on 15 November 1952.
19. Joint Intelligence Committee, *Magnitude and Imminence of Soviet Air Threat to the United States,* Joint Chiefs of Staff 1924/75, 20 October 1953, 1210.
20. NII-1011 absorbed the short-lived Laboratory B, established at the site years before. It was in the village of Snezhinsk near the Kyshtm processing center. This facility is today called the All Union Scientific-Research Institute for Technical Physics (VNIITF: Vsesoyuzny nauchno-issledovatelsky institut tekhnicheskoi fiziki). B. Yemelyanov, *Raskryvaya perviye stranitsy: K istorii goroda Snezhinsk (Chelyabinsk-70)* (Yekaterinburg: Uralsky Rabochy, 1997).
21. Details of Soviet weapons designs after 1956–57 are generally lacking. A certain amount can be inferred from data about missile warheads, and in recent histories, the two nuclear-warhead development bureaus have begun to cautiously reveal which weapons they designed.
22. Rostislav Angelsky, "Kak odin nemetsky 'FAU' stal vdrug russkim 'Desyat Kh,'" *Tekhnika i oruzhiye* 8 (1996).
23. Col. Gen. Viktor Yesin, "At the Dawn of the Strategic Missile Forces," *Armeysky sbornik,* May 1996 (trans. FBIS-UMA-96-168-S).
24. Rabe was an acronym for Raketenbau und Entwicklung: Missile Production and Development.
25. An excellent English-language biography is available. James Harford, *Korolev: How One Man Masterminded the Soviet Drive to Beat America to the Moon* (New York: John Wiley & Sons, 1997).
26. Viktor Yesin, "Na zare RVSN," *Armeyskiy sbornik* 5 (1996): 67–69.
27. The ostensible reason for Yakovlev's arrest was his failure in managing the development of antiaircraft artillery systems due to the problems of the new S-60 57 mm antiaircraft gun in Korea. A recent study suggests that the closing of the SAM (surface-to-air missile) bureaus at NII-88 and Yakovlev's removal may have been connected. Andrew Aldrin, "Innovation, the Scientists, and the State: Programmatic Innovation and the Creation of the Soviet Space Program" (Ph.D. diss., University of California, Los Angeles), 267–72. After Stalin's death, Yakovlev was released from prison and assigned to the commission overseeing the acceptance trials of the Berkut missile system.

28. This was a new plant that had been created around machine tools taken as war reparations from the German automobile industry.

29. N. Ya. Lysukhin, *RVSN v sisteme natsionalnoi bezopastnosti Rossii: Istoriko-Politologicheskiy analiz* (Moscow: RVSN, 1997), 48.

30. "Soviet Surface-to-Surface Missile Units: Deployment Augments Tactical and Strategic Strike Capability," *Intelligence Review* 255 (October 1962): 35.

31. Aleksandr Shirokorad, "Raketny boy: Armeyskiye i frontoviye ballisticheskiye," *Aviatsia kosmonavtika/tekhnika i oruzhiye* 20, no. 9 (1996): 2–3.

32. Yu. P. Semyonov, *Raketno-kosmicheskaya korporatsia Energia imeni S. P. Korolyova* (Kaliningrad: Energia, 1996), 38.

33. S. G. Kochemasov et al., *Khronika osnovnykh sobytii istorii RVSN* (Moscow: RVSN, 1994), 6.

34. Yesin, "At the Dawn of Strategic Missile Forces"; A. Dolinin, "Soviet Missiles on German Soil," *Krasnaya zvezda,* 10 April 1999, 6.

35. However, U.S. intelligence believed that only thirty-two launch sites were actually built, so the regiments may have been below full strength.

36. The best English-language account of the early Soviet missile programs can be found in Asif Siddiqi, *Challenge to Apollo: The Soviet Union and the Space Race, 1945–1974* (Washington, D.C.: NASA, 2000).

37. The oxidant accounted for about 65 percent of the weight in these early liquid-fueled missiles.

38. Semyonov, *Raketno-Kosmicheskaya korporatsia Energia,* 61–62.

39. The requirement established in October 1953 was for a 5.5-ton payload containing a 3-ton thermonuclear device.

40. Aldrin, "Innovation," 334.

41. Hypergolic fuels ignite on contact with one another and are generally storable at normal operating temperatures without the need for refrigeration. The most common combination of these fuels in the early 1950s was kerosene and nitric acid. Cryogenic fuels require refrigeration of their components to keep them in a liquid state. The oxidizer is normally liquid oxygen (LOX). Korolyov at first believed that hypergolic engines would never be efficient enough to provide intercontinental ranges. The development of a new fuel, heptyl/NDMG (unsymmetric dimethylhydrazine), in 1956–59 in the Soviet Union, as well as improvements in chemical oxidizers such as inhibited red fuming nitric acid, led some engine designers such as Glushko to believe that hypergolic engines could serve as the basis for intercontinental missiles. Regarding heptyl, see Aldrin, "Innovation," 327.

42. Specific impulse is a measure of the relation between thrust and fuel flow per second, providing an indicator of the efficiency of the engine.

43. Unlike Korolyov's OKB-1, no official history of Yangel's design bureau has been published. There are a number of essay collections by bureau officials, including V. Gubarev, *Yuzhny start* (Moscow: Nekos, 1998).

44. This program began in the late Stalin years but was accelerated under Khrushchev. G. Shizrin, "Methods of Practical Decision-Making in the Soviet Defense Industry," in E. Melikov et al., *Soviet Defense Decision Making: An Integrated View,* ed. Andreas Tamberg (Falls Church, Va.: Delphic, 1989), 87–89.

45. Accuracy was measured as CEP (circular error probable). A CEP of 5 km (3.1 mi) means that more than half of all missiles fired would land within a circle of 5 km radius around the target.

46. N. M. Korneyev and V. N. Neustroyev, *Generalny konstruktor, akademik Vladimir Pavlovich Barmin* (Moscow: Sozvezdiye-4, 1999), 79–98.
47. S. Derevyashkin and I. Baichurin, "Trudniye starty znamenitnoi Semerski," *Novosti kosmonavtiki* 10 (2000): 66–69.
48. It should be noted that the official defense budget did not include all or even most of total defense expenditures. Nevertheless, the cost of the R-7 launch sites was extremely high.
49. The Atlas silo launcher cost $3.7 million each, compared to about $500,000 for the Minuteman silos. J. Lonnquest and David Winkler, *To Defend and Deter: The Legacy of the U.S. Cold War Missile Program* (Rock Island, Il.: USACERL, 1996), 85.
50. Ernest R. May et al., *History of the Strategic Arms Competition, 1945–1972* (Washington, D.C.: Office of the Secretary of Defense, Historical Office, 1981), 375. The second R-7A site, code-named Volga, began construction near Salekhard, in northwest Siberia on the Ob River. A. V. Bal et al., *Poligon osoboi vazhnosti* (Moscow: Izd. Soglasie, 1997), 9. The conditions there were so severe that the launchers were not completed. It was abandoned as a potential missile site when the range of later missiles increased and the local permafrost conditions made the construction of underground silos impossible.
51. These units were code-named UAP (*uchebny artillerisky poligon:* artillery training grounds). The four other UAPs were at Kirov, Tyumen, Vladimir, and Razdolnoye.
52. I. V. Bystrova, *Voyenno-Promyshlenny kompleks SSSR v gody kholodnoi voiny: Vtoraya polovina 40-kh- nachalo 60-kh godov* (Moscow: IRI-RAN, 2000), 113.
53. The time required to prepare the R-7A for launch varied considerably, depending on the preconditions. Some former OKB-1 engineers suggest that the actual launch-preparation time was shorter, only eight to ten hours, probably under conditions where the missile had already been prepared at the assembly hall. Chertok, *Rakety i lyudi: Goryachiye dni kholodnoi voiny,* 23.
54. This was more de facto than de jure, as the Soviet and American efforts in antisatellite (ASAT) weapons over the next decade would suggest. For an examination of the impact of the early spy satellites, see David Lindgren, *Trust but Verify: Imagery Analysis in the Cold War* (Annapolis: U.S. Naval Institute, 2000).
55. M. D. Yevstafyev, *Dolgy put k Bure* (Moscow: Vuzovskaya Kniga, 1999), 81.
56. The Meridian radio navigation system was deployed in the mid-1950s at five sites but could reach only about 3,000 km (1,860 mi) from any of the shore locations. For an overview of Soviet naval navigation technology, see S. Alekseyev et al., "Morskiye sredtsva navigatsii: Istoria i perspektivy razvitia," *Morskoi sbornik* 9 (2000): 63–68.
57. Robert Divine, *The Sputnik Challenge: Eisenhower's Response to the Soviet Satellite* (Oxford: Oxford University Press, 1993); Rip Bulkeley, *The Sputnik Crisis and Early U.S. Space Policy* (Bloomington: University of Indiana Press, 1991).
58. May et al., *History of the Strategic Arms Competition,* 414.
59. Peter Roman, *Eisenhower and the Missile Gap* (Ithaca: Cornell University Press, 1995); Andreas Wenger, *Living with Peril: Eisenhower, Kennedy, and Nuclear Weapons* (Oxford: Rowman & Littlefield, 1997).
60. On the roots of Khrushchev's "nuclear romanticism," see Vladislav Zubok and C. Pleshakov, *Inside the Kremlin's Cold War* (Cambridge: Harvard University Press, 1996), 188–94.
61. Khrushchev's use of the Soviet Union's growing missile strength as a rationale for troop cuts is very evident in his memo to the Central Committee Presidium on 8 December 1959, which can be found in Vladislav Zubok, "Khrushchev's 1960 Troop Cut: New Russian Evidence," *Cold War International History Project Bulletin* 8–9 (winter 1996/97): 418–20.

62. See chapter 5 in Matthew Evangelista, *Unarmed Forces: The Transnational Movement to End the Cold War* (Ithaca: Cornell University Press, 1999).
63. Simonov, *Voyenno-Promyshlenny kompleks,* 294. The usual caveats should be noted about the unreliability of Soviet defense budget figures, even the formerly secret ones. Some of the cuts in the defense budget may have been illusory, because Khrushchev introduced a cost-cutting program aimed at reducing the ostensible price of certain weapons without any real changes in productivity or input, which would have represented a real decrease.
64. This figure includes all types of missile weapons, including tactical air defense, antitank, antiship, and air-to-air and other types of missiles. The relative breakdown of strategic missiles versus tactical missiles is not available. Simonov, *Voyenno-Promyshlenny kompleks,* 303. Curiously enough, this change was reflected in Warsaw Pact budgets of the time, in large measure due to Khrushchev's insistence that the pact countries' armies follow the Soviet trends. So, for example, in the Czechoslovak Army, the 1965 procurement budget devoted 47.2 percent of its funds to missiles and the remainder to more conventional weapons, a very high fraction for a nation without a strategic-arms effort. M. Pucik, "The East-West Security System and the Czechoslovak Army in the First Half of the 1960s," *Journal of Slavic Military Studies* 10, no. 4 (December 1997): 77.
65. Simonov, *Voyenno-Promyshlenny kompleks,* 249.
66. For an examination of the doctrinal debate, see chapter 9 in Yosef Avidar, *The Party and the Army in the Soviet Union* (University Park: University of Pennsylvania Press, 1983).
67. For an account of the public debate over control of the missile force, see *The Formation of the Soviet Strategic Rocket Forces: A Study in Interservice Rivalries* (Washington, D.C.: CIA Directorate of Intelligence, 1972), copy at National Security Archives.
68. The "Soviet Army" actually encompassed four combat arms: the Ground Forces, the Air Force, the Strategic Air Defense Force, and, after 1959, the Strategic Missile Force. The Ground Forces were the Soviet analog of the U.S. Army.
69. In the early 1960s GAU was reorganized as GURVO (Main Administration for Missile Weapons). This organization controlled the NII-4 research center at Bolshevo, the main think tank of the RVSN, as well as the RVSN proving grounds at Plesetsk and Tyuratam.
70. Aleksandr Medved, "Frontovaya udarnaya aviatsia na poroge raketnoi epokhi," *AviaMaster* 4 (1998): 42–43.
71. N. Lysukhin, *RVSN v sisteme natsionalnoi bezopastnosti Rossii* (Moscow: Military Academy of the RVSN, 1999), 67.
72. The Russian name, literally translated, means Missile Force for Strategic Missions. This name is frequently mistranslated as Strategic Rocket Force, or SRF.

Chapter 3. Deploying the First Generation: 1960–1965

1. For the U.S. perspective, see May et al., *History of the Strategic Arms Competition,* 422.
2. On the U.S. perspective, see Campbell Craig, *Destroying the Village: Eisenhower and Thermonuclear War* (New York: Columbia University Press, 1998). On Khrushchev's perspective, see Vladislav Zubok and Hope Harrison, "The Nuclear Education of Nikita Khrushchev," in *Cold War Statesmen Confront the Bomb: Nuclear Diplomacy since 1945* (Oxford: Oxford University Press, 1999).
3. Sergei Khrushchev has stated that his father thought that a force of two hundred ICBMs was sufficient to deter the United States. Other sources have suggested the force size was intended to be about three hundred ICBM launchers. Sergei Khrushchev, "The Cold War,"

lecture, University of California at Irvine, 19 July 1997. These figures are supported by recent evidence on the intended production rate of ballistic missiles under the 1959–65 five-year plan, which envisioned producing 500 ICBMs (210 R-7's, 100 R-9's, and 190 R-16's). It should be kept in mind that the number of missiles produced always exceeded the number of intended launchers to provide a reserve of missiles for trials, operational testing, and a maintenance float. In addition, a portion of the R-7 missiles were undoubtedly intended as boosters for satellite launches. The production plan for IRBMs included 1,800 R-12's, 200 R-14's, and 100 R-15's. I. V. Bystrova, "Razvitiye voyenno-promyshlennovo kompleksa," in *SSSR i Kholodnaya Voina,* ed. V. S. Lelchuka (Moscow: Mosgorarkhiv, 1995), 193. This information is further supported by evidence from other defense sectors. For example, the contemporary Soviet ABM network around Moscow was designed to defend against a very small number of warheads, about six to eight, which suggests that the Soviets expected the United States also to field a very modest ICBM force.

4. The nuclear-powered space booster was authorized on 30 June 1958.

5. It dropped from 5 metric tons to 2.2 metric tons.

6. In a shameless attempt to push his rival out of business, Korolyov proposed to develop both a storable-fuel and a cryogenic-fuel version of his R-9 design, but he was only authorized to proceed with the latter.

7. David Snead, *The Gaither Committee, Eisenhower, and the Cold War* (Columbus: Ohio State University Press, 1999).

8. This version of the story is amplified in Sergei N. Khrushchev's biography of his father, *Nikita Khrushchev and the Creation of a Superpower* (University Park: Pennsylvania State University Press, 2000), 288–89, 297–98. This book was originally published in Russian in two volumes as *Nikita Khrushchev: Krizisy i rakety* (Moscow: Novosti, 1994), and there are some differences.

9. Three basing options for the R-7 had been considered: surface, underground, and in tunnels in mountains. Bystrova, "Razvitiye voyenno-promyshlennovo kompleksa," 204.

10. A firsthand account of the R-16 trials by one of the test range's senior commanders can be found in K. V. Gerchik, *Nezabyvayemy Baikonur* (Moscow: Tekhnika Molodezhi, 1998), 60–82.

11. The casualties included Marshal Mitrofan Nedelin, head of the RVSN; two of Yangel's chief designers, L. A. Berlin and V. A. Kontsevoi; engine designer V. P. Glushko's main assistant, G. F. Firsov; the designer of the missile's guidance system, B. M. Konoplyov, from the Kharkov NII-692; and the first assistant of the state commission, L. A. Grishin.

12. This was probably due to the fact that the first launch did not use telemetry, but was a simple dynamic flight test. During this period, U.S. intelligence relied heavily on intercepting the radio telemetry signals broadcast from the missile-to-ground stations that were used by the designers to monitor the progress of key components and subsystems. Later, bases in border areas such as Turkey would employ radars to track the missiles as well.

13. Some American gyro systems were kept running continuously for fourteen years, though the average time before repair was shorter. On the Soviet systems, see Chertok, *Rakety i lyudi: Goryachiye dni kholodnoi voiny,* 58.

14. Chertok, *Rakety i lyudi: Goryachiye dni kholodnoi voiny,* 32.

15. The first set of state trials examines whether the missile has reached its design objectives and can proceed to production. These are called developmental tests in the United States. The second set are conducted by the missile force using missiles incorporating modifications developed during the first test series. These are intended to determine whether the

missile is ready for deployment and are comparable to what are called operational tests in the U.S. system.

16. The United States monitored the tests from neighboring countries such as Turkey, Iran, and Pakistan. U.S. stations intercepted radio-telemetry signals from the missiles, which provided data to the Soviet engineers on the performance of the fuel system, flight controls, and guidance. In addition, parts of the test could be tracked by radars.

17. The R-16 missile cost R 1.42 million, while the R-9 missile cost R 1.37 million. However, the R-9 launch complex cost R 3.82 million, compared to R 1.42 million for the R-16, presumably due to its more demanding fuel-handling system. Simonov, *Voyenno-Promyshlenny kompleks,* 250.

18. This differs from the usual Western approach, which views the R-7 as the first generation, and the R-9 and R-16 as the second. This difference in outlook is prompted by the Russian view that the R-7 was never deployed in significant enough numbers to warrant such a distinction, and some Russian designers refer to the R-7 as "generation zero."

19. The R-7A ICBM was manufactured at the GAZ No. 1 Progress Plant at Kuibyshev, while the R-16 was manufactured at the Yuzhmash plant in Dnepropetrovsk and later at the Polyot plant in Omsk. Korolyov's R-9 was first produced in Kuibyshev and later extended to the new Plant No. 1001 in Krasnoyarsk (now called Krasmash). Chertok, *Rakety i lyudi: Goryachiye dni kholodnoi voiny,* 39.

20. Its formal military title was the 6th State Central Proving Ground: 6GTsP (6 Gosudarstvenny tsentralny poligon). B. I. Ogorodnikov, *Yaderny arkhipelag* (IzdAt: Moscow, 1995).

21. The best overview of the industry in English is *Making the Russian Bomb: From Stalin to Yeltsin,* by Thomas Cochra, Robert Norris, and Oleg Bukharin (Boulder: Westview Press, 1995).

22. The first test of a bomb developed by the new NII-1011 was a 680-kiloton blast at the Semipalatinsk test range on 10 April 1957. Yemelyanov, *Raskryvaya perviye stranitsy,* 162.

23. I. I. Velichko, *Ballisticheskiye rakety podvodnykh lodok Rossii* (Miass: GRTs Makeyeva, 1997), 8–9.

24. V. A. Kucher et al., *Podvodniye lodki Rossii: Atomnoye pervoye pokoleniye, 1952–1996,* vol. 4, pt. 1 (St. Petersburg: TsKBMT Rubin, 1996), 105–40.

25. Robert Herrick, *Soviet SSBN Roles in Strategic Strike,* pt. 1, *Final Report on Soviet Naval Mission Assignments,* Report to the Assistant Director for Net Assessment, April 1979.

26. M. N. Avilov, "Polyot iz moskovskikh glubin: Iz istorii sozdania raketnovo kompleksa D-4," *Taifun* 3 (2000): 33–39, and 4 (2000): 20–25.

27. M. Muratov, *Otechestvenniye atomniye podvodniye lodki* (Moscow: Tekhnika i Vooruzenie, 2000), 54.

28. Rostislav Angelsky, "Tsar raketa," *Krylya rodiny* 3 (2000): 5–7.

29. Ye. V. Arsenyev et al., *Istoria konstruktsii samolyotov v SSSR 1951–65 gg.* (Moscow: Mashinostroyeniye, 2000), 345–46.

30. Desmond Ball, *Politics and Force Levels: The Strategic Missile Program of the Kennedy Administration* (Berkeley: University of California Press, 1980), 132–33.

31. The number of Minuteman missiles planned for deployment varied for several years, including options up to three thousand missiles, and was finally fixed at one thousand missiles in November 1964.

32. See, for example, chapter 4 in Christopher Bluth, *Soviet Strategic Arms Policy before SALT* (Cambridge: Cambridge University Press, 1992).

33. Although there is a growing body of information on the history of the original Soviet Zenit space reconnaissance satellite program, there is very little evidence on when the system offered the resolution to pinpoint U.S. missile silos. The Soviet GRU conducted a significant number of Zenit-2 missions beginning in 1962, but it was not accepted for service until after the conclusion of tests on 10 March 1964. The Ftora camera on the first Zenit-2 satellites had a requirement for a resolution of only 10 m (33 ft), which suggests that the early satellites could not detect a completed silo, even though its actual resolution proved to be 5–7 m (16–23 ft). The later Zenit-4 had a resolution requirement for 3 m (10 ft). Chertok, *Rakety i lyudi: Goryachiye dni kholodnoi voiny,* 89–98.

34. The Russian term for launch-on-warning is *otvetno-vstrechny udar* (OVU), or counter-response attack; the term for launch-on-attack is *otvetny udar* (OU), or response attack.

35. May et al., *History of the Strategic Arms Competition,* 475.

36. Khrushchev, *Nikita Khrushchev,* vol. 2 (Novosti: Moscow, 1994), 158–59.

37. It must be noted that by this time, Khrushchev had abolished the former ministries in his failed attempt to replace them with the Sovnarkom organizations. Nevertheless, in the defense industries, these previous ministerial structures and rivalries continued to play an important role in weapons decision making.

38. See, for example, A. Fursenko and T. Naftali, *One Hell of a Gamble: Khrushchev, Castro, and Kennedy, 1958–1964* (New York: W. W. Norton, 1997), 171.

39. On the U.S. missile concessions, see Philip Nash, *The Other Missiles of October: Eisenhower, Kennedy, and the Jupiters, 1957–1963* (Chapel Hill: University of North Carolina Press, 1997).

40. This force structure is detailed in a declassified chart from 20 June 1962 reproduced in A. I. Gribkov et al., *U kraya yadernoi bezdni* (Moscow: Gregori-Peidzh, 1998), 50.

41. These ships were armed with antiship missiles, not ballistic missiles.

42. In June 1962 the RVSN planned to deploy the 43rd Missile Division to Cuba with one R-12 regiment (664th) and two R-14 regiments (665th and 668th), supplemented with two R-12 regiments from other divisions (the 79th Regiment from the 29th Missile Division and the 181st from the 80th Missile Division). In the end, the 43rd Division was left in place, and a new divisional structure was formed to control the regiments.

43. Of the forty-two missiles, six were training missiles; hence there were only thirty-six nuclear warheads.

44. Yury Grekov, "Operatsia Anadyr," *Armeisky sbornik* 12 (1999): 73.

45. Both are variations of the Mikoyan Kometa (AS-1) air-to-surface cruise missile. The naval Sopka is fitted with an active radar seeker with a conventional shaped-charge warhead, while the Meteor version is fitted with an inertial guidance system and a nuclear warhead.

46. These regiments were under-strength compared to the normal regimental organization, with only eight missile launchers in two batteries each, instead of the usual sixteen in four batteries. *Guided Missiles and Rockets,* USEUCOM Intelligence Report, Annex 16, 14 June 1966, 16–17, from a declassified copy in the holdings of the National Security Archives, Washington, D.C. This report provides details on the FKR-1 regiment attached to the 24th Tactical Air Army in the Soviet Group of Forces, Germany.

47. The nuclear-warhead inventory included six Model 407N free-fall bombs for IL-28 bombers, twelve Model 901A4 warheads for Luna (FROG) tactical ballistic rockets, thirty-six warheads for the R-12 (SS-4) ballistic missiles, and twenty-four warheads for the R-14 (SS-5) ballistic missiles.

48. The MiG-21 fighters deployed to Cuba were under the PVO Air Defense Command.
49. Gribkov, *U kraya yadernoi bezdni,* 88.
50. The confusion in U.S. intelligence was due to the fact that the Sopka coastal antiship missile batteries deployed on Cuba used a missile similar to the FKR-1 land-attack missiles, both systems employing a version of the Mikoyan Kometa (AS-1) missile. The coastal missiles were detected and identified, and the FKR-1 units were probably mistaken as reserves for the conventionally armed coastal units.
51. This force is listed on the declassified order-of-battle document dated 20 June 1962 and reprinted in Gribkov, *U kraya yadernoi bezdni,* 50.
52. A. Pochtarev and V. Yaremenko, "Operatsia Anadyr," *Nezavisimoye voyennoye obozreniye,* 3–9 October 1997, 5.
53. Whether or not the cruise missiles were ever armed remains clouded in controversy. A recent collection of essays by participants states that the FKR missiles were armed in late October, but accounts by officers in charge of the nuclear custodial units deny that this ever occurred. Gribkov, *U kraya yadernoi bezdni,* states on page 119 that the missiles were armed, but Beloborodov, in charge of the Object S nuclear custodial unit in Cuba, denies it. Mark Kramer, "Lessons of the Cuban Missile Crisis for Warsaw Pact Nuclear Operations," *Cold War History Project Bulletin* 8–9 (winter 1996–97): 353.
54. According to accounts by veterans, two regiments and one battery were at combat readiness on 25 October, and another battery became operational on 27 October, bringing the force to a total of three complete regiments with twenty-four launchers. V. I. Yesin, ed., *Strategicheskaya operatsia Anadyr: Kak eto bylo* (Moscow: MOOBIK, 1999), 68–69, 291.
55. A debate on this issue can be found in Mark Kramer, "Tactical Nuclear Weapons, Soviet Command Authority, and the Cuban Missile Crisis"; and James G. Blight et al., "Kramer vs. Kramer," *Cold War International History Project Bulletin* 3 (fall 1993): 40–46. The text of the 27 October 1962 message reiterating this order can be found in Gribkov, *U kraya yadernoi bezdni,* 364
56. S. Moroz, *Myasishchev M-4/3M* (Kiev: Arkhiv-Press, 1999), 28.
57. Chertok, *Rakety i lyudi: Goryachiye dni kholodnoi voiny,* 52. An account of a missile officer at the Baikonur missile site during the crisis can be found in Ivan Yevteyev, *Eshcho podnimalos plamya* (Moscow: Inter-Vesy, 1997), 78–82.
58. The silo-based versions of the missiles had the suffix "U" added, which meant "unified," that is, capable of launch from either a surface or silo launcher.
59. For a look at the internal politics of the design bureaus, see William Barry, "The Missile Design Bureaux and Soviet Manned Space Policy" (Ph.D. diss., University of Oxford, 1996).
60. No complete biography of Chelomey has yet appeared. An eighty-fifth anniversary tribute was published as Ivan Yevteyev, *Operezhaya vremya* (Moscow: Bioinformservis, 1999).
61. The Myasishchev bureau was transferred to Chelomey's control in October 1960.
62. The best Russian account of the formal stages of missile design is a handbook on designing air defense missiles. I. S. Golubev and V. G. Svetlov, *Proyektirovanie zenitnykh upravlyayemykh raket* (Moscow: Izd. MAI, 1999).
63. Kaliningrad was renamed Korolyov in the 1990s after the famous designer.
64. This process was expedited by Iu. A. Mozzhorin's appointment as head of NII-88 in 1961. Mozzhorin had antagonistic relations with Korolyov and was intent on reestablishing NII-88 as an independent research center, and not a subordinate to Korolyov's growing missile and space endeavors. Barry, *Missile Design Bureaus,* 201.

65. OKB: Experimental Design Bureau; SKB: Special Design Bureau; KB: Design Bureau.
66. For a guide to the many design bureaus of the Russian missile and space industry, see V. I. Lukyashchenko et al., *50 let vperedi svoyego veka, 1946–1996 gg.* (Moscow: RKA, 1998).
67. He took this post when he was appointed assistant to the Council of Ministers for defense affairs in 1957.
68. In the early days, missile design bureaus were headed by chief designers. The practice of naming the head of a bureau as general designer was taken from the aviation industry. The practice became common in the late 1950s and eventually became more systematically applied. Some small design bureaus remained headed by a chief designer. In the 1980s, the practice shifted again, and subordinate chief designers were given the loftier title of deputy general designers.
69. In Russian, such a draft project was called *eskizny proyekt,* also sometimes known by the acronym OKR (special design study).
70. Intermediate-range missiles and some solid-fuel missile tests were conducted at Kaputin Yar until 1964, when most of the tests were shifted to Plesetsk.
71. *Lyotno-konstruktorskaya ispytania,* or LKI.
72. *Gosispytania.* They were sometimes called joint trials because they would be monitored both by the military and the industrial ministries.
73. *Seriiny kontrolny otstrel,* or SKO.
74. For example, the 15A35 (SS-19 Mod 3) is a new production missile and not a rebuilt 15A30 (SS-19 Mod 2).
75. O. Volkov and V. Umnov, "Who Taught the President's Phone to Holds Its Tongue: We Have an Entire Industry Unknown to Anybody," *Komsomolskaya pravda,* 1 May 1992 (trans. FBIS-SOV-92-089, 7 May 1992, 31).
76. A. Dollin, "Communications in the RVSN are more than just communications," *Krasnaya zvezda,* 30 January 1997 (trans. FBIS-SOV-97-021, 30 January 1997).
77. Stepan Pronin, "Who Is at the Red Button?" *Rossiiskaya gazeta,* 3 June 1995 (trans. JPRS-TAC-95-002, 14 June 1995); A. Dolinin, "Vlasikha strategicheskaya," *Krasnaya zvezda,* 30 April 1996.
78. This is called the TsKP: *tsentralny kommandny punkt,* central command post.
79. The Russian term is *nesanktsionirovannoye deistviye* (NSD).
80. For an overview of the Soviet Navy's efforts to develop command-and-control systems, see Yu. Aleseyev, "Korabelniye avtomatizirovanniye sistemy upravlenia," in *Rossiiskaya nauka: Voyenno morskomu flotu* (Moscow: Nauka, 1997), 352–56.
81. These were located at Krasnodar (code name Gerakl), Gorky (Goliaf), Arkhangelsk (Atlant), Frunze (Prometei), Khabarovsk (Gerkules), and Molodechno (Antei). Development of the long-range communication systems was undertaken by the Radiotechnology and Electronics Institute of the Academy of Sciences and the Scientific Research Institute for Communications of the navy (NII-Svyazi VMF). Gen. Lt. V. Gekov and Col. V. Adamsky, "Supersvyaz dlya atomnykh submarin," *Krasnaya zvezda,* 29 April 1995.
82. Kathleen Broome Williams, *Secret Weapon: U.S. High-Frequency Direction Finding in the Battle of the Atlantic* (Annapolis: Naval Institute Press, 1996).
83. Development of command-and-control systems for the bomber force were entrusted to Chief Designer R. Atoyan of the NII for Mathematical Machines in Yerevan (Armenia). Production of these systems was undertaken by the Elektron Assembly Plant in Yerevan.
84. Desmond Ball, "The Soviet Strategic C3I System," in *C3I Handbook* (Palo Alto: EW Communications, 1986), 207.

85. A. V. Karpenko, *Protivoraketnaya i protivokosmicheskaya oborona* (St. Petersburg: Nevsky Bastion, 1998), 3.
86. Grigory Kisunko, *Sekretnaya zona* (Moscow: Sovremmenik, 1996). Two other radar design bureaus worked on the associated early warning radars: the NII-RT (Scientific Research Institute of Radio Technology), headed by Alexander L. Mints; and the NII-37 (later NII-DAR: NII-Dalnei Radiosvyaz, or Scientific Research Institute for Long-Range Communications), headed by V. P. Sosulnikov.
87. This radar, designated Hen Roost by U.S. intelligence, was developed by NII-37.
88. O. V. Golubev et al., "Zadachi upravlenia i otsenki effektivnosti v razrabotkakh otechestvennoi sistemy PRO-Eksperimentalny poligony kompleks PRO Sistem A," *Tekhnicheskaya kibernetika* 6 (1992): 166–74.
89. This effort was undertaken by Pyotr Pleshakov's M-3 division of NII-108 in Moscow. Mikhail Pervov, *Raketniye kompleksy RVSN* (Moscow: Novosti, 1999), 45, 75–76.
90. The RAM absorbed the radio energy from the ABM radar and converted it to heat rather than reflecting it back. The tests concluded that the early versions of RAM reduced the radar reflectivity of the warhead by a factor of ten.
91. The technical requirement called for the system to deal with six to eight pairs of targets, that is, six to eight separate warheads and the final stage of the missile, which would also follow the warhead. The requirement was based on the assumption that it would require several ABM missiles to deal with each pair of targets, hence the plan to deploy at least one hundred ABM missile launchers to deal with six to eight ICBMs.

Chapter 4. The Race for Parity: 1965–1973

1. A. Saveleyev and N. Detinov, *The Big Five: Arms Control Decision Making in the Soviet Union* (Westport, Conn.: Praeger, 1995), 3.
2. Dale Herspring, *The Soviet High Command, 1967–1989* (Princeton: Princeton University Press, 1990), 53–54.
3. In 1957–58 Khrushchev replaced the ministries with regional Sovnarkhoz, which were responsible for the management of major plants and industrial facilities. However, most of the defense ministries were kept intact by the creation of an alternate organization, the State Committee. So the Ministry of the Defense Industry became the State Committee for Defense Technology (GKOT), and the Ministry of the Aviation Industry became the State Committee for Aviation Technology (GKAT). The heads of these state committees retained the rank of minister of the Soviet Union, and the Council of Ministers retained its role in the direction of the defense industries. The missile programs were primarily managed by the GKOT under K. N. Rudnev, though some bureaus under GKAT control, such as Chelomey's OKB-52, continued to play a role. Rudnev was replaced by Deputy Chairman L. V. Smirnov in June 1961, an administrator with a long association with Yangel's design bureau. The missile industries were further protected by the appointment of V. N. Novikov as head of the Gosplan state economic planning agency in 1960.
4. The new MOM was headed by Sergei A. Afanasyev, who had been involved in 1952 in converting the Dnepropetrovsk automobile plant into the main Soviet ICBM plant. He remained as head of MOM through the Brezhnev years, until 1983.
5. *Heptyl* is the Russian term for unsymmetric dimethylhydrazine (UDMH).
6. There was already some significant work under way on smaller solid-fuel tactical-rocket engines by Boris P. Zhukov, chief designer of the NII-125 rocket propulsion institute, but

this engine technology did not readily translate to ICBMs, since the engine-core diameters were so small.

7. Grabin's bureau had been one of the main developers of field artillery in World War II. V. Grabin was retired by Khrushchev's orders in 1958, and his TsNII-58 artillery design bureau was transferred to OKB-1 on 27 June 1959. Khrushchev had been displeased with Grabin's advocacy of super-heavy artillery for the tactical nuclear delivery role, epitomized by his Obyekt 271 Kondensator self-propelled 406 mm heavy gun. Chief designer Igor Sadovsky was assigned to head the new OKB-1 division working on solid-fuel missile design. The solid-fuel rocket design effort was coordinated with the new chemical production facility at Biisk, where a significant solid-fuel rocket-engine test facility was erected.

8. The term RT stood for *raketa tverdotoplivnaya* (solid-fuel missile) and was also known under its GURVO designation, 8K95.

9. Even this small force created some controversy within the bureau. Korolyov's assistant, V. Mishin, was very upset by the diversion of so much talent into this project, given the heavy commitment of the bureau to other high-priority programs, including the R-9 ICBM, the Zenit spy satellite, and many space programs.

10. This was due to the use of older Nylon-B (NMF-2) solid fuel developed by Zhukov's NII-125, which was a form of ballistite. This limited the casting of engines to a 0.8 m (2.6 ft) diameter. The Soviets were not able to cast larger-diameter engines until the advent of Nylon-S propellant, which was developed by V. S. Shpak's team at the Leningrad Institute of Applied Chemistry (GIPKh) and which was about 30 percent more energy efficient as well.

11. It was 2.7 km (1.7 mi) to the right of the intended target and 12.4 km (7.7 mi) downrange.

12. Semyonov, *Raketno-Kosmicheskaya korporatsia Energia,* 131.

13. This was a stillborn scheme for the aviation ministry to enter the ICBM business with Myasishchev and Sukhoi's bureaus, each developing one stage of the missile, and with Chelomey coordinating the effort.

14. Chertok, *Rakety i lyudi: Goryachiye dni kholodnoi voiny,* 115.

15. Kosberg's design bureau had previously worked on second- and third-stage engines. It is located in Voronezh and is now called KB Khimavtomatika (Chemical Automation Design Bureau). The second-stage engines were developed by P. Izotov's OKB-117 in Leningrad, a design bureau previously specializing in jet-engine development.

16. The semiofficial history of the UR-100 program can be found in Gorodnichev et al., *GKN-PTs imeni M. V. Khrunicheva: 80 let* (Fili: Khrunichev State Research and Production Space Center, 1996).

17. This skirted around the weight limits by using air as the oxidant in the first stage, rather than requiring the missile to carry its own oxidant.

18. The guidance system for the RT-2 was originally assigned to Pilyugin's team at NII-885 in Monino. However, after a dispute in the institute over the guidance approach, Pilyugin's team was allowed to secede and set up a separate guidance design bureau in Moscow, which formed the basis for the NII-AP (NII avtomatiki i priborostroyeniye: Scientific Research Institute for Automation and Instruments, now NPO AP), which became one of the Soviet Union's primary guidance institutes.

19. The first silo launch took place on 17 July 1965.

20. Dates on service introduction differ. Some sources state that the acceptance date was 24 November 1966. "Intercontinental Ballistic Missile UR-100 (RS-10)," *Voyenny parad,* September–October 1996, 144.

21. This presumably would have been the Sokol Aviation Plant, a fighter plant long associated with Mikoyan.

22. The best account of the early tribulations of the Soviet solid-fuel program can be found in the third volume of Chertok's memoirs, *Rakety i lyudi: Goryachiye dni kholodnoi voiny,* 105–22; as well as in Igor Pavlov, "Polemics: Who Doesn't Like the Topol Missile System and Why?" *Nezavisimoye voyennoye obozreniye* 10 (15–21 March 1997) (trans. FBIS-UMA-97-075-S).

23. Pavlov, "Polemics." The Chertok memoirs suggest that the transfer of the RT-2 program from OKB-1 to Arsenal was largely initiated by Zhukov, while the Pavlov article suggests that it was an effort by Ustinov to keep alive his cherished solid-fuel program.

24. Moskovsky institut teplotekhniki: Moscow Institute of Thermotechnology. The institute's chief designer was A. D. Nadiradze, the former head of the GosNII-642 guided-weapons institute. In 1965 MIT had been assigned to develop the Temp-2S (NATO: SS-12) frontal ballistic missile for the army's Ground Forces.

25. The TsKB-7 design bureau at Arsenal was working on the unsuccessful RT-15 (8K97) IRBM version of the RT-2 at the time. The RT-2 program was transferred to the Arsenal plant rather than the original prime contractor, SKB-172, in Perm, because by this time the Perm plant had been connected with several failed solid-fuel missile efforts, such as the Ladoga tactical ballistic missile, while Arsenal was being assigned the development of the navy's solid-fuel SLBM effort.

26. This resulted in the Temp (SS-16).

27. Chertok, *Rakety i lyudi: Goryachiye dni kholodnoi voiny,* 132.

28. In the original versions of this system, two radio stations emitting coded signals in the 3 cm (1.2 in) band were positioned about 500 km (310 mi) from one another, perpendicular to the launch direction of the missile. In later versions of the system deployed after 1959, a single radio transmitter could be used, usually consisting of a continuous wave signal for range information and a pulsed wave signal for flight corrections. On the contemporary R-9 system, the transmitters were in silos that were automatically elevated near the time of launch. The flight-control system onboard the missile received these signals and processed them to determine the missile's relative position to the coded beams, providing flight corrections to the engines to reorient the missile if necessary.

29. The requirements called for a probable accuracy of 1.3 to 1.9 km (.8 to 1.2 mi) CEP and a maximum error of 5.0 km (3.1 mi). The RVSN defined maximum error as 2.3 times the probable error, so these two figures are essentially similar. A. V. Karpenko et al., *Otechestvenniye strategicheskiye raketinye kompleksy* (St. Petersburg: Nevsky Bastion, 1999), 178.

30. *Odnichnoi start.* Although the OS system was preferred, the design bureaus were also instructed to offer less expensive, soft-basing options. Ye. B. Volkov et al., *Mezhkontinentalniye ballisticheskiye rakety SSSR (RF) i SShA: Istoria sozdania, razvitia, i sokrashenia* (Moscow: RVSN, 1996), 136.

31. Guidance was handled by the usual institutes: N. A. Pilyugin's bureau for the inertial system in cooperation with V. A. Kuznetsov's gyroscope bureau, and M. S. Ryazan's bureau for the radio-telemetry systems.

32. Chertok, *Rakety i lyudi: Goryachiye dni kholodnoi voiny,* 70.

33. Sergei Khrushchev, *Khrushchev on Khrushchev* (New York: Little, Brown, 1990), 103–4.

34. May et al., *History of the Strategic Arms Competition,* 498.

35. This debate went public in the late 1960s. See for example, Michael Getler, "Arms Control

and the SS-9," *Space/Aeronautics,* November 1969. For a recent summary of this debate, see Kirtsen Lundberg, *The SS-9 Controversy: Intelligence as a Political Football,* Case Program C16-89-884 (Cambridge: Kennedy School of Government, Harvard University, 1989).

36. Vincent Dupont, "The Development of the Soviet ICBM Force, 1955–1967" (Ph.D. diss., Columbia University, 1991).

37. The missions might include missile silos, but also softer targets such as bomber bases, which were still a significant target in the 1960s and early 1970s. Volkov et al., *Mezhkontinentalniye ballisticheskiye rakety,* 130.

38. *Globalnaya raketa.* O. Urusov, "Kosmosy dlya shturma Ameriki," *Novosti kosmonavtiki* 7 (2000): 65–67, and 8 (2000): 68–71; Asif Siddiqi, "The Soviet Fractional Orbiting Bombardment System," *Quest* 7, no. 4 (2000): 22–32.

39. Jeffrey Richelson, *America's Space Sentinels: DSP Satellites and National Security* (Lawrence: University of Kansas Press, 1999).

40. M. A. Sakovich, "Slavnoe desyatiletiye morskovo raketostroenia," *Taifun* 5 (2000): 14.

41. This bureau was designated TsKB-7 GKOT and is now known as KB Arsenal. It was traditionally involved in the development of ship artillery. V. G. Degtyabr et al., *50 let KB Arsenal imeni M. V. Frunze* (St. Petersburg: Nevsky Bastion, 1999), 69.

42. These rockets are better known in the West as the FROG (free rocket over ground).

43. This was a cooperative effort between Tyurin's TsKB-7 and the army artillery design bureau SKB-172 in Perm.

44. It was called SS-NX-13 by the United States, because U.S. intelligence incorrectly did not believe that it had been deployed. Aleksandr Shirokorad, *Rakety nad morem* (Moscow: Tekhnika i Vooruzheniye, 1997), 9.

45. The Project 705B was also known as the Project 687. A. V. Kuteinikova, *TsKB No. 16–TsPB Volna,* vol. 2 (St. Petersburg: Malakhit, 1995), 93–101.

46. This project began in 1958, and there were various armament schemes, including the old D-4, the newer solid-fuel D-6. This project was undertaken by S. N. Kovalev's team at TsKB-18 (now the Rubin design bureau) in Leningrad.

47. The first four missiles could be salvoed about eight seconds apart. But the second and third salvoes had to have a twenty- to thirty-five-minute interval between them to adjust the boat's trim due to the water filling the launch tubes. M. Muratov, *Otechestvenniye atomniye podvodniye lodki* (Moscow: Tekhnika i Vooruzheniye, 2000), 57–58.

48. The R-27 had an accuracy of about 1.3 km (0.8 mi) CEP, while the U.S. Navy's Polaris A3 had a CEP of 0.6 km (0.4 mi). The first boats of the Project 667A class were fitted with the Sigma navigation system. The Soviet Navy's first submarine inertial navigation system, the Tobol, developed by O. V. Kishchenkov's design bureau, was installed in the final production Project 667AU submarines starting at the end of 1972; eight earlier submarines were refitted with the system. Later, some of the navigation systems were upgraded with the Tsiklon system, which received navigation data from satellites.

49. This version was designated the R-27K and was part of the 4K18 weapon system.

50. This proposal was first aired at the February 1962 military conference at Gagra/Pitsunda. Khrushchev, *Nikita Khrushchev,* vol. 2 (Moscow: Novosti, 1994), 155–56.

51. Shirokorad, *Rakety nad morem,* 8.

52. The Navaga class had an endurance of seventy days. The earlier Project 658/Hotel nuclear ballistic-missile submarine had a nominal endurance of fifty days.

53. Bruce W. Watson, *Red Navy at Sea: Soviet Naval Operations on the High Seas, 1956–1980* (Boulder: Westview Press, 1982), 26. Other sources state it was in 1969. May et al., *History of the Strategic Arms Competition,* 725.

54. There are no detailed Soviet budget figures yet available beyond the early 1960s. This is a U.S. estimate based on CIA estimates. A. S. Becker and E. D. Brunner Jr., *Evolution of Soviet Military Forces and Budgets, 1963–1972,* DARPA WN(L)-9326-ARP, November 1975, 6.

55. G. A. Sukhina et al., *Raketny shchit otechestva* (Moscow: RVSN, 1999), 103–4.

56. In 1961 the U.S. missile site program involved 21,300 construction workers and about 3,000 administrators, compared to an average of about 300,000 workers in the Soviet program. This was largely due to the far more extensive use of prefabricated structures in the United States and an economy that placed higher emphasis on labor productivity. Lonnquest and Winkler, *To Defend and Deter,* 81; Sukhina et al., *Raketny shchit otechestva,* 104.

57. Accounts by missile officers of the time can be found in S. G. Kochemasov, *Veterany-Raketchiki vspominayut* (Moscow: RVSN, 1994).

58. The additional troops were those assigned to the R-12 and R-14 intermediate-missile divisions, which declined in strength from about 134,000 in 1963 to 119,000 in 1972. Becker and Brunner, *Evolution of Soviet Military Forces,* 25.

59. The composition of these divisions shifted through time. In 1962 there were eighteen IRBM divisions and twenty ICBM divisions; in 1972 there were only fourteen IRBM divisions, while there were twenty-two ICBM divisions.

60. These consisted of the 43rd Missile Army in Vinnitsa, 50th Missile Army in Smolensk, 3rd Missile Corps in Vladimir, 5th Missile Corps in Kirov, 7th Missile Corps in Omsk, 8th Missile Corps in Chita, 9th Missile Corps in Khabarovsk, 18th Missile Corps in Orenburg, and 24th Missile Corps in Dzhambul.

61. While not widely discussed, the early Soviet bases depended on encrypted teletypes for transmitting messages to the remote bases, which could be intercepted by U.S. signals-intelligence units based along the Soviet frontier.

62. Irukhim Smotkin, *Hardening Soviet ICBM Silos* (Falls Church, Va.: Delphic, 1991), 42.

63. Dmitry Litovkin, "Snaipersky vystrel: Konstruktora Tyurina," *Voyennoe znaniye* 10 (1997): 26.

64. N. S. Popov et al., *Bez tain i sekretov: Ocherk 60-letnei istorii tankovovo konstruktoskovo biuro na Kirovskom zavode v Sankt-Peterburge* (St. Petersburg: Prana, 1996), 259.

65. V. Degtyabr et al., *50 let KB Arsenal imeni M. V. Frunze* (St. Petersburg: Nevsky Bastion, 1999), 123.

66. Steven Zaloga, "The Tu-22 Blinder and Tu-22M Backfire," *World Airpower Journal* 33 (1998): 56–80.

67. Valery Yarynich, *Sistema upravlenia strategicheskimi yadarnymi silami,* paper presented at "Russian Missile Programs, the MTCR, and the Future of U.S.-Russian Arms Control," Monterey Institute, 21–22 July 1995, 7–8.

68. It was 300 m (990 ft) long and 25 m (82 ft) high. Its performance and operating features have more in common with the conventional American AN/FPS-50 nonarray radar of the period than later phased-array radars. The Dnestr radar used simple one-dimensional electronic scanning.

69. These were at Olenegorsk, on the Kola Peninsula; Skrunda, in Latvia; Mishelevka, near Irkutsk; Genichesk, near the Black Sea; and Pinsk.

70. The A-35 ABM system command and control was based around the 5E92-B computer system, developed by V. S. Burtsev, while the Dnestr early-warning radar used the incompatible 5E73 computer system of M. A. Kartsev. The computers used different data-transmissions systems, making data sharing between the radars of the two systems impossible. A temporary fix enabled data sharing, but the fix consumed 30 percent of the computer memory and speed. V. G. Repin of TsNPO Vympel was assigned as chief designer of the upgraded missile-attack warning system. In 1973 a new unified command post was established to handle data input from the Dnestr-M BMEWS radar and the A-35 engagement radars. The TsNPO Vympel (Central Scientific Production Association Vympel) was formed on New Year's eve 1970 from Kisunko's OKB Vympel, Mints's Radio Engineering Institute, Georgy Kuzminsky's NII DAR, Bubnov's KB Radiopripor, the Dnepropetrovsk Radio Plant, and other supporting production facilities to consolidate ABM efforts.

71. Yury Leshchenko, "Rules of Life for Academician Semenikhin: About the Nuclear Button and Those Who Created the System for Controlling the Country's Strategic Forces," *Krasnaya zvezda*, 30 November 1993 (trans. JPRS-UMA-93-044, 8 December 1993, 17) .

72. Yarynich, *Sistema upravlenia*, 8–10.

73. NII-4 MO (Scientific Research Institute-4 of the Ministry of Defense) is the RVSN's advanced research center. It examines new technologies and plays a key role in determining future strategic-missile system technical requirements and strategic warfare doctrine. Aleksandr Dolinin, "Secrety sekretnovo NII v gody 'kholodnoi voiny' zdes proschityvali yaderniye stsenarii," *Krasnaya zvezda*, 23 December 1994.

74. Yu. P. Maksimov, *Raketniye voiska strategicheskovo naznachenia* (Moscow: RVSN, 1992), 126.

75. The launch battalions controlled an individual silo. The regiment was responsible for the launch-control center (LCC), which netted together several silos. The command sequence in the missile force was the General Staff command post (Level 1), RVSN central command post at Vlasikha (Level 2), missile army (Level 3), missile division (Level 4), missile regiment (Level 5), and launch battalion (Level 6).

76. Bruce Blair, "Russian Control of Nuclear Weapons," in *The Nuclear Challenge in Russia and the New States of Eurasia*, ed. George Quester (Armonk, N.Y.: M. E. Sharpe, 1995), 60.

77. Aleksandr Dollin, "On the Second Floor . . . Down: Reporting from the Strategic Missile Forces Communications Control Center," *Krasnaya zvezda*, 29 September 1995 (trans. FBIS-UMA-95-192-S, 29 September 1995).

78. The development work was undertaken by chief designer V. V. Alekseichik of the Mars Design Bureau in Ulyanovsk, and series manufacture took place at the NPO Komintern in Leningrad.

79. The associated command-and-control systems on the submarine included the Rotator, Integral, and BKTS (*bortovy kompleks tekhnicheskikh sredstv:* onboard technical equipment system). Yarynich, *Sistema upravlenia*, 27–29.

80. In Russian, POSYaS (Plan operatsii strategicheskikh yadernykh sil). Pavel Podvig, *Strategicheskoye yadernoye vooruzheniye Rossii* (Moscow: IzdAT, 1998), 46–47.

81. The S-25 Berkut program was estimated to cost R 12 billion, and the S-75 through 1961 was estimated at R 26 billion. J. E. Loftus and A. W. Marshall, *Forecasting Soviet Force Structure: The Importance of Bureaucratic and Budgetary Constraints* (Santa Monica: Rand Corporation, July 1963), 53. By way of comparison, the contemporary U.S. Nike Hercules program cost half a billion dollars for development and $2.7 billion for procurement for 500 launchers. The Soviet S-75 program was nearly ten times the size, including

some 4,800 launchers by 1968. While Soviet unit costs were probably lower due to a larger production run, a lower level of sophistication, and a smaller number of reload missiles, the program was still of very significant size, probably equivalent to about $30 billion in 1968 dollars. This figure is based on the sale of 18 launchers and associated missiles and radars to India in 1964–65 for $112 million. To provide a further comparison, the wartime U.S. Manhattan research program was estimated to cost about $1 billion.

82. This system was later called ABM-1a Galosh by Western intelligence. Kisunko, *Sekretnaya zona,* 379.

83. The system was designed to defeat six to eight "pairs" of targets, meaning both a separable warhead and the main missile body, the presumption being that the radars of the time could not distinguish between the two. Kisunko, *Sekretnaya zona,* 471.

84. A two-volume official history of the Military Space Force was published as T. G. Melnik, ed., *Voyenno-Kosmicheskiye sily* (St. Petersburg: Nauka, 1997).

85. Dwayne Day et al., *Eye in the Sky: The Story of the Corona Spy Satellites* (Washington, D.C.: Smithsonian Institution Press, 1998), 164.

86. Victor Gobarev, "Soviet Policy towards China: Developing Nuclear Weapons, 1949–69," *Journal of Slavic Military Studies* 12, no. 4 (December 1999): 42.

87. *A History of Strategic Arms Competition, 1945–1972,* vol. 3, *A Handbook of Selected Soviet Weapon and Space Systems,* U.S. Air Force Supporting Studies (1976), 180–86.

88. I. D. Sergeyev, ed., *Khronika osnovnykh sobytii: Istorii raketnykh voisk strategicheskovo naznacheniya* (Moscow: RVSN, 1994), 39.

89. *Soviet Forces for Intercontinental Attack,* CIA Report NIE-11-8-71 (Washington, D.C.: CIA, 1971), 33.

90. Daniel Buchonnet, *MIRV: A Brief History of the Minuteman and Multiple Reentry Vehicles* (Livermore, Cal.: Lawrence Livermore Laboratory, 1976), declassified copy at National Security Archives.

91. For example, Volkov et al., *Mezhkontinentalniye ballisticheskiye rakety,* mentions that the program considered three warhead types for the R-36: the monoblock, orbital, and MRV.

92. V. V. Bulavkin and E. A. Goncharov, *NPO Tekhnomash: 60 let* (Moscow: Tekhnomash, 1998), 260–61.

93. Karpenko et al., *Otechestvenniye strategicheskiye raketniye kompleksy,* 183.

94. This version was also called the SS-11 Mod. 2B by Western intelligence.

95. In two of the tests, the warheads were released for a symmetrical cross-range spread about 18.5 km (11.5 mi) across, or about 9 km (5.6 mi) between each other.

96. V. Popov, "O vtorom ispytatelnom upravlenii," *Kosmodrom* 1 (2000): 7.

97. Stephen Whitefield, *Industrial Power and the Soviet State* (Oxford: Clarendon Press, 1993).

Chapter 5. Beyond Parity: 1973–1985

1. Robert Campbell, "Resource Stringency and Civil-Military Resource Allocation," in *Soldiers and the Soviet State,* ed. Timothy Colton et al. (Princeton: Princeton University Press, 1990), 126–63.

2. The most detailed account of this affair is found in a two-part essay by Vladimir F. Utkin and Yury Mozzhorin. Utkin was a chief designer at the Yangel design bureau at the time and took over as general designer when Yangel died of a heart attack in 1971. Mozzhorin was assistant head of the main RVSN think tank, NII-4, in Bolshevo, in 1955–61 and headed the studies department at TsNIIMash at the time of the controversy. "Raketnoye i

kosmicheskoye vooruzheniye," in *Sovetskaya voyennaya mosch ot Stalina do Gorbacheva,* ed. A. A. Brish et al. (Moscow: Voyenny Parad, 1999), 173–242.

3. TsNIIMASH (Central Scientific Research Institute for the Machine Building Industry) was the main NII of the Ministry of General Machine Building and the new name for NII-88 starting in 1967.

4. For a look at the social aspects of the Soviet armed forces during the Cold War, see chapter 6 in Roger Reese, *The Soviet Military Experience* (London: Routledge, 2000).

5. For example, the French army in the 1930s was faced with a similar problem of absorbing new tank technology into a force based on conscripts. Eugenia Kiesling, *Arming against Hitler: France and the Limits of Military Planning* (Lawrence: University of Kansas Press, 1996).

6. Sokolov was head of the main research institute of the RVSN missile force, NII-4, in Bolshevo.

7. Raymond L. Garthoff, *Détente and Confrontation: American-Soviet Relations from Nixon to Reagan* (Washington, D.C.: Brookings Institution, 1994).

8. On the roots of Brezhnev's détente policy, see chapter 10 in Richard Anderson, *Public Politics in an Authoritarian State: Making Foreign Policy during the Brezhnev Years* (Ithaca: Cornell University Press, 1993).

9. Arkady Shevchenko, *Breaking with Moscow* (New York: Knopf, 1985), 202.

10. Saveleyev and Detinov, *Big Five,* 9. For a more critical review of the Soviet aims, see William Odom, *The Collapse of the Soviet Military* (New Haven: Yale University Press, 1998), 83–87.

11. V. Yu. Marinin, "Seredina 1960-x gg.-nachalo 'zolotovo veka' otechesvennovo korablestroyenia," *Taifun* 2 (1997): 9–12.

12. May et al., *History of the Strategic Arms Competition,* 566.

13. Anatoly Dobrynin, *In Confidence* (New York: Random House, 1995), 193–94.

14. For a firsthand account by one of the civilian analysts, see Vitaly Tsygichko, "Strategic Decision Making in the Former Soviet Union," in *Russia on the Brink of the Millennium,* ed. A. Voskressenski et al. (Commack, N.Y.: Nova Science, 1998), 149–62.

15. Saveleyev and Detinov, *Big Five,* 35.

16. Dobrynin, *In Confidence,* 165.

17. D. Sahal, *Patterns of Technological Innovation* (London: Addison Wesley, 1981).

18. The original OS silos had a hardness of 200–284 psi, while the improved OS-84 silos raised this to about 1,140 to 1,470 psi. The levels varied by silo type. Smotkin, *Hardening,* 42.

19. From 1964 to 1972, the RVSN added 103,000 troops, bringing the total to 274,000. A. S. Becker and E. D. Brunner Jr., *Evolution of Soviet Military Forces and Budgets, 1963–1972* (Washington, D.C.: DARPA, 1975), 3–4.

20. These were the 7th Missile Corps (Omsk), 8th Missile Corps (Chita), and 18th Missile Corps (Orenburg).

21. The MR-UR-100 designation did not follow the usual Yangel pattern and stood for *Modernizirovannaya raketa-UR-100:* modernized missile for the UR-100 requirement.

22. *Boyevoi zheleznodorozhny raketny kompleks:* Combat Railway Missile System.

23. Ye. Kaluga, "No More Political Ambition: Disarm, but Sensibly," *Pravda,* 30 December 1992 (trans. FBIS-SOV-92-252, 31 December 1992, 6).

24. V. Pappo-Korystin et al., *Dnepropetrovsky raketno-kosmichesky tsentr: Kratky ocherk stanovlenia i razvitia* (Dnepropetrovsk: KB Yuzhnoe, 1994), 93.

25. This organization was an expansion of the former NII-1 MO. Volkov et al., *Mezhkontinentalniye ballisticheskiye rakety,* 337.

26. A. V. Karpenko, *Podvizhniye raketniye kompleksy strategicheskovo naznachenia* (St. Petersburg: Nevsky Bastion, 1996), 10–14.

27. Popov et al., *Bez tain i sekretov,* 345.

28. For example, an experimental test unit for the Temp-2S had already been organized at Plesetsk in 1968 under the command of Lt. Col. N. V. Mazyarkin. Bal et al., *Poligon osoboi vazhnosti,* 41.

29. *A Soviet Land-Mobile ICBM: Evidence of Development and Considerations Affecting a Decision on Deployment* (Washington, D.C.: CIA, 1974).

30. Strobe Talbott, *Endgame: The Inside Story of SALT II* (New York: Harper & Row, 1980), 134.

31. Saveleyev and Detinov, *Big Five,* 24.

32. The CIA's 1976 *National Intelligence Estimate* reported that "the similarity between the two systems will make it difficult for us to determine whether the Soviets are deploying SS-X-16 ICBMs with the SS-X-20 launch units."

33. *NIE 11-3/8-76 Soviet Forces for Intercontinental Conflict through the Mid-1980s* (Washington, D.C.: CIA, 1976), 28. In a 1986 report on Soviet noncompliance with SALT II, the U.S. Arms Control and Disarmament Agency concluded that the SS-16 had been deployed at Plesetsk, but that remaining launchers had been dismantled by 1985. In 1985 systems related to the SS-16, such as warhead transporters, were spotted being moved to railcars at Plesetsk, presumably for dismantlement.

34. *NIE 11-3/8-77 Soviet Capabilities for Strategic Nuclear Conflict though the late 1980s* (Washington, D.C.: CIA, 1977), 8.

35. Kochemasov et al., *Khronika,* 30.

36. Soviet RVSN divisions have special engineer camouflage units attached. "Inzhenery v RVSN," *Armeisky sbornik* 5 (1999): 57–59.

37. Pavlov, "Polemics," 6.

38. V. P. Kuzmin and V. I. Nikolsky, *Voyenno-Morskoi flot SSSR, 1945–1991* (St. Petersburg: Morskoye Obshchestvo, 1996), 445.

39. See appendix 1 in Evgeny Miasnikov, *The Future of Russia's Strategic Nuclear Forces: Discussion and Arguments* (Moscow: Center for Arms Control, Energy, and Environmental Studies at MIPT, 1998; www.armscontrol.ru/subs/snf/).

40. Capt. 1st Rank I. K. Kudrin, "Vospominania komandira K-241," *Taifun* 2 (2000): 45–46.

41. S. Sontag and C. Drew, *Blind Man's Bluff: The Untold Story of American Submarine Espionage* (New York: Harper, 1999), 171–96.

42. During their career, the thirty-four Navaga class performed 590 patrols.

43. The associated missile system was designated D-8. M. A. Sakovich, "Slavnoye desyatiletiye morskovo raketostroyenia," *Taifun* 5 (2000): 18–20.

44. A. M. Vasilyev, "Proyekt Skorpion: Zamaskirovaniye nadvodniye raketonostsy," *Taifun* 4 (1997): 26–31.

45. Unlike the earlier R-27, the R-29 was launched from the tube like the American Polaris.

46. Kuzmin and Nikolsky, *Voyenno-Morskoi flot,* 54. The Murena had modest noise reduction (sound-level discrete frequencies in the 5–200 hertz spectrum/dB relative to 1 Pa at 1 m) of 130–35, compared to 140–45 for the Navaga. This noise level was comparable to that of late–World War II diesel submarines.

47. A. A. Zapolsky, *Strategicheskim raketonostsam-byt!* (St. Petersburg: Malakhit, 1998), 127.

48. Russian sources indicate that the CEP of the missile was 900 m (2,970 ft).

49. The Navaga initially cost R 35–40 million, rising to R 60–70 million by the end of the production run, while the later Project 667BRDM cost R 150–350 million. G. G. Kostev, *Voyenno-Morskoi flot strany, 1945–95* (St. Petersburg: Nauka, 1999), 368.

50. The Project 941 Akula was called Typhoon by NATO due to a misunderstanding of a Soviet statement during an arms-control conference in which the name of the weapon system, Taifun (Typhoon), was mistaken for the name of the submarine itself. The issue is all the more confusing, because a class of attack submarines, the Project 971 Shchuka, was called Akula by NATO.

51. A view of the loading system for the LCC can be found in N. Spassky et al., *Russia's Arms,* vol. 4, *Strategic Missile Forces* (Moscow: Voyenny Parad, 1997), 296.

52. Yarynich, *Sistema upravlenia,* 18–20.

53. These included the Almaz, Bazalt, and Sopka systems, developed by the NII for Mathematical Machines in Yerevan. Yarynich, *Sistema upravlenia,* 31–32.

54. It is not clear when this feature was introduced, but most likely it was in the Tu-22M3/ Tu-95MS/ Tu-160 generation of strategic bombers. Blair, "Russian Control," 61.

55. The submarine-based communications element of the system is called P-790 Tsunami-BM. Aleksandr B. Shirokorad, *Sovetskiye podvodniye lodki poslevoyennoi postroiki* (Moscow: Arsenal, 1997), 98.

56. V. Zakolodyazhny and V. Panteleyev, "Radionavigatsionniye sredstva opredelenia mesta i tendentsii ikh razvitia," *Morskoi sbornik* 6 (1995): 69.

57. Kostev, *Voyenno-Morskoi flot strany,* 397–98.

58. V. Kotelnikov, "In Support of Guaranteeing Security: Certain Problems of the Organization of Radio Communications between Shore and the Sea," *Morskoi sbornik,* September 1996 (trans. FBIS-UMA-96-235-S, 1 September 1996).

59. "The nuclear football" is the American nickname for these types of systems, since the officer in charge of the presidential suitcase often carries it under his arm like a football. The Russian nickname for these devices is "nuclear briefcase" *(yaderny chemodanchik).*

60. The suitcase was developed under Chief Designer Nikolai Devyanin. Oleg Volkov and Vladimir Umnov, "Is the 'Nuclear Briefcase' Really Necessary?" *Moscow News* 13 (1–17 April 1994); and "We Never Knew Them: Briefcase Is Tired, Nuclear Briefcase Designer Visits Editorial Office for First Time," *Komsomolskaya pravda,* 28 January 1992 (trans. FBIS-SOV-92-019, 29 January 1992, 7–12); Aleksey Arbatov, "The Mysteries of the Nuclear Button," *New Times* 4 (January 1992): 20–23.

61. One suggestion is that each of the sanctioning levels adds its own code to a sequence, thereby sanctioning the release. For example, the national leader issues his code through the Cheget of 153, to which the minister of defense adds his code of 609, to which the executing branch command post such as the RVSN adds its code of 731, resulting in the full code of 153609731. However, this raises the question of how the command link would survive in the event of a nuclear emergency that removed one link in the chain. Presumably, there would be some means to add an alternate sequence in the code if a portion of the sanctioning team is unavoidably removed. Gen. Lt. Yu. Kardashevsky, "In Whose Hands Is the Nuclear Button?" *Argumenty i fakty,* 26 December 1991 (trans. FBIS-SOV-91-003, 6 January 1992, 17–18).

62. Bill Gertz, "Mishaps Put Russian Missiles in Combat Mode," *Washington Times,* 12 May 1997.

63. Vladimir Yegorov and Foma Aksyonov, "Underground: The Legend of Metro-2," *Tekhnika molodezhi* 5 (1991) (trans. FBIS-UMA-95-159-S, 17 August 1995, 7).

64. *Military Forces in Transition, 1991* (Washington, D.C.: Department of Defense, 1991), 43.

65. The Gorky area (now Nizhny-Novgorod) was the planned site for the Supreme Leadership relocation in World War II. The new bunker complex was a short distance southeast of Arzamas, the center of Soviet nuclear weapons design. Details of this facility will be found in *Soviet Military Power: An Assessment of the Threat, 1988* (Washington, D.C.: U.S. Department of Defense, 1988), 60–61.

66. Bruce Blair, *The Logic of Accidental Nuclear War* (Washington, D.C.: Brookings Institution, 1993), 143.

67. Piotr Butowski, *Lotnictwo wojskowe Rosji,* vol. 2 (Warsaw: Lampart, 1995), 79.

68. As a result, Western intelligence called these radars Pechora LPAR (large phased-array radar).

69. This program was about 15 percent the size of the missile silo construction program of the late 1960s. Votintsev, "Neizvestniye voiska ischeznuvshei sverkhderzhavy," *Voyenno-Istorichesky zhurnal* 11 (1993): 22.

70. The Duga chief designer was F. A. Kuzminsky of the NII-DAR (Scientific Research Institute for Long-Range Communication). The Duga-2 test bed OTH-B radar was between Gomel in Belorussia and Chernobyl in Ukraine. A. Babkin, "Fortresses Alone Are Ineffective, or Why the OTH Radar System Was Shut Down," *Kommunist vooruzhonnykh sil,* 11 February 1991 (trans. JPRS-UMA-91-012, 3 May 1991, 45).

71. This led to considerable shake-ups in the design team. Kuzminsky was demoted from his leadership of the NII-DAR and subordinated to a new program head, V. Markov, the former deputy minister of the Ministry of the Radio Industry. However, disagreements between the two led to Kuzminsky's resignation, and F. F. Yevstratov took over leadership of OTH radar development. Votintsev, "Neizvestniye voiska ischeznuvshei sverkhderzhavy," *Voyenno-Istorichesky zhurnal* 10 (1993).

72. Although work continued on the radar, the Chernobyl nuclear power plant accident forced the abandonment of the Gomel test-bed radar. The only completed radar at Komsomolsk was judged to require R 300,000 in upgrades, without the assurance that the modifications would solve the problems. As a result, the upgrade program was canceled in 1989, and in November 1989 the radar was withdrawn from service. The other radar site was abandoned after a fire destroyed much of its equipment.

73. The program for a space-based detection system was headed by General Designer A. I. Savin's TsNII Kometa (Central Scientific Research Institute Comet) in Khimki. Design of the satellite itself was undertaken by Chief Designer V. M. Kovtunenko of the Lavochkin NPO. The infrared telescopes were developed by Mikhail M. Miroshnikov's GOI imeni S. I. Vavilova (State Optical Institute named after S. I. Vavilov) in Leningrad and manufactured by the Leningrad Optical Mechanical Association (LOMO). Boris Kagan, *Soviet ABM Early Warning System: Satellite-Based Project M* (Falls Church, Va.: Delphic, 1991), 7–8.

74. Tests of the Project M optical sensor began in 1975 at a test facility in Sosnovy Bor. Two different approaches were examined: an electron beam scanner and an electromechanical scanner. The electron beam scanner was the first type tested in space.

75. E. Babichev, "V polyote Kosmos-2368," *Novosti kosmonavtika* 2 (2000): 46–49.

76. The U.S. strategic-bomber force consisted of 1,277 aircraft in 1964 and 521 in 1972. *U.S. Department of Defense Posture Statement for Fiscal Year 1972* (Washington, D.C.: Department of Defense, 1971), table 9.

77. Steven Zaloga, *Soviet Air Defense Missiles: Design, Development, and Tactics* (Coulsdon, England: Jane's, 1988), 49, 83.

78. John Collins, *U.S./Soviet Military Balance, 1970–82* (Washington, D.C.: Congressional Research Service, 1983), 31

79. G. A. Sukhina et al., *Raketniy shchit otechestva* (Moscow: RVSN, 1999), 179.

80. Saveleyev and Detinov, *Big Five,* 7.

81. TsNPO Vympel (Central Scientific Production Association Vympel) was formed from Kisunko's OKB Vympel, Mints's Radio Engineering Institute, Georgy Kuzminsky's NII DAR, Bubnov's KB Radiopripor, the Dnepropetrovsk Radio Plant, and other supporting production facilities.

82. U.S. intelligence believed that about two to four hundred of the SS-11 force were aimed against regional targets. May et al., *History of the Strategic Arms Competition,* 702.

83. Benjamin Cole, "British Technical Intelligence and the Soviet IRBM Threat, 1952–60," *Intelligence and National Security* 14, no. 2, 70–93.

84. Robert Norris et al, *British, French, and Chinese Nuclear Weapons* (Boulder: Westview Press, 1994), 101.

85. Jacques Vilain, *La Force de dissuasion française: Genese et evolution* (Paris: Docavia, 1987).

86. Volkov et al., *Mezhkontinentalniye ballisticheskiye rakety,* 337.

87. Dmitry Ustinov insisted that the Soviet Ministry of Defense begin using names for most major missile programs started in the late 1960s, largely due to the confusion in the ranks of party officials over the UR-100, UR-100N, and MR-UR-100 controversy, and the increasing use of GURVO industrial designations in official documents. The names were intended to make it easier to keep track of the various programs.

88. While the threat study for the Pioner has not been described, those for Soviet antitactical ballistic-missile programs during this period have been discussed in some detail in a study by the 3 TsNII MO, which conducted them. S. I. Petukhov and I. V. Shestov, *Istoria sozdania i razvitia vooruzhenia i voyennoi tekhniki PVO sukhoputnykh voisk Rossii,* pt. 2 (Moscow: Izd. VPK, 1997), 3–8.

89. This included the Minsk Automotive Plant (MAZ), responsible for the chassis, and the Barrikady plant in Volgograd, which manufactured the associated launcher equipment.

90. The U.S. Navy deployed a small number of submarines with the Regulus cruise missile in the 1950s, but the missile was so large that only one could be carried per submarine. In addition, the weapon was so cumbersome that it limited the role of the submarine to a single mission.

91. Jonathan Haslam, *The Soviet Union and the Politics of Nuclear Weapons in Europe, 1969–87* (Ithaca: Cornell University Press, 1990).

92. Talbott, *Endgame,* 71–72.

93. V. Markovsky, "Bekfair-Proryv iz neizvestnosti," *Aerokhobbi* 1 (1993): 4.

94. Production of the Tu-22M2 in 1972–83 was 211 aircraft, all manufactured at the State Aviation Plant No. 22, in Kazan.

95. *A History of Strategic Arms Competition, 1945–1972,* vol. 3, *A Handbook of Selected Soviet Weapon and Space Systems* (USAF Supporting Studies, June 1976), 13.

96. V. E. Ilin et al., "Kratky spravochnik po rossiiskim i ukrainskim samolyotam i vertolyotam," *Aviatsia i kosmonavtika* 6 (1995): 41. This figure is repeated in Russian official documents made available during confidence-building efforts in the early 1990s. *Iskhodniye danniye dlya raschota koeffitsientov soizmerimosti obraztsov vooruzhenia i voyennoi tekhniki i voiskovykh formirovany SSSR i NATO* (Moscow: USSR Armed Force General Staff Operational-Strategic Research Center, 1991).

97. Ironically, this concession came just as evidence began to emerge that the new Backfire C variant might have range advantages over the standard Backfire B.
98. David Dunn, *The Politics of Threat: Minuteman Vulnerability in American National Security Policy* (Basingstoke, England: Macmillan, 1997).

Chapter 6. To the Brink of Collapse: 1985–1991

1. Details of Soviet missile-certification life are not complete. The ICBMs of the fourth generation had a certification life of ten years, though there was always the capability of keeping a particular type in service much beyond the certification life of a single missile, since the USSR manufactured far more missiles than the total number of silos. Under pressure, the life expectancy could be extended by factory rebuilding, as was done with the SS-11, and as is planned with the SS-19. The SS-19 life-extension program is expected to keep the system viable for an additional fifteen years.
2. Graham Spinardi, *From Polaris to Trident: The Development of U.S. Fleet Ballistic Missile Technology* (Cambridge: Cambridge University Press, 1994), 125–26.
3. Yu. P. Maksimov, *Zapiski vyvshego glavkoma strategicheskikh* (Moscow: RVSN, 1994), 231.
4. For a view of Soviet "bastion" doctrine, see Jan Breemer, "The Soviet Navy's SSBN Bastions: Why Explanations Matter," *RUSI Journal,* winter 1989, 33–39.
5. The Fili organization later became known as KB Salyut and is now part of a major space consortium with the neighboring Khrunichev manufacturing plant.
6. This left Chelomey in control of the original NPO Mashinostroyeniye bureau in Reutov.
7. This version was different enough from the preceding R-36M, known internally as the 15A14, that it received a new designation, 15A18.
8. A test on 18 October 1979 toward Kamchatka demonstrated an accuracy of 0.15 nautical miles (300 m, or 990 feet).
9. This missile had the GURVO designation of 15A16 and was known in the West as the SS-17 Mod 3.
10. Volkov et al., *Mezhkontinentalniye ballisticheskiye rakety,* 338.
11. Kochemasov et al., *Khronika,* 31.
12. This was called the ABSU variant (*avtonomnaya bazirovannaya samokhodnaya ustanovka,* or autonomously based self-propelled launcher). Sergeyev, *Khronika osnovnykh sobytii,* 32.
13. The Yuzhmash design bureau (KBYu) was the renamed Yangel SKB-586 design bureau in Dnepropetrovsk. Following Yangel's death in November 1979, it was led by B. F. Utkin.
14. U.S. intelligence did not spot the first launch because it failed so soon into the flight. "Soviets Fail in Second Test of PL-4 (SSX-24) ICBM," *Defense Daily,* 2 June 1983, 178.
15. The RT-23 silo version had the industrial designation of 15Zh44; the rail-based version was designated 15Zh52. The new RT-23UTTKh (UTTKh = improved technical-tactical characteristics) versions were 15Zh60 for the silo version and 15Zh61 for the rail version.
16. This version is sometimes called by its treaty pseudonym of RS-22B. Volkov et al., *Mezhkontinentalniye ballisticheskiye rakety,* 340.
17. The road-mobile version of the SS-24 was not identified until recent Russian revelations. A. V. Karpenko, *Podvizhniye raketniye kompleksy strategicheskovo naznachenia* (St. Petersburg: Nevsky Bastion, 1996).
18. Two very large TEL (transporter-erector-launcher) vehicles were developed for this role,

differing in their engine power: the MAZ-7906 with a 1,200 hp engine, and the MAZ-7907 with a 1,500 hp diesel engine. Karpenko, *Podvizhniye raketniye kompleksy,* 23–24.

19. Twenty-eight tests of the silo-based 15Zh60 and thirty-two tests of the rail-mobile 15Zh61 were conducted at Plesetsk through 1997. Bal et al., *Poligon osoboi vazhnosti,* 45.

20. Bill Gertz, "U.S. Satellites Detect Marked Increase in Mobile Soviet ICBMs," *Washington Times,* 14 October 1988.

21. This included the reconstruction of neighboring bridges and overpasses, new signaling equipment and switches, and other costly upgrades. Aleksandr Dolinin, "BZhRK: Raketny bronepoyezd," *Krasnaya zvezda,* 28 September 1994 (trans. FBIS-SOV-94-192, 4 October 1994, 26–27).

22. S. G. Kochemasov et al., *Khronika osnovnykh sobytii istorii RVSN* (Moscow: RVSN, 1994).

23. "Blast Reported at Soviet Plant that Makes Vital Missile Part," *New York Times,* 18 May 1988; "Explosion Hits Soviet Missile Plant," *San Diego Union,* 19 May 1988.

24. This submarine should not be confused with the nuclear attack submarine that NATO called the Akula, which was actually called Project 971 Shchuka by the Soviet Navy. Sergei Ptichkin, "The Birth of the Typhoon," *Soviet Soldier* 10 (1992): 32–35.

25. The name Vodonosets (water carrier) was a play on its official designation, Raketonosets (missile carrier).

26. M. Muratov, *Otechestvenniye atomniye podvodniye lodki* (Moscow: Tekhnika i Vooruzheniye, 2000), 72.

27. The accuracy was stated to be a CEP of 250 m (825 ft).

28. Muratov, *Otechestvenniye atomniye podvodniye lodki,* 77.

29. Butowski, *Lotnictwo wojskowe Rosji,* 74; G. Jacobs, "Soviet Strategic Command and Control and the Tu-142 Bear J," *Jane's Intelligence Review,* April 1991, 161–65.

30. The Tu-95M-5 Volga program examined the K-26 complex and its associated KSR-5 (AS-6 Kingfish), a missile developed earlier for the Tu-16 Badger medium bomber. The Tu-95K-22 program adapted the K-22 complex and Kh-22 missile (AS-4) of the Tu-22K Blinder bomber.

31. Butowski, *Lotnictwo wojskowe Rosji,* 33–37.

32. Myasishchev was allowed to open another design bureau after Khrushchev's ouster, but it was very small and lacked the influence of the previous OKB-23.

33. Piotr Butowski, "Blackjack Profile," *Air International,* May 2000, 285–92.

34. Ye. A. Fedosov, ed., *GosNIIAS: Ocherki istorii, 1946–1996* (Moscow: GosNIIAS, 1996), 188–94.

35. The Strategic Air Command backed into cruise missiles while attempting to design a new decoy missile, the SCAD, to replace the old ADM-20 Quail.

36. There were two versions manufactured. The initial Tu-95MS-6 version carried six Kh-55 missiles on an internal MKU-6-5U rotary launcher. Later production Tu-95MS-16's carry six missiles internally and an additional ten missiles externally on launch pylons.

37. The culmination of this criticism was the "B-Team" reassessment of CIA estimates of Soviet intentions. A version of this study can be found in Donald Steury, ed., *Intentions and Capabilities: Estimates on Soviet Strategic Forces, 1950–1983* (Washington, D.C.: CIA, 1996), 365–90.

38. No Russian figures for missile production beyond the 1950s have been released, so these figures are based on U.S. intelligence estimates. *NATO and Warsaw Pact Weapons Production Trends, 1975–1989* (Washington, D.C.: DAMIS, U.S. Department of Defense, 1990),

36; "DIA Tables Detail Soviet Weapons Production," *Aerospace Daily*, 31 August 1984, 350. The U.S. figures are based on *U.S. Strategic Missile Procurement FY65-FY90* (Greenwich, Conn: DMS, 1980).

39. These operations became a major preoccupation of the Soviet General Staff during this period. S. F. Akhromeyev and G. M. Kornyenko, *Glazami marshala i diplomata* (Moscow: Mezh. Otnoshenia, 1992), 22.

40. See especially the chapter "The Vulnerability of Soviet Command," in Blair, *Logic*.

41. Pappo-Korystin et al., *Dnepropetrovsky raketno-kosmichesky tsentr*, 84.

42. Col. Valery Yarynich, "Op-Ed: The Doomsday Machine's Safety Catch," *New York Times*, 1 February 1994.

43. IONDS, *Electronics Systems Market Intelligence Reports* (Greenwich, Conn.: DMS, 1986).

44. This point was made by Valery Yarynich during a panel discussion at the conference "Russian Missile Programs, the MTCR, and the Future of U.S.-Russian Arms Control," held on 21 July 1995 at the Monterey Institute of International Studies in Monterey, California.

45. The Perimetr was developed by the design bureau of the Leningrad Polytechnic Institute (KB LPI), headed by Taras Sokolov (now called NPO Impuls); and the Scientific Research Institute of the Strategic Missile Forces (NII-4 RVSN), in Bolshevo. The launch system was designed by the TsKB-TM (Central Design Bureau for Heavy Equipment Production) and was responsible for suitable changes to the existing launch silos. In June 1987 the key designers working on the Perimetr system were granted state prizes.

46. The launch sites for the 15A11 command missiles were at Yedrovo/Vypolzovo, in the Valday hills, about 150 km (93 mi) from Moscow; and/or at the Kostromo base, which is about 250 km (155 mi) from Moscow. According to an essay by Bruce Blair, the Perimetr command transmitter in the Moscow region had an effective range of about 950 km (589 mi), which would make either SS-17 base acceptable. The SS-20 bases nearest Moscow at the time were in Belorussia and Ukraine, several of which were within range. Blair, "Russian Control," 76.

47. At least thirty Perimetr tests launches were conducted. Blair, *Logic*, 79.

48. Blair, "Russian Control," was followed up by an article by the science editor at the paper, who interviewed former CIA chief Robert Gates. Gates's reaction to the story was, "My instinctive reaction is that they wouldn't do that." Former National Security Agency head William Odom stated that the story was implausible, though not impossible. William Broad, "Russia Has Computerized Nuclear Doomsday Machine, U.S. Expert Says," *New York Times*, 8 October 1993.

49. The Pershing 2 could be fuzed to air burst or to penetrate before detonating. Its publicly announced penetration capability was 100 feet. "Pershing," *DMS Market Intelligence Reports: Missiles/Spacecraft*, 1985, Analysis Section, 1.

50. The Soviet military tended to exaggerate the capabilities of the Pershing II. The United States stated that its range was 1,600 km (992 mi), which limited its effectiveness in targeting Moscow. But the Soviet military claimed its range was 2,500 km (1,550 mi). It is not clear if the Soviet military position was based on a simple mistake in assessment or the result of internal debates within the Soviet government, in which the military used the exaggerated Pershing threat to win concessions from the Kremlin for its own procurement programs. See Saveleyev and Detinov, *Big Five*, 57.

51. Steven Zaloga, "SA-12 Tactical Ballistic Missile Defense: The Antey S-300V," *Jane's Intelligence Review* 2 (1993): 52–58.

52. Although it has not been described, this facility was probably part of the Golitsino-2 facility, near Krasnoznamensk in the Moscow region, which is used by the Military Space Forces (VKS: Voyenno-Kosmicheskiye sily) to control military space satellites. V. Baberdin and I. Ivanyuk, "Golitsino-2: Tsentr sekretnykh kosmicheskikh orbit," *Krasnaya zvezda,* 21 April 1992; Oleg Falichev, "Bez grifa sekretno: Glaza i ushi presidenta, ili nekotoriye priklyuchenia rossiskikh voyennykh sputnikov na okolozemnoi orbite," *Krasnaya zvezda,* 17 January 1996.

53. See chapters 7 and 8 in Mikhail Alexseev, *Without Warning: Threat Assessment, Intelligence, and Global Struggle* (New York: St. Martin's Press, 1997).

54. The Soviet satellites had a life expectancy at the time of about eighteen months. Paul Podvig, "The Operational Status of Russian Space-Based Early Warning System," *Science and Global Security* 4 (1994): 363–84.

55. The first three of these appear to have been slight modifications of the existing Oko design. The second generation of Prognoz satellites, related to the Lavochkin Spektr design, appeared on 26 April 1990. In recent years the Prognoz network has consisted of three satellites. These require a more powerful booster than the Oko and are launched on the Proton-K boosters from Tyuratam. Philip Clark, "Russia's Geosynchronous Early Warning Satellite Programme," *Jane's Intelligence Review,* February 1994, 61–64.

56. Stephen Cimbala, "Year of Maximum Danger? The 1983 War Scare and U.S.-Soviet Deterrence," *Journal of Slavic Military Studies* 13, no. 2 (June 2000): 1–24.

57. Votintsev, "Neizvestniye voiska ischeznuvshei sverkhderzhavy," *Voyenno-Istorichesky zhurnal* 10 (1993): 38.

58. Interview with S. Petrov on BBC International, 21 October 1998.

59. For an intriguing look at other occasions when the command-and-control system nearly failed, see Peter Pry, *War Scare: Russia and America on the Nuclear Brink* (Westport: Praeger, 1999).

60. These were located at Pechora (northern Russia), Lyaki (near Iran), Mishelevka (near Irkutsk), Sary Shagan (Kazakstan) and Karlovka (near Murmansk on the Barents Sea). By 1987 three more new radars were under construction in the western USSR at Mukhachevo, Baranovichi, and Skrunda, bringing the total to nine. Construction began on a tenth site near Sevastopol in 1988 to cover approaches from the Mediterranean and to fill the final gap in the new network. These last four sites used the improved Daryal-UM version of the system.

61. The most reliable description of this debate can be found in the account by the former head of the Soviet ABM force, Gen. Col. Yu. V. Votintsev. "Neizvestniye voiska ischeznuvshei sverkhderzhavy," *Voyenno-Istorichesky zhurnal* 10 (1993): 35–36.

62. Pavel Felgengauer, "Russia Will Have to Build Its Defense on Strategic Nuclear Weapons," *Nezavisimaya gazeta,* 19 November 1992 (trans. FBIS-SOV-92-235, 7 December 1992, 10).

63. Bill Gertz, "Moscow Builds Bunkers against Nuclear Attack," *Washington Times,* 1 April 1997.

64. They were originally called IL-76VPK (*vozdushny komandny punkt:* airborne command post). Dmitry Komissarov, *IL-76: Istoria samolyota* (Moscow: Press-Solo, 1995), 30–31.

65. Thomad Nichols, *The Sacred Cause: Civil-Military Conflict over Soviet National Security, 1917–1992* (Ithaca: Cornell University Press, 1993).

66. Vladislav Zubok, "Gorbachev's Nuclear Learning," *Boston Review,* April/May 2000, 7–12.

67. For an examination of the trends in the late 1980s, see Nikolai Sokov, "From the Soviet Union to Russia: Changes in the Patterns of Interest Group Impact upon National Security Policy" (Ph.D. diss., University of Michigan, 1996).

68. For an examination of the influence of state think tanks outside the military on Gorbachev's reforms, see Jeffrey Checkel, *Ideas and International Political Change: Soviet/Russian Behavior and the End of the Cold War* (New Haven: Yale University Press, 1997).

69. William Green et al., *Gorbachev and His Generals: The Reform of Soviet Doctrine* (Boulder: Westview Press, 1990).

70. Georgy Arbatov, *The System: An Insider's Life in Soviet Politics* (New York: Random House, 1992), originally published as *Zatyanuvsheyesya vyzdorovleniye* (Moscow: Mezh. Otnoshenia, 1991).

71. The most thorough look at Gorbachev's military policies can be found in Odom, *Collapse.*

72. Henry Rowen et al., *The Impoverished Superpower: Perestroika and the Soviet Military Burden* (San Francisco: ICS Press, 1990).

73. Akhromeyev's selection over Ogarkov was engineered by Ustinov. Arbatov, *System,* 277.

74. S. F. Akhromeyev and G. M. Kornyenko, *Glazami marshala i diplomata* (Moscow: Mezh. otnoshenia, 1992),

75. D. Tikhanov, "Interview with Col.-Gen. Yury Votintsev," *Vecherniy almaty,* 2 June 1993, 3 (trans. JPRS-UMA-93-035, 22 September 1993, 8–9).

76. Steven Zaloga, "Red Star Wars," *Jane's Intelligence Review,* May 1997, 205–8.

77. The Terra-3 was developed by TsNPO Vympel starting in 1969, and the test bed included a high-energy ruby laser and a high-energy carbon dioxide laser. TsNPO Vympel was headed at this time by Ustinov's son, Nikolai Ustinov. Vympel was primarily responsible for the overall conception and design of Terra-3, but the lasers were developed by NPO Astrofizika. Although the complex provided the Soviet program with considerable detail about laser interaction with typical ICBM and reentry vehicles, Terra-3 did not prove practical as a weapon. Ustinov's son was ousted as general designer at Vympel following his father's death in December 1984. Votintsev, "Neizvestniye voiska ischeznuvshei sverkhderzhavy," *Voyenno-Istorichesky zhurnal* 11 (1993): 17.

78. See chapter 6 in Christoph Bluth, *The Collapse of Soviet Military Power* (Aldershot: Dartmouth Publishing, 1995).

79. These patrols lasted from January 1985 to April 1987. M. I. Musatov, *Strategicheskiye sily sderzhivania i sistemy oboronnoi bezopastnosti Rossii v sovremennykh geopoliticheskikh usloviyakh* (Moscow: Shkola, 1999), 159.

80. The average patrol rate of the Yankee class was very low: only about 1.1 patrol per year per submarine. In 1978 the 3rd Submarine Flotilla made only twenty-seven combat patrols, but it made forty-five patrols in 1979, forty-eight in 1980, forty-two in 1981, and fifty-two in 1982. While the pattern had been to have at least two Navagas on combat patrol at any one time, during this period it increased to as many as six or seven at a time. I. K. Kudrin, "Vospominania komandira K-241," *Taifun* 2 (2000): 42.

81. This was a Project 667AU Navaga, *K-219* of the 3rd Flotilla. It was the second missile-tube accident suffered by *K-219,* and on its ill-fated patrol, one of its sixteen missile tubes was permanently welded shut as the result of an earlier accident. The submarine had sizable turnover of crew and prior to its September 1986 sortie had lost twelve of its thirty-two officers. Kudrin, "Vospominania komandira K-241." For a dramatized account of the loss of *K-219,* see Peter Huchthausen et al., *Hostile Waters* (New York: St. Martin's Press, 1997).

82. Haslam, *Soviet Union,* 164–68.
83. It would appear that the Soviets actually planned more than 180 Topol launchers prior to the 1991 expansion contract, because more than 180 were deployed when the decree was signed. From other sources, it would appear that the original plan called for about 270 launchers, and the 1991 agreement increased this force to 150 percent of its original planned size, up to 405 launchers by 1994.
84. Maksimov, *Zapiski vyvshego glavkoma strategicheskikh,* 249.
85. The Polyus, also known as the 17F19DM Skif-DM, was developed by KB Salyut (http://www.friends-partners.org/~mwade/craft/polyus.htm, May 2000).
86. These positions are described in the autobiography of the chief of the RVSN at the time, Yu. P. Maksimov, *Zapiski vyvshego glavkoma strategicheskikh,* 249–51.
87. The most insightful examination of the internal Soviet debates over START appears in Savelyev and Detinov, *Big Five.*
88. Maksimov, *Zapiski vyvshego glavkoma strategicheskikh,* 269.
89. In fact, the program had already been canceled in 1991, and authorization of the launch of a single Kuryer was approved only as a gesture after the United States had test launched one of its Midgetman missiles.
90. Pervov, *Raketniye kompleksy RVSN,* 159.
91. There is a growing cottage industry in books on the causes of the Soviet collapse. For an examination of the demoralization of the Soviet elite, see Paul Hollander, *Political Will and Personal Belief: The Decline and Fall of Soviet Communism* (New Haven: Yale University Press, 2000).
92. For an account of the role of the difficulty of reform in the collapse of the Soviet Union, see Philip Roeder, *Red Sunset: The Failure of Soviet Politics* (Princeton: Princeton University Press, 1993).
93. Clifford Gaddy, *The Price of the Past: Russia's Struggle with the Legacy of a Militarized Economy* (Washington, D.C.: Brookings Institution, 1996).
94. Noel Firth and James Noren, Soviet Defense Spending: A History of CIA Estimates, 1950–90 (College Station: Texas A&M University Press), 111.
95. The PVO-Strany absorbed about 10 percent of the Soviet defense budget in 1951–90, compared to 11 percent for the strategic offensive forces, according to CIA estimates. Conventional forces absorbed about 40 percent.
96. There is no Russian data on missile-production rates. This information is based on U.S. intelligence assessments. *NATO and Warsaw Pact Weapons Production Trends, 1975–1989* (Washington, D.C.: U.S. Defense Analysis and Management Information System, 1990), 36.

Chapter 7. Soviet Becomes Russian: 1991–2000

1. For a more detailed breakdown of the shifts in strength, see Steven Zaloga, "Strategic Forces of the SNG," *Jane's Intelligence Review,* February 1992, 79–85.
2. For overviews of the nuclear policies of the successor states, see *The Nuclear Challenge in Russia and the New States of Eurasia,* ed. G. Quester (Armonk, N.Y.: M. E. Sharpe, 1995); and Graham Allison et al., *Avoiding Nuclear Anarchy: Containing the Threat of Loose Russian Nuclear Weapons and Fissile Material* (Cambridge: MIT Press, 1996).
3. The initiative to remove tactical nuclear weapons from the republics actually began in

October 1991, before the Soviet breakup, as part of Gorbachev's response to President Bush's unilateral initiative to withdraw tactical nuclear forces from Europe and from naval forces.

4. "Russia's Dispute with Ukraine over Nuclear Weapons Is Removed," *Nezavisimaya gazeta,* 19 June 1996 (trans. FBIS-UMA-96-145-S).

5. A small number of land-based weapons were returned in July 1992, and all naval weapons had been returned by mid-1993.

6. William Potter, *Nuclear Profiles of the Soviet Successor States* (Monterey: Monterey Institute for Nonproliferation Studies, 1993).

7. These were deployed to Yoshkar Ola. Aleksandr Dolinin, "Another Regiment Equipped with Topol Missiles on Combat Alert Duty," *Krasnaya zvezda,* 21 April 1994 (trans. JPRS-UMA-94-022, 7).

8. Ian Kemp, "Russia: NATO expansion may prompt retargeting," *Jane's Defence Weekly,* 4 December 1996, 5; "New Regiment of Strategic Missile Troops Formed," First Channel Network, 29 December 1996, 1200 GMT (trans. FBIS-SOV-96-251).

9. Taras Kuzio, *Ukrainian Security Policy* (Washington, D.C.: CSIS, 1995), 89–121.

10. The START I treaty was ratified on 18 November 1993, but with reservations. A second vote on 4 February 1994 removed the reservations and accepted the related Lisbon Protocols, as well as accepting the Nonproliferation Treaty, which committed Ukraine to eventual denuclearization.

11. "A Superpower's Final Attribute," *Moscow Interfax AiF* 10 (10–16 March 1997) (trans. FBIS-UMA-97-057-S).

12. Two aircraft were retained for museums, two Tu-95MS's were kept for research, and the remaining twenty-three aircraft were scrapped by October 2001. "Last Two Strategic Bombers Leave Ukraine for Russia," *Kommersant,* 23 February 2000, 3.

13. N. Poroskov and A. Dolinin, "Reserves of Combat Readiness: The RVSN," *Krasnaya zvezda,* 14 July 1997 (trans.: FBIS-SOV-97-195).

14. Most of the ICBM guidance platforms were developed by the AiP NPO (NPO avtomatiki i priborostroyenia: Automation and Instrument NPO, formerly NII-885) and manufactured at the T. G. Shevchenko Instrument Building Plant, both in Kharkov.

15. Nikolai Sokov, *Russian Strategic Modernization* (Lanham, Md.: Rowman & Littlefield, 2000), 107–8.

16. This figure came from the RVSN commander in 1997. Valery Borisenko, "Both the Missiles and the People Are Always in Complete Readiness," *Moskovskaya pravda,* 4 June 1997 (trans. FBIS-SOV-97-110).

17. "RVSN Commander Supports Ratifying START 2," *Moscow Interfax,* 1537 GMT, 9 March 1997 (trans. FBIS-SOV-97-068).

18. Most Russian ICBMs from this period had certified lives of seven years, meaning that most deployed missiles had been in use for about fifteen years. The service life of missiles can be extended by rebuilding programs, but this was a problem for Russia in the mid-1990s, since so many of the rebuild facilities were in Ukraine. "Sergeyev Bemoans State of Russian Military Equipment," *Interfax,* 11 December 1998.

19. William Ritter Jr., "Soviet Defense Conversion: The Votkinsk Machine Building Plant," *Problems of Communism,* September–October 1991, 47; *ITAR-TASS Release,* 5 July 1994 (trans. FBIS-SOV-94-129).

20. This was former general Alexandr Lebed, who was the regional governor in Krasnoyarsk

territory in Siberia. "Lebed Considers Taking over Local Russian Missiles," *Reuters,* 24 July 1998.

21. Most of the activities of the proving grounds were consolidated at the tactical ballistic-missile proving ground at Kapustin Yar, which in 1999 was restructured as the State Central Interbranch Proving Ground.

22. For the effect of the Soviet collapse on Russian defense industries, see Kimberly Zisk, *Weapons, Culture, and Self-Interest: Soviet Defense Managers in the New Russia* (New York: Columbia University Press, 1997).

23. In the past, the engineering-development phase of major weapons programs was initiated by a Council of Ministers decree. This pattern has changed due to Yeltsin's attempts to wrest more control from the industrial ministries. Aleksandr Dolinin, "'Topol M' startuyet budushcheye," *Krasnaya zvezda,* 21 December 1994.

24. "Topol-M Ballistic Missile Enters Service," *Agenstvo voyennykh novostei,* 26 April 2000.

25. The annual RVSN budget appropriation was about 45–50 percent of the funding needed, but in fact, due to government funding problems, even this amount was seldom actually provided. "Interview with RVSN Commander V. N. Yakovlev," *Nezavisimoye voyennoye obozreniye,* 17–23 December 1999, 1–3.

26. Borisenko, "Both the Missiles and the People."

27. The staffing levels of 112,000 troops at the end of 1996 was 86 percent the authorized strength of the time, which was 130,000. "A Superpower's Final Attribute," *Moscow Interfax AiF* 10 (10–16 March 1997) (trans. FBIS-UMA-97-057-S).

28. E. M. Kutovoi et al, "Ballisticheskiye rakety podvodnykh lodok," *Taifun,* May 1999, 28.

29. The lead boat of the class is called the *Ivan Dolgorukhy.*

30. "Interview with the director of the Makeyev Design Bureau Vladimir Degtyar," *Nezavisimoye voyennoye obozreniye,* 18 May 2000.

31. In March 2000 there were reports again that the Russian Air Force would fund the design of a new bomber that would be deployed in 2015. "Air Force Finalizing Tender Results for New Bomber," *Agentsvo voyennykh novostei,* 28 March 2000.

32. Sergei Ovisyenko, "Threads Run from Pechora to the President's Black Suitcase," *Rossiyskiye vesti,* 12 April 1995 (trans. JPRS-UMA-95-020, 2 May 1995, 25).

33. Phillip Clark, "Decline of the Russian Early Warning Satellite Programme," *Jane's Intelligence Review,* January 2001, 14–17.

34. David Hoffman, "Russia Blind to Attack by U.S. Missiles," *Washington Post,* 1 June 2000.

35. Nicholas Johnson and David Rodvold, *Europe and Asia in Space, 1993–1994* (Colorado Springs: Kaman Sciences Corporation, 1995), 344–46.

36. ELF Communications, *Command, Control, Communications, and Intelligence Market Intelligence Report* (Greenwich, Conn.: DMS, 1985).

37. SACDIN, *Electronic Systems Market Intelligence Report* (Greenwich, Conn.: DMS, 1986).

38. Gertz, "Mishaps."

39. Viktor Litovkin, "Missilemen's Commander-in-Chief Wants to Go on Reducing His Troops," *Izvestia,* 20 February 1998 (trans. FBIS-TAC-98-051, 20 February 1998).

40. Gertz, "Mishaps."

41. Nikolai Devyanin, "All that Has Happened, Alas, Had to Happen," *Moskovskiye novosti* 7 (29 January–5 February 1995) (trans. JPRS-TAC-95-001, 14 February 1995). Devyanin was one of the designers of the Cheget nuclear suitcase. Presumably his claim that this

was the only time the Kavkaz system was activated excludes training operations. The Kazbek system is regularly tested and has been used on a number of occasions to remotely launch missiles during training exercises, including SLBMs. See Vladimir Gundarov, "The Presidential Button Worked," *Krasnaya zvezda,* 4 October 1996.

42. Amy Woolf and Kara Wilson, "Russia's Nuclear Forces: Doctrine and Force Structure Issues," *Current Politics and Economics of Russia* 8, no. 4 (1997): 195–231. For a perspective by Russian civilian security specialists, see A. Arbatov, ed., *The Security Watershed: Russians Debating Defense and Foreign Policy after the Cold War* (Amsterdam: Gordon & Breach, 1993).

43. For a formal view of Russian thinking on deterrence, see the RVSN textbook. V. V. Prozorov, *Yadernoye sderzhivaniye v teorii primenenia RVSN* (Moscow: RVSN Military Academy, 1999).

44. Some sources, such as Yarynich, *Sistema upravlenia,* indicate that the Signal-A system was designed to download the targeting data in ten to fifteen seconds. Other sources indicate that the SS-25 mobile launcher requires fifteen to twenty seconds. Yury Zinchuk, "ICBMs Can Be Targeted 'Very Quickly,'" *Moscow NTV sevodnya,* 0600 GMT, 23 May 1997 (trans. FBIS-TAC-97-157, 6 June 1997); Bruce Blair, *Testimony at Hearing on Russian Missile Detargeting and Nuclear Doctrine Held by Congressman Curt Weldon, Chairman, Research and Development Subcommittee,* 13 March 1997.

45. The RVSN accounted for 90 percent of the missions in a launch-on-warning operation, and 60 percent of the missions in a launch-on-attack operation. "Interview with RVSN Commander General of the Army Igor Sergeyev," *Armeisky sbornik* 12, December 1996 (trans. FBIS-UMA-97-050-S).

46. Response to Joshua Handler, U.S. Office of Naval Intelligence, Freedom of Information Act, Princeton Center for Energy and Environmental Studies.

47. This was a Murena (Delta I) of the Northern Fleet. "Nuclear Drama on Russian Submarine," *Jane's Defence Weekly,* 20 May 1998, 6; David Hoffman, "Russia Is Warned of Missile Menace," *Washington Post,* 14 May 1998.

48. "Russia's Insurance Policy: The RVSN," *Armeisky sbornik* 12 (1998) (trans. FBIS-SOV-1999-0301).

49. Obyedinyonnoye glavkomandovaniye strategicheskikh sil sderzhivania, or OGSSS. Minister of Defense Sergeyev received permission to organize this headquarters from Yeltsin at a meeting in Sochi on 3 November 1998.

50. Nikolai Sokov, "Rocket Union?" *Jane's Defence Weekly,* 10 February 1999, 22–26.

51. A. I. Lebed, "The New Step of Military Reform Is Fraught with Strategic Error," *Nezavisimoye voyennoye obozreniye,* 20–26 November 1998 (trans. FBIS-UMA-98-331); "Russia Still Plans Joint Command for Deterrence Force," *Interfax,* 9 December 1999.

52. The air defense missile units and interceptors units of the PVO-Strany were absorbed by the Russian Air Force.

53. Dean Wilkening, *The Evolution of Russia's Strategic Nuclear Forces* (Stanford: Stanford University Center for International Security and Cooperation, 1998); David Foy, *Standing on One Leg: The Future of the Russian Nuclear Triad* (Maxwell Air Force Base: Air Command and Staff College 1999).

Index

293